DOMESTICATING SLAVERY

Jeffrey
Robert
Young

Domesticating
Slavery

The
Master Class
in Georgia
and
South Carolina,
1670–1837

The
University
of North
Carolina
Press

Chapel Hill
and
London

Library of Congress Cataloging-in-Publication Data

Young, Jeffrey Robert.

Domesticating slavery: the master class in Georgia and

South Carolina, 1670–1837 / Jeffrey Robert Young.

p.   cm.

Includes bibliographical references and index.

ISBN 0-8078-2490-9 (cloth: alk. paper). —

ISBN 0-8078-4776-3 (pbk.: alk. paper)

1. Slaveholders—Georgia—Attitudes—History.

2. Slaveholders—South Carolina—Attitudes—History.

3. Slavery—Georgia—Justification.   4. Slavery—South

Carolina—Justification.   5. Plantation life—Georgia.

6. Plantation life—South Carolina.   7. Georgia—Politics

and government—1775–1865.   8. South Carolina—

Politics and government—1775–1865.   I. Title.

E445.G3Y68   1999

306.3'62'0975709033—dc21   98-49757   CIP

03 02 01 00 99   5 4 3 2 1

For JIM ROARK,

whose support has meant far more to me than he knows

CONTENTS

ACKNOWLEDGMENTS

After many years of benefiting from assistance offered by sympathetic institutions and individuals, I take great pleasure in acknowledging those who made this work possible. First and foremost, I must thank the librarians and archivists—too numerous to name individually—who patiently answered questions about collections, provided access to manuscript collections, ordered obscure titles through interlibrary loan, and expressed the kind of interest in a project that maintains the author's own level of excitement. In particular, I received the finest imaginable treatment from the staff at the Charleston Library Society, the Clements Library at the University of Michigan, the Georgia Department of Archives and History, the Georgia Historical Society, the Manuscripts Division of the Library of Congress, the New York Public Library, the New-York Historical Society, the Newberry Library, the Perkins Library at Duke University, the South Carolina Department of Archives and History, the Southern Historical Collection at the University of North Carolina at Chapel Hill, and the Virginia Historical Society. The South Caroliniana Library at the University of South Carolina became my home for three productive and happy months. There, Laura Costello and Henry Fulmer steered me toward valuable collections and, just as important, made me feel welcome.

In my travels around the country, I encountered no finer library staff than the one serving the Emory University community. Eric and Marie Nitschke hunted down answers to questions that made merely mortal reference librarians stumble, and Jerrold Brantley's friendship brightened my mood during many long months in the microfilm room. The staff at the interlibrary loan office demonstrated an inexhaustible reservoir of goodwill as they tracked down countless sources.

The Department of History at Emory University provided me with a first-class graduate education. Patrick Allitt, William Beik, Michael Bellesiles, Geoff Clark, Elizabeth Fox-Genovese, Margot Finn, Eugene Genovese, Fraser Harbutt, John Juricek, Jamie Melton, Mary Odem, Randy Packard, Susan Socolow, and Sharon Strocchia created a supportive and stimulating environment for graduate coursework and research. Jonathan Prude carefully reviewed the manuscript, pressed me to develop my ideas about capitalism and culture, and offered me much-needed encouragement. Dan Carter took time to answer my questions, to write countless letters of recommendation, and, on one very memorable occasion, to tell me how to install a tape deck in my car (our friendship survived the electrical fire).

The roots of this project extend backward to the old Cox Hall dining room at Emory, where I participated in a number of highly caffeinated, high-cholesterol discussions with Ellen Barnard, Dan Costello, Sarah Gardner, and Diane Burke. Their perspectives on southern history enriched and challenged my own. Sarah Gardner also graciously agreed to split my housing expenses in a memorably filthy sublet apartment in Chapel Hill—physical surroundings that were grim enough to keep us in the archives during every waking hour. Laura Crawley, Christine Jacobson Carter, Stacey Horstmann, and Andrew Silver helped to make my experience in the Mellon Southern Studies Seminar both rewarding and enjoyable. Dave and Vicki Haviland opened their home to me in Washington, D.C., and Ursula Pallares provided me with a wonderful place to stay in Columbia, S.C.

I received crucial financial assistance from the Department of History, the Graduate School of Arts and Sciences, and the Mellon Southern Studies Program at Emory University. The Pew Program in Religion and American History at Yale University funded me for a year while I wrote a significant portion of the manuscript. I am also deeply grateful for grants that I received from the Georgia Chapter of the Colonial Dames of America and the North Caroliniana Society.

At conferences that I attended and archives that I visited over the years, I have made the acquaintance of many scholars willing to listen to my ideas and to offer their own advice, some of which I have been wise enough to act on. Peter Coclanis agreed to read my prospectus back in 1993. Since then, he has read the entire manuscript several times and has strengthened it immeasurably with his keen insight into the history of the South and the early modern world. I am also especially grateful for support and advice offered by Robert Forbes, Lacy Ford, Grace Hale, John Inscoe, Jane Pease, William Pease, David Shields, and Mart Stewart.

A number of my former colleagues at Illinois State University shared with me their historical expertise on subjects that made their way into the manuscript. For their help, I thank Mari-Paz Balibrea-Enríquez, Jorge Canizares Esguerra, John Freed, and Lou Perez. I survived the midwestern winters because of the friendship offered by, among others, Lee Beier, Maura Doherty, John Gill, Virginia Gill, Jin Lee, Richard Soderlund, Jennifer Travis, and Mohamad Tavakoli-Targhi. My new colleagues at Georgia Southern University—Jon Bryant, Walter J. Fraser, Georgina Hickey, Annette Laing, and Anastatia Sims—have welcomed me back to Georgia and have shared with me their vast knowledge of southern history. Jerry Steffen deserves praise for encouraging my research and easing my transition into a new university system. I also thank Lewis Bateman, Pamela Upton, Nancy Raynor, and the rest of the staff at the University of North Carolina Press for guiding this work to publication.

I have not had the privilege of meeting Willie Lee Rose, but I most certainly profited from her pathbreaking work on the question of slaveholder ideology. I selected the title of this book to pay tribute to her essay "The Domestication of Domestic Slavery," which first led me to ponder the timing by which the slaveholders developed their world view.

A portion of Chapter 5 first appeared as part of my article "Ideology and Death on a Savannah River Rice Plantation, 1833–1867: Paternalism amidst 'A Good Supply of Disease and Pain,'" *Journal of Southern History* 59 (November 1993): 673–706. Advice offered by John Boles, the journal's anonymous readers, and the journal's editorial staff enabled me to make fruitful revisions of this material.

Without the love and support of my family and friends, I could never have embarked on (let alone completed) this project. My parents, Jack and Joanne; my brothers, Jonathan and Jason; and my grandmother Frances Kass have been extremely generous, both emotionally and financially. I hope the publication of this book convinces them that I have not been sleeping too late and relaxing too much all these years. Todd Mages has been a source of reliable and sensible counsel since I met him in 1971. Jon Feldman has joined me in many valuable discussions about race relations and American history. And my friends Eric Wallen and John Wollaeger have provided much amusement and, more recently, free medical advice dispensed over the phone. I must also thank both Cynthia Bansak (for helping me to survive my initial move to Atlanta) and Louis Corrigan (for listening patiently to my ideas about literature and culture).

My deepest personal debt is to Laurie Watel, whose influence led me finally to put my ideas in writing. I burdened her with numerous chapter drafts and interminable conversations about slavery and capitalism. In return, she offered me tender words of encouragement and, when necessary, sharp criticism. Our son, Paris, took shape at roughly the same time as my manuscript. He has since introduced into our lives a measure of happiness that I never knew existed.

This book is dedicated to my mentor Jim Roark. His seminar on the Old South was a formative intellectual experience for me. As my dissertation adviser, he has listened and responded wisely to my ideas, my concerns, and my complaints. His own scholarship on slavery has provided me with a model of careful research and eloquent expression. He is the finest teacher I have known, and I am fortunate to be able to count myself among his friends.

DOMESTICATING SLAVERY

This people are so domesticated,

or so kindly treated by their masters,

and their situations so improved,

that [an entire] host [of abolitionists]

cannot excite one among twenty to

insurrection. They are able to compare

their comforts and their labor, and

are fully sensible that their comforts

are as great, and their labor not

more arduous, than any other class

of laboring people.

Senator William Smith

of South Carolina, 1820

INTRODUCTION

When prominent authors Harriet Martineau and William Gilmore Simms clashed over the question of human bondage in 1837, their exchange reverberated across the American South. Hailing from Norwich,
England, Martineau had traveled through the United States for the better
part of two years before penning the memoir that touched off her feud with
Simms, the quintessential writer of the antebellum South. To the dismay of
her southern hosts, she used the account of her journey, *Society in America*,
to excoriate the institution of human bondage and to champion the cause
of an abolitionist movement that had been gathering momentum during
the previous decade. Martineau charged the South with retarding its own
economic and social development by clinging to an abusive, obsolete mode
of labor. In effect, she turned the chronicles of her travels into a catalogue of
the slaveholders' crimes against humanity. She reported, for example, that
"upon a mere vague report, or bare suspicion, persons travelling through

the south have been arrested, imprisoned, and, in some cases, flogged or otherwise tortured, on pretence that such persons desired to cause insurrection among the slaves." She bemoaned the "management of the female slaves on estates where the object is to rear as many as possible, like stock, for the southern market." And she observed, sadly, that "one of the absolutely inevitable results of slavery is a disregard of human rights; an ability even to comprehend them."[1]

Indicted on both economic and moral grounds, slaveholders hastened to defend themselves in the court of world opinion. None responded more forcefully than did Simms. At the time of their exchange, the Charleston author, like Martineau, was in his early thirties and had emerged during the previous half-decade as a major literary figure. In November 1837 Simms reviewed Martineau's work in the *Southern Literary Messenger*. He sought, in the process, to dismantle her most sacred assumptions about justice, economics, and individual rights.[2] According to Simms, slavery provided the foundation for a stable and moral society. Spurning Martineau's charge that southern masters routinely abused their slaves, Simms presented slavery as a humane institution. "We have been apt to think and say," he wrote, "that there were few people so very happy, hearty, and well satisfied with their condition, as the southern negro." "A brutal master is sometimes punished, and always known," he continued, "and his offences against law and humanity in the treatment of his slaves, are quite . . . often the subject of public inquiry and prosecution." For Simms, moreover, the unfree labor system that linked the masters' financial fortune to the well-being of their workers naturally resulted in the humane treatment of slaves: "No better security has ever yet been devised by man for the safety of man, and [for] the proper observance of humane laws by the citizen, than that given by the southern slaveholder, in the continual presence of their leading interests."[3]

Rejecting Thomas Jefferson's notion that "all men are created equal," Simms rejoiced that "God has not created the physical man, or the mental man, alike." "All harmonies," he asserted, "arise, entirely, from the inequality of the tone, and all things, in art, nature, moral and political systems, would give discord or monotony, but for this very inequality." For Simms, a clearly delineated hierarchy—one in which masters and slaves, superiors and inferiors, fulfilled reciprocal responsibilities—provided the key to a harmonious social order. In such a society, maintained Simms, "no despotic power" denied justice to the slave; rather, "*providence has placed him in our hands, for his good, and has paid us from his labor for our guardianship.*" Interpreted from this perspective, slavery benefited the slaves by rescuing them from the chaos of their African homeland; it benefited society as a whole by eliminating the "utter enervation, sluggishness, and shame of body and mind alike" that Simms believed characterized "some of the *unlaboring* people of Europe." Whereas Martineau had presented slavery as a disease that steadily undermined the ideals of the United States, Simms tendered it as a cure from the destructive "equality insisted upon by the levellers"— equality that "would result in the necessary forfeiture of names to things" and the destruction of "all barriers of present distinction."[4]

For the better part of the past century, scholars have struggled to situate Martineau's and Simms's arguments within the broader cultural context of anti- and proslavery thought that emerged in the early nineteenth century. While scholars exploring the antislavery movement have certainly established no consensus about the relationship between capitalism and antislavery sentiment, there can be little doubt that Martineau's views on individual liberties extended logically from the capitalistic framework of nineteenth-century England.[5] For centuries, England had experienced a slow yet dramatic transition toward wage labor. As this economic shift occurred, political economists defended the right of laborers to negotiate the terms for their work. Indeed, by the late eighteenth century, pioneering students of the proper relationship between economy and society—the classical political economists such as Adam Smith and James Mill—had already identified the protection of personal liberties as a crucial step in the growth of a profitable economy and, equally important, a just society.[6] Exposed to these authors' texts during her youth, Martineau not surprisingly adopted their arguments and turned her work into a forum for their criticism of unfree labor.[7] In this sense, Martineau's writings highlighted the emerging tendency toward bourgeois individualism in England. Even as her views on specific issues such as women's rights were sometimes dismissed as radical, her broader system of values conformed perfectly with the middle-class ethos that was coalescing on both sides of the Atlantic during this era.

Although historians can therefore trace the intellectual lineage of Martineau's antislavery arguments and gauge their wider cultural significance, scholars have experienced far greater difficulty determining the roots or resonance of Simm's proslavery stance in the American South. In the early twentieth century, leading historians of southern slavery accepted Simms's words at face value. In *American Negro Slavery* (1918), for example, U. B. Phillips depicted the slaveowners as humane gentlemen and ladies who cared far more for their slaves' welfare than for their plantations' profitability. Influenced by his own racist beliefs about the natural limitations of

African Americans, Phillips concluded that the values espoused by Simms had matured gradually and were as crucial to the development of the slave-owners' world as were the crops in their fields and the thoroughbreds in their stables. These values, according to Phillips and the many scholars per-suaded by his work, laid the foundation for a distinctive southern society that provided for the welfare of both whites and blacks.[8]

In the decades following World War II, historians became more and more uncomfortable with Phillips's rosy assessment of human bondage. As the civil rights movement reshaped the contemporary social landscape, it also fostered studies of slavery that depicted in graphic detail the slaveown-ers' callous disregard for the plight of their slaves. By the late 1950s, leading historians had recast the southern planters as vicious entrepreneurs willing to shed African American blood to avoid the red ink of an unprofitable plantation balance sheet. Although Kenneth Stampp entitled his influential history of southern slavery *The Peculiar Institution* (1956), his and similar works placed the slaveowners firmly within the transatlantic context of cap-italistic development. In such a historiographical climate, scholars rejected Simms's claim that the slaveowners were uniquely dedicated to the ideals of Christian stewardship. Historians interpreted elaborate paternalistic pro-slavery arguments as empty words cynically designed to counter abolition-ist charges but utterly divorced from the daily reality of plantation life.[9]

Since the 1960s, scholarly interpretations of the planters' world view have gravitated toward two distinct historiographical poles—one depicting the slaveowners as racist but savvy entrepreneurs who embraced liberal demo-cratic values, and the other presenting them as would-be paternalistic stew-ards who defended their hierarchical society from the specters of capitalism and egalitarianism.[10] As this debate has grown increasingly stale, historians (including some of the principal participants in the old historiographical battle) have sketched out a more nuanced understanding of how the slave-holders made sense of themselves and their society.[11] But even as scholars such as Robert Olwell and John Boles have presented evidence belying "any simple dichotomy" between the slaveowners' paternalism and their partici-pation in a capitalistic economy, the old schools of interpretation have re-tained their force.[12] Indeed, studies published in the 1990s demonstrate how the questions that once inspired pathbreaking analysis of the Old South now undermine productive debate about the region's fundamental ideolog-ical orientation.[13]

What we lack is an interpretive approach that explicitly incorporates the valid evidence presented by both sides in this ongoing debate—an approach, moreover, which illustrates that, far from simply coexisting, market capitalism and ideals of organic reciprocity evolved in tandem in the slave-owning South. Although the last decade of scholarship has established a need for an intellectual bridge between the existing schools of interpretation, we still lack a theoretical vocabulary that can accommodate evidence that the slaveowners immersed themselves ever more deeply in the market during the very period when the paternalistic defense of slavery matured. I proceed from the assumption that the current historiography of slaveholder ideology has taken on something of a life of its own and that the dull weight of historiographical inertia has created a gulf not only between capitalistic and paternalistic interpretations of the South but also between all the works replicating this dichotomy and the more recent scholarship that fits neatly within neither existing school of interpretation.[14]

In the ensuing pages, I present a new paradigm for the historical analysis of slaveholder ideology.[15] Tracing the evolution of the slaveowners' identity in Georgia and South Carolina from colonization to 1837, I chronicle the cultural and political developments that made possible William Gilmore Simms's tirade against Harriet Martineau. As we shall see, Simms's embrace of organic metaphors for slavery and his hostility toward unbridled individualism masked a bizarre paradox that historians must unravel to make sense of the slaveowners' sectional culture. The story of the early Deep South reveals that by the 1830s the defense of slavery had itself taken shape as a form of cultural capital, speeded across at least some parts of the South with the same efficiency as were bales of cotton and barrels of rice. The dynamic of this market for culture, moreover, ensured that the content of the slaveowners' ideals would reflect many of the same "modern" concerns permeating England and the northern United States during this period. Indeed, only through their extensive participation in a transatlantic intellectual community could the southern slaveowners develop the system of ideas that would ultimately lead them into a state of political exile from the rest of the Western world.

Before turning to events in Georgia and South Carolina, a few words about the theories driving this work are in order. First, although I build on the insights of both the capitalistic and paternalistic schools of interpretation, my analysis departs from both historiographical camps by presenting a different model for the slaveowners' perspective on the relationship between slavery and family. In fact, scholarly disagreement over the slaveholders' understanding of plantation domesticity rests at the center of the historiographical impasse over planter identity. Those scholars presenting the

South as a bastion for organic, hierarchical values have, of course, built their case around the concept of paternalism—a concept introduced to professional historians by U. B. Phillips and then considerably refined by more recent authors. Scholars such as Eugene D. Genovese have employed the term "paternalism" to evoke the slaveowners' image of an extended plantation household encompassing unfree African Americans as well as free whites, all bound together by a network of reciprocal responsibilities.[16] Again and again, historians have contrasted the paternalistic, slaveowning family dynamic with bourgeois "nuclear" households in the North that hinged on affective relationships between immediate family members and a growing distinction between the domestic sphere and the outside world. This line of analysis has enabled scholars from the paternalistic school of interpretation to stress the "premodern" or, at the very least, "nonmodern" characteristics that differentiated the planters from capitalists in the northern United States and Western Europe.[17] On the other hand, scholars who deny that the South was paternalistic have argued that slaveowners did not reject but rather embraced bourgeois domesticity. By the early nineteenth century, according to such historians as Rhys Isaac and Jane Turner Censer, the slaveowners were retreating toward more tightly defined families that excluded blacks and therefore made impossible the idealized organic bond between the self-styled paternalistic master and the seemingly obedient, grateful slave.[18]

These historiographical approaches, however, preclude a crucial historical possibility. It is entirely plausible that southern planters imbibed deeply from a wellspring of bourgeois domesticity even as they extended their idealized conception of family to include their black slaves. Of course, to make this claim is to suggest that the slaveowners developed their conceptions of family relations in accordance with the transatlantic trend toward bourgeois domestic values. Elizabeth Fox-Genovese and Eugene Genovese have considered this possibility but have ultimately chosen to emphasize the differences between the paternalism that materialized in the context of the slaveowners' political needs and the paternalism that (Genovese acknowledges) "enters into every form of human relations, including the most bourgeois."[19] In so doing, they and even the scholars who have defined the planters in opposition to paternalistic categories of analysis have unwittingly obscured the fact that the southern slaveholders' understanding of domesticity reflected the same moral concerns about individual welfare that would eventually become the hallmark of modern, bourgeois society.[20] Indeed, to make sense of the slaveowners' complicated relationship with romanticized images of home that were becoming more and more prevalent in the nineteenth century, one must reconsider their impression of the individual's proper place in both the family circle and in society at large.[21]

In the late-eighteenth-century South, growing numbers of slaveowners recognized and at least claimed to respect the humanity of their social inferiors. One need only consider the eighteenth-century diary of Virginia planter Landon Carter to see how this period marked a transition away from traditional patriarchal demands for unlimited power over household dependents.[22] To be sure, Carter at times certainly adhered to long-honored patterns of patriarchal conduct. Not surprisingly, he deemed his slaves "villains" when they dared to disobey his commands. Wary of showing affection for fear that it might undermine his mastery, he asserted that "the more particular we are in our charges and the fonder we show ourselves of anything the more careless will our slaves be." Carter also demanded absolute obedience from his children and carefully recorded those instances when they ignored his instructions. In 1766, he reflected on the "domestic gust" that occurred when he disciplined his grandson for "impudent" behavior. Irritated that his son and daughter-in-law refused to castigate the child for impertinence, Carter took it upon himself to give the boy "one cut over the left arm with the lash of my whip." He recounted that his son responded with outrage, moving toward "his father with some heavy God damnings" before "prudently" deciding not to attack him. Carter observed that his "whip handle should have settled" the matter had his son actually dared to attack him.[23]

But if this incident demonstrates the patriarchal nature of southern plantation life during the colonial era, it also reveals that the region's slaveholders had initiated a transition in family values that would attain full force in the following century. That Carter's son and daughter-in-law protested his actions with screams of horror reminded him of mounting expectations that patriarchal authority be tempered by affectionate, paternalistic concern. Without irony, he considered it inappropriate when his "rascally grandson" pretended to whip his younger sister. And Carter himself struggled with his own sense that his bondservants should be treated with some measure of tenderness. Thus, the same slaveowner who exclaimed on one occasion that "slaves are devils and to make them otherwise will be to set devils free" also insisted that he "enjoy[ed] the humanity" of making personal sacrifices in order to indulge his slaves with considerate care. Despite his contempt for neighborhood doctors, Carter stated that providing medical care for one's slaves "is the duty of the Master and I have sent for [medical assistance for an ailing slave] to satisfye that [duty]." Although Carter consistently experienced difficulties maintaining order among his enslaved workers, his feelings for his favorite slaves reinforced his hope that at least some of his workforce were "gratefully endeavouring to serve a very kind master."[24]

The trend toward greater sensitivity to the needs and desires of individual members of society accelerated in the nineteenth century—exactly the period when capitalistic markets proliferated and an emerging American bourgeoisie projected a vision of the home as a sanctuary of love and comfort.[25] Despite the efforts of proslavery ideologues to distance the South from the destructive influences supposedly overtaking the North, their defense of slavery proceeded from the same domestic standards that underpinned middle-class family life in the North. However much a southern ideologue such as Simms denounced the principle of universal "equality insisted upon by the levellers," his defense of slavery turned on the recognition of the slave's individual claim to well-being. Unlike thinkers in previous ages, Simms and other southern authors repeatedly concerned themselves with the question of the slave's happiness and potential for personal development. A hierarchy was moral only insofar as it provided subordinate members of society with the opportunity to make the most of their abilities. "In the South the negroe is not an object of dislike or hatred," wrote Simms in "The Morals of Slavery." "There he never offends by obtrusiveness; he occupies his true position, and while he fills it modestly, he is regarded with favor, nay, respect and love, and is treated with kindness and affection." For Simms, the "morality of slavery" was established by slaves' moral improvement under the tutelage of concerned white masters. "Regard the slave of Carolina," he urged, "with a proper reference to the condition of the cannibal African from whom he has been rescued, and say if his bondage has not increased his value to himself, not less than to his master." Simms concluded that southern slavery had increased the slaves' "health and strength" and elevated their "mind and morals."[26]

Just as parents in the sentimentalized home defined childhood as a period for nurturing their children's morals, so too did masters in the South reconceptualize their plantation households as an environment that would foster their bondservants' spiritual and physical growth. When critics of slavery projected idealized domestic images to establish the brutality of chattel slavery, proslavery authors defended their region by drawing on the same domestic sensibility that appealed to their northern opponents. The Baptist luminary Richard Furman, for example, insisted that "a master may, in an important sense, be the guardian and even the father of his slaves." Like many of his peers, Furman considered it crucial to point out how the slaves themselves acknowledged that the institution fulfilled their individual needs. "There appear to be many . . . truly enlightened and religiously disposed" slaves, he claimed, who were cognizant that bondage served "their own true interests." For those eager to defend plantation slavery, such imagery provided a powerful counterpoint to stock antislavery images of slave families separated at the auction block and individual slaves suffering at the hands of sadistic masters.[27]

Antebellum slaveowners, then, celebrated an organic ideal that measured the needs of every individual to determine whether a particular institution served the needs of the community. Whereas ancient philosophers such as Aristotle had justified human bondage by discounting the slave's individuality and denying that the larger social good was even remotely predicated on the slave's personal welfare, southern thinkers explicitly referred to the humanitarian advance that they had made over the brutally patriarchal slaveowning societies of earlier ages.[28] Building their modern defense of hierarchical slaveowning society with fundamentally bourgeois domestic conceptions of the loving family, the southern slaveowners articulated a philosophy that I would call "corporate individualism." This system of relations distinguished itself from the classic patriarchy of antiquity by linking the welfare of the entire society to the well-being of every individual. And although corporate individualism manifested itself in the social relations of the eighteenth- and nineteenth-century North as well as the South, the value system's subordination of individual freedom to the needs of the corporate social whole distinguished it from the radical egalitarianism of the emerging antislavery movement.[29]

The slaveowners' paternalistic impulses certainly composed a crucial element of the philosophical framework of slaveowner ideas that I define under the rubric of corporate individualism. I would suggest, however, that the concept of paternalism does not adequately convey a critical theme around which the cultural dynamic of the slaveholders' world view turned. As we have seen from Simms's remarks, increasing numbers of slaveholders not only recognized the humanity of African American slaves but also acknowledged their individual human potential for growth and moral action of their own. This individualistic component of southern proslavery thought is too often obscured by the conventional paternalistic paradigm that contrasts the planters' organic society with bourgeois individualism in the North. Genovese and Fox-Genovese's formulation of the slaveowners' paternalistic ideology as "in but not of the capitalist world" misses the crucial point that the planters articulated their familial metaphors for slavery using a vocabulary of bourgeois individualism and domesticity. And since the historiography of southern slavery has cast paternalism as a system of ideas harkening back to a more traditional social order, the use of this term inevitably leads to confusion over the distinguishing intellectual and cultural characteristics of the slaveowners' world view. In proposing the paradigm of corporate individualism, I do not want to dismiss the small mountain of evidence demonstrating that many slaveowners conceptualized their mastery in familial terms. It is the recognition of individual rights inherent in the slaveowners' family metaphor which is of historical interest and which is more effectively evoked by the concept of corporate individualism.[30]

At the same time, however, the individualism manifesting itself in slaveholder ideology was consistently tempered by an ideal of personal restraint—an ideal that is not adequately explored by the historians who have rejected or downplayed the paternalistic school of interpretation in favor of charting the increasing influence of democratic, market-oriented values. The notion that individuals must temper their passions for the greater benefit of their own households and society at large forms a second major element of the planters' proslavery culture. Corporate individualism defined freedom in a manner that separated the liberty of mature, moral members of society from the licentiousness of those whose judgments were impaired by sin or the limitations of gender and race. In other words, corporate individualism called not only for the recognition of individual human potential but also for restraint against personal urges that threatened the integrity of a moral, Christian republic. "While men remain in the chains of ignorance and error, and under the dominion of tyrant lusts and passions, they cannot be free," declared ideologues such as Furman. "And the more freedom of action they have in this state, they are but the more qualified by it to do injury, both to themselves and others."[31] According to this rationale, society subordinated certain individuals out of respect (rather than contempt) for their personal welfare and potential for moral growth.

Because historians have for so many years considered capitalism and organic values as antagonistic, even mutually exclusive categories, they have not sufficiently recognized that most southern slaveowners encountered corporate individualism only because they had immersed themselves in an expanding market culture—that is, the capitalistic market provided the venue through which the message of corporate individualism and enlightened mastery was transmitted to the generations of American slaveowners who came of age during the antebellum era. Far from being theoretical alternatives that scholars must choose between when describing the antebellum South, the slaveowners' market economy and their fixation on organic values emerged historically in dialectical fashion. As I shall consider, notions of corporate individualism became cultural capital—messages encapsulated in domestic fiction, religious tracts and periodicals, and published sermons, all packaged for effective presentation to white slaveowners, who eventually turned the romanticized domestic sensibility toward sectional political ends.

Historians have already broached the possibility that the very structure of the global market led to increasing sensitivity to the needs and suffering of people living around the world. In an essay that has attracted considerable attention, Thomas Haskell connected the rise of humanitarian sentiment in the late eighteenth and early nineteenth centuries with the rapid growth of capitalistic markets. Arguing that market transactions reinforced participants' sense of restraint and extended their sense of compassion to include distant strangers, Haskell explained the genesis of the antislavery movement by identifying a crucial shift in the structure—the very form—of capitalistic culture.[32] Joyce Chaplin has quite rightly applied this insight to the southern planters' proslavery strand of humanitarian thought, noting that the planters confronted "progressive notions about how to treat blacks" without surrendering their prerogatives as masters. Rooting humanitarian sentiment in the words of Enlightenment authors, Chaplin traces the trajectory of the concept from its European origins to its arrival (through the medium of the publishing industry and "a variety of popular sources" including "legal codes, sermons, local histories, and newspapers") in the eighteenth-century South.[33] Chaplin approaches proslavery trends in the South from a secular perspective, but given the overwhelming influence of Protestant churches on antebellum southern values, persuasive analysis of the relationship between planter ideology and the market must also consider how religion impacted the slaveowners' world view. After all, as Larry Tise has suggested, ministers penned more than half the proslavery tracts published in America.[34]

Over the past few years, scholars of American religion have paid increasing attention to evangelical Protestant efforts to marshal the resources of the capitalistic market in order to "sell" religion to the masses. Notwithstanding Christ's admonition that it is "easier for a camel to pass through the eye of a needle than for a rich man to enter the kingdom of God," R. Laurence Moore and William Leach have suggested that "commerce and religion" were not always "in conflict." Their work moves significantly beyond Weber's famous formulation of the Protestant work ethic in that these more recent scholars reveal how religious reformers competed with secular alternatives by commodifying their faith (in forms ranging from Bibles mass-produced on steam-powered printing presses to interdenominational evangelical institutions such as the Young Men's Christian Association [YMCA] and the Salvation Army).[35] These insights certainly apply to the slaveowning South, where, as we shall see, Christianity triumphed after religious reformers learned to work with rather than against emerging markets.

The rise of the publishing industry and, in particular, the rise of the novel also figure heavily into the story chronicled in these pages. That a transatlantic literary culture should provide an ideological foundation for a sectional proslavery argument presents an intriguing paradox. Certainly readers in England and the northern United States read the work of chivalric novelists such as Walter Scott (and even Simms) without turning fictive themes into a blueprint for sectional political posturing.[36] In the South, however, certain characteristics of a slave-based plantation economy created an intellectual and political context in which the values of corporate individualism resonated. Literary critics who approach reading as "a process of construction" provide important reminders that, based on their own backgrounds and political needs, individual readers can derive very different meanings from the same works.[37] As I demonstrate in this book, the slaveowners' particular political needs and their peculiar fears (not to mention the isolation and boredom that they routinely experienced on their plantations) drove them to embrace the sanctuary of a fictive domestic realm. How that world (so vividly crafted by antebellum novelists) impacted the slaveowners' ideology as a ruling class will be one of my primary considerations. Although historians have offered trenchant studies of individual southern ideologues and authors, they have not yet uncovered the workings and political consequences of a southern community of readers. My own analysis proceeds from a cultural model that is much more diffuse than the one implicitly offered by the scholars studying the contributions of individual intellectuals to a defiantly proslavery system of thought. In a certain sense, I attempt to rethink the long-standing question about the relationship of southern intellectuals with proslavery doctrine. Rather than ask what factors compelled certain authors to write from a proslavery perspective, I question how (and at what point in time and places in space) communities of white southern readers coalesced around values that promised great rewards for intellectuals who articulated an explicitly southern slave-owning identity.[38]

Finally, I should explain my unusual periodization of southern history. Because I am interested primarily in how the southern household evolved in tandem with wider political and social developments in the Deep South—in how the slaveowners' shifting ideas about race, gender, and family provided the foundation for their identity as a master class—I have structured my analysis around a chronological framework. Here, I follow the advice offered by Willie Lee Rose, one of the first and most perceptive scholars to study the historical timing for the emergence of a proslavery rationale that was grounded in domestic imagery.[39] I begin my historical account during the earliest period of colonization because religious institutions and literary sources were already influencing the slaveowners' political stance in the early eighteenth century. I end my story in 1837 because the broad contours of a mature proslavery culture had emerged by that date and had begun to shape the political stance adopted by southern statesmen and theologians during this period of sectional crisis. Before the end of this decade, the slaveowners' private conceptions of plantation domesticity, their public defenses of slavery as a moral institution, and their political attacks on northerners who questioned slaveholder morality intersected to form a vibrant political culture that boded ill for the future of the country. Tracing how that proslavery culture contributed to the slaveowners' ultimate decision to shatter the Union would have made this a significantly longer book but would not have materially altered my central line of interpretation, which, of course, involves the interplay of religious, literary, economic, familial, and political factors in the creation of a self-conscious, slaveowning world view.

My thesis consists of the following contentions: In the colonial period, slaveowners in South Carolina and Georgia carved out their plantations on the periphery of a burgeoning network of global exchanges for profit. They developed a culture in accordance with their economy—one that valued the accumulation of wealth over the Christian ideals trumpeted by visiting missionaries and imperial authorities. As the American Revolution vested the slaveowners with chief political authority over the new American nation, they struggled to reconcile their status as masters with the organic principles that they then adopted to justify their break from England. Paradoxically, even as the southern slaveholders intensified their commitment to the international market economy, their modern commercial infrastructure became the medium through which they internalized the ideals of corporate individualism. Hence, the slaveowners embraced an ethos of corporate individualism only after experiencing the influence of a market society that they would eventually revile as the bane of moral society. Forged in the context of global capitalism, their ideology enabled them to cohere as a ruling class but had the unintended effect of isolating them politically and socially—this time within the very nation that they helped to establish. By the 1830s, these planters were struggling to overcome a dilemma of their own making. Their simultaneous desire for profit and noblesse oblige—a duality that had always caused them distress—laid the foundation for a regional culture that threatened to tear them and their nation apart.

In lifting up the slaveowners' perceptions of slavery and linking them to their regional political stance, I do not mean to suggest that their perspective should speak for their slaves and for the poorer white southerners, who both consistently struggled against the elite planters' hegemony. Clearly, African American slaves crafted an identity that offered them some sanctuary from the role assigned to black southerners by their masters' notions of corporate individualism.[40] And as Lacy Ford Jr., J. Mills Thornton III, and Steven Hahn have demonstrated, the antebellum yeomanry fiercely defended its independence and, in many cases, guarded slavery as an institution that permitted democracy to flourish among white males.[41] My own approach to the question of an antebellum southern identity recognizes that these tensions existed and seeks to uncover how the planter elite constructed domestic imagery that enabled them to prevent the resistance offered by blacks and whites from bursting through the seams of the planters' idealized social vision. In fact, the slaveowners' authority rested on their ability to reconcile notions of corporate individualism with bourgeois conceptions of equality and Jacksonian enthusiasm for democracy. To sketch the nuances of this process is not to de-emphasize African Americans and poorer whites as historical actors in their own right but rather to highlight the historical forces that ultimately frustrated the ambitions of the many southerners who sought to diminish or to eradicate the planters' political influence.

It is my most sincere desire that no one misinterpret this study of slaveholder ideology as an apology for slavery. Forcing African Americans to labor under threat of violence and death and profiting greatly from their exploitation, slaveowners routinely committed atrocities. Worse, they did so in an era that denounced their acts as crimes against humanity. And worse still, they had the temerity to congratulate themselves for their benevolence as they benefited from the misery of their slaves. I have at every turn attempted to distinguish between the slaveholders' perception of themselves and the more unsavory image that should be their historical legacy. I believe that the slaveholders' world view must be studied to understand how they clung to the institution of slavery in an age of emancipation and to make sense of the political culture that eventually drove them out of the Union. In tracing the evolution of a southern proslavery culture and that culture's influence on sectional relations in the antebellum United States, I am not suggesting that the benevolent self-image held by owners led to improved conditions on their plantations. To the contrary, the slaveowners' world view acted to blind white southerners to the hideous circumstances of plantation slavery.

The slaveholders aspired to chivalry, as did Cervantes's Don Quixote, a literary character whom they knew well and even mentioned when they discussed the question of slavery. Like the nineteenth-century planters, Quixote had been a prosperous landholder who became obsessed by the ideals set forth in works of literature. As was the case with the planters, Quixote's dedication to these values warped his perceptions of his surroundings and led him to abandon the identity that had originally enabled him to acquire the books that had changed his life. Yet Cervantes crafted a farce around his central character's escapades through his imagined realm, whereas the southern slaveholders were destroying lives as they played out the cherished role of honorable planter. The southern slaveowners never realized that they were jousting with windmills when they attempted to reconcile slavery with the ideals of Christian stewardship. Their delusions enabled them to develop into a master class that inflicted very real misery on millions of African American slaves. In this sense, their story can be told only as a tragedy.

CHAPTER ONE

Slavery and the Cultural Marketplace in the Colonial Deep South

The desire for profit motivated Europeans to risk their lives and capital in colonizing the New World. And from the first journeys of Columbus, European exploration and settlement of the Americas entailed an international slave trade—one that originally moved slaves from the West Indies to the courts of Spain and ultimately transported some twelve million African bondservants to new, infinitely more miserable homes in the New World.[1] Over the course of the early modern period, the proliferating international market for staple crops and precious metals enabled Europeans to transform the sufferings of these slaves into vast fortunes. White families such as the Manigaults—Huguenots who fled France for the New World in the late seventeenth century—rose to positions of social prominence in just a few generations. Judith Giton Royer, the matriarch of the Manigault family, arrived in South Carolina as an indentured servant and was forced to work in the field "like a slave."[2] But within decades, her children acquired their own slaves and, eventually, became the colony's wealthiest residents. In many ways, the story of the Deep South can be told in such terms of explosive economic growth and the attendant suffering inflicted by whites on African American slaves.

By the 1760s, elite slaveowners in South Carolina and Georgia had begun to reflect on the image that they presented both to their neighbors in the colonies and to powerful segments of English metropolitan society. Enriched by international commerce, white planters were discovering that global fiscal, political, and religious connections posed fundamental challenges to prevailing colonial conceptions of mastery. Even as their lives and fortunes depended on their ability to maintain absolute authority over their slaves, leading planters realized that their status as masters was undermining their campaign to be recognized as English gentlemen and ladies. Eighteenth-century government and church officials had struggled to reform plantation slavery—a crusade that faltered against the slaveowners' unwillingness, as a group, to recognize their slaves as human beings. Amid the mounting tensions between England and America in the years following the French and Indian War, the planters staked their understanding of political liberty on their right to exploit their unfree labor force without interference from meddling representatives of church and state. A market for cosmopolitan culture was simultaneously heightening colonial planters' preoccupation with English standards for gentility and, ironically, cultivating a political critique of mercantilism that the slaveowners could use to defend their pretensions to unlimited power over black and white dependents.

From the earliest days of English settlement in South Carolina, white colonists focused almost exclusively on extracting a fortune from the swampy wilds of their new home. The colony was first established as an extension of the plantation economy in the British West Indies. Coveting the vast tracts of uncultivated land in North America, Caribbean planters—particularly those on Barbados—lobbied King Charles II for permission to colonize the mainland. In 1663, the king granted a charter to a proprietary group organized by Barbados slaveowner John Colleton. When English settlers established Charlestown in 1670, they were extending a market-oriented system of slave-based production that had originated centuries earlier.[3]

Upon their arrival, entrepreneurial settlers experimented with different exports. Drawing on their African slaves' agricultural knowledge, the South Carolina slaveowners quickly discovered that the cultivation of rice along the coastal swamplands could yield tremendous profits.[4] Like businesspeople in any century, the planters sought to maximize the fiscal return on their investment by improving their methods of production and marketing.[5] In 1691, for example, the colonial assembly passed legislation encouraging "ingenious and industrious persons" to build machines that would result in "the better propagation of any commodityes of the produce of this Collony."[6] By the middle of the eighteenth century, the rice planters had learned to construct elaborate irrigation systems for their rice fields—an advancement that typified their ongoing efforts to harness technology for their own profit.[7] The plantation complex that evolved in the New World therefore rested on knowledge that circulated from diverse and distant points. The rice that grew in the Carolina lowcountry was the product of African ideas as well as African labor. The southern planters who financed these agricultural operations applied emerging western European standards of rational, efficient productivity to achieve the greatest possible profit from markets that required an intimate knowledge of economic trends in numerous European and Caribbean ports.

Just a few generations after establishing a beachhead in a hostile wilderness, South Carolina planters were annually producing millions of pounds of rice in an economy that linked their fortunes with those of distant traders and consumers.[8] As rice traveled from the colony to markets around the world, consumer items from England and other developed countries poured into the southern market. In 1747, for example, Charlestown merchant Henry Laurens observed that the city was "glutted with European Goods."[9] Nine years later he noted that "a shocking Earthquake" which "almost totally destroy'd the whole City of Lisbon" also rattled the Charlestown financial community. The transatlantic economy had linked South Carolina's fortunes to ports thousands of miles away.[10] On one level, these global economic connections promised to turn the southern planters' attention toward cultural imperatives emerging in western Europe. The transatlantic market for staple crops required colonists to think in terms of rational production of those commodities that could command a healthy price from distant consumers. The willingness of southern planters to orient their economy to derive maximum gain from the global market manifested itself in their rapid embrace of indigo as a new staple crop in the 1740s. Crucial information about indigo cultivation flowed into South Carolina in 1745 by way of Antigua—a movement of knowledge toward the periphery of the English imperial network that carried in its wake a burgeoning traffic in human property. By 1748 Laurens was expressing his certainty that "our Indigo Manufactory will prove an advantageous staple in this Colony." Seven years later, he noted that "the cultivation of Indigo create[s] such a demand" for slaves that slave traders were commanding unprecedented prices during public auctions.[11] As this economy gathered momentum, elite colonists began to express contempt for those settlers interested only in subsistence farming. For example, Laurens complained about "the Dutch People" who "continue but in low circumstances making very little if any thing more than a subsistence for their Familys." The Charlestown merchant regretfully concluded that "all that the bulk of them aim at is victuals & Clothing no matter how mean. Few of them seem to covet more."[12] Having embraced profit from the international market as the centerpiece of their economy, wealthy residents in the Deep South were mystified by those who rejected the potential fruits of international commerce. Localism had become an inscrutable economic riddle to a planter elite whose existence rested on a global perspective. Yet, at the same time, even the wealthiest members of colonial society could not completely immerse themselves in cosmopolitan culture.

Despite the slaveowners' thorough integration into a thriving international market, a sense of isolation and vulnerability plagued them for the better part of their colony's first century. English settlers were persistently threatened by disease and the possibility of a painful and early death.[13] The swamps that provided a hospitable environment for the cultivation of rice also harbored numerous pathogens such as malaria and dysentery, meaning that settlers could lose lives far more quickly than they could gain riches through distant business connections. In addition to incredibly high rates of disease-induced mortality, the colonists faced a disturbing human threat. Many Native American tribes already populated the land that the English king had awarded to the Carolina Proprietors. Although disease carried by European settlers thinned the ranks of the Cherokee, the Creek, and the Yamasee, these native inhabitants of the Deep South spent the colonial period making intermittent attacks on white interlopers. On an equally ominous note, the specter of violent reprisal also came from African slaves. By providing the Carolina planters with a captive labor force, the international market fostered a local demographic structure with unsettling implications for white masters. By 1708, blacks outnumbered whites in South Carolina; by 1740, twice as many slaves as free whites inhabited the colony, and in certain lowcountry parishes, slaves made up 90 percent of the population.[14]

In 1739, the slaveowners confronted their worst fears about their isolated position in the global economy. Seeking to foster discord in English settlements, Spanish authorities in St. Augustine, some two hundred miles south of Charlestown, announced a royal edict offering freedom to any slave escaping from English territory. As a result, according to South Carolina lieutenant governor William Bull, the colony's slaveholders worried that "their Negroes which were their chief support may in little time become their Enemies, if not their Masters, and that th[eir] Government [would be] unable to withstand or prevent it." Pointing to the defection of several slaves to Spanish territory, Bull warned imperial authorities that the affair might "entirely ruin" the colony.[15] White fears escalated when a band of slaves rebelled against their masters in a region near the Stono River some twenty miles from Charlestown. According to Bull, the insurrection began when "a great number of Negroes arose in Rebellion, broke open a Store where they got Arms[,] killed twenty one White Persons, and were marching the next morning in a Daring manner out of the Province, killing all they met."[16] Although white authorities captured and executed most of the insurgents the following day, those slaves that eluded pursuit kept white colonists in a constant state of alarm. By November 1739, according to records kept by the colonial assembly, a number of slaveholders in the Stono region had abandoned their plantations to live with other white families "at particular Places, for their better Security and Defence against those Negroes which were concerned in that Insurrection who were not yet taken."[17] One year later, South Carolina governor James Glen complained to Parliament about the colonists' most "dangerous Enemies[,] their own *Negroes,* who are ready to revolt on the first Opportunity and are Eight Times as many in Number as there are white Men able to bear Arms."[18] In their quest for wealth, slaveowners in South Carolina sacrificed not only the well-being of their slaves but also their own peace of mind.

Cognizant of the threats posed by potentially rebellious slaves, the Trustees of Georgia envisioned a different path for the colony that they had established in 1733. They hoped that Georgia would strengthen the English empire in two ways. First, they intended for the new colony to fortify South Carolina against Spanish territory on the Florida peninsula; second, they planned Georgia as a haven for unemployed Englishmen and their families.[19] Far more concerned with achieving these goals than with relieving the plight of suffering black bondservants, the Trustees banned slavery from Georgia in 1735.[20] They reasoned that the presence of large numbers of African Americans would undermine the colony's security and alienate the poor white settlers. Although the Anglican ministers involved in launching the colony insisted that "religion is the best Guardian of the publick Peace," they doubted that even a slave population exposed to Christian teachings could be controlled. "Perhaps it is imagined," wrote Benjamin Martyn in 1741, "that by gentle usage the negro may be made a trusty servant; this cannot be depended on. Every man is naturally fond of liberty, and he will struggle for it when he knows his own strength."[21] Had the Trustees' plan come to fruition, Georgia would not have developed the slave-based plantation economy that had played a formative role in the shaping of South Carolina. In planning the future of their colonial project, the Trustees sought to channel the colonists' individual desires in directions that would serve the corporate whole. Without slavery, the colony promised to serve the interests of poorer whites, not to mention the geopolitical interests of the English government and the holy interests of the Anglican Church.

The prohibition of slavery, however, quickly proved untenable. To be a sure, a few settlers objected to slavery on moral grounds. In 1739, eighteen Scots from the town of Darien signed a petition characterizing slavery as "shocking to human Nature" and a certain source for racial warfare—for a future "Scene of Horror." Their words reflected the first stirrings of an antislavery movement that, within a century, would sway the course of the mightiest nations. In the first half of the eighteenth century, however, such pleas fell largely on deaf ears.[22] Most white colonists denied that "the people of Georgia can ever get forward in their settlement or even be a degree above common slaves, without the help and assistance of negroes."[23] The Reverend John Martin Bolzius observed that his opposition to the importation of black slaves into Georgia made him an outcast. "All from the highest to the lowest" in the colony, he complained, "Vote for Negroes and look upon me as a Stone in their way . . . and they will, I suppose, not rest until they have removed it one way or other."[24]

By midcentury, colonists driven by the desire to profit from slavery overwhelmed government efforts to proscribe human bondage. Determined to acquire coastal land suitable for rice cultivation, slaveowners poured into Georgia from South Carolina.[25] In the face of widespread violation of the stricture against slavery, the Trustees formally repealed the ban in 1750.[26] Like their counterparts in South Carolina, Georgia settlers gained the freedom to experiment with different slave-produced staple crops to determine which ones promised the most wealth—a freedom they exercised with "the greatest pleasure."[27] As was the case in South Carolina, those colonists with sufficient access to slaves and the rich soil along the coast focused their efforts on the production of rice. By the 1760s, Georgia's economy and social structure greatly resembled those of South Carolina. The allure of profits from the international economy overpowered the Georgia Trustees, who were attempting to extend their Christian culture into a distant colony. The structure of the market, in other words, cultivated the thirst of individual settlers for personal profit. The Trustees' corporate social vision had little chance of competing with a market for staple crops that promised fabulous wealth to those individuals willing to manage an unfree labor force for personal gain.

The plantation economy of the Deep South promised to enrich England as well as the slaveowners. Nevertheless, the slaveowners' obsession with fiscal gain troubled representatives of the Anglican Church and the imperial government—organizations charged with maintaining order throughout God's kingdom. Although the Georgia Trustees capitulated on the question of slavery, English authorities still attempted to influence the settlers through structures of religion and government. Church emissaries and the king's officials worked to channel the colonists' entrepreneurial urges in a very specific direction—one that would provide the greatest benefit to the mother country. The colonists, on the other hand, sought to protect their economic liberties from interference. They had little use for macroeconomic theories about the benefits of mercantilism and even less for theological pronouncements about moral relationships between masters and slaves. Slavery played a paradoxical role in this tension between the drive for personal enrichment and the need to care for society as a whole. It provided the slaveowner with the opportunity for wealth. At the same time, however, it subjected the larger community to the risks of slave rebellion and introduced troublesome questions about society's obligations to every individual member—even the "lowliest" African slave.

Drawing on Christian tradition, many of the ministers who traveled to America believed that God's mandate for organic society would resolve the tension between individual profit and the welfare of the larger community. Over the course of centuries, Christian thinkers had rationalized slavery as an institution that helped to contain humankind's sinful nature within a hierarchy stretching from heaven to earth. Although theologians such as Saint Thomas Aquinas argued that slavery resulted from human imperfections, they also maintained that it combated those deficiencies by subordinating them to higher authorities.[28] The Reformation placed new emphasis on the conscience of the individual adherent and criticized the Catholic Church for its corruption, but Protestant authorities seldom wished to level earthly distinctions between unfree workers and their masters. Martin Luther, for example, denounced the German serf revolt of 1525, just eight years after he had posted his theses at Wittenberg; successive Protestant thinkers likewise tended to accept Catholic teachings about the need for masters and slaves to internalize Christian doctrines respecting mutual responsibilities.[29]

As a result, holy justification for earthly hierarchy and bondage followed the English colonists to all parts of America. In 1630, John Winthrop lectured his fellow settlers in Massachusetts—the future stronghold of the American antislavery movement—that "God Almighty in His most holy and wise providence hath so disposed of the condition of mankind as in all times some must be rich, some poor; some high and eminent in power and dignity, others mean and in subjection." According to Winthrop, this difference in worldly station did not create injustice because God would compel the highest members of society to care properly for their inferiors. The Almighty was "moderating and restraining" the wicked, "so that the rich and mighty should not eat up the poor, nor the poor and despised rise up against their superiors and shake off their yoke." Winthrop insisted that the tension between private gain and public good must always be resolved in favor of the latter. God's organic community enabled him "to account ourselves knit together by this bond of love" and to conclude that "the care of the public must oversway all private respects by which not only conscience but mere civil policy doth bind us; for it is a true rule that particular estates cannot subsist in the ruin of the public."[30]

Although Winthrop was a religious dissenter who risked his life to obtain liberty of conscience in the New World, the Anglican emissaries following him to America offered a similar message respecting the need for carefully structured hierarchy. Eager to promote religion in the colonies, Anglican missionary Thomas Bray organized the Society for the Propagation of the Gospel in Foreign Parts (SPG) in 1701. Through its economic and political clout, the organization secured funding for numerous American missions.[31] In 1706 SPG missionary Francis Le Jau arrived in Charlestown hoping to instill "the Dutys of Christian love and Humanity" among the masters, slaves, and American Indians living in South Carolina.[32] Following the theological course charted by Winthrop, Luther, Aquinas, and the many Christian authorities preceding the SPG's founding, Le Jau by no means disapproved of slavery in the abstract. Attempting to convey this fact to the suspicious Carolina slaveowners, he drew a clear distinction between the slaves' participation in church rites and emancipation from earthly bondage. "You [will] not ask for the holy baptism," insisted Le Jau to the slaves, "out of any design to free yourself from the Duty and Obedience you owe to your Master while you live."[33]

Despite these reassurances, slaveowners in South Carolina rebuffed Le Jau's efforts, fearing that his Christian mission would foment rebellion among their enslaved workers. Le Jau himself confronted this possibility when "the best Scholar of all the Negroes" in his parish "told his Master abruptly there wou'd be a dismal time and the Moon wou'd be turned into Blood." The incident caused Le Jau temporarily to doubt whether slaves had "judgment enough to make good use of their Learning." While his faith overcame such reservations and eventually enabled him to assert that slaves converted to Christianity "do better for their Masters profit than formerly, for they are taught to serve out of Christian Love & Duty," the slaveowners continued to suspect that Christianity would undermine their authority.[34] Given the Christian perspective on the slaveholders' ambition for personal riches, their fears had some foundation. Although Protestant theology developed the capacity to interpret the individual accumulation of great wealth as a sign of inner virtue, early-eighteenth-century ministers tended to associate abundant earthly riches with moral corruption.[35] Le Jau, for his part, believed that "the heart of a Christian" should never contain the desire "of getting easily great Estates."[36] Not surprisingly, Christian reasoning on this point did not convince the settlers who willingly risked all the uncertainties of the New World to enrich themselves.

White residents of the Deep South viewed Le Jau's proselytizing about proper interracial relationships as the meddling of an uninvited outside agitator. Pointing to the slaveholders' "Whispers" of disapproval and "Conduct" against him, Le Jau observed that they would "not have me urge of Contributing to the Salvation, Instruction, and human usage of Slaves and free Indians."[37] Le Jau realized that the slaveowners had rejected his appeal for a holy interracial community. "Many Masters," he concluded with sorrow, "can't be persuaded that Negroes and Indians are otherwise than Beasts, and use them like such."[38] The spg had hoped that the religious wisdom flowing from England into the colonies would reform the practices of American slaveowners. Instead, their ministers sent back to England a steady stream of bad news about colonial slaveowners' intransigence. "Permit my zeal My Lord to Implore your favour and Charity in behalf of the poor Slaves that live amongst us," wrote Le Jau to the bishop of London in 1712. "They are suffered; some forced to work upon Sundays, having no other means to subsist, they are used very cruelly many of them, the generality of Masters oppose that they should know any thing of Christianity."[39]

Reflecting on his failed mission during the last year of his ministry, Le Jau wrote that "indeed few Masters appear Zealous or even pleased with what the Missionaries try to do for the Good of their slaves, they are more Cruel Some of them of late Dayes than before, they hamstring, maim & unlimb those poor Creatures for Small faults." Le Jau's successors likewise reported that "the generality of people here wholly neglect their necessary duty" to their slaves' spiritual welfare.[40]

Undaunted by the slaveowners' response to religion in South Carolina, other ministers attempted similar missions in Georgia. In 1723, supporters of Thomas Bray, the missionary who had engineered the spg's initial efforts, formed an organization dedicated to Christianizing African Americans. The Associates of Dr. Bray played a pivotal role in securing royal support for the new colony.[41] In 1751, following the decision to legalize slavery in Georgia, they sent the Reverend Joseph Ottolenghe to Savannah to bring Christian faith to the slaves and masters living in the coastal swamplands.[42] At first, Ottolenghe reported to his superiors in London that "God has been very Merciful to me in Blessing my poor Endeavours with Good Success." Many of the slaves, he wrote with pride, had "gone thro' the Catechism, & several begin to read tolerably well."[43] His optimism, however, soon retreated in the face of the realization that the "penurious Masters" believed "that they should be great Losers should they permit their Slaves to learn what they must do to be saved." Like Le Jau before him, Ottolenghe argued that Christianity would transform an "immoral dishonest Domestic" into "a faithful Servant," but the missionary discovered that many slaveowners "will upon no Account whatever suffer their Slaves to be instructed in the Christian Religion alledging . . . that a Slave is ten times worse when a Christian, than in his State of Paganism."[44]

Although Ottolenghe and Le Jau failed miserably in their efforts to Christianize slavery in the colonial Deep South, their frustrations did not result from a fundamental disparity between Christian doctrine and the institution of slavery. Ottolenghe spent much of his time in Georgia directing his own slaves to cultivate silk for profit on the transatlantic market, and the Associates of Dr. Bray had been named for a man who sanctioned slavery both as a means of saving the African soul and as a labor system that would finance missionary activity.[45] For that matter, the Congregationalists of New England maintained John Winthrop's legacy by continuing to approve of slavery. Cotton Mather, for example, implored African Americans in Massachusetts to renounce their "fondness for freedom."[46] Even the Baptists— the denomination most associated with the leveling of earthly social ranking—maintained that slavery did not violate Scripture. In 1710 the Baptist Church in Charlestown debated a slave code provision that implemented castration as punishment for certain crimes committed by slaves. Concerned about the morality of such brutal castigation, the South Carolina Baptists consulted with the Baptist Church in South Moulton, England, which upheld the righteousness of slave castration when performed in the spirit of "preserving order" and protecting the "common good." The Baptists concluded that Scripture permitted masters to keep their slaves "in order, and under government; and for Self preservation, [to] punish them to prevent farther Mischief."[47] Although interdenominational rivalry prevented the Baptists and Congregationalists from cooperating with the efforts of Anglican organizations such as the SPG and the Associates of Dr. Bray, the early-eighteenth-century Christian world largely agreed about the moral grounding of human bondage.

Yet slaveowners in the Deep South and throughout the Western Hemisphere bristled in the presence of missionaries. In no small part this antipathy resulted from the planters' troubled relationship with the cultural structures linking the colonies with England—in this case, religious organizations such as the SPG and the Associates of Dr. Bray. Notwithstanding the tremendous wealth engendered by plantations in the Lower South, the slaveowners' vulnerable position within the larger world of international commerce and culture denied them the confidence of an entrenched elite. Facing threats from disease, hostile Indians, and rebellious slaves, they derived their wealth on the periphery of what they deemed civilization. The prospect of early death undermined the confidence of slaveowning families, and the great distance separating them from metropolitan England frustrated their efforts to translate riches into social stature. Having taken the first steps toward transforming themselves into members of the English upper class and having discovered numerous obstacles blocking them from their ultimate goal, colonial slaveholders had little patience for the criticism of proselytizing outsiders, however well meaning. On the question of managing their enslaved workforce, the colonists in the Deep South preferred to remain on the periphery of the empire, safe from the prying eyes of overly sensitive missionaries.[48]

More to the point, slaveowners resisted missionary efforts because they feared that religion would undermine their authority over their slaves and jeopardize their market-oriented economy. They resented transatlantic religious organizations that judged their communities by the standards of a universal morality. Although the Baptists in Charlestown no doubt appreciated the vote of confidence offered by their spiritual brethren in England in the early eighteenth century, slaveowners across the Deep South must have found it troubling that people four thousand miles away would pass judgment on their society. Denied direct access to the slaves, Anglican authorities could at least present their organic perspective on the master-slave relationship in print. Authors such as William Fleetwood, Edmund Gibson, Stephen Hales, and Samuel Smith emphasized that the Scripture instructed slaves to "obey in all things, your Masters according to the Flesh." But they also enjoined slaveowners in the Deep South to fulfill their own responsibilities to God.[49] In language foreshadowing the themes that would be repeatedly evoked by later generations of proslavery writers, ministers such as Smith called for the colonial plantation household to become a religious family whose needs would be overseen by a benevolent master. In a sermon to the Georgia Trustees in 1733 that would later be published, Smith averred that "every house . . . should be a render'd in some sense a temple, and every planter a priest." Notwithstanding Anglican efforts to disperse these tracts in the colonies, the collective spiritual voices of Anglican activists totaled nothing more than a tiny whisper amid the desolate religious environment of the early colonial South. Never one for brevity, William Fleetwood called for organic family relations in an expensive, weighty tome of five hundred pages that was far beyond the intellectual and financial grasp of most white southerners. And slaveowner hostility toward the Anglican Church ensured that pamphlets which were effectively dispersed in the South (such as Gibson's) managed to change very few slaveowners' opinions about their responsibilities toward their slaves. Thus early efforts to extend a Christian infrastructure across the Atlantic met with almost complete failure because the slaveowners considered the missionaries' product to be dangerous and unnecessary.[50]

A number of ministers also directly contributed to colonial reservations about transatlantic religious organizations by conducting themselves with little regard for Christian teachings. Dissipation posed a common problem for visiting clergy. Le Jau, for example, reported in 1712 that he and his fellow ministers had expelled from their ranks the Reverend Mr. Gignilliat for repeatedly abandoning his parish and abusing his wife.[51] Alexander Garden, the bishop of London's commissary in Charlestown, complained in 1737 about John Boyd, the spg's minister in North Carolina. Garden wrote to the bishop to give "some Hints of [Boyd's] Idleness & Inclination to Drunkenness," noting that he had been spotted "Lying dead Drunk & fast asleep on the Great Road to Virginia, with his Horses Bridle tyed to his Leg."[52] That such behavior persisted throughout the colonial period was evident when, in 1762, Savannah minister John Moore informed his superiors about William Duncanson, a minister "dismissed from the Service of the Society on account of some gross Misdemeanours; such as Excess of Drinking, profane Swearing, &c."[53] Hesitant to surrender their power to missionaries reporting to church officials residing far away from the southern plantations, planters in South Carolina and Georgia were especially dismayed to learn, firsthand, that the ministers charged with governing moral life in the colonies had difficulty restraining their own inclinations toward vice. The onset of evangelicalism in the 1740s, moreover, intensified the slaveowners' foreboding that religion would unravel the cords binding slaves to their masters.

Amid the slaveowners' alarm over the Stono Rebellion and a fire that destroyed a large portion of Charlestown in 1740, George Whitefield initiated his efforts to integrate the Deep South into his sophisticated religious network. At first, anxieties of the white settlers heightened the appeal of Whitefield's call for spiritual rebirth. Marshaling his unparalleled talent as a preacher, Whitefield drew crowds in South Carolina and Georgia that were sufficiently large and unruly to alienate Anglican authorities such as Alexander Garden.[54] Garden denounced Whitefield's style of preaching for generating too much enthusiasm on the part of the laity—enthusiasm that might undermine the authority of the Anglican Church and the stability of southern society. On these grounds, he condemned Whitefield for the "Frenzie" that he had aroused among "the People" and for "the Bitterness and Virulence wherewith he raved against the Clergy of the Ch[urch] of England in general."[55] "He boasts himself to be some great One indeed, sent forth from God . . . to give Light to the World," reported Garden to the bishop in April 1740. Much to Garden's displeasure, "the Multitude ran to hear [Whitefield]; and the Ears and Passions, not the Understanding of the Lower Sort, Specially Dissenters[,] were taken."[56] Garden especially feared the "Trances, Visions and Revelations, both 'mong Blacks and Whites," that Whitefield's preaching had generated "in abundance."[57]

As Frank Lambert and Harry S. Stout have suggested, this burst of religious enthusiasm was not simply an otherworldly affair. In addition to their fervent and contagious faith, mid-eighteenth-century figures such as Whitefield depended on an extremely sophisticated international network of supporters to promote their messages. At the same time that Whitefield (as Stout observes) explicitly "condemned peddlers, entertainers, dancers, jugglers, and actors" who personified an expanding, presumably Godless, market culture, the religious orator cleverly tailored his appeal to "draw crowds away" from them. For all the emotional overtones of the New Birth, Whitefield's commercial savvy led him into a mutually profitable relationship with the emblematic figure of the American Enlightenment, Benjamin Franklin. Lambert presents Whitefield as a "powerful salesman" whose "immersion in a thoroughly commercialized society . . . provided him with the means of constructing a new religious discourse." And both Lambert and Stout note that Whitefield's individualistic theology reinforced his earthly preoccupation with commercial matters. By the middle of the century, well-organized committees of letter-writing supporters were narrowing the cultural distance between the continents, mastering the art of advertising to maximize attendance at Whitefield's sermons (which drew crowds of up to thirty thousand), and increasing demand for his published sermons (which became commodities to be marketed globally).[58]

Here, the transatlantic cultural market offered to the colonists a new paradigm for family relations—a paradigm that centered on a philosophy of corporate individualism. Evoking sentimental conceptions of the parent-child and master-servant relationship, Whitefield appealed to men to fulfill their responsibilities to their household subordinates. To parents, he stated that "love and pity" for "the darling of their hearts" should motivate a greater regard for their spiritual welfare. To masters, Whitefield argued that the principle of reciprocity made it unjust for them to demand "bodily work" from their servants only to deny them "some spiritual as well as temporal wages." Whitefield ultimately emphasized that household dependents had the capacity for personal growth. Far from encouraging "children and servants to disregard their parents and masters according to the flesh," the "improvement of their souls" would lead them to "perform their duties" to their earthly superiors with greater enthusiasm.[59]

Whitefield confronted monumental obstacles when he attempted to apply these principles to slaveowning society. On his arrival in the South, Whitefield struggled to demonstrate to local slaveholders that Christianity posed no threat to their mastery. Entering the debate over the Georgia Trustees' ban on slavery, for example, Whitefield had asserted that denying slaves to the settlers was like "tyeing their legs and bidding them to walk."[60] Nevertheless, Whitefield ultimately alienated the slaveholding elite by invoking the moral standards of the expanding transatlantic religious community and chastising the planters for their failures before God. Disgusted by the slaveowners' refusal to acknowledge their Christian duties toward their slaves, Whitefield published a tract in 1740 charging that "God has a quarrel" with the southern masters for their "Abuse and Cruelty to the poor Negroes." Slaves led such a wretched existence that in Whitefield's opinion, "perhaps it might be better for the poor Creatures themselves, to be hurried out of Life." Although Whitefield reiterated his belief that Christ required slaves "to be Subject, in all lawful Things, to their Masters," the minister confessed that "considering what Usage they commonly meet with, I have wondered, that . . . they have not more frequently rose up in Arms against their Owners." Whitefield prayed that "they may never be permitted to get the upper hand" but observed that "should such a Thing be permitted by Providence, all good Men must acknowledge the Judgement would be just."[61] Central to Whitefield's religious project was his insistence that African Americans were human beings who were "naturally capable of the same Improvement" as whites. His regard for the potential moral progress of the most degraded members of society forced Anglican authorities to draft their own response to this challenge against the slaveowning elite.[62]

Dismayed by Whitefield's rebuke, Alexander Garden stepped forward to defend the southern status quo. Although other missionaries visiting the Deep South had corroborated Whitefield's assertions about the brutality of plantation slavery, Garden publicly attacked him for questioning the morality of the slaveowning colonists. According to Garden, "the Generality of Owners use their slaves with all due Humanity, whether in respect of Work, of Food, or Raiment." The Charlestown minister agreed with Whitefield that God would, in fact, "have a Quarrel with any of the Human Race, for their Abuse of and Cruelty to others," but he characterized the charge as "false and injurious" when leveled against southern planters. He even asserted that far "from being miserable," southern slaves were "more happy and comfortable in all temporal respects (the Point of Liberty only excepted) than the Lives of three fourths of the hired farming Servants, and Day Laborers, either in Scotland, Ireland or even many Parts of England." Wage laborers, noted Garden, constantly worried "how to provide for their Families," a burden "which Slaves are entirely exempted from, their Children being all provided for at the Owners' Charge." That the slaves remained "ignorant of Christianity" Garden attributed to "the want of one certain uniform Method of teaching them," rather than to the slaveowners' ill intentions.[63]

As the first resident of the Deep South to make a public justification of slavery—one that presented the same tenets of corporate individualism articulated by southern proslavery writers over the next 125 years—Garden demonstrated that slaveholders could place critics of slavery on the defensive by employing Christian notions of reciprocal responsibilities between master and slave. And while Garden clearly deluded himself when he denied the brutality of plantation slavery, the minister did attempt to practice what he preached. Upon his arrival in Charlestown as a representative of the bishop of London and the SPG, he struggled to establish a school for African Americans. Garden envisioned an educational system in which black schoolmasters would teach slave children who would, in turn, enlighten their parents. He believed that within "the Space of Twenty years, the knowledge of the Gospel 'mong the slaves . . . (excepting those newly Imported) would not be much inferiour to that of the lower sort of white People, Servants & day Labourers." Through religious instruction, Garden hoped to raise black slaves almost to the level of productive, God-fearing white workers.[64]

Although Garden had employed Christianity in defense of southern slavery, his plans to incorporate the slaves into a wider religious community encompassing both whites and blacks received little support from local slaveholders. Garden observed that because his proposal "contains in it the loss of the Annual Profit from the labour" of the slaves serving as schoolmasters, "no body would be prevailed with to put it into Practice." The SPG ultimately agreed to purchase two slaves to serve as schoolmasters, and Garden, with some assistance from the Associates of Dr. Bray, managed to establish his school in Charlestown during the early 1740s. South Carolina slaveholders, however, never shared his enthusiasm and probably applauded when a hurricane leveled the school in 1752. Persistent to the end, Garden rebuilt it, but his death four years later marked the downfall of efforts to educate the colony's slaves. In 1759, Richard Clarke, Garden's successor as the institution's supervisor, predicted doom for South Carolina before fleeing the country for England. He left in his wake rampant fears of slave insurrection and the slaveholders' marked aversion to all efforts at incorporating the slaves into a larger religious community.[65]

Clarke's dramatic exit reminded the planters that despite the explicitly proslavery viewpoints articulated by such missionaries as Garden, Ottolenghe, and Le Jau, Christianity carried a potentially incendiary message to the enslaved. If the Scripture set forth the ideal of servitude to God and Christ as the key to salvation, it also announced that the lowliest slave possessed a soul as worthy as that of the most powerful king. The moral structure of the universe hinged on the Lord's carefully planned hierarchy of spiritual and animal life, but within that hierarchy righteous men and women were supposed to recognize their religious bond with the rest of humanity. By emphasizing one element of this duality over the other, proslavery and antislavery forces could each claim that certain passages in the New Testament supported their respective arguments. For example, ministers proselytizing in favor of human bondage pointed to Paul's decision to return Onesimus to his master, Philemon; they observed that the apostle could not decide the slave's fate without knowing his owner's will. On the other hand, critics of slavery could note that Paul had implored Philemon to receive Onesimus "no longer as a slave, but as more than a slave: as a dear brother, very dear to me, and still dearer to you, both as a man and as a Christian."[66] During the colonial period, the antislavery implications of such biblical reasoning had a profound impact on slaveowners in the Deep South. However much missionaries attempted to reassure the slaveowners that religion would make their slaves more faithful workers, masters in South Carolina and Georgia feared the legacy of biblical prophets who promised to "loose the fetters of injustice, to untie the knots of the yoke, and set free those who are oppressed."[67] By the middle of the eighteenth century, Christian concern for the downtrodden was beginning to spark the first widespread rejection in world history of slavery as an institution. Representative of this ideological movement were the men and women of conscience who complained, as did one resident of Barbados, that there was "no Such thing as being a Christian" in places where "so many wretched Slaves" made life "a Kind of Hell."[68] The planters of the Lower South quickly learned that such Christian spiritual awakenings could jeopardize their mastery. In 1741, George Whitefield's sermons aroused Hugh Bryan, a resident of both Georgia and South Carolina, to a new sense of responsibility toward the multitude of slaves supposedly lingering in spiritual darkness around him. In the wake of the Stono Rebellion and the Charlestown fire, Bryan's actions unleashed another specter that threatened to destroy the slaveholders' world.

Unlike Whitefield, who had tempered his criticism of the southern slaveholders' transgressions by firmly upholding the righteousness of human bondage as an earthly institution, Bryan denied that God compelled the slaves' obedience toward earthly masters. The Georgia Trustees learned that Bryan had instructed slaves belonging to other colonists to "not go to work but [to] go & seek Christ [for] he was their master." Thrilled that a white authority figure had encouraged them to disregard their owners' commands, the slaves replied "in the Height of Joy & Transport" that "Christ was a very good Master" and then "went raving in the Woods for some time" until "their Masters were oblig'd to take them under discipline."[69] Bryan himself then retired to the woods, where he prophesied that the coastal slaveowners would "be destroyed by fire and sword" at the hands of their slaves.[70]

Aghast by these proceedings, a Charlestown jury indicted Bryan for assembling "great Bodies of Negroes" on the "Pretence of religious Worship" and for making "sundry enthusiastick Prophecies" concerning "the Destruction" of the city and the "Deliverance of the Negroes from their Servitude."[71] City authorities also detained Whitefield after they confirmed that he had edited an incendiary letter that Bryan published in the *South Carolina Gazette*. In this letter, Bryan ominously observed (amid the owners' fears of slave revolt) that "God's just Judgements are upon us." The situation resolved itself in March 1742, when Bryan apologized to the colonial assembly for his actions; moreover, in the following years, he and his brother Jonathan learned how to reconcile plantation slavery with Christian notions of organic hierarchy and eventually became prominent, respected planters in Georgia.[72] Most slaveowners, however, hardly noticed the evolution of his views. They had already concluded that Christianity threatened slavery.[73]

The ministers who believed that Christianity should buttress the slaveholding order struggled to distance themselves from Bryan's revolutionary efforts, but to little avail. Garden, for example, condemned Bryan's religious fervor and applauded when Bryan confessed that he had "had his eyes opened, and saw himself under the Delusion of the Devil."[74] Yet these denunciations of radical religious behavior could not overcome the owners' belief that Christianity in any form carried ominous implications for the master-slave relationship. Slaveowners ignored even respected clergymen such as Garden when they sermonized about the slaveholders' holy obligations. However much the Anglican commissary approved of the social boundaries delineating masters from slaves, Garden proved no more successful than Bryan in exposing the plantations to the teachings of the Lord.[75] For the Anglican missionaries, a global market for religious culture offered the means by which the distant colonies could be subordinated within a holy social hierarchy characterized by reciprocal responsibilities between superiors and inferiors. "Our great Metropolis," observed Samuel Smith, "is the common Receptacle of the Wealth of the Plantations, and enrich'd by the Drudgery of our *Negroe* Slaves." "If we think the Gospel too chargeable a Commodity to import to them in Return," he continued, "we must be lost to all that is generous in our Religion and Nature." Smith insisted that white English subjects who benefited from "the Distinctions of our Complexion and Station" fulfill "the Duties of Common Benevolence and Christian Charity" to pay off their debt to the Lord. It was exactly this sense of obligation, however, that the colonists in the South eagerly wanted to avoid. Southern slaveowners ignored even the proslavery rhetoric of ministers such as Garden because they wanted to remain unencumbered by a religious dynamic that would bind their actions toward their slaves.[76]

Despite decades of missionary activity in the Deep South, the Anglican and evangelical campaign to Christianize the plantations made little discernible progress. Although a few colonial planters attested that their "negroes were instructed in the Christian religion," Anglican minister Charles Martyn reported in 1762 that out of a slave population numbering some forty-six thousand, he "imagine[d] there are five Hundred who are Christians"—a figure representing only 1 percent of the total number of slaves. Christianity had hardly advanced from its atrophied state earlier in the eighteenth century, when SPG ministers offered similar estimates for slave participation in Christian rituals.[77] In this depressing religious atmosphere, Christian activists continued to exert their energies. In 1762, one of George Whitefield's associates reported from the colony that "religion in these provinces is dreadfully languid! Now & then one is converted—but our Souls long for thousands, even for a Number equal to the Drops of the Morning Dew."[78] Try as they might, however, the ministers had failed to establish a holy transatlantic community that included both slaves and their masters. Despised as a savage domestic presence over the first two-thirds of the eighteenth century, African Americans would "converse almost wholly among themselves" and would continue to exist, in Garden's words, as "a Nation within a Nation."[79]

Like the religious emissaries sent from England, officials of the royal government attempted to knit the colonies more tightly into the fabric of the British Empire. Le Jau, Ottolenghe, Garden, and many other missionaries had insisted that the Lord cared for every human being's fate—that God's compassionate demands linked all living creatures. When considering the proper course for governing the colonies, the King's representatives echoed this holy call for organic unity. In their opinion, England had established the colonies to strengthen her standing as a nation. Eighteenth-century British economic policy—referred to as "mercantilism" by later scholars—assigned a tributary role to the settlements in the New World.[80] By supplying England with needed commodities and by serving as a market for her manufactured goods, the colonies were supposed to enrich the mother country and the empire as a whole. Although the planters rejected missionary efforts to integrate them into a transatlantic religious community, they responded more ambiguously to the colonial government established by the Crown.

In most instances the settlers desired closer ties with the British metropolis. Surrounded by dangers, southern slaveowners looked to their distant king for support. The colonists, for example, applauded the king's decision to finance the construction of a fort on the Altamaha River in 1738. "From so Signal an Instance of His Majesty's Paternal Care," wrote William Bull, "the Inhabitants of Carolina have the greatest Encouragement to hope that his Majesty will be Graciously pleased to continue his Protection and to Support the Possessions which have been acquired at the Expense of so much Blood, and so many of the Lives of His faithfull and Loyal Subjects."[81]

Unfortunately, from the colonists' perspective, the British government seldom provided such support. The Carolina Proprietors formally surrendered their colonial power to the royal government in 1729, and the Georgia Trustees lost control of their colony to the king in 1752. Yet the vast distances between the colonies and England undermined royal efforts to administer daily life in the Deep South. In the same letter in which Bull acknowledged the king's aid, he also bemoaned the insufficient military strength of the colonies in the Deep South. "The Provinces of Carolina and Georgia," according to Bull, could not "raise above three or four Thousand fighting men" — hardly a sufficient number to confront the impending danger posed by French and Spanish forces. As Bull reminded his superiors in England, "an army of Seven Thousand men (most of them disciplin'd Troops) were ready to Embark from Havanna" to be "Joyned by fifteen hundred French" in order to conquer both South Carolina and Georgia. The southern slaveowners, moreover, faced dangers even more terrifying than their European enemies. The colonists consistently reminded imperial officials that the benefits of a slave-based plantation economy carried with them the constant risk of slave insurrection—a risk that could be sufficiently minimized only with appropriate military assistance from the English metropole.[82]

If the colonists' lives depended on the maintenance of close ties with England, so too did their fortunes. As we have already seen, English credit financed the colonization of the South; English ships carried the slaveowners' commodities to European and Caribbean markets and supplied their plantations with African slaves. By the middle of the eighteenth century, settlers in the Deep South looked to British expertise to derive greater financial returns from their agricultural ventures. In 1755 Alexander Garden II, the son of the Anglican minister in Charlestown, conveyed to the Royal Society of Arts his desire to increase plantation efficiency. Writing to an English correspondent, Garden speculated that "the Models which you have received of Machines for improvements in the Manufactures must be extremely curious" and expressed his "hope that in some time they will be communicated." Garden wanted the slaveowners to benefit from machines that could "pound as much rice in one day as 16 Negros."[83]

Separated from England's scientific discoveries by a vast ocean, the colonies remained isolated from a progressive European sensibility that, according to reformers such as Garden, would make society more efficient and humane. Garden lamented that "we have but very few Ingenious Machines here in this province to facilitate labour." In the place of labor-saving technology, the planters relied on "the poor slaves hard labour & the loss of many of their lives testified [to] the fatigue they underwent in satiating the inexplicable Avarice of their Master[s]." Like the religious reformers who chastised the slaveowners for placing short-term financial gains before the eternal profit of God's organic community, Garden criticized the planters for fixating on immediate gains and losses at the expense of their long-term prospects. "As every trial is not attended to great advantage," wrote Garden, "the very first disappointment in not finding their desired profits makes them relinquish the most advantageous projects." In his opinion, the "tedious, laborious & slow Method of Cultivating" employed by the slaveholders resulted in the unnecessary death of valuable slaves. "And how can it well be otherwise," wrote Garden, "the wretches being obliged to labour hard to compleat their task," which "soon rids them of cruel Masters or more cruel overseers & ends their wretched beings here." Clearly the younger Garden did not share his father's optimism concerning the slaveowners' willingness to sacrifice their temporary financial interests for the long-term good of society. He believed that greater cultural intercourse with England might liberate the slaveowners from the "heavy dull trodden path" of inefficient production to which they had "been accustomed."[84]

Other prominent colonists, however, suspected that the transatlantic framework for the exchange of culture and commerce would limit America to a peripheral position as a supplier of commodities, as a land lacking its own mature economy and social institutions. Garden himself expressed this fear when the Swedish naturalist Peter Kalm visited America and "went home to Sweden laden [with] the Spoils" of his scientific foray—namely, the privilege of classifying for the first time various species of plant and animal life. Disgusted "that not only the advantages of such discoveries but the entire honour shall be the invaluable possession of Sweden," Garden complained that the British colonies would not "reap the advantages of their Labours & public spiritedness."[85] Although Garden limited his charge of exploitation to such foreign nations as Sweden, American critics of British mercantilist policy noted that England itself was purposely impeding the development of autonomous institutions in the colonies.[86]

Southern conceptions about the proper relationship between America and England shifted dramatically in the wake of the French and Indian War. Although the conflict ultimately solidified England's position as the dominant power in North America, British imperial policy during the nine-year struggle jeopardized the slaveowners in the Deep South. News of General Braddock's disastrous attempt to capture Montreal reached the planters in summer 1755, sparking their contention that the "Ministry would do well to prosecute a War in America with Americans." Frustrated with the weakness of the British military campaign, Henry Laurens asserted that the "English Veterans" should have "staid at home as the advantage the Enemy have gain'd by their shamefull behaviour will put us to ten times the inconveniency in this part of the World tha[n] their coming has been of service."[87] Slaveowner resentment intensified the following year when British officials resettled approximately one thousand French Acadians in the Deep South. These prisoners of war represented a new domestic threat to the planters — one that led South Carolina governor James Glen to complain to his superiors. "The danger that many People apprehend" from the French prisoners, wrote Glen, "gives the utmost uneasiness, for tho' their number is not sufficient to attempt anything by force, yet they may watch opportunitys and join with the Negroes."[88]

Episodes like these prompted the slaveowners to question why the Crown provided them with so little assistance and so many headaches. In December 1756, merchants and planters "interested in the Trade & Prosperity of South Carolina and Georgia" reminded the king that "by means of their Negroes" their colonies returned greater wealth "to Great Britain than any Colony on the Continent of an equal number of White Inhabitants." The petitioners realized that their status as slaveholders placed them "in a more dangerous situation in Case of an attack from the French than any others, as their whole domestick force would in Such a Crisis be required to Keep their Negroes . . . in proper subjection."[89] As such, southern planters framed their proposals for military aid in terms of their special needs as slaveowners. South Carolina slaveowner and official Charles Pinckney, for example, informed British authorities of the need to "leave a considerable part of the militia at home in their several Districts to guard against the insurrection of their Slaves, as they will be incited by the French to rise upon their masters and cut their throats in hopes of obtaining freedom."[90]

The disappointment of the slaveowners must have been profound when British officials responded to their dilemma not with military assistance but with a moratorium on rice exports—a policy designed to prevent the commodity from falling into the hands of the French.[91] In addition, colonists such as Christopher Gadsden complained bitterly about British interference with the South Carolina militia. When English officer James Grant accused the southerners of cowardice, Gadsden published several essays returning the charge.[92] By the time the French capitulated in 1763, many white southerners had begun to suspect that imperial policy potentially threatened their mastery. Over the course of the ensuing decade, more and more slaveholders would respond to British authority with the same resentment they had reserved for Christian missionaries trying to temper the master-slave relationship with the gospel. Notwithstanding the explosive growth of their economy, planters in the Deep South turned a wary eye across the Atlantic Ocean. Global fiscal connections were enriching them, but the slaveowners remained suspicious of the organic doctrines offered by church and state. In the slaveowners' minds, those doctrines threatened to subordinate their mastery to a greater common good and leave them penniless, or even dead, on the shores of a continent four thousand miles from London's bustling streets.

From the earliest days of colonization, the settlers had viewed England as the fountainhead of civilization—as the place where one could acquire the social graces that differentiated refined citizens from wealthy but mannerless nabobs.[93] In 1748, for example, Henry Laurens had promised his stepmother that a "Voyage to London should Polish me & make me quite Polite."[94] Educating their sons at English schools and filling their libraries with English books, the wealthiest colonists structured their notions of elite behavior around the traditional standards of the English aristocracy. Of course, slaveowners in the Deep South faced an uphill battle in emulating a British elite that had managed to separate courtly manners and country estates from mundane monetary transactions. Unlike English manors, southern plantations revolved around the naked oppression of slavery. The institution of human bondage enriched the slaveowners of the Deep South, but it also hindered their efforts to attain the desired status of a landed elite. In printed works ranging from travelogues to novels, authors working in the English metropolis articulated a fierce contempt for the colonial planters' crude exploitation of an enslaved African labor force. British authors such as Edward Kimber (who published an account of his visit to the Chesapeake in *London Magazine* in 1746) acknowledged the slaveowners' "considerable Marks of Opulency" but denounced them for conducting auctions in which slaves were handled "as the Butchers do the Beasts in *Smithfield*, to see if they are Proof in Cod, Flank, and Shoulders." As the historian Michael J. Rozbicki has suggested, the British elite's perceptions of slavery as a distasteful violation of polite standards for society cast a shadow over the very wealth on which colonial planters staked their claims to the status of a gentry.[95]

Nevertheless, by the 1760s at least a few wealthy white settlers were attempting to reconcile English precepts for mannered behavior with the grim realities of plantation slavery. Slaveholders chased away the ministers who dared to preach about the reciprocal aspects of the master-slave relationship, but they did not divorce themselves entirely from the widely celebrated ethos of noblesse oblige or, for that matter, from mainstream British culture. Concerns that Christianity might threaten their profits had fostered the slaveowners' hostility toward religious reform; ironically, however, involvement in the international market also exposed white southerners to prescriptions for elite behavior that downplayed vulgar emphasis on individual profit. Through avid reading, many of the wealthiest planters and merchants encountered such authors as Shakespeare, who denounced the single-minded pursuit of personal riches as an activity detrimental to society. In *Merchant of Venice*, for example, Shylock's ugliness as a character stemmed from his assertion that wealth alone provided life with meaning:

> You take my house when you do take the prop
> That doth sustain my house; you take my life
> When you do take the means whereby I live.[96]

Scholars such as David S. Shields have demonstrated that by the mid–eighteenth century, a network of coffeehouses and salons had linked American colonists to a cosmopolitan corporate sensibility that was typically articulated in works of literature. It was, of course, ironic that the very global economic connections that had spawned a cruel traffic in human flesh also provided a venue for the expression of an aesthetic that valued sociability and humanity more than the coldhearted pursuit of individual gain.[97]

Although colonial entrepreneurs had more in common with Shylock than they cared to admit, some of the most prominent southern landowners formulated identities as virtuous citizens. Hoping to disassociate themselves from Shylock's willingness to exact "a pound of flesh" to enforce the repayment of a debt, elite southerners eschewed the charge of selfishness. Alarmed by an accusation of "ungenteel" behavior, Henry Laurens assured an anxious debtor in 1747 that "I counted so Little upon the money you Receiv'd of me, that I should [have] been content to Let it remain unpaid 'till your Convenience."[98] Eight years later, Laurens demonstrated his willingness to sacrifice money for the sake of maintaining his reputation as a righteous member of his community. "The money is a thing we dont in the least mind," he informed a partner. "We are only endeavouring to avoid the censure of our Neighbours that they should not charge us with making Innovations on the Commissions they have been always accustom'd to."[99]

In fact, by the second half of the eighteenth century, prosperous colonial merchants such as Peter Manigault, Henry Laurens, and James Habersham were transforming themselves into genteel landowners, acquiring lowcountry plantations and marrying into prominent families.[100] Exchanging their mercantile operations for what they deemed the more settled life of plantation ownership, these men anticipated filling their days with pleasurable intellectual and social pursuits. "I am at this middle state of Life," observed Laurens in 1764, "retreating by gradual Steps from that bustle & hurry that my attention to commerce had unavoidably led me into." "I think there can hardly be a greater" misfortune, he announced on another occasion, "than for a Man either thro' habit or necessity to be drudging all his days in a constant hurry of Trade."[101] Two years later, Charlestown merchant Richard Hutson expressed the same goal: "I am going now to turn Planter & shall reside a great part of my time in the Country, where I shall be always at leisure to receive your letters."[102] Framing plantation ownership in ideal terms, these men hoped to disassociate themselves from the vulgar pursuit of wealth. Laurens, for instance, preferred the life of the planter to the "retail Trade," which he dismissed as "mean" and which he believed "Lessen[ed its practitioners] in the esteem of people whose respect they must endeavour to attract."[103]

As a cultural impulse, the desire to play the role of the landed country gentleman sprang from a transatlantic exchange of values. The colonists most exposed (through their own commercial activity) to society in the English metropolis demonstrated the greatest eagerness to emulate standards of gentility that required the wealthy to distance themselves from overt preoccupation with personal gain. When colonial merchants acquired plantations, they not surprisingly fitted them with all the trappings of polite British society, a feat made easier by the steady flow of consumer goods from England into the slaveowning economy. Hence, Elias Ball, Henry Laurens's brother-in-law, stocked his plantation household with fine china, Windsor chairs, and mahogany furniture. Indicating the geographic orientation of his aspirations for social status, Ball named his plantations Kensington and Hyde Park and decorated them with "two handsome Landscapes" of these London suburbs.[104] As we have seen, religious and literary institutions provided the means by which an influential minority of slaveowning society attempted to convey these standards of gentility to the colonies. Anglican reformers offered a message of universal salvation, a creed that washed over the boundaries between regions and races with a common fealty to a loving deity. For this reason, Henry Laurens claimed that "Members of various outward denominations & professions amongst Christians" were "all Led by the same Spirit."[105] Likewise, the Bible belonging to the Mackay family, prominent merchants in Savannah, contained an inscription reaching out to "All Persons black or White, bond or free, who are willing to save themselves and be happy." The Mackays conceptualized God as a "gatherer of . . . all members from the East & from the West from the North and from the South of all nations & all colours to one Grand Body to join in the Universal Songs of Praise."[106] Successful colonial businesspeople also pursued this corporate social agenda through institutions such as the Charleston Library Society, an organization managed by men like Henry Laurens. In justifying its mission, the society equated civilization and political power with literary refinement and social grace and looked to England as the source for texts that would prevent the colonists from "sinking" into the state of "gross Ignorance" exhibited by "the naked Indian."[107]

Although wealthy planters increasingly dreaded isolation from the metropolis, closer cultural ties to England posed difficulties for slaveowners who had grown accustomed to exercising absolute authority over their bondservants.[108] Campaigns to ameliorate plantation slavery—to make southern slaveholders accountable to God and to their British sovereign— had consistently originated in the British metropolis. In the first half of the eighteenth century, the crusade to reform slavery had been waged almost exclusively by missionary organizations that the slaveholders could ignore with impunity. But as England began to administrate the colonies more closely in the 1760s, government officials began to echo Christian doctrine concerning masters and slaves. In 1766, King George III directed South Carolina's new governor, Charles Montagu, to "endeavour to get a Law passed (if not already done) for the restraining of any inhuman severity, which if by ill Masters or Overseers may be used toward their Christian Servants & their Slaves, and that Provision be made therein, that the willful killing of Indians and Negroes may be punished with Death."[109] Such instructions only alienated the southern slaveowners, who feared that imperial interference would undermine their ability to keep the slaves in subjection. Angry Georgia colonists had already forced Governor James Wright to dismiss the colony's chief justice for, among other offenses, sympathizing with a slave who "Pretended to be free." According to Wright, the chief justice disregarded testimony verifying that the man in question was in fact a slave, insisting that "the Negro" was "Free, and should be so"—that the judge "would make him so."[110] Such behavior from an official charged with interpreting the king's laws in America must have caused deep foreboding among the slaveholders, who studiously ignored their sovereign's imperatives about slavery. Reflecting the sympathies of his Charlestown community, South Carolina lieutenant governor William Bull pleaded in 1770 that royal mercy be extended not to the suffering slaves but to the very few masters unlucky enough to be prosecuted for killing slaves "in a sudden passion."[111]

Aware that acceptance of corporate doctrine implied deference to imperial authority, only a few white southerners internalized an organic conception of slavery during the colonial period. Their unusual views can be explained by their peculiarly strong relationship with the English metropolis. Many served Anglican or evangelical organizations. Alexander Garden, for example, had reported directly to the bishop of London. Others, such as Savannah merchant and slaveowner James Habersham, also maintained official ties to the imperial government and to the global network of evangelical reformers. For his part, Habersham had journeyed to the New World as George Whitefield's assistant. At the end of his life, in the years preceding the Revolution, he served as Georgia's acting governor. Habersham lived in Savannah, but his work for the government and his religious concerns rooted his conscience in the corporate values promulgated from the distant mother country. As such, he insisted that "both bond and free are equally entitled" to the "Common Salvation" provided by religious instruction. Habersham lamented that "ignorant people" had "foolishly insinuate[d]" that black slaves were "scarcely reasonable Creatures, and not capable of being instructed in the divine Truths of Christianity." Considering his slaves to be human beings, he insisted that he could not "divest [him]self of Humanity" when their troubles came to his attention. Indeed, when rabies resulted in the death of an enslaved boy, the Georgia slaveowner's sympathies led him to recount in gruesome detail the "Cries and Intreaties of the Mother begging her Child to be put to Death" and "the dreadfull shreiks of the Boy." According to Habersham, the horror had "rung such a Peal in my Ears, that I never can forget [it]." "It is impossible for me to describe," he concluded, "and hope never to meet the like again."[112]

The bond of humanity linking Habersham to his slaves likewise affected prominent merchants whose work necessitated a transatlantic perspective.[113] Richard Hutson, one of Habersham's acquaintances in Charlestown, did not hesitate to have disobedient slaves whipped but nevertheless valued the principle of treating them with humanity. In 1767 he expressed dismay over the mistreatment of a number of his slaves who had fled the plantation to seek his compassion in town. Initially resolved to give "every one a severe flogging at the Workhouse," Hutson changed his mind when he learned that they "had scarcely any Victuals" and had been assigned overly burdensome tasks. Hutson called this treatment "unreasonable" and even went so far as to assert that slaves could potentially work without their overseers' "severity."[114]

Henry Laurens also exhibited a growing humanitarian concern for his slaves in the 1760s. In previous decades, Laurens had not sympathized with the many Africans he had shipped to the Americas. In 1757, for example, one of his customers unknowingly purchased an African man who was mentally impaired and physically deformed. The slave in question was malnourished and covered with sores, but Laurens felt compassion only for the white colonist who had mistakenly bought "defective" human property. "The poor man is really very much to be pittied," wrote Laurens, because "he has got a Negro to pay for, that no one will take off his hands at any rate" and because henceforth he would be forced to keep "in View [a slave whom he considered to be] shocking to human Nature."[115] By 1762, however, Laurens's correspondence began to reflect a nagging concern about his obligations toward the Africans he held in bondage. In December of that year, he advised a partner that a "Negro man" consigned for sale in Charlestown had "alleg'd that he was a Free Man & made such pretensions to his Liberty & procur'd such advocates on his part as [to] give me a good deal of uneasiness." Although Laurens eventually confined and sold the man, his claims to liberty roused Laurens's conscience. By insisting that none of his business partners should "attempt to enslave a Free Man," Laurens was acknowledging that Africans were human beings who, in certain circumstances, could claim the liberties enjoyed by whites.[116]

Upon acquisition of numerous plantations in the 1760s, Laurens increasingly attempted to manage his slaves according to the principles of humanity. In his opinion, compassion toward the bondservants did not threaten the monetary gain that he expected from their labor. By insisting on "proper care" for pregnant slave women in 1763, Laurens was simultaneously fulfilling his obligations toward humane treatment and ensuring that his holdings would increase through the birth of healthy children.[117] During that same year, Laurens again demonstrated his concern for both profit and humanitarianism when he dismissed an overseer for becoming sexually involved with a slave. Such conduct, concluded Laurens, "besides being wrong & unwarrantable in itself must be extremely offensive to me & very hurtful to my Interest, as it must tend to make a good deal of jealousy & disquiet amongst the Negroes."[118]

As the decade progressed, moreover, Laurens's sense of obligation toward his slaves became an imperative that overshadowed purely fiscal concerns. In November 1764, Laurens feared that "the poor creatures" on his plantation would not receive sufficient winter clothing. "My heart aches for them," observed Laurens in Charlestown, "until that is done."[119] In subsequent communication with his overseers and partners, Laurens explicitly instructed that the slaves "be well fed & humanely treated."[120] By 1765, Laurens's aspiration to humanitarianism was raising troublesome questions about the morality of the slave trade that had helped to build his fortune. When an estate sale following his brother-in-law's death threatened to "seperat[e] & t[e]ar assunder" slave families on the Hyde Park plantation, he responded with outrage toward this potential "inhumanity." "I wanted no profit," asserted Laurens, "but only a gratification in a tender concern which I had set my heart upon & which I was willing to pay well for." Indeed, according to Laurens, nothing "could have been contrived to distress" him more than "this unnecessary division of Fathers, Mothers, Husbands, Wives, & Children who tho Slaves are still human Creatures." "I cannot be deaf to their cries," he concluded, "lest a time should come when I should cry & there shall be none to pity me."[121]

Pointing to such evidence, scholars have asserted that by the mid–eighteenth century southern slaveowners were aspiring to a paternalistic ideal.[122] These historians, however, seriously overstate the case for a transformation in colonial slaveholders' values. The attitudes expressed by Habersham, Hutson, and Laurens in no way signified a wide-scale reformulation of white conceptions about black slaves. The vast majority of slaveholders in the 1760s viewed their black bondservants with the same contempt that had existed from the earliest European encounters with Africa.

Beginning in the sixteenth century, social convention had encouraged English explorers to associate sin with the color black; two centuries later, when slave ships began transporting significant numbers of slaves to North America, English colonists institutionalized racial difference in the form of laws that prescribed special (and invariably harsher) treatment for blacks.[123] Racism enabled white colonists to construe African Americans as dangerous beasts, as mentally inferior savages — in short, as a distinct branch of the human race. Because these racial stereotypes justified the brutal conditions to which black slaves were routinely subjected and because alternative corporate theories of slavery threatened to reduce the planters' power over their bondservants, Christian activists met with no success when they campaigned against the inhumane treatment of southern slaves. In 1736, Charles Wesley complained of "the cruelty of masters toward their negroes" in Charlestown, recounting specific instances of slave dismemberment and torture for offenses as minor as "overfilling a tea cup."[124] Three decades later, white authorities in the Deep South were still branding slaves, punishing them through castration and immolation, and placing the severed heads of executed slaves on posts to mark the sites of the slaves' crimes.[125] Earlier in the eighteenth century, ministers such as Joseph Ottolenghe had struggled to bring the gospel to black slaves, to integrate and bind them to the larger white culture through "cords of love." Like Ottolenghe and their other forerunners in the Deep South, however, missionaries in the 1760s collided with a racial wall when they attempted to extend the boundaries of religious community to encompass blacks as well as whites. In 1765, angry community reaction to Anglican minister Isaac Amory's efforts to preach to African Americans forced him to resign as rector of St. John's Church in South Carolina. Traveling through the backcountry four years later, Baptist minister Oliver Hart encountered an indelible racial line literally drawn with blood from "a horrible murder committed a few years [earlier] by a Negro Fellow." "The Blood still remaining on one of the Doors" informed such visitors as Hart that racial divisions precluded the possibility of an interracial religious community.[126] Laurens himself testified that "the difficulties [met by the] few who would wish to deal with [their] servants as with brethren in a state of subordination . . . are almost insurmountable."[127]

As it turned out, racism blunted the impact of humanitarianism even among the planters whose business and religious activities exposed them to the value system of the English metropolis. For instance, when eight of Habersham's slaves died in 1764, the Georgia slaveowner dwelled on his own economic misfortune rather than on the loss of so many human lives. "I cannot replace them," lamented Habersham, "for Four Hundred Pounds Sterling." Habersham later admitted that the demise of another slave woman "affected me more than all the negroes I have ever lost." But this emotional response stemmed less from Habersham's sympathy for his slave and more from his longing for departed members of his own white family. Because the slave in question had been "a favourite of [Habersham's] dear deceased wife and nursed two of [his] Daughters," her death brought to his "remembrance those dear Innocents and their now happy Mother." As a result, observed Habersham, "I have really been obliged to lay down my pen several times to give Vent to those Feelings only known to a tender Husband, and Parent." While tender husbands and parents mourned the loss of their loved ones, "tender" masters routinely framed the loss of their slaves in economic terms.[128]

Humanitarian ideals did play some part in Henry Laurens's renunciation of the most overtly exploitative aspects of the business of human bondage. "I quitted the Profits arising from that gainful branch" of the international slave trade, he announced in 1768, "principally because of many acts, from the Masters & others concerned toward the wretched Negroes from the time of purchasing to that of selling them again."[129] In addition, on one occasion Laurens expressed his wish "that our oeconomy & government differ'd from the present system," bemoaning that "those laws which now authorize the custom" of slavery remained "in force." Yet the transatlantic intellectual community that helped to inspire Laurens's humanitarianism also equipped him with ideas that forestalled an active campaign against slavery—namely, the cultural construction of racial identity. Henry Laurens, for his part, recognized the need for racial distinction between rulers and their inferiors. Commenting on an overseer of mixed racial descent, Laurens asserted that the man must "carry a steady command otherwise the Blacks will drown him . . . for of all Overseers they love those of their own colour least."[130]

If Laurens sometimes sympathized with his slaves, he also generalized that "Negroes are faithless." And after his "ten or twelve Years experience" with the slave trade, Laurens forwarded the incredible claim that he had never seen "an instance of Cruelty" equal to that exercised upon an unfortunate group of Irish immigrants shipped to South Carolina without proper provisions.[131] Although these Irish families surely experienced horrors, their white complexions no doubt heightened Laurens's sensitivity toward their plight. Conversely, Laurens remained involved with the slave trade throughout the 1760s, despite his growing reservations about the trade's morality.[132] Humanitarian concerns led southerners to reassess their treatment of French prisoners of war, hostile American Indians, and white criminals.[133] But notions of racial difference prevented any wholesale reconsideration of the treatment of slaves. To the contrary, most slaveowners maintained that kind treatment of slaves encouraged them to resist their masters' authority. The *Georgia Gazette* provided evidence of this sentiment in 1763 when it reported the "most shocking murder" of a white family at the hands of its slave. According to the newspaper, the deceased plantation owners "used the barbarous destroyer of their family and substance with remarkable tenderness and lenity."[134] Clearly, the most significant aspect of the humanitarian campaign to ameliorate colonial slavery was its failure—a failure that resulted from the imperial political framework in which reformers were operating. As long as the slaveowners associated organic metaphors for slavery with their own subordination to authorities in the metropolis, they would continue to embrace an individualistic slaveowning ethos that granted them complete power over bondservants.

The English campaign to more closely regulate the colonies in the 1760s extended far beyond imperial efforts to reform the master-slave relationship. Following the costly crusade against France and her Native American allies, Parliament passed acts designed to increase revenue generated by the colonies. The most controversial of these, the Stamp Act of 1765, required the colonists to purchase stamps before transacting official business (such as recording wills and signing contracts). Such imperial supervision of routine economic transactions infuriated the colonists, many of whom resisted with violent measures.[135] Parliament repealed the Stamp Act the following spring but could not allay colonial suspicions about the British imperial system. "It seems highly probable," predicted Henry Laurens in September 1766, "that all America will undergo many pangs yet before there is a hearty reconciliation between the Mother Country & her colonies."[136] Laurens's fears came to pass when Parliament enacted the Townshend Duties in 1767. By the later part of the decade, settlers who had deferred to British authority during the Stamp Act crisis were denouncing the new taxes as outrageous violations of their liberties. Laurens himself provides us with a case in point. In 1765, he had rebuffed an angry mob that accused him of harboring stamped paper in his Charlestown residence. Although Laurens had "most heartily" wished for a repeal of the Stamp Act, he nevertheless had maintained that the colonies owed a "humble & dutiful acquiescence to an Act of Parliament however oppressive it may be," criticizing the

Sons of Liberty—a group that had organized to resist British taxation—for "their pretended Patriotism" and "unbounded acts of Licentiousness & at length Burglary & Robbery."[137] Yet following his own confrontation with customs officials in 1767, Laurens construed English imperial policy as a greater threat to the colonial social order than were the mobs that had attempted to batter down his front door two years earlier.[138] "The Cloud is gathering thick in the North," he wrote to his friend in Georgia, "& will soon spread over America if not dispel'd by wise Measures in Britain." South Carolina and Georgia, according to Laurens, would "not subscribe to the Right of a British Parliament to lay internal Taxes upon America, & tho' feeble, have gather'd Strength among themselves [and] will be keen in asserting their Liberty."[139]

Although colonists such as Laurens still considered themselves "Loyal and faithful Subjects" and asserted that "the Word Rebellion is most discordant and ungrateful to the Ear of a British American," their struggle against Parliament eroded their faith that the mercantilist imperial system would serve their future interests. "It cannot be a wonder to you who know Mankind," lectured Laurens to Lord Grenville in 1769, "that Americans should complain a *little* of *great* Oppressions." And although colonists could not yet imagine a prosperous future outside the English empire, the specter of revolution against English authority had nonetheless been raised. "The time *may* come," predicted Laurens, "when Americans from Oppressive Laws, Oppressive Informers, Oppressive and unjust Decrees and final Sentences, may be driven through their despair to Acts destructive of *their own happiness* and detrimental to *that* of the Mother Country."[140]

As England attempted to tighten its administration of the colonies, the slaveowners perceived great risks to their autonomy lurking within their sovereign's regard for the welfare of southern slaves. In 1770, South Carolina slaveowners stridently resisted the Crown's entreaty that the assembly pass a law "for the restraining of any inhuman severity" on the part of "ill Masters or Overseers" toward "their Christian Servants and their Slaves, and that provision be made therein that the wilful killing of Indians and Negroes may be punished with Death."[141] William Bull acknowledged in 1770 that "the Royal humanity has often recommended to Governors, that a white man who murders a Negro should be punished with Death," but he countered that "in *Maryland, Virginia & all Southern Colonies and Islands,* it has been thought dangerous to the public safety to put them on a footing of equality in that respect with their masters." Bull feared such legal protection "might tempt Slaves to make resistance, and deter Masters and man-

Slavery and the Cultural Marketplace | 49

agers from inflicting punishment with an exemplary severity tho' ever so necessary." In his opinion, "the happy temperament of Justice and Mercy in our Negro Acts, and the general humanity of the Masters" made legal reform unnecessary.[142]

The slave code proposed by the Georgia Assembly in 1765 sparked a similar controversy. In May 1768 Georgia officials learned that the king had disallowed their act for "the better Ordering and Governing of Negroes and other Slaves," despite their contentions that they could not "possibly subsist without" it. The veto perplexed James Habersham, who noted that the assembly had framed the revised slave statutes "on more extensive and humane principles than our former Law or [the one] now in Force in So[uth] Carolina."[143] He discovered two years later that the Crown had rejected the legislation because the Board of Trade believed that "Slaves should be made Real Estate and go with the Lands they were employed upon." This remarkable plan would have raised American slaves to the status of serfs, affording them protection from the auctions that separated parents from children and husbands from wives. Although Habersham himself was devoted to ameliorating colonial slavery, he denounced the Board of Trade's provision as an impediment to Georgia's plantation economy. "In a young and extensive Country like this, where Property must necessarily be frequently Alien[at]ed and new Settlements daily made," wrote Habersham, "many cogent Reasons might be urged against such a Measure."[144] Imperial officials retreated from their dramatic strategy but continued to press for a "suspending clause." This clause antagonized colonists by preventing legislation from taking effect until the board approved it—a delay that could stretch to years. Georgia Assembly members ultimately conceded this point to the governor, but not without expressing their indignation. They resolved "that this House agrees to the suspending clause solely from the necessity of the case and not from any conviction," for they looked "upon suspending clauses to be of such pernicious consequences."[145]

By the end of the colonial period, British officials such as William Knox personified the growing threat posed by organic conceptions of society. Appointed Georgia's provost marshal in 1756, Knox managed to irritate his fellow planters on both religious and economic grounds. Repeating the long-standing Christian doctrine on slavery, Knox declared that the slaves' "stupidity" did "not authorize us to consider them as beasts for our use, much less to deny them all knowledge of common salvation." Echoing authorities such as Whitefield and Garden, he insisted that masters "would be much better served" by "Negroes instructed in religion and taught to serve their masters for conscience sake." Knox, however, did more than simply call for closer imperial scrutiny of the master-slave relationship. As a representative of the Crown, he also defended the "right of the supreme legislative power [of Parliament], acting pursuant to their trust, to dispose of any part of the property of the people for the public safety and advantage." Although Knox himself was one of Georgia's largest slaveowners, his mercantilist ideals prompted his conclusion that southern masters should surrender some measure of power to the proper religious and civic authorities.[146] Knox's beliefs signified the English church and state's converging sentiments respecting colonial slaveowners. Although Knox expressed concern for the slaves' welfare, he was more deeply troubled about their masters. Whatever their pretensions to the status of English gentlemen and ladies, whatever their professions of fealty to God and to the king, southern planters perceived nothing but ruin in Knox's organic vision for America's future.

During the 1760s, cultural tensions were emerging not only between the slaveowners and imperial officials reporting to England but also between the slaveowners and poorer white residents of the southern backcountry. The relationship between the backcountry settlers and the wealthy landowners along the coast reflected, in many ways, the same dynamic of periphery and core that characterized American intercourse with England. Dominating their colonial assemblies, the coastal planters refused to divert precious resources to the settlers struggling to establish residences hundreds of miles from the tidewater region. In 1764, South Carolina governor Thomas Boone complained that "the Assembly has made no sort of Provision for the Protection of the Frontiers." Moved by the dilemma of an Irish upcountry settlement that "must either be starved or murdered, having no Arms nor money to purchase them," Boone lamented that "the Members of the Commons House of Assembly having their Plantations near the Sea Coast, and in a state of security, are deaf to the cries of the back Settlers."[147] Despite Boone's pleas on behalf of the backcountry colonists, a prominent lowcountry leader "declared in full Assembly that he would rather submit to the destruction of one half of the Country than to give up the point in dispute with the Governor."[148] Suffering from a paucity of schools, churches, and courts to suppress (as William Bull declared in 1765) "the Idlers and Vagabonds, who now infest and Injure the Industrious remote Settlers too often with Impunity," the backcountry residents clamored for relief.[149] To further complicate matters, Georgia authorities (cognizant of their colony's relatively tenuous political position) likewise resented the Carolina planters' presumptuous claim to power over the entire region. In 1763, for example, Georgia governor James Wright accused the South Carolina coastal slaveowners of improperly speculating in lands that belonged to Georgia. Noting that the Carolina planters were claiming fifty-acre headrights for each of their slaves "with no intention to remove there or settle them" but only to sell them in the future, Wright accused the "wealthy Settlers in Carolina" of rupturing the commonwealth for their own selfish gain. Like the backcountry settlers in South Carolina, the Georgia governor worried about the ability of his "Frontier Province" to sustain itself in the face of the Carolina lowcountry's arrogance.[150]

By the late 1760s, tension between settlers in different regions of the Deep South had reached dangerous levels. Colonists braved the hardships of frontier life because they expected the unsettled territory to provide them with fortunes of their own. When their pleas for a circuit court system went unanswered, the backcountry settlers decided that they were serving as "a Barrier between the Rich Planters and the Indians, to secure the former against the Latter—Without Laws or Government, Churches[,] Schools or Ministers." They lamented that "the Lands, tho' the finest in the Province" remained unoccupied because "rich Men [were] afraid to set Slaves to work to clear them, lest they should become a Prey to the Banditti."[151] The British officials struggling to resolve these tensions realized that an isolated backcountry undermined the imperial system that was designed, after all, to channel the resources of the entire region back to England. Imperial authorities suggested such measures as improved transportation to reorient the backcountry economy toward the transatlantic market. "The opening [of] an easy way down those Rivers to Markets where South Carolina Products may be bartered for European Goods, is the most likely way to prevent establishing Manufactures in those inland parts of home Materials for Home consumptions," suggested the authors of one government report in 1768.[152] As William Bull demonstrated that same year, the king's officials did sympathize with the plight of backcountry residents and attempt to redress their grievances. The previous year, residents had acted on their own initiative to organize vigilante groups known as the Regulators, through which they enforced their own brand of order on backcountry life. Bull assured his superiors that the Regulators were "not idle Vagabonds" nor "the mere dregs of Mankind" but rather "an industrious hardy Race of men, each possessed of and expert in the use of Fire Arms, each Master of one Horse,

[and] many of several, besides Cattle and Slaves."[153] Clearly, the backcountry residents were prepared to participate in a holistic imperial society, if only the local prejudices of the planter elite did not interfere.

The coastal slaveowners' political power, however, hinged on their ability to resist organic doctrine that would have subordinated their class interests to the greater needs of the British Empire. When the conflict with backcountry residents finally exploded, the planter elite in Carolina confronted the prospect of a chaotic world in which their property and their claim to political authority would no longer be respected. Marshaling thousands of armed men, the Regulators threatened to march on Charlestown in September 1768.[154] Fearing that "half of the people" in the colony had mobilized against the lowcountry, the South Carolina Assembly felt compelled to end the immediate crisis by extending a circuit court system into the backcountry.[155] Reluctantly surrendering some of their precious resources to the backcountry residents, the lowcountry slaveholders vented their wrath on the British officials whose organic perspective on colonial life had led them to sympathize with the Regulator movement. The coastal planters no doubt noticed that support for draconian mercantilist policies went hand in hand with a sensitivity toward backcountry grievances. The itinerant Anglican minister Charles Woodmason, for example, became an outspoken advocate of the backcountry after his willingness to serve as a stamp distributor lost him the affection of Charlestown neighbors.[156] Likewise, South Carolina chief justice Charles Shinner—an official despised by the lowcountry elite because he had attempted to enforce the Stamp Act—had embarked on a personal crusade to bring justice to the backcountry.[157] These alliances and antipathies had profound implications for the identity of slaveowners in the Deep South during the late colonial period. Conflicts with England and with less developed regions of the southern frontier reinforced the sense of embattled isolation felt by lowcountry planters. Seeking to protect their own fortunes, these planters rejected grandiose economic or religious plans asking them to sacrifice for the greater glory of the British Empire or God's holy community.

Ironically, slavery itself provided the colonists with another powerful metaphor with which to condemn English tyranny. By the 1760s, settlers on the periphery of the empire complained that mercantilist policies were reducing them to a state of dependence no better than slavery. Henry Laurens, for example, asserted that the Deep South would "sullenly & stubbornly resist against all ministerial Mandates & admonitions tending to enslave them."[158] Christopher Gadsden likewise observed that the colonies were "riveted in a Slavery beyond Redemption, and by far exceeding that of the Subjects of any absolute Monarch in Europe."[159] Fearing unbridled political power, southerners hinged their criticism of British mercantilism on thoroughly modern (and, ironically, thoroughly British) ideas about reciprocity between rulers and subjects. Because Parliament had not tempered its authority with respect for the colonists' rights, prominent settlers in the Deep South could complain that they had been reduced to bondage.

Of course, given the lowcountry planters' determination to maintain their ascendancy over the backcountry settlers as well as their African American slaves, such imagery raised embarrassing questions. Advocates of the backcountry noted that "those who call themselves *Sons of Liberty*" made "such Noise with the Words *Freedom[—]Birth-Right — Privilege —* and Rights — *Liberty of the Subject —* and such Sounds" despite the fact that they "Lord it over their fellow Provincials with all the Insolence of Human Pride, and Imperiousness of Arbitrary Law givers."[160] In a petition read before the South Carolina assembly, the backcountry residents argued that they were "Free-Men" and "Not Born Slaves."[161] On an even more disturbing note, the planter elite discovered that political allusions to slavery could subvert their mastery over their own bondservants. According to Laurens, such had been the case during the Christmas season of 1765 when "some Negroes had mimick'd their betters in crying out '*Liberty*,'" sparking fears of impending slave revolt.[162] Although coastal slaveowners insisted on a reciprocal relationship with imperial authority, they aspired to absolute mastery over their enslaved workforce.

From the earliest days of the colonies, the desire for organic society had competed with the struggle for individual profit. Missionaries and imperial authorities had attempted to integrate the southern colonies into a wider religious and political community even as the settlers maintained their individual pursuit of wealth. By the 1760s, southern slaveowners had concluded that excessive imperial authority would shatter the familial bond between England and the colonies; at the same time, however, the planters ignored the complaints of the most miserable American subjects — their own black slaves, who were parceled into lots and forced to toil like animals. Building their fortunes on African American suffering, white colonists in the Deep South staked out an untenable ideological position.

Although slavery remained the key to their social status, the planters attempted to divest the institution of ideological significance. Their social station depended on slavery, but the tidewater elite viewed the institution of human bondage in strictly economic terms and not as the basis of a class identity that superseded the boundary between the backcountry and the coast. Their ideology, in short, celebrated their identity as a landed, genteel class without trumpeting their role as masters of African American slaves. The slaveowners sought, in other words, to remove slavery from public debate over the structure of colonial society—to secure for individual masters a free hand in governing their slaves. Amid the chaos unleashed by the Revolution, however, southern planters discovered that without considerable government assistance, they could not keep their slaves in subjection. As they campaigned for political liberties, white colonists unwittingly raised the possibility that the slaves whom they forced to till the land would one day reap the glories of universal freedom.

*What a stupendous,
what an incomprehensible
machine is man! who
can endure toil, famine,
stripes, imprisonment &
death itself in vindication
of his own liberty, and the
next moment . . . inflict on
his fellow men a bondage,
one hour of which is
fraught with more misery
than ages of that which he
rose in rebellion to oppose.*
THOMAS JEFFERSON,
1786

CHAPTER TWO

An Unhappy Breach

Slaveholder Ideology in the Age of Revolution, 1770–1786

In practically every historical setting, slaveowners have abhorred rapid social innovation. Given this propensity toward tradition, one might question why so many southern slaveowners embraced the radical cause during the revolutionary era. Certainly, during the colonial period, masters in the Deep South had resisted missionary reform of plantation life. How, then, could these same slaveowners come to champion the campaign for radical political reform of the imperial system—particularly when their very lives and fortunes depended on the maintenance of the status quo? The mystery deepens when we consider the incredible economic success of Georgia and South Carolina. By the 1770s, slaveowners in the Deep South had become the wealthiest colonists on mainland British North America. For families such as the Manigaults, the New World provided the opportunity for fantastic wealth. By the middle of the century, Gabriel Manigault had expanded his father's mercantile activities and made the transition to plantation ownership. By the 1760s, his son Peter, the third generation of Manigaults in America, capitalized on his family name to gain the position of speaker of the colonial assembly. And yet, despite this rags-to-riches story, Gabriel and Peter Manigault made crucial contributions—both financial and political—to the patriotic cause.

To understand why so many successful planters rejected British authority, one must consider how their position as slaveowners affected their ideas about the relationship between imperial government and family life. Amid increasing tension between England and the colonies, southern slaveholders charged imperial officials with two serious crimes. First, the planters accused the imperial government of violating the standard of reciprocity central to corporate individualism, a standard that was recognized as the foundation for enlightened domestic relations in the late eighteenth century. Second, the planters came to believe that English administrators were contemplating the emancipation of American slaves, a possibility that promised the immediate destruction of southern plantation households. Both assumptions flowed from the slaveowners' ever increasing cultural contact with the English metropolis, yet both notions motivated the planters ultimately to break from England. As a destructive war decimated southern plantation society, white antipathy toward African Americans increased. By the 1780s, the political break with England had resulted in a reformulated conception of household relationships. Having obtained their independence as a nation, slaveholders in the Deep South faced the challenge of reconciling their ideas about family with the values on which they had staked their claim to freedom.

Although Parliament's mercantilist policies served as the catalyst for American unrest, colonists in the Deep South were protesting far more than economic loss. Indeed, many prominent southerners contended that their problems stemmed from a prevailing obsession with material gain—an obsession that had supposedly corrupted Parliament and threatened to undermine the moral structure of colonial society. Virginia planter Landon Carter captured the essence of colonial fears when he denounced economic activity "that kicks Conscience out of doors like a fawning Puppy." In the Deep South, a variety of printed material reminded prominent merchants and planters of Carter's assertion that "the love of money is the incentive of evil men."[1] As historian Bernard Bailyn has demonstrated, the campaign by English Whigs against government corruption generated numerous political pamphlets that profoundly affected colonial ideas about power.[2] Works of fiction also contributed to American assumptions about corruption. South Carolina slaveholder Isaac Ball, for example, acquired in 1770 a copy of *Fables and Stories Moralized*, an anthology of Aesop's tales. The volume reminded Ball that "'Tis with Men in the World, as it is with Beasts in the Market: They are all to be Sold if the Bidder can but come up to the Price: only One Man is a Slave to his Pleasures; Another, to his Ambition, a Third, to his Avarice, a Fourth to his Revenge." Pointing out "Every Man's Weakness," one tale presented the argument that, in the end, "we shall All be found Mercenary."[3] Amid such grim assessments of human nature, the colonists yearned for virtuous government. Unfortunately, Parliament's efforts to increase American revenues suggested to the colonists that greed had debased the British imperial system.

Notwithstanding the vast distances separating their plantations from the English metropolis, fears of parliamentary corruption troubled the southern slaveholders on a very personal level. From the earliest days of colonization, American colonists had viewed the question of imperial authority through the prism of family morality. The king and Parliament traditionally demanded colonial obedience in much the same way that a righteous father insisted on the allegiance of his children—by asserting that patriarchal authority would benefit the entire family.[4] Linking the government of nations to the government of families, the domestic justification for imperial authority meant that colonial slaveholders could not challenge Parliament without confronting embarrassing questions about their own position within the plantation household. At the same time that slaveholding colonists charged Parliament with undermining the colonies' welfare, they themselves confronted the accusation that they were mercilessly exploiting their own black bondservants. In fact, criticism of imperial government unfolded hand in hand with increasing doubts about the morality of unlimited patriarchal authority. Ideas about the proper allocation of power, in other words, inextricably linked the public sphere of imperial politics to the private world of household relationships.

By the latter half of the eighteenth century, authorities in Europe and America were grappling with new standards for enlightened leadership. Fostered by Christian theology and by capitalism's need for self-motivated workers, a philosophical emphasis on individual rights had begun to reshape traditional notions of social hierarchy. For centuries, rulers ranging from biblical patriarchs to early modern Tuscan merchants had sacrificed social inferiors to the greater good of the community—to a vision of corporate welfare articulated by (and limited to the needs of) those in power. By the 1760s, however, concern for every individual's well-being forced social authorities toward a more inclusive definition of community welfare, one that recognized the concerns of even the lowliest members of society. At the level of the colonial household, this ideological trend toward corporate individualism resulted in increasingly sentimental relations between parents and children; parents rephrased their demands as pleas offered primarily for the child's benefit. Thus, to warn his son about the potential danger of visiting London in 1768, Georgia merchant James Habersham wrote, "Let me enjoin[,] rather let me request you, as a proof of the filial duty you owe a Parent, anxious, very anxious for your wellbeing both for Time and Eternity to give the few following remarks a fair and candid reading."[5] Fathers—even powerful and wealthy fathers—wanted their authority to be affirmed by children who consented through love rather than force.

Participants in the burgeoning debate over the application of imperial authority hastened to employ the language of enlightened domesticity to justify their positions. Characterizing the imperial system as a happy family, British officials attempted to depict the king as a source of "Paternal Goodness" and the colonists as grateful children who would "ever merit his most Paternal Affection." Southern slaveowners likewise invoked the standards of a family life operating on the principles of corporate individualism to frame their critique of British tyranny. Turning a blind eye toward their ruthless subjugation of their slaves, the planters accused the imperial government of violating the most significant element of the modern affective family—the reciprocal obligations that tempered paternal authority with concern for the child's welfare. Thus, when Henry Laurens characterized the colonies as "forward children" for their opposition to Parliament's acts in 1768, he also observed that such children "Sometimes deter indiscreet Parents from shewing too freely their wrath & bitterness, to the benefit of the more docible Brethren." If parents unwisely indulged their thirst for power at the expense of their dependents (Laurens suggested), then it fell on subordinate members of the family to uphold the dynamic of corporate individualism.[6]

In response to this ideological challenge, some defenders of British mercantilist policy unabashedly rejected the new standard for paternal authority and reiterated the old-fashioned rationale for Parliament's recent statutes. "Every Act of a Dependent Provincial Government," wrote one proponent of the empire, "ought to Terminate in the Advantage of the Mother State, unto whom it owes its' being." The author of this blunt logic argued that "all advantageous Projects, or Commercial Gains in any Colony, which are truly prejudicial to, and inconsistent with the Interest of the Mother State, Must be understood to be illegall." He even applauded the mercantilist system for encouraging rivalry rather than cooperation between the colonies. For the most part, however, the authorities seeking to bind the colonies more closely to the standards of the English metropolis maintained that their plans would benefit the individual colonies and the individuals within the colonies, as well as England itself. In 1769, for example, South Carolina lieutenant governor William Bull chose not to dissolve the colonial assembly for concurring with the Virginia House of Burgesses' resolutions about American rights. Demonstrating his sensitivity to the colonists' demands, Bull informed his superiors that "I should not accordingly Act to His Majesty's most gracious and paternal Intention if I put a stop to their Proceedings by a dissolution or immediate prorogation, especially as experience had shewn that a repetition of such marks of displeasure . . . tended rather to furnish the more turbulent and factious with popular arguements to keep up their clamors."[7] Although officials in both South Carolina and Georgia did on other occasions dissolve colonial assemblies for obstructing imperial policy, their hesitancy to do so indicated their distaste for despotism.

Ironically, imperial efforts to foster enlightened government in both the colonies and the empire at large ultimately encouraged the southern movement for independence. Far from mercilessly exploiting the colonies, British authorities had supported the growth of thriving plantation economies. In doing so, however, they unwittingly created a resident elite composed of exceptionally wealthy planters.[8] On the eve of the Revolution, the coastal rice planters in the Deep South had amassed the largest fortunes in North America. Their privileged place within the empire—their freedom from unduly heavy economic and political burdens—afforded them the resources to conduct a campaign of resistance against imperial authority. If imperial authorities succeeded all too well in fostering a prosperous colonial economy, they also proved to be too effective at integrating the far-flung colonies into one cultural infrastructure. The British campaign for organic unity between England and the colonies unexpectedly created the very network through which the American colonies coordinated their resistance. As early as the Stamp Act controversy of 1765, officials in Georgia and South Carolina had attributed local political unrest to a radical message that originated in the northern colonies and was conveyed through the market structures fostered by the imperial system. In South Carolina, for example, Bull asserted that before accounts of radical resistance arrived from New England, "the People of this Province, tho' they conceived [of the stamp tax as] too great a burthen seemed generally disposed to pay a due obedience to the Act." In Georgia, Governor James Wright lamented that "too much of the Rebellious Spirit in the Northern Colonies has already Shown itself here, indeed the People have been for many Months Past Stimulated by letters Papers &c. sent here from the Northward to follow their Example." Charlestown merchant Richard Hutson similarly observed that "the people of this province appeared at first too easy and unconcerned about [the Stamp Act], but the laudable example of the northern provinces in endeavoring to repell the manifest encroachments thereby made on their liberty, seems to have had an happy influence on them, in opening their Eyes and communicating a noble sense and spirit of freedom."[9]

Likewise, when radical activity forced acting governor James Habersham to dissolve the Georgia Assembly in 1772, he blamed the incident on the lines of communication linking the colony to its incendiary neighbors. Habersham noted that "the example of the Assembly of Carolina has I am afraid infatuated our People here," observing that "some People since have fed our Gazette with inflammatory Doctrines, in order to keep up the Spirit of Party and Opposition."[10] Although British authorities attempted to limit their most repressive measures to the specific colonies where unrest was most profound—for example, Massachusetts in the wake of the Boston Tea Party—the colonies had become too closely integrated for localized imperial response. By 1774, observers across the South were reporting the genesis of a unified colonial mentality. "The general Voice" in Virginia, wrote the plantation tutor Philip Fithian, "is *Boston*."[11] In Charlestown, Bull blamed colonial resistance on "the Spirit which had been raised in those [northern] Towns with great threats of violence to hinder the landing and disposing of the Tea there"—a spirit "communicated to this Province by Letters, Gazettes & Merchants." Cultural and political boundaries between the American colonies were giving way to coordinated colonial resistance to British policy.[12]

Ironically, this unifying culture of radical protest extended all the way back to England. Avid readers, the colonists were well acquainted with "country" tracts lambasting the English court for its corruption.[13] Savannah bookseller James Johnston, for example, routinely advertised works by authors such as Thomas Gordon and John Trenchard.[14] The slaveowners in the Deep South drew on the logic of these authors when they articulated their grievances against imperial policy. Ralph Izard displayed a "country" conception of government and human nature in his argument that "when

Americans become Governors, Chief Justices, Attorney Generals, &c. they have no more virtue to boast of than other people. Self-Love is the strong ruling passion of mankind."[15] In fact, American patriots penned numerous pamphlets of their own. Their tracts sometimes lacked the aesthetic quality of such works as *Cato's Letters* but nevertheless evoked the same republican principles. Appropriately enough, Henry Laurens's pamphlet cataloguing the corruption of Charlestown's imperial officials began with a quotation from Trenchard. In 1773, frustrated members of the Governor's Council in South Carolina attempted to police American authors' radical ideas by imprisoning a Charlestown printer. After the Commons House of Assembly quickly "countermanded" the council's instructions and released the printer, however, imperial authorities realized to their dismay that they could not control a transatlantic print culture that was contributing to colonial resistance.[16]

The imperial government's regard for the welfare of individual African American slaves sparked an ideological crisis among the planter elite in the Deep South. Although radical colonists complained that England wanted to reduce them to a state of slavery, they were even more concerned that imperial authorities might lift their slaves to a state of freedom. Of course, the imperial leadership fully acknowledged that the colonial economy hinged on slavery, and they had no intention of emancipating the hundreds of thousands of African Americans held in brutal subjectivity throughout the South. The Crown agreed with Habersham's contention that "white people were unequal to the Burthen in this Climate and therefore it was absolutely necessary to allow us the free use of Slaves."[17] Indeed, royal officials even instructed colonial governors to veto any legislation restricting the importation of African slaves into the Deep South—a measure that South Carolina had adopted in 1766 to redress the skewed black-white population ratio and minimize the possibility of insurrection. By improving the conditions of American slavery, the king's officials merely wanted to ensure that revenue would continue to flow from the coastal rice plantations into the royal coffers.

Still, by the early 1770s the planters of the Deep South had good reason to worry about their security as slaveowners. When South Carolina ended its three-year prohibition against the slave trade in 1769, thousands of slaves poured into the region. By 1772, Charlestown traders were entreating their overseas business partners to send greater numbers of slaves. The firm of

Leger & Greenwood, for example, informed their suppliers that "the Planters in general are now grown so oppulent that We are convinced We should meet with no Difficulty to make good the payments."[18] In 1773 alone, Charlestown merchants sold some nine thousand slaves.[19] Although the booming plantation economy enriched both planters and merchants, the influx of African slaves exacerbated the threat of slave resistance and insurrection. In February 1772, for example, a Charlestown jury complained about the inability of the slave patrols to maintain order, charging that "the Negroes in general do disregard them."[20] The problem grew worse over the ensuing years. In 1774 Charlestown newspapers were reporting the need for legislative action because blacks in Charlestown had become "so irregular and disorderly in their Conduct, and so superfluous in their Number."[21] That same year, Georgia slaveholders confronted even more compelling problems with their slaves. According to the *Georgia Gazette*, ten lowcountry slaves killed their overseer in the field and several other whites before authorities regained control.[22] Imperial officials such as Bull continued to insist that the slave population could be trusted to reinforce the militia, but they too worried about insurrection. Bull himself noted that "to observe good order among the Slaves, one fourth of the Militia must be left at home, which furnishes a constant Patrol to keep all quiet there." To the planters of the Deep South, African American slaves remained dangerous outsiders who were more inclined to murder their owners than to demonstrate the faithfulness of "trustee negroes."[23]

Southern slaveowners in the 1770s continued to reject suggestions that they treat their slaves with greater humanity. James Habersham's fruitless struggle to Christianize the plantations of the Georgia lowcountry provides a case in point. He had encouraged the missionary activities of Cornelius Winter, a Methodist preacher who was endeavoring to "remove some Peoples weak Objections against having their poor ignorant Servants instructed in the Principles of the Christian Religion." Winter had preached at Habersham's plantation in the late 1760s, prompting "visible signs of decency and Attention among" his slaves. Well aware that fellow plantation owner William Knox had "expressed a Desire to have [his] Negroes instructed," Habersham "recommend[ed] this young Man to [Knox's] Friendship."[24] Over the next few months, Habersham contacted other influential acquaintances about Winter's mission to the slaves. He wanted his friends to help Winter to become ordained by the Anglican Church, giving him a credential that might allay the slaveowners' suspicions about his proselytizing. In the end, Habersham hoped that Winter's efforts would refute those "ignorant people" who "foolishly insinuate" that the slaves were "scarcely reasonable Creatures, and not capable of being instructed in the divine Truths of Christianity."[25]

In May 1771, however, Habersham learned that the bishop of London had refused to ordain Winter, thereby ending his campaign to bring the gospel to the slaves. The episode reinforced the spiritual isolation of the few resident slaveowners seeking to reform the master-slave relationship. Not only were planters such as Habersham rebuffed by their fellow slaveowners, but they also remained far removed from the administrative powers that managed the religious campaign to integrate the colonies into one organic community. Notwithstanding the support of Habersham and other elite planters, Winter's credentials as a local religious activist obviously did not impress Anglican authorities (who believed that instructions should flow from England to the slaveowning South). This institutional dynamic frustrated the best efforts of the tiny number of planters whose cosmopolitan perspectives had fostered a desire to Christianize slavery. "The souls of my poor benighted Blacks," confessed Habersham four years later, "have long lain heavy on my Heart." Despite his intentions, the Georgia slaveowner realized that no "saving Impressions" had "reached any of [his slaves'] Hearts." In a burst of pessimism, Habersham concluded that future missions to the lowcountry plantations would "meet with all the opposition and reproach that men and Devils can invent."[26]

In the months preceding his death in 1775, James Habersham witnessed the failed ministry of David, a free African American preacher in the South Carolina and Georgia lowcountry. Noting that David had fallen into disfavor with the local white community, Habersham sadly informed the preacher's patron in England that slaveowners were "determined to pursue, and hang him, if they can lay hold of him." After preaching that "God would send Deliverance to the Negroes, from the power of their Masters, as He freed the Children of Israel from Egyptian Bondage," David had little choice but to flee "in the first vessel, that sails for home." To the slaveowners of the Deep South, the age of humanitarian reform threatened to become an age of emancipation. Habersham himself bitterly complained that England harbored "a mistaken kind of compassion" for the slaves "because they are black," despite the fact that "many of our own colour and Fellow Subjects, are starving through want and Neglect."[27] In the northern colonies, speakers and authors equated British oppression of America with the injustice of subjecting African Americans to a state of perpetual servitude. "We, the patrons of liberty," asserted one Massachusetts minister in 1770, "have dishonored the Christian name, and degraded human nature" by ignoring "the cause of our African slaves."[28] Samuel Hopkins employed even more dramatic rhetoric when he addressed this question in 1776. According to the Rhode Island minister, the slavery that Americans complained of "is lighter than a feather compared to [the African American slaves'] heavy doom, and may be called liberty and happiness when contrasted with the most abject slavery and inutterable wretchedness to which they are subjected."[29]

Indeed, by the 1770s, southern slaveowners were confronting increasingly personal attacks against their morality. Visitors to the plantation South tended to criticize the southern slaveholders for disregarding the humanity of their slaves and for violating the emerging standards of the modern, affective family. Traveling from Massachusetts to South Carolina in 1773, for example, Josiah Quincy indicted the slaveowners for their lack of domestic virtue. "The enjoyment of a negro or mulatto woman," complained Quincy, "is spoken of as quite a common thing: no reluctance, delicacy or shame is made about the matter." The northern-born visitor considered it ludicrous that the planters "were called men of worth, politeness and humanity," terms that such enlightened individuals as Quincy increasingly reserved for household heads who treated their dependents—male and female, black and white—with love and respect.[30] Stung by such criticism and compelled by their desire to condemn British authorities for patriarchal tyranny, residents of the Deep South reconsidered the virtues of their household relationships. Seeking to balance their own political claims with the ideals of the late eighteenth century, slaveowners stumbled over new dynamics of both race and gender.

During the colonial era, elite southerners had harbored conflicting ideas about female identity. On one hand, European tradition had instilled the idea that women suffered from dangerous passions and emotional instability. During the medieval and early modern periods, this notion had contributed to the archetypal image of the evil witch whose deranged impulses threatened surrounding men with moral oblivion. When the plantation tutor Philip Fithian contemplated the character of his female charge, he revealed that these unflattering assumptions about women lingered in the eighteenth-century South. His pupil, wrote Fithian in 1774, was "not without some few of those qualities which are by some . . . said to belong [e]ntirely to the fair Sex" — "great curiosity, Eagerness for superiority, Ardor in friendship, But bitterness and rage where there is enmity."[31] Although

Fithian asserted that there was "little or no truth" to the stereotype, so many people harbored degrading conceptions about women that his employer's wife questioned whether God had even endowed women with souls. Disturbed by such doubts, Fithian concluded that "many among the Fair" maintained such "private Sentiments" concerning women's debased nature. The Virginia planter Landon Carter gave voice to the traditional colonial stereotype of women's character when he stated that "from the knowledge I have of some Ladies' tempers, I don't think there can be a more treacherous, [e]nterprising, Perverse, and hellish Genius than is to be met with in a Woman. Madam Eve, we see, at the very hazard of Paradise suffered the devil to tempt to her; and of such a tendency has her sex been."[32]

At the same time, however, elite members of colonial society conceptualized an ideal female identity that was the perfect antithesis of the popular stereotype. In contrast to the unbridled emotion typically associated with women, prominent southerners assumed that their wives and daughters would demonstrate circumspection and refinement. Thus when George Milligen-Johnston described the ladies of South Carolina in 1763, he emphasized their "Goodness of Heart, Sweetness of Disposition, and that charming Modesty and Diffidence, which command Respect whilst they invite Love, and equally distinguish and adorn the Sex."[33] In 1771 Henry Laurens instructed his daughter Martha "to be virtuous, dutiful, affable, courteous, [and] modest."[34] Through careful dress and the mastery of such social skills as dancing and music, elite women hoped to present an irreproachable image to society at large. The distance they had traveled from their "natural" tendency toward dangerous passion was supposed to indicate their families' impeccable quality.

Not surprisingly, these conflicting images of them meant that women occupied no clearly defined economic or social role in late-eighteenth-century society. At times, the lack of a coherent, rigorous ideology for gender relations resulted in economic opportunities for women that became unthinkable in the following century. For example, when a Georgia plantation owner searched for an overseer in 1778, he stated his preference for "a single Man" but conceded that "if a prudent woman cou'd be got I shou'd have no Objection as she might be usefull on the Plantation."[35] In this case, the demands of an expanding market economy coincided with a popular image of women that did not preclude hard labor. Yet the contrasting image of genteel, refined ladies fostered a gender dynamic that divorced women entirely from daily economic activity. Within plantation households such as the one that employed Fithian, women were valuable to the extent that they served as "ornaments in their family."[36] As such, the suggestion that women were participating in plantation management enraged respectable landowners in the Lower South. For example, when Florida governor Patrick Tonyn implied in 1778 that Alexander Gray's wife had interfered with Gray's management of his estate, the planter responded with indignity. "I never suffered her, nor did she ever shew an inclination to have the least direction or concern relating any of the plantations," responded Gray. "The white people as well as [the] Negroes are [e]ntirely at my Command." Elite women who resisted the authority of their husbands exposed themselves to public ridicule. When Elizabeth Oates defied her spouse by setting up a household in Savannah in 1765, her husband humiliated her by taking out an ad in the *Georgia Gazette* to warn creditors that he would not pay any debts accrued by his disobedient wife.[37]

Although riddled with inconsistency, eighteenth-century conceptions of women turned on the common assumption that female nature prevented their participation in significant political debate. Obviously, notions of the debased nature of women served to justify their exclusion from the political process. At the same time, elite women who aspired to a refined station in society were accepting an ornamental role that blocked them from overtly political activity. The American Revolution, however, prompted a sweeping transformation of this gender dynamic. When residents of the Deep South confronted British authorities for violating modern notions of enlightened government, they likewise reassessed the role of women in the household and in the nation. The colonists coveted an organic rather than a despotic relationship with their imperial superiors. Thus they expected Parliament to consult the colonies before altering traditional policies. When Americans applied that standard of reciprocity to their own conception of gender, they awarded women with a more active role in the political process. Radicals such as Christopher Gadsden and William Tennent called on the women of South Carolina to support the colonies' nonimportation agreement. "I could wish, as our political salvation, at this crisis," wrote Gadsden in 1769, "depends altogether upon the strictest oeconomy, that the women could, with propriety, have the principal management thereof; for 'tis well known, that none in the world are better oeconomists, make better wives or more tender mothers, than ours."[38]

According to the Charlestown Presbyterian minister William Tennent, English authorities had "persuaded themselves" that American women would rather "suffer this Empire to be enslaved, & your Husbands' throats to be cut" than "give up your darling Tea dish Ceremony." Asserting that

"I cannot think you so divested of all love to your Country as to be willing to partake of any trivial pleasure at the Expence of the Liberties if not the blood of your Husbands & Children," Tennent exhorted southern women to take political action to prove the English wrong.[39] The shifting political and ideological context of the late eighteenth century was prompting a wholesale reassessment of female identity. Turning traditional prescriptions for elite female behavior upside down, Tennent called for colonial women to renounce refined social rituals in favor of political purpose. Gadsden likewise insisted that South Carolina women "so far from laying out at this time any thing unnecessarily" would "be rather much grieved and distressed to find herself obliged, upon any occasion, to buy the least article of British manufacture that her family cannot do without." "I am very sure," he concluded, "our Women will not bear the thought that the ruin of their family may be laid at their door."[40] In formulating this new conception of gender, Americans were harnessing the principles of corporate individualism to serve the patriotic cause. The recognition of individual female political agency allowed activists such as Tennent and Gadsden to channel the energies of American women into the campaign for colonial resistance.

Amid the privation caused by war, American wives and daughters measured themselves by this new conception of womanhood. In June 1780, for example, South Carolina plantation owner Eliza Pinckney fretted about the "frights and hardships" experienced by her daughter-in-law Betsy. But if Eliza Pinckney felt compassion "in a great degree" for the younger woman's "distress," she also insisted that Betsy react with strength to the ongoing political crisis: "Exert your utmost efforts to keep up your spirits, and imitate your husband[']s fortitude, [as] it is as much a female, as a masculine virtue, and we stand in as much need of it to act our part properly."[41] By 1782, those women engaged in the revolutionary struggle felt compelled to criticize and to revile their reluctant counterparts. "I dare say you exclaim against our young Ladies for their want of patriotic spirit which has so peculiarly distinguished the Carolinians," wrote Camden resident Mary Clay to her sister; "you may be assured I shall be very scrupulous what persons I associate with."[42] Indeed, by the later stages of the Revolution, some women had begun to buckle under the political burdens so recently assigned to them. In 1781, for example, Anne Hart wrote to her husband from occupied Charleston, exasperated that he seemed to "think a poor Weak Woman is hardy enough to bear more than he Could." "Wou'd he not Contrive to fetch her to him," she asked bitterly, and not "leave all for her to do"—especially since "she is liable to Banishment, to transportation for Actions not her own"?[43]

This reassessment of female roles, however, carried ominous implications for slaveholding society. The same individualistic values that provided the framework for a new gender dynamic could also foster the burgeoning antislavery movement. Men and women internalizing the principles of bourgeois individualism confronted the individual rights not only of women but also of African American slaves. By invoking an enlightened standard of domesticity in their struggle against English authority, the slaveowning colonists made themselves vulnerable to charges of inhumanity and exploitation. Tory opponents of the Revolution highlighted southern inconsistency on this issue when they asked, "How is it that we hear the loudest *yelps* for liberty among the drivers of the negroes?"[44]

Virulent racial prejudice enabled southern slaveowners to downplay questions about their selective embrace of individual rights. By ascribing subhuman qualities to African Americans, white slaveholders believed they could rightfully deny their slaves the liberties otherwise accorded to every human being. In the northern colonies, revolutionary ideology promoted the cause of slave emancipation and, by the turn of the nineteenth century, led to the abolition of unfree labor. As historians such as Gary Nash have demonstrated, the process of emancipation was complex and often contested.[45] Nevertheless, the region's ultimate embrace of abolitionism set it apart from the South, where a plantation economy necessitated an ongoing commitment to slavery. In the years preceding the Revolution, very few masters in Georgia and South Carolina emancipated their slaves. In these cases, moreover, owners tended to free only their mulatto offspring. Thus, in 1774, South Carolina relatives of the recently deceased Benjamin Williamson freed three mulatto slaves because they had "reason to believe they are his Issue."[46] Four years earlier, South Carolina planter Jonathan Drake had "left a Mulattoe Child named Molly her freedom & fifteen Negroes."[47] By recognizing individuals of mixed racial descent as their relatives, these slaveowners were taking an unusual step. Yet, as was revealed by Drake's decision to bequeath his mixed-race daughter an estate that included slaves, even these exceptionally benevolent white southerners stopped well short of a campaign against human bondage.

The same held true for Henry Laurens, who kept himself informed about the budding abolitionist movement. His response demonstrated how ostensibly humane planters could convince themselves that slavery retained at least some virtues. Visiting London in May 1772, Laurens followed the development of the *Somerset* case—a court battle that resulted in the first major victory for the English abolitionists. Despite his professed sympathies for the sufferings of many American slaves, Laurens characterized the Somerset affair as "a long and comical Story." Writing to a fellow slave-owner in South Carolina, Laurens noted that "my [slave] Man Robert Scipio Laurens says, the Negroes that want to be free here, are Fools." Henry Laurens then observed that Robert Scipio had not departed from Laurens, even after Laurens instructed him "to go about his Business."[48] Notwithstanding his unusual consideration for his slaves' feelings, Laurens did not advocate abolition in the early 1770s. Following the *Somerset* verdict, he even helped a business partner avoid the potential fiscal sacrifice of emancipating a slave that the man had transported to England. Laurens ordered the slave to be sent "by first Vessel for Charles Town & that proper precautions may be taken immediately upon arrival . . . to prevent Elopement."[49] Robert Scipio's subsequent conviction for theft no doubt reinforced Laurens's beliefs about the undesirability of free blacks. Informing an acquaintance of Scipio's fate, Laurens confessed that his "wishes are to See the [British] Kingdom cleaned from every one of [Scipio's] Colour" to prevent the mongrelization of the English race and the further corruption of Parliament.[50]

In fact, the southern planters' dedication to the institution of slavery set the stage for their rejection of imperial authority.[51] In the months preceding the Revolution, the slaveholders increasingly feared that England would devastate their society by freeing their bondservants. An Englishwoman visiting North Carolina in March 1775 reported rumors of a royal proclamation supposedly "ordering Tories to murder the whigs, and promising every Negroe that would murder his Master and family that he should have his Master's plantation."[52] That same month, South Carolina slaveowner Ralph Izard learned about an English plan to "emancipate all their negroes [in the South], and protect them after they have done it."[53] In Georgia, word circulated that British authorities planned to "liberate the slaves and encourage them to attack their masters." Although Georgia governor James Wright characterized these rumors as "absurd & improbable," he credited them with throwing "the people in Carolina and in this province, into a ferment" and rightly predicted they would "have an exceeding[ly] bad effect and . . . will involve us all in the utmost distress."[54]

Asserting that the people of Georgia had fallen into "a State of Madness, and Desperation," James Habersham anticipated the impending Revolution with "Horror and Grief." Although British administration of the colonies had enabled the planters to develop into a powerful elite, the prospect of racial Armageddon drove them to strike for independence. And because new ideas about domestic relationships had undergirded that political break, it was only appropriate that southerners conceptualized the Revolution in terms of broken families. "Father against Son," predicted the prominent Georgia colonist, "and Son against Father, and the nearest relations and Friends combatting with each other [and], I may Perhaps say with Truth, cutting each others throats."[55] The Revolution did in fact tear apart prominent southern families such as the Gardens and the Manigaults. Whereas Gabriel and Peter Manigault pitted themselves against British tyranny, Peter's son Gabriel Manigault II vacillated between the rebels and the Tories. Disgusted by the colonists' disloyalty to the Crown, Alexander Garden fled for England even while his son Alexander Garden III served as an officer in the Continental army. As one of Ralph Izard's acquaintances correctly foretold in 1774, the struggle against England was marked in every sense by "all the horrors of a civil war."[56]

Within weeks of the first shots at Concord and Lexington, whites in the Deep South confronted the menace of a vast slave population struggling to arm itself. Joseph Manigault, for example, informed his brother that a schooner "loaded with Goods to go in the Country, was robbed by some negroes," who seized "Nothing else but Powder."[57] As Continental and British troops clashed in the North, restless slaveowners fixated on the possibility of Tory-inspired slave insurrection. Particularly disturbing news had arrived in May 1775 from Arthur Lee, a Virginian living in London, who (according to William Campbell, the newly appointed royal governor of South Carolina) sent word of an imperial plot "not only to bring down the Indians on the Inhabitants" of the Deep South "but also to instigate, and encourage an insurrection amongst the slaves."[58] In South Carolina, rumors abounded that royal officials planned to emancipate and to arm the colony's slaves.[59] When the Charlestown General Committee formally declared their willingness to fight for the patriotic cause, they pointed to "the dread of instigated Insurrections at home" as a cause "sufficient to drive an oppressed People to the use of Arms."[60] In late October, the House of Commons exacerbated matters by debating plans to foster slave rebellions in the South. Although Parliament rejected that course of action, Ralph Izard reported from London that former South Carolina governor William Lyttelton "was particularly rancorous against America, and plumed himself much on the expedient of encouraging the Negroes in the Southern Colonies, to drench themselves in the blood of their masters."[61]

As Edward Rutledge asserted in December 1775, the possibility that England would incite slave insurrections tended "more effectually to work an eternal separation between Great Britain and the Colonies . . . than any other expedient, which could possibly have been thought of."[62] In February 1776 Henry Laurens reported "discoveries which have lately been made of a Settled plan to involve us in all the horrible Scenes of foreign & domestic Butcheries." The slaveowners fully believed that "while Men of War & Troops are to attack us in front the Indians are to make inroads on our backs [while] Tories & Negro Slaves [were] to rise in our Bowels."[63] By March 1776, fearful whites had written these fears into South Carolina's first state constitution. The document asserted that the British had "excited domestic insurrections—proclaimed freedom to servants and slaves, enticed or stolen them from, and armed them against their masters."[64] For slaveowners such as Rutledge, the imagined spectacle of slaves being "emancipated for the express purpose of massacreing their Masters" provided the catalyst for political independence.[65] The English policy concerning the slaves brewed similar resentment in Georgia. American general Lachlan McIntosh stated that British forces were "encouraging our slaves to desert to them, pilfering our sea islands for provisions."[66]

In response, the Continental army attempted to formulate a military strategy that would minimize British interference with southern slavery. In March 1778, Rutledge chastised Thomas Pinckney for overlooking the fact that the moment his forces in South Carolina "quitted Purrysburgh the Enemy would have . . . decreased the riches of this Country by near 2000 Negroes."[67] As soldiers battled for control of the lowcountry, Charleston minister Oliver Hart concluded that "Negroes are [of] a very precarious Tenure, any where near the Environs of Georgia." Five months later Hart postulated that British "Plunderers never had the pleasure of ravaging so opulent a Country before," insisting that the "Havoc they have made is not to be described."[68] Southern planters, moreover, also lost slaves to marauding American soldiers as well as to common thieves.[69] When the American general Nathanael Greene attempted to restore order to the southern countryside in 1781, he discovered that the "savage fury" of the war and the prevailing "spirit for plundering" had left not even "the shadow of government" in Georgia and South Carolina.[70]

Slaveholders in the Deep South had always regarded their slaves with a mixture of contempt and fear. As thousands of slaves liberated themselves or were removed from the slaveholders' control, white hostility toward African Americans became even more pronounced. A few slaveowners abandoned colonial arguments about the superior virtues of slave labor and attempted to hire white servants as household laborers.[71] And most southern planters resorted to a grisly array of violent punishments and executions to maintain control over their black slaves. When Thomas Pinckney's slave John lost one of his master's letters, the slaveowner ominously announced that the boy was "now under sentence" and "shall severely expiate his offense."[72] Slaveowners such as Charleston resident William Ancrum discouraged their overseers from any "lenity" that might "encourage" the slaves to resist.[73] By 1779, slaves fleeing "to the woods to shun labour or punishment" were being "hunted down or shot as wild beasts" by their owners.[74]

British imperial authorities had once attempted to protect slaves from murder at the hands of unduly cruel masters. By contrast, the revolutionary government institutionalized state-sanctioned executions for resisting slaves. Indeed, radical organizations such as the Charleston General Committee rose to power largely by opposing the Crown's humanitarian concern for southern slaves. During summer 1775, for example, South Carolina governor Campbell struggled to protect slaves and free blacks who he believed had been wrongly accused of plotting insurrection. Forced to retreat to warships in Charleston Bay, he watched helplessly as revolutionary authorities sentenced one "unfortunate man," Thomas Jeremiah, "to be hanged and afterwards burned."[75] Upon learning "on what grounds they had doomed a fellow creature to death," Campbell's "blood r[a]n cold." His efforts on Jeremiah's behalf, however, "raised such a clamour amongst the people as is incredible, and they openly and loudly declared if I granted the man a pardon they would hang him at my door." Given the slaveowners' obsession with the prospect for slave revolt, "this heartrending story" could have only one ending—the execution of Jeremiah.[76] Over the next six years, many other African Americans fell victim to the campaign for independence, sacrificed on the pyre of a white crusade for political liberty. What planters in the Deep South most coveted was the freedom to maintain their mastery over tens of thousands of African Americans. Years of war did nothing to soften the ruthlessness of revolutionary officials. In September 1781, South Carolina governor John Rutledge instructed General Francis Marion to make "severe examples" of "all negroes who carry any provisions of any kind, aid or assist or carry any intelligence to or for the enemy." "Agreeable to the laws of this State," ordered Rutledge, "all such negroes shall suffer death."[77]

Rutledge's inhumanity suggests a broad affinity between the form of government authority and the content of government social policy. Given that the British Empire had integrated diverse regions into one imperial system, it made perfect sense for the king to sanction a philosophy of Christian stewardship. The monarchy's interests were obviously well served by a theology that compelled individuals, however distant from the center of authority, to sublimate their interests to the greater good of the corporate enterprise. When royal officials intervened on behalf of the slave, they were also obliging the colonists to defer to the king's wisdom respecting the common good. On the other hand, when the colonists denounced cohesive imperial political structures for violating their liberties, they were denying that the metropolis could judge the righteousness of activity occurring in distant locales. Risking their lives to decentralize the form of government authority, southern revolutionaries had every reason to reject the Christian ideal of organic society. The lesson they had drawn from their experience with England warned them against surrendering the political autonomy of their communities to the strictures of an all-encompassing moral code. In this context, revolutionary officials such as Rutledge felt few qualms when they advocated harsh measures in their campaign for liberty. It would have made little sense for them to allow universal prescriptions for proper conduct to interfere with their political campaign against centralized power.

Conversely, the few revolutionary slaveowners whose wartime responsibilities exposed them to a global perspective on human bondage were the ones who exhibited unusual concern for individual slave welfare. Surveying the isolated instances in which American masters adopted principles of Christian reciprocity, one is struck by how often they expressed their humanitarian impulse from foreign locations. As the eighteenth-century historian Alexander Hewatt observed, "good masters and mistresses, whose humanity and a sense of interest will not permit them to treat their negroes in a harsh manner, do not always reside at their plantations." Ralph Izard demonstrated that a lack of physical proximity did not preclude masters' humanitarian concern for their slaves. While serving as an American diplomat in France, Izard insisted that his South Carolina overseer provide his slaves with necessary provisions, regardless of the cost. "The Negroes ought to be comfortably cloathed if there is any possibility of doing it," directed Izard in 1777; "I cannot think of their not being so, without the greatest uneasiness, & I would take my chance of borrowing money for the maintenance of my family, & have the whole of my crop appropriated to that purpose, rather than they should be subjected to such distress."[78] Writing from

London that same year, Gabriel Manigault recounted a story that defined the master-slave relationship in terms of mutual responsibility and affection, describing how "a Violent Storm" had destroyed a ship transporting a slaveowner named Mr. Wragg to England. The slaveowner perished at sea, and "if it had not been for the Care and attention of the Negro Mr. Wragg had brought with him," observed Manigault, "his Son might probably have been lost likewise."[79] Distance from the chaotic revolutionary setting enabled both Izard and Manigault to sentimentalize the master-slave relationship.

Their idealized conception of slavery stood in dramatic contrast to the one articulated by their counterparts remaining in the Deep South, who complained about being "rob'd and deserted" by slaves. Summing up the opinion of local slaveowners in 1780, Charleston slaveowner Eliza Pinckney attributed the slaveholders' pessimistic assessment of the institution's prospects to the fact that "the slaves in this country in gen[era]l have behaved so infamously and even those that remain'd at home so insolent and quite their own masters." By the end of the war, slaveowners were describing those slaves who had "never deserted to the British" as "remarkably" obedient.[80] Even before the Revolution, southern slaveowners had resisted idealists seeking to reform the master-slave relationship. After years of hardship and destruction, after experiencing the dislocation of thousands of slaves from their plantations, southern planters became livid when revolutionary politicians such as Thomas Jefferson raised questions about the morality of the unfree labor system. Already isolated before the war by their humanitarian pretensions, planters such as Henry Laurens discovered that the wartime intellectual climate in the Deep South made it ever less likely that the slaveowners, as a class, would embrace corporate individualism as a component of their identity.

Immersed in the progressive intellectual currents of the eighteenth-century Enlightenment, Jefferson had denounced the African slave trade as a monstrous barbarity—one that he blamed on English imperial policy. Indeed, Jefferson's original draft of the Declaration of Independence had indicted the king for "captivating and carrying" a distant people "into slavery in another hemisphere." Yet, despite the fact that Jefferson's perspective on slavery offered a blistering critique of the British Empire for "suppressing every [southern] legislative attempt to prohibit or to restrain this execrable commerce," the Deep South rejected his views out of hand.[81] The clause "reprobating the enslaving of the inhabitants of Africa," reflected Jefferson, "was struck out in complaisance to South Carolina and Georgia," which (Jefferson wrongly claimed) "had never attempted to restrain the importation of slaves" and which (Jefferson rightly speculated) "on the contrary still wished to continue it."[82]

Like Jefferson, Laurens averred that "Negroes were first enslaved by the English," that "Acts of Parliament have established the Slave Trade in favour of the home residing English." And unlike his fellow slaveowners in the Deep South, Laurens had genuine reservations about the morality of the institution. Although his fortune rested on a foundation of unfree labor, Laurens confessed to his son John that he "abhor[red] Slavery." The charge of hypocrisy bothered the South Carolina planter, who claimed not to be "one of those who dare trust in Providence for defence & security of their own Liberty while they enslave & wish to continue in slavery, thousands who are as well intitled to freedom as themselves." Yet Laurens himself noted that such views would make him "appear to many as a promoter not only of strange but of dangerous doctrines." He therefore vowed to "proceed with caution."[83] On these points his son clearly agreed: "The equitable Conduct which you have resolved upon with respect to your Negroes, will undoubtedly meet with great Opposition from interested Men—I have often conversed upon the Subject and I have scarcely ever met with a Native of the Southern Provinces or the W. Indies, who did not obstinately recur to the most absurd Arguments in support of Slavery."[84]

As the war progressed, John Laurens hoped that military expediency would promote greater acceptance of emancipation. In a letter to his father, he proposed the liberation of slaves who were willing to serve as American soldiers. "My plan," wrote Laurens, "is at once to give freedom to the Negroes and gain Soldiers to the States." "When can it be better done," he asked, "than when their enfranchisement may be made conducive to the Public Good, and be so modified as not to overpower [the slaves'] weak minds"?[85] Laurens, however, could barely convince his father, let alone a wider community of slaveowners, that his plan merited execution. Noting that his son's "mind is enveloped in the Cloud of that project," the elder Laurens "undert[ook] to say there is not a Man in America of your opinion."[86] Henry Laurens's skepticism was not misplaced. When the Continental Congress suggested that South Carolina implement John Laurens's scheme in 1782, the planters responded with outrage. Simply put, the slaveowners' racial views and economic dependence on slavery prevented any consideration of African Americans as fellow citizens.

Whereas the slaveholders rejected a humanitarian approach to slavery,

Tories not surprisingly demonstrated a greater inclination toward Christian paternalism. Maintaining their loyalty to the imperial hierarchy, they quite naturally embraced an ideology that mandated organic relations between social superiors and inferiors. In 1775 Gabriel Johnston, former governor of North Carolina, argued in the House of Commons that "the state of slavery cuts off all the great magnanimous inventive powers of the human mind, but it rather strengthens fidelity and attachment; the Roman history fully confirms this: amidst the multiplied treachery of friends and relations . . . the slave was seldom or ever unfaithful to his master." In his opinion, slaveowners "in general" were "kind to their slaves."[87] Although the war threatened the mastery of every slaveholder in America, Tory narratives of the Revolution emphasized the mutual affection supposedly binding loyal slaves to caring masters. Thus, in August 1777, a Tory planter named Burgwin recounted how his trusty slave foiled the plans of a Whig "marauding party" at his property in South Carolina. After "curry[ing] the favor" of the rebels with "a dusty quart Bottle of what he told them was 'Master's best old Wine,'" wrote Burgwin, "the faithful old Negro carried off the chest" filled with his valuables and "buried it out of sight."[88]

In Burgwin's account, the loyalty of his slaves went hand in hand with the loyalty that he believed many South Carolina residents still felt toward the English monarchy. Noting "a conspiracy in favor of Gt. Britain among the back[country] inhabitants," the Tory asserted that if imperial authorities "wou'd send over a sufficient force to the Southern Colonies with arms and ammunition to receive and give protection to the friends of [royal] Govern[men]t, matters wou'd take quite a different turn." Burgwin asserted that "the People are most heartily tired of the present [revolutionary] masters"—that a sense of organic fealty to traditional structures of both slaveowning and royal authority persisted in the South. Like their revolutionary counterparts, however, Tory slaveowners did worry that imperial policy would cost them their slaves, who would in "great Numbers . . . endeavour to join the King's Troops in Expectation of being declared and made free." In 1779, a number of prominent Loyalist planters in Georgia beseeched Lord George Germain to resist the temptation to utilize African Americans in defense of the Empire. They complained that hundreds of slaves had already "dispersed themselves on board [Tory] Transports and Merchant Ships and were carryd away in the same and totally lost to their Owners."[89]

Of course, as historian Sylvia Frey has noted, humanitarian concern for the slaves did not motivate British policy respecting the question of bondage in revolutionary America.[90] As a rule, royal officials cared less about the plight of the African American bondservant than they did about restoring order in the colonies. The few British officers struggling to improve the slaves' welfare realized that English military command did not share their feelings. James Moncrief felt it necessary to remind General Henry Clinton that "the Number of slaves, who have attached themselves to the Engineer[ing] Department, since my Arriv[a]l in this part of the Country, and who look up to me for protection, has been for some time past a matter for serious concern." Moncrief stressed the "many advantages which His Majesty's service has derived from their labour," imploring Clinton to "direct upon what footing they are to be fixed." Fearing that no provision would be made to protect the slaves when British forces evacuated South Carolina, Moncrief suggested that England form "a Brigade of the Negroes of this Country."[91] Subsequent events validated the officer's worst suspicions. When imperial troops withdrew from North America, they did not liberate the thousands of slaves that accompanied them; sadly enough, the British transported many American slaves to the miseries of plantation life in the West Indies.[92]

Such monstrous treatment of the slaves, however, did not negate the connection between the structure of imperial authority and an organic understanding of slavery. Although British military officials had placed practical concerns ahead of humanitarian ones, the war nevertheless highlighted the long-standing tendency of planters with strong links to the metropolis to embrace the doctrine of corporate individualism. As these Tory planters fled America in the wake of British military defeat, they continued to aspire to frame their identities as masters on an ideal of Christian stewardship that recognized their slaves' humanity. South Carolina slaveowner Elias Ball, for example, took refuge in St. Augustine in 1783 before relocating to London the following year. In correspondence with his cousin who had stayed in South Carolina, Ball expressed pleasure that a favorite slave would remain in the white family's service. "I shall be satisifyed [if] his children may be of service to mine by & by," wrote Ball, but only on the condition that the slave was actually "desirous of liveing" with Ball's cousin.[93] In subsequent years, Ball took the trouble to send gifts to his former bondservants in the hopes that they would realize he would "not forget [his] old friend[s]." Ball obviously preferred his former slaves to free English servants, whom he deemed "a very Troublesome sett of people"; he favored an organic society in which superiors and inferiors exchanged reciprocal responsibilities to one atomized by rampant individualism.[94]

Meanwhile, a very different ideological dynamic had pervaded the postwar Deep South. While refugees such as Ball confronted an economy based on free labor, white southerners were struggling to rebuild a plantation system that hinged on slavery; while many Tories clung to romanticized ideas about slavery, their revolutionary counterparts reflected on wartime experiences that undermined idealistic conceptions of human bondage. Through slave desertions, deaths, and forced removals, the war had decreased the slave population of the Lower South by as many as twelve thousand African Americans.[95] Slaveowners such as Georgia planter John Berrien denounced "the desertion of those villainous negroes." Berrien, for his part, went so far as to "curse the hour that I became a Georgian."[96] Even the wealthiest slaveowners, moreover, bemoaned the "Difficulties in which our Estates were involved" and expressed fears that their "Patrimony which was once considerable will be greatly diminished." Yet slavery remained the bedrock of the southern economy. "The Negroe business is a great object with us," asserted Georgia merchant Joseph Clay in 1785, "both with a view to our Interest individually, & the general prosperity of this State & its Commerce. It is to the Trade of the Country, as the Soul [is] to the Body."[97]

In spite of this fierce commitment to slavery and an equally intense hostility toward the slaves, the transatlantic ideological current of corporate individualism inspired a few unusual southerners to press for humanitarian reform. Clinging to his ideals during the last years of his life, Henry Laurens struggled to improve the standing of his South Carolina slaves. "They are as happy and contented as laboring people can be," wrote Laurens in 1785, "and some of them to whom I proffered absolute freedom wisely rejected it." Laurens insisted that he would "prevent their ever being absolutely slaves," noting that "to some of them I already allow wages—to the whole every reasonable indulgence."[98] Recognizing his slaves' capacity for personal growth, the planter even maintained that he could "see the rising gradations to unlimited freedom and view[ed] the prospect with pleasure." "When we shall be wise enough to stop the importation" of African slaves, he continued, "such happy families [as his own] will become more general and time will work manumission or a state equal to it."[99]

Ultimately, however, Laurens punctuated his vision of the future with sober reflection rather than unbounded optimism. The wartime experience of massive slave resistance and dislocation and a continuing dependence on the exploited labor of African slaves made the region decidedly inhospitable terrain for humanitarian reform. "But alas!," he complained in 1785, "these

Southern States are not at this moment in a disposition to be persuaded" to take such measures, "tho' one should rise from the dead" advocating them. "A whole country is opposed to me," confessed Laurens in one frank exchange with a British antislavery activist. "God forbid our conversion by too long a delay," he wrote on another occasion, "shall be the effect of a direful struggle."[100] To a large extent, Laurens's ideological isolation stemmed from the dearth of a Christian infrastructure in the postwar South. Had a network of churches been in place to promote an organic religious community, Laurens might have anticipated the future with optimism instead of despair. And given Christianity's tendency to reconcile humanitarian individualism with carefully delineated social hierarchy, he might even have echoed colonial religious authorities by defending slavery as an expression of God's order. The Revolution, however, decimated the meager foundation laid by Christian activists during the colonial period.

The Anglican Church obviously suffered the most. As Patricia Bonomi's study of colonial religious patterns has made clear, American resentment toward the imperial system had resulted in mounting disaffection with Anglican authority in the 1770s.[101] The Savannah minister Haddon Smith described the outraged response of his community when he "refused to comply" with the call for a general fast to protest imperial policy in 1776. "A number of People" approached Smith to "forbid him doing any more Duty in the Town of Savannah; and the next Day, being Sunday, they fastened the Doors of the Church." Several days later, the Anglican minister retreated to Tybee Island to avoid being tarred and feathered by angry American patriots. When the colonists finally declared their independence, dissenting denominations in South Carolina justified their campaign for disestablishment by appealing to "the free & equal rights of mankind." Arguing before the South Carolina assembly in 1777, Presbyterian minister William Tennent denounced "all religious establishment" as "an infringement of religious liberty."[102] The assembly found such logic compelling and unanimously agreed to protect the right of all Protestants to "enjoy free & equal privileges." Stigmatized by their association with British authority and increasingly denied state revenue, Anglican churchmen were forced to surrender their dream of incorporating the backcountry into a unified religious domain.[103]

While Anglican authorities fled the war-torn South, Presbyterian and Baptist ministers played prominent roles in the campaign for American independence. William Tennent stepped forward in the 1770s to denounce Parliament and to rally the South around the nonimportation agreement. Working tirelessly for the Revolutionary cause, Baptists such as Oliver Hart denounced Tories as "some of the basest Creatures under the Heavens."[104] Indeed, one imperial official observed from Charleston in 1780 that "at the commencement of the rebellion there was nothing that conduced more to foment the disturbances and set the minds of the people in a flame than the exertions of some itinerant preachers who were sent throughout the country where they poisoned the minds of the people with groundless fears and false apprehensions."[105]

The ministers' political efforts, however, did not result in a general religious awakening. In fact, the destruction and dislocation wrought by the war handicapped the efforts of every denomination, whatever their respective wartime politics. "All things Continue to grow Worse & Worse for the more Extortion increases the more pride & vanity & all sorts of Vice prevail. There is no more appearance of a Reformation th[a]n [there] was before the Enemy Came among us," lamented one religious Charleston resident in 1779.[106] John Joachim Zubly, a Congregationalist minister from Georgia, observed in 1780 that "in these Southern Provinces . . . the publick worship of God in all denominations [is] almost totally set aside or neglected." Four years later, Baptist Mary McDonald announced that religion "is at a very low ebb in Charleston—it is quite unfashionable even among professors of every denomination."[107] And because the degree of religious adherence in Charleston had always compared favorably with "the lamentable state of religion" in the backcountry, McDonald's report suggests that Christianity made little headway into the postwar Deep South.[108] Reflecting on Christianity's fortunes during this chaotic era, South Carolina Baptist minister Richard Furman concluded that "our Churches have suffer[e]d greatly by the Death of Ministers and members, as also by their removal."[109]

In private, ministers such as Charles Woodmason and Oliver Hart aspired to the role of Christian steward. Before the war, Woodmason had approved of South Carolina statutes that restrained the power of slaveowners to discipline their slaves. The Anglican described such legal protection as "a wise Provision lest the Owners of the Slaves may have them maltreated, or injur'd thro Passion, or Malice or Revenge as there are too many warp'd, and rancourous Minds" who "would vent their Resentment on a Poor harmless Negroe."[110] Likewise, Oliver Hart's correspondence with his wife reveals that they valued affectionate relations with their black bondservants. Writing from Charleston in 1781, Anne Hart observed that "the poor black members [of the family] hang about me and wish for Master." Internalizing the ideal of Christian benevolence, the Harts structured their relationships with their slaves around the principle of reciprocity. Anne Hart recognized the humanity of the slaves and even confessed that their feelings for her husband "sometimes make me drop a tear."[111]

And yet religious torpor and widespread white antipathy toward blacks prevented itinerant preachers in the Lower South from Christianizing the master-slave relationship. The war had buttressed long-standing colonial suspicion that Christian benevolence would erode the mastery of southern slaveowners. In 1779, for example, Georgia Indian trader George Galphin observed that the slaves had deserted "every indulgent master upon the river." Noting that the British had taken thirteen of his own bondservants, Galphin complained that "some Ba[ptist] preacher has been the ruin of all our negro[e]s."[112] Blaming Christianity for their woes, such embittered slaveowners shunned humanitarian conceptions of human bondage.

Notwithstanding his private sympathies for the slaves, the revolutionary threat of slave insurrection forced Woodmason to assume a hostile public stance toward the southern slave population. Disturbed by bickering between backcountry Presbyterians and Episcopalians, he pointed to the need for white unity amid the dangers of slavery. "We have an *Internal* Enemy of not less than 100[,000] *Africans* below us (and more daily importing)," he asserted. "Over these We ought to keep a very Watchful Eye, lest they surprize us in an Hour when We are not aware, and begin our [interdenominational] Friendships towards each other in Common Death." In a similar manner, Oliver Hart's wartime fears of slave revolt overshadowed his recognition of slave humanity. Hart, for example, complained bitterly in 1775 when backcountry whites refused to assist coastal slaveowners against their slaves.[113]

The uncertain social order engendered by the Revolution led both Woodmason and Hart to cultivate menacing images of the African American slave in order to establish a unified white mentality. But even as racial prejudice and fear banded white southerners together, geographically specific concerns continued to divide them. Throughout the war, murderous antipathy persisted between lowcountry and backcountry residents. Although South Carolina's passage of a Circuit Court Act in 1769 redressed many of the backcountry Regulators' grievances, the regions embarked on opposite paths during the Revolution. Catering to the backcountry's resentment toward the rice-planting coastal elite, royal authorities found numerous allies in the interior of the state. In August 1775, a lowcountry delegation consisting of William Drayton and William Tennent attempted to improve relations between the regions but could not overcome the hostility of backcountry settlers. Noting that a "Pamphlet sent up by the [royal] Governor has done much Damage," the dejected delegates concluded that "nothing could be done here, as they have industriously taught the People that no Man from Charleston can speak the Truth."[114] Over the next eight years, backcountry Tories engaged in bloody guerrilla warfare against patriot forces. As a result, the fall line separating the coastal plains from the South Carolina piedmont delineated starkly hostile regional political cultures.

In addition, the boundary between South Carolina and Georgia demarcated two distinct political sensibilities. As a frontier colony vulnerable to the attack of American Indians and foreign powers, Georgia had relied on imperial support for its survival. When the revolutionary crisis began to unfold, Georgia quickly earned a reputation as one of the least radical American colonies. Much to the irritation of revolutionaries in South Carolina, Georgians consistently violated the nonimportation agreements and did not send representatives to the First Continental Congress in 1774.[115] Although the revolutionary forces in the two states often cooperated, the war did not erase their mutual suspicions. In fact, at one point during the Revolution, leading South Carolina patriots threatened "to *compel* Georgia to submit" to a political "Union with Carolina, [so] that the two Provinces should in future be considered as one *State.*" As the royal governor of Georgia, James Wright, gleefully recounted, the Carolinians "immediately decamped" upon making the threat so as to avoid being "Tarred & Feather'd" by angry Georgians.[116] Moreover, tension between Georgia and South Carolina during the colonial period persisted after the Revolution. As late as 1787, South Carolina governor Thomas Pinckney was denouncing Georgia's territorial claims as "repugnant to the spirit of the Confederation." Notwithstanding their shared plantation economies and their common interest in the subordination of a rebellious slave population, Pinckney likened Georgia to "a hostile nation" and lamented the dearth of friendly relations "between States strictly connected by the Bond of Confederation and endeared to each other by social sufferings and mutual assistance in the common cause" of the Revolution.[117] Despite their shared malevolence toward African American slaves, white residents in the Lower South had not yet developed a common regional mentality.

Depending on their affiliations of race, class, gender, and geography, southerners arrived at very different conclusions concerning the Revolution. White women in the Deep South, for example, drew from their wartime experiences an emboldened sense of agency. Traditionally marginalized from colonial debates about government, southern women discovered during the war that their gender no longer shielded them from the responsibility and danger of political struggle. The transition to a new understanding of gender, however, was fraught with tension. In 1781, for instance, Whig officer Hugh Hughes felt compelled to treat his commander's wife, Catherine Greene, as an autonomous individual by giving her news of her husband's activities. Yet, at the same time, old assumptions about the need to protect women from dangerous knowledge led Hughes to believe that he had transgressed appropriate conventions of gender. "I won't tell the general [Greene] that I purposely made a long Digression in writing to you Ma'am," noted a somewhat embarrassed Hughes, "lest he should suspect me of insensibility to your delicate Situation & Sex, which would be an ineffable Mortification to any Vanity."[118]

Although individualistic ideals and the exigencies of the Revolution had endowed American women with greater political responsibility, traditional patriarchal power continued to limit their freedom. Jane Bruce, the daughter of a South Carolina family, unhappily discovered this to be the case in 1786. Having fallen in love with her suitor Mr. Jones, she agreed to marry him before consulting her parents. When they discovered her intentions, they responded with the "severest treatment." "My parents are determined never to consent . . . and have forbid me ever seeing you in their house," wrote their chagrined daughter to Jones, before informing him that "all correspondence between us must now be at an end and we must endeavor to forget each other." Bruce's desire to act autonomously had led her to consent to marriage without her parents' knowledge. And when her father exerted his household authority, his daughter paused before submitting. "When my father receives your letter, I know he will make me declare whether I am determined to obey or disobey him," wrote Bruce to Jones. "If I was sure it would give uneasiness to none but myself I would not hesitate a moment in declaring [my love], but I never would disobey him."[119] Torn between her own desires and the pressure to obey her father, Bruce eventually married her suitor. Whether she did so with her father's consent remains unclear, but in any event, her struggle sprang from the era's conflicting prescriptions for womanhood.

In this period of transition, women were expected simultaneously to defer to male authority and to guard the nation's political virtue. For the wives of exiled loyalists to England, these expectations could spell disaster. Confiscation statutes passed by the victorious Americans allowed the states to claim all marital property belonging to the Tory men, regardless of their wives' political stance during the war. Thus, even though prevailing gender codes required women to accept their husbands' supposedly superior political judgment, women unfortunate enough to have married Tories lost their dowries to the state. One such woman was Florence Cooke, a Charleston resident who petitioned the South Carolina General Assembly in 1783 to prove her "sincere affection for the independence, and freedom of her Country"—an affection that flourished during the war despite her husband's capitulation to Tory pressures that were "too powerful for his Situation and Circumstances to withstand."[120] Notwithstanding their contributions to the Revolution, American women continued to confront a gender code that denied them leadership over men. "A woman is the most unfit person on earth to have the management of boys," observed one prominent South Carolina woman in 1783, "as they cannot have them under the least *subordination*."[121] In the following decades, women in the Deep South would struggle toward an identity encompassing both their aspiration to become "Republican Mothers" and their desire to fulfill the mandate of the patriarchal household.

The Revolution also marked a turning point in male identity—even for the elite slaveholders of the Deep South. The expectation that authority be tempered by a concern for the welfare of the governed had undergirded the colonial movement for independence. In making their case against the king, southern planters had invoked the principle of reciprocity. Whereas previous philosophies of government had largely ignored the individual when defining the needs of corporate society, the slaveowners' revolutionary ideology embraced the concept of corporate individualism in order to denounce mercantilism. These same slaveholders, however, correctly perceived that a system of ideas which recognized the humanity of individual members of society threatened their claim to unbridled authority over their slaves. As they rebuilt the plantation system following the war, they therefore attempted to govern their unfree labor force according to the very tyrannical precepts that they believed had marred the imperial system.

Although most planters gamely ignored their own hypocrisy, some whites correctly perceived that the coastal slaveholding elite threatened the safety of the emerging democratic order. In the South Carolina backcountry, inhabitants resented the state government for awarding a disproportionately large share of power to the lowcountry districts. And even in Charleston, prominent revolutionary figures like Christopher Gadsden questioned the future of a republic built on slavery. "The inhabitants near the sea are principally concerned in negroes—has their conduct during this campaign been so particularly meritorious?" wrote Gadsden to South Carolina's governor in 1782. According to Gadsden, the coastal slaveowners' "interest has indisputably occasioned more danger to the State than their fellow citizens, with less of that kind of property." "Have they not excepting a very few," he continued, "been the most backward in the State during these critical times to turn out?"[122] Concurring with this sentiment, Henry Laurens observed that "at present the number of wretched slaves, precarious riches, is our greatest weakness." To be sure, only a small minority of southern whites voiced such doubt about slavery's future; indeed, as they reestablished their profitable plantations, most inhabitants of the Deep South clamored for more instead of fewer slaves. Gadsden himself remained a slaveholder, bequeathing his slaves to his children.[123] Nevertheless, the Revolution had led a few slaveowners to question slavery's righteousness and many more to doubt the institution's viability in an age of freedom.

Sensing that the Revolution had enhanced their need for a coherent system of values, forward-thinking planters stressed the value of education as a means of instilling political virtue and resolving troublesome ideological tensions. In May 1782, for example, George Walton exhorted a young friend in Georgia to "continue [to] improve your mind by reading, or rather studying some modern author"—advice that echoed John Laurens's wartime contention that South Carolinians advance their understanding "in all Branches of useful Knowledge." Through intellectual and moral self-discipline, southerners sought to ensure the survival of their new republic. "The Cup is in our Hands," wrote Christopher Gadsden in 1784, "& if we prove so lazy as not to Bear it up to our Lips, we must deservedly be ruin'd, & so far from meriting any Pity cannot but expect the highest Degree of Laughter & Contempt." In the wake of the political split with England, authors such as David Ramsay of South Carolina sought to establish an American system of publishing and literature that would help to forge an admirable national character. Whether or not the undertaking would aid the slaveholders with their quest for mastery, however, remained to be seen. On an ominous note, two prominent texts published by Americans in the 1780s—Thomas Jefferson's *Notes on the State of Virginia* and J. Hector St. John de Crèvecoeur's *Letters from an American Farmer*—condemned the cruelty of slavery. Instead of reinforcing the righteousness of the slaveholders' hegemony, Jefferson's writings denounced the slaveholder for inflicting "on his fellow men a bondage, one hour of which is fraught with more misery than ages of that which he rose in rebellion to oppose."[124]

To withstand such charges, the southern planters needed a philosophical framework that justified social hierarchy and, at the same time, incorporated the individualistic legacy of the American Revolution. Since the early 1700s, Christian missionaries had offered the slaveowners a theology that fulfilled both requirements; ironically, however, the planters of the Deep South had rejected their message and stymied their efforts to establish a network of Christian churches. Stung by charges of ruthless exploitation and by the wartime defection of their slaves, white southerners dehumanized their African American bondservants instead of uniting with them in an interracial religious community. Alexander Hewatt asserted in 1779 that "the negroes of that country [of South Carolina and Georgia], a few only excepted, are to this day as great strangers to Christianity, and as much under the influence of Pagan Darkness, idolatry and superstition, as they were at their first arrival from Africa."[125]

Only such unusual slaveholders as Laurens construed mastery in terms of love. Noting in 1785 that he had "forbidden" the lash on his plantations, Laurens claimed to maintain order by appealing to his slaves' affections. "If you deserve whipping," he lectured them, "I shall conclude you don't love me and I will sell you[;] otherwise I will never sell one of you, nor will I ever buy another negro."[126] But Laurens stood practically alone in these sentiments. Obsessed with the prospect of generating huge fortunes from their plantations, Laurens's fellow citizens rejected out of hand the notion that they should subordinate the commercial aspects of slavery to the principles of Christian morality. Slaveowners such as Georgia merchant Edward Telfair, for example, occasionally proved willing to keep slave families intact when purchasing them at public auction, but only insofar as they received fiscal compensation for their humanitarianism.[127]

To vanquish their British oppressors, the southern slaveowners had cloaked themselves in the loftiest ideals of their era. Asserting that only the consent of the governed could establish the foundation for virtuous government, the campaign by white southerners for political liberty had heralded the arrival of an age of freedom. But even as the citizens of the new American republic clamored for a moral political existence, they maintained a society built on the sufferings of a vast African American slave population. Blinded by their racist, dehumanizing mores, the slaveowners aspired to an absolute dominion over their black household members—a dominion of unrestrained tyranny. Herein lay the American Revolution's most tragic legacy. During the war, the one hundred thousand slaves of the Deep South had struggled valiantly against the plantation order. To no segment of the population did the ideal of freedom mean more, and to no group of Americans was its denial more crushing. After 150 years of bondage in America, the slaves remained outsiders, largely removed from mainstream culture by their own desire for autonomy, as well as by white convictions about their inferiority. Surrounded by such dangerous company and by the egalitarian ideals sparked by the Revolution, few slaveowners believed without reservation that their mastery was secure.

We have painful
reports here respecting
[slave] insurrections in
the two Carolinas. . . .
Our property in Carolina
is held by a slender tye.
. . . This is one of the
many abuses of the rights
of Man.
PIERCE BUTLER,
1793

CHAPTER THREE

Building a Nation Safe for Human Bondage

Slaveholders in the Early Republic, 1787–1800

During the colonial period, the location of slaveowners on the periphery of the British Empire had colored their understanding of social relations. Independence from England forced masters in the Deep South to recast time-honored assumptions about individual rights and state authority. Although one might expect the Revolution to have fostered a greater emphasis on political liberties, the slaveowners drew exactly the opposite lesson from their struggle against England. As long as ultimate authority rested with the Crown, planters in the Deep South had every incentive to minimize government interference with the master-slave relationship. In the 1780s, however, the new dynamic of core and periphery led the slaveowners toward a greater respect for government authority. Influential planters suddenly occupied the central political position in the new American nation. Having gained final responsibility over their own society, the slaveholders turned an increasingly critical eye toward popular protest.

The Manigault family once again provides a case in point. As speaker of the South Carolina Assembly, Peter Manigault had spearheaded colonial resistance against imperial policy in the 1760s. Twenty years later, Manigault's children yearned for stability in a world threatened by the French Revolution and the attendant (successful) slave uprising on St. Domingue. Although "the horrors of preceding times" prevented them from thinking "this [one] the worst of ages to live in," the Manigaults and their peers believed that theirs was a "wicked world." Like other members of the slave-owning elite, they grew tired of "always patroling & guarding" and even came "to dread the future."[1] The genesis of a new federal government provided much-needed reassurance that Americans could regulate the passions threatening their new nation. To buttress their insecure position, however, the slaveholders required more than a political solution to the problem of slavery in an age of revolution. During this turbulent period, planters in the Deep South took their first halting steps, as a ruling class, toward the construction of a culture that embraced corporate individualism as the principal pillar of a stable, moral society.

By the late 1780s, the new American nation was faltering amid a host of economic and social problems. The revolutionary generation had vanquished the British, replacing imperial authority with a decentralized confederation of virtually autonomous states. Americans quickly learned, however, that the absence of hierarchical government could lead to chaos instead of freedom, to licentiousness instead of liberty. In 1786, for example, settlers in western Massachusetts armed themselves in protest of state taxes that they deemed to be overly burdensome. Although Shays's Rebellion resulted in minimal bloodshed, it raised the question of whether exalted notions of individual rights would permit Americans to preserve order. In Charleston white mechanics verbally and physically protested perceived violations of their democratic liberties. Revolutionary leaders, who had previously courted the favor of the white working class by advocating rebellion against England, now hastened to reaffirm their commitment to social stability. Christopher Gadsden, for example, complained that "we have too many amongst us [who] want again to be running upon every Fancy to the Meetings of [the] liberty Tree." Although he had built a reputation as a champion of the Charleston artisans, Gadsden questioned "whether this [tendency toward popular protest] is not a Disease amongst us far more dangerous than any thing that can arise from the whole present Herd of contemptible exportable Tories."[2] Responding to artisan riots that occurred in 1783 and 1784, he contended that "it must distress and alarm every good Citizen to see the many insults on Government so frequently happening." Addressing a grand jury at the Court of General Sessions in Charleston in 1783, Aedanus Burke raised the same concerns: "Although a life of warfare favours the higher passions, ambition, a love of country and friends, and inspires a contempt of toils and death; yet it begets also a contempt for laws and civil order, a love of pleasure and dissipation, and in some degree unhinges the mind from principles of religion and morality."[3]

Troubled by the chaos that seemingly surrounded them, as well as by the Confederation's inability to implement a foreign policy, prominent Americans from across the country called for a stronger national government. Slaveowners in the Deep South were among the most enthusiastic advocates of a new constitution. Giving voice to the concerns of his region, Charles Pinckney of South Carolina wrote that "it is the anarchy" or, "rather worse than anarchy," a "pure democracy, which I fear"—one in which "the laws lose their respect, and the Magistrates their authority; where no permanent security is given to the properties and privileges of the Citizens."[4] In 1787 Pinckney, along with prominent politicians from every state except Rhode Island, convened in Philadelphia to establish a constitution that would protect the American people from their own passionate whims.

The Georgia and South Carolina delegations arrived with the intention of buttressing the institution of slavery, but they collided with a powerful antislavery movement. When John Rutledge of South Carolina introduced a resolution forbidding federal interference with the international slave trade, northern delegates insisted that they "never would concur in upholding domestic slavery." Gouverneur Morris of Pennsylvania denounced slavery as "a nefarious institution," claiming that it was "the curse of heaven on the States where it prevailed."[5] Joining in the attack on slavery, Rufus King of Massachusetts questioned the wisdom of a new union as long as the South had "the liberty to introduce a weakness which will render defence more difficult." "There was so much inequality and unreasonableness in all this," he concluded, "that the people of the Northern States could never be reconciled to it."[6] Even the delegates from the Upper South criticized slavery as a crime against humanity. George Mason of Virginia, for instance, argued that "slavery discourages arts & manufactures" and "produces the most pernicious effect on manners." Fearing "the judgment of heaven on a Country" filled with slaves, Mason "held it essential in every point of view, that the Gen[era]l Gov[ernmen]t should have [the] power to prevent the increase of slavery."[7]

In response, the statesmen representing the Deep South vowed to reject any agreement that threatened the institution of human bondage. Charles Cotesworth Pinckney boldly stated that "S[outh] Carolina & Georgia cannot do without slaves"; John Rutledge declared that the constitution's position respecting slavery would ultimately dictate "whether the southern states shall or shall not be parties to the Union."[8] The delegates from Georgia made their point with equal force. Abraham Baldwin, for example, insisted that his state would reject any "attempt to abridge one of her favorite prerogatives."[9] Over the course of the convention, the southern statesmen locked horns with the opponents of slavery and successfully lobbied for a number of concessions toward their regional labor system. First, the delegates agreed that three-fifths of the number of slaves be included in the population figures used to apportion each state's representatives in Congress. Second, they compromised on the question of the international slave trade by forbidding congressional interference until 1808. Finally, they assented to a fugitive slave clause mandating the return of runaway slaves who had crossed state lines.[10]

Notwithstanding these concessions to slavery, the proceedings in Philadelphia alienated the Georgia and South Carolina delegations. Verbally assaulted by the most eloquent voices of their generation, the statesmen of the Deep South confronted evidence that powerful politicians would henceforth attack plantation society as immoral. Georgia representative Pierce Butler captured their sense of vulnerability when he noted that the South desired "security." Slaveowners, according to Butler, wanted assurance that "their negroes may not be taken from them which some gentlemen within or without doors, have a very good mind to do." Given their belief that emancipation would leave their states "a desert waste," southerners could ill afford to ignore even the most abstract abolitionist rhetoric. As a result they looked to the future with misgiving, no doubt noting that even the northern politicians who acknowledged the South's right to protect slavery nevertheless anticipated the institution's demise. The delegations from the Deep South therefore drew little comfort when men such as Oliver Ellsworth of Connecticut promised not to "intermeddle" with the southern labor system but, in the very next breath, predicted that "slavery in time will not be a speck in our Country."[11]

The manner in which slaveowners in Georgia and South Carolina reacted to such sentiment demonstrates the Deep South's ideological commitment to slavery. Historians have often argued that southerners defended slavery as a "necessary evil" during this period—that eighteenth-century slaveowners willingly conceded the immorality of human bondage and argued for its continuance solely for practical reasons. Abraham Baldwin provided evidence for this interpretation when he claimed that Georgia would "probably put a stop to the evil" of the slave trade without federal coercion. Making a similar argument, Charles Cotesworth Pinckney stated that "if the S[outhern] States were let alone they will probably of themselves stop [the slave] importations." Indeed, he even assured the delegates that "he w[oul]d himself as a Citizen of S[outh] Carolina vote for it."[12]

To a large extent, however, expediency rather than genuine embarrassment or guilt motivated Baldwin's and Pinckney's comments about slavery. The Georgia and South Carolina delegations realized that antislavery sentiment placed them in the minority at the constitutional convention. By appearing to sympathize with their critics, the statesmen of the Deep South hoped to minimize any threat to the institution of human bondage. Over the course of the constitutional debates, Pinckney in particular emerged as a man biting his tongue—avoiding confrontation that might push the opponents of slavery toward a more extreme position. For example, when Gouverneur Morris launched into his tirade against slavery, Pinckney denied his charges but then cut short debate, claiming that his thesis "could be demonstrated if the occasion were a proper one."[13] When antislavery delegates heaped further abuse on the Deep South several weeks later, they finally exhausted his patience. Pinckney reminded the convention that "if slavery be wrong, it is justified by the example of all the world." He "cited the case of Greece[,] Rome & other an[c]ient States," as well as "the sanction given [to slavery] by France, England, Holland & other modern States," before arguing that "in all ages one half of mankind have been slaves."[14] The position staked out by southern delegates such as Pinckney left little doubt about Georgia's and South Carolina's commitment to unfree labor. Had these elite planters already formulated an organic perspective on slavery, the constitutional convention would have provided them with a perfect opportunity to highlight a reciprocal relationship between masters and slaves. As we have already seen, however, southern planters associated the organic defense of slavery with British imperial administration—with efforts to curtail their liberties to control their own human property. For this reason (rather than from any profound distaste for the institution), southern representatives at the convention refrained from offering any elaborate defense of human bondage.

In many ways, Pierce Butler epitomized the attitudes of the statesmen representing the Deep South in Philadelphia. During the proceedings, he exerted himself to protect slavery but avoided extended discussion about the morality of the institution. When an Irish correspondent confronted him four years later with an "opinion respecting the treatment of the wretched Affricans," Butler responded with ambivalence. On one hand, he observed that "had it pleased God to allow the benign beam of Civilization to reach [the slaves'] Country, it would not [have been] in the power of Europe to enslave them." Defending slavery, Butler expressed "much doubt [that the slaves'] situation in their own Country is freer or better" than conditions in the South. On the other hand, however, Butler conceded that such reasoning "does not perhaps justify the [slave] trade." Eager to maintain the friendship of his correspondent, Butler acknowledged that "we should leave them to their own fate," before concluding that "indeed, I wish I had never owned one of them."[15] Facing an antislavery audience, Butler struggled to deliver the expected lines about slavery but could not divorce himself from the notion that the institution had its virtues. And his voluminous correspondence leaves little doubt that his ownership of slaves caused him far less anguish than did the prospect of emancipation. "I assure you I am apprehensive that the folly of some idle people in America will sooner or later give us some trouble with our Negroes," wrote Butler to a friend in 1792. "It must at all times be crushed in the Bud for if it gets any head we must suffer even in the Supression, by the numbers that wou'd fall."[16]

When the convention adjourned and the slaveowners of the Deep South discussed the constitution among themselves, they never referred to the doctrine of slavery as a necessary evil, nor did they look forward to a brighter future without it. To the contrary, South Carolina residents such as Rawlins Lowndes exalted slavery as a positive good, arguing that the slave "trade could be justified on the principles of religion, humanity and justice; for certainly to transport a set of human beings from a bad country to a better, was fulfilling every part of these principles." Trumpeting the constitution's merits to the voters of South Carolina, David Ramsay insisted that slavery would play a crucial role in the nation's future prosperity. Noting that, under the terms of the compact, northerners were "bound to protect us from [the] domestic violence" of slave insurrections, Ramsay rosily predicted that "though Congress may forbid the importation of negroes after 21 years, . . . it is probable that they will not."[17] Charles Cotesworth Pinckney noted with pride that despite the "religious and political prejudices of the Eastern and Middle States, . . . by this settlement we have secured an unlimited importation of negroes for twenty years." More important, in his opinion, the constitution offered the "security that the general government can never emancipate them, for no such authority is granted."[18] Thus in conversation among themselves, the slaveowners of the Deep South demonstrated no guilt about their mastery. Anxieties sparked by the ideals of the Revolution were limited to fears that misguided reformers would somehow rob them of their slaves.

In the end, residents of the Deep South decided by overwhelming margins that ratification of the constitution served their best interests. In Georgia, the looming presence of hostile Creek Indians fostered the desire for a stronger federal government. The summer preceding the constitutional convention, James Robertson had observed that "we are at present in a very uncomfortable situation in Georgia, . . . apparently on the eve of an Indian war." According to reports forwarded to James Madison later in 1787, residents of the state believed that "the Indians derive their motives as well as their means from their Spanish neighbours." Individual slaveowners, moreover, complained "that their fugitive slaves are encouraged by East Florida."[19] Caught between this formidable triangle of enemies—the Indians, the Spanish, and their own runaway slaves—delegates to the Georgia constitutional convention rapidly and unanimously ratified the constitution in January 1788.[20]

In South Carolina, not surprisingly, much of the debate also turned on the question of slavery. Antifederalist critics of the new government such as Rawlins Lowndes pointed to the slave trade clause as evidence that "the Northern states would so predominate [the new nation], as to divest us of any pretensions to the title of a republic." "What cause was there for jealousy of our importing negroes?" asked Lowndes. "Why confine us to 20 years, or rather why limit us all?" Most prominent citizens of the state, however, insisted that the constitution would strengthen the slaveowners' hold over their human property. David Ramsay, for example, depicted Lowndes as "almost alone" in his opinion that the new government gave "all the advantage" to antislavery reformers. In Ramsay's opinion, the northerners "never did a more political thing than in standing by those of South Carolina about our negroes. . . . The language now [being heard in the South] is [that] 'the Eastern states can soonest help us in case of invasion & it is more in our interest to encourage them & their shipping.'" Ramsay could only conclude that "in short . . . a revolution highly favorable to union has taken place."[21] And Charles Cotesworth Pinckney stepped forward to defend the document that he had helped to write. According to Pinckney, the constitution granted southerners "a right to recover our slaves in whatever part of America they may take refuge, which is a right we had not before." "In short, considering all the circumstances," he concluded, "we have made the best terms for the security of this species of property [that] it was in our power to make. We would have made better if we could; but on the whole, I do not think them bad."[22] Swayed by this reasoning, the South Carolina convention ratified the constitution in May 1788 by a vote of 149 to 73.

The adoption of a new federal government did not permanently allay the slaveholders' fears about the future. Saddled by debt, merchants and planters in the Deep South anxiously wondered whether "the best times [we]re over."[23] By the 1780s, shifting international markets had undermined the wealthiest segment of southern society—the planters and merchants who derived their fortunes from the production of rice. Noting that Brazil had gained control of the once lucrative Portuguese market, Ralph Izard gloomily concluded in 1789 that "this is a loss to us which there seems to be no hope of recovering." One year later, South Carolina senator Pierce Butler observed that money was "not to be had in Georgia and Carolina."[24] Pressed by their creditors, slaveowners such as Butler found it necessary to sell many of their slaves, an indignity that led them to repudiate "dependence on the will of others" as "a great curse." "I shall never know happiness," asserted Butler, "while I owe a shilling."[25]

Mired in a stagnant economy, planters in the Deep South began to suspect that their new federal government would erode rather than reinforce their hegemony. At the very least, Congress had proven reluctant to protect the region's increasingly peculiar interests. Slaveowners in Georgia had anticipated that the new federal government would act to stop Spanish assistance to "fugitive Negroes." In 1789, however, southern congressmen could not prevail on the American ambassador even to broach the topic in negotiations, let alone to force the Spanish to desist.[26] One year later, Congress exacerbated matters by approving a treaty with the Creek Indians that, according to Pierce Butler, "was not satisfactory to the Georgia Members." Butler criticized the clause respecting "the Negroes taken from the Georgians" by the Creeks as "vague and weakly worded."[27]

Episodes like these set the stage for the sectional conflict that would haunt Congress over the next seven decades. By the 1790s, the notion that a commercial economy hinging on free labor somehow threatened the slave-owning states had begun to infiltrate southern politics. In 1787, for example, Thomas Jefferson had contended that American virtue centered on the nation's "mass of cultivators." For this reason Jefferson argued against the "principle that every state should endeavour to manufacture for itself." He advised that the "work-shops remain in Europe," thereby preventing the "mobs of great cities" from debilitating "pure government, as sores do the strength of the human body."[28] Although sectionalism did not immediately pervade Jefferson's ideas about pastoral virtue, agrarianism encouraged other southerners to view the northern states with suspicion. As early as January 1789, politicians in the Deep South were predicting that the differences in regional economics would result in "strong opposition" to the South in Congress.[29]

In the opinion of such southern congressmen as Pierce Butler, regional antipathy sprang from the northern obsession with monetary gain. Butler conceived of Congress as a battleground in which a southern society based on the production of staple crops would battle with the representatives of commerce. "My apprehensions of a lasting harmony," he wrote in 1790, "are awakened by the self-interestedness of the [North-]Eastern States."[30] When the Senate contemplated Alexander Hamilton's proposal for a national bank, Butler denounced the plans as a plot against the South. He maintained that despite "the Title of National," the bank would become "the Instrument of draining the Southern States of the little Cash [that] they have."[31]

Like Jefferson, Butler believed that "commerce should be the consequence [and] not the means of Agriculture." Invoking this principle, he denounced Hamilton's fiscal plans as an effort to place the "Landed interest in a very subordinate situation—a very painful one."[32] In the ensuing years, Butler continued to fear that a banking monopoly favoring the "monied Interest of America" would leave "the landed Interest" to "shift for itself."[33] Believing that "too great attention" to "money transactions must injure [one's] character," Butler construed Hamilton's efforts to foster America's commercial economy as a grave threat to national virtue. "The moment I read Mr. Hamilton's report," he wrote in 1792, "I was alarmed." Just a few months later Jefferson informed President Washington that "the great discontents in the South" were "grounded on [their] seeing that their judgments & interests were sacrificed to those of the Eastern states on every occasion" in Congress.[34]

Despite their efforts to engender a proslavery constitution in 1787, slaveowners confronted a federal government that appeared unwilling or unable to protect their society from the dangers of unbridled individualism. In 1790, a group of Quakers presented an antislavery petition to Congress itself—a maneuver that outraged southern politicians. "I don't like it at all," remarked Charles Cotesworth Pinckney. "I much approve of the proceedings of the federal government hitherto," he continued, "but I have no idea of their intermeddling with our Negroes."[35] Pinckney's troubled response epitomized the slaveholders' fears in the 1790s. While their consciences remained largely untroubled by the decade's swirling political and ideological currents, the slaveowners fixated on the possibility that humanitarian reform would ignite a slave rebellion.

With or without the assistance of white antislavery activists, African Americans risked their lives to vanquish the authority of their masters. In March 1787, for example, the South Carolina legislature requested Governor Thomas Pinckney to "take the most effectual & decisive measure to extirpate the runaway Negroes who have lately committed depredations in the Vicinity of Purrysburg." Pinckney characterized their actions as an "insurrection" and arranged for a "Select Body of Men" to hunt them. Five years later, fears of slave rebellion once again unsettled white authorities. Military officials were instructed to "direct the utmost attention" to "the strict and regular performance of the duties of [the slave] patrol." The stakes, according to Charles Pinckney, were nothing less than the survival of slaveholding society: "The intelligence we have received of some recent discoveries [of slave insurrection plots] in Virginia & Maryland ought to assure us that the peace and security of this country may very much depend on the strict and unceasing performance of the Duties I have enjoined."[36]

As Pinckney's comments made clear, the fear of slave rebellion radiated across the Western Hemisphere. In October 1793, for example, military officials in Georgia reminded "the Captains commanding Companies in the Chatham Regiment to be particularly attentive to the operation of the Patrol Law" because of "recent information" concerning slave insurrection plots in "sister states." The threat also emanated from more distant locations. Writing from Jamaica in 1792, Mary Smith asserted that William Hammet of Charleston "should be acquainted with" the fact that "there is great reason to apprehend an Insurrection at the [island's] North Side."[37] Global trading connections therefore carried fear as well as profit to the southern slaveowners. They realized that they were risking their lives as well as their capital to obtain profit through the international market for staple crops.

Despite the inaccuracy of many reports concerning slave insurrections, the planters could ill afford to ignore them. Their lives depended on the news about their slaves' activities, and more and more frequently, that news was grim. The course of emancipation in the northern states, not to mention the transatlantic abolitionist movement, had created a climate of pessimism in the slaveholding South. Even the wealthiest slaveowners sometimes concluded that the future boded ill for their mastery. Ralph Izard, for example, predicted that the ownership of eighty slaves would not enable his son "to maintain a Family in the stile of a gentleman." "It is my opinion," wrote the venerated South Carolina planter, "that the time is at no very great distance when the property in Negroes will be rendered of no value. The enthusiasm of a considerable part of this Country, as well as of Europe, on this Subject, can not fail of producing a convulsion which will be severely felt by the Southern States."[38] With more dramatic flair, Margaret Izard Manigault expressed her fears of "les vilains Noirs." "These horrible ideas [obsess me] at night," she confessed, "when nothing interrupts them, & I almost envy those who have already died peaceably in their beds." Slaveowners attributed these dire circumstances to the modern notions of universal freedom that were supposedly corrupting their slaves. Noting that "our [human] property in Carolina is held by a slender tye," an alarmed Pierce Butler characterized the scandalous impertinence of African Americans as "one of the many abuses of the rights of Man."[39]

The reaction of southern slaveowners to the French Revolution—the pivotal political event of the 1790s—exemplified their ambivalence about the future. At first, white southerners such as Joseph Manigault looked favorably on the Revolution, observing that the French "have imbibed [American] Ideas of Liberty." Pierce Butler gave voice to this view when he "ardently hope[d] the French Nation will accomplish their object & secure to themselves & their posterity the equal operations of Laws; perfect freedom and the enjoyment of property." "Every humane breast must be interested in the issue," continued Butler on a later occasion. "If the French succeed, and I trust they will, they will give a benevolent useful lesson to Rulers & the Ruled: they will open the eyes of one and teach Caution to the other—they will teach Princes that there is a reciprocity in all compacts."[40] Hence the slaveholders of the Deep South welcomed the French Revolution because they believed it was motivated by the central principle of enlightened society—the desire for an organic, affective bond between superiors and inferiors.[41]

And yet, for the same reasons, the Jacobin attack on all vestiges of social hierarchy in France alarmed the southern planters. With the violent downfall of the French king, the slaveowners directed their sympathies toward the nation's former rulers. Noting that "the King of France's Escape and capture" was "the general subject of conversation" in Charleston, Joseph Manigault observed that while "he is certainly blam[e]able for not behaving with more candour," he nevertheless "had a very difficult part to act, and as he is said to be a man of good heart I cannot help feeling for his Misfortune." One year later, Pierce Butler admitted that "the affairs of France wear a gloomy aspect."[42] By limiting political liberties to white men, the slaveowners had managed to reconcile them (at least temporarily) with hierarchical society. When "strange accounts" of the Jacobin campaign against social ranks reached the Deep South, many slaveholders responded with disgust. Margaret Izard Manigault, for example, predicted that "religion must soon be driven from among them."[43]

The slaveowners' greatest worry was that the French Revolution would become the catalyst for a general leveling of all social distinctions between rich and poor. By 1793, the planters were receiving reports from England suggesting the possibility that class warfare would be exported from the Continent. Although Englishmen such as Elias Ball insisted that a "spirit of Loyalty & attachment to the constitution of the Country & so harty a detestation of the French Leveling principals" pervaded the country, others British residents spoke with less certainty. J. B. Petry of Scotland claimed that "the Merchants, the tradesmen, the manufacturers and Some of the land owners tremble at the idea" that the working class might rebel against their authority. He conceded that "the unthinking labourers or workmen care little about it now" but predicted that if the economy soured, they would "imbibe soon their minds with the ideas of their rights & will seek in insurrection the means & ways to support themselves and families."[44] Uncertain of their ability to maintain control over their own society, white southerners saw their worst political nightmares coming to pass in France. Richard Furman spoke for many in his community when he concluded that "the Liberty a great Part of [the French] seem to wish and are contending for, is [the] Liberty to act the Infernal."[45]

With violent clarity, events in the colony of St. Domingue demonstrated that French political principles could unleash anarchy on a slaveholding society. Led by the brilliant Toussaint L'Ouverture, slaves in St. Domingue had successfully rebelled against their masters in 1791 and, against all odds, had managed to establish an independent nation. Needless to say, these events horrified white southerners. Writing from Charleston in 1793, James Ladson asserted that it was of "no consequence" which country gained control of St. Domingue so long as "tranquility" was restored "to that ill-fated Island."[46]

L'Ouverture and his newly freed supporters, however, defied both British and French campaigns to reestablish white order. When the French Assembly formally abolished colonial slavery in 1794, southern slaveowners faced the terrifying prospect of global emancipation.

By the mid-1790s, concerned planters were seeking to isolate their society from the pernicious influence of the radical French.[47] Notwithstanding mounting hostility toward England for interfering with American shipping, white southerners such as Ralph Izard argued against a military alliance with the French. Corresponding with Thomas Pinckney in 1793, he contended that if the Jacobites succeeded, "South Carolina would be one of the first victims to the principles contained in the Rights of Man, which are applicable, without distinction, to persons of all Colors."[48] "In consequence of the Convention of France having emancipated all the Slaves in their Colonies," wrote Izard in 1794, "the Southern States would be exposed to great danger from the number of Frenchman who would come among us for the purposes of War [against England], & who have always shewn the strongest inclination to propagate the opinions of their Government." Izard insisted that exposure to French political principles "would plunge all descriptions of Persons in Carolina into distress, & the Planters probably into destruction."[49] Alarmed that some southern statesmen ignored these risks to advocate war with Great Britain, he insisted that "a prodigious number of the lower order of Frenchman" would "fraternize with our Democratical Clubs, & introduce the same horrid Tragedies among our Negroes, which have been so fatally exhibited in the French Islands." "Are the Inhabitants of South Carolina ignorant of these things," he asked in dismay, "or is it the will of God that the Proprietors of Negroes should themselves be the Instruments of destroying that Species of Property?"[50] Secretary of State Thomas Jefferson himself warned that agents from St. Domingue might incite a slave insurrection in the Deep South. Jefferson informed South Carolina governor William Moultrie of news that several men "were setting out from this place [Philadelphia] for Charleston, with a design to excite an insurrection among the negroes." Their efforts were supposedly part of "a general plan, formed by the Brissotine party at Paris, the first branch of which has been carried into execution at St. Domingo."[51]

As it turned out, slaveowners were neither ignorant of the threat to their authority nor hesitant to exercise every available option in defense of their mastery. The French Revolution had posed too powerful a threat to the slaveowners' hegemony to be ignored. In November 1797, for example, Charleston authorities battled rioting African American slaves who had been transported to the United States by slaveowners fleeing Haiti. "The account of the intended designs of the Fr[ench] Negroes" gave the slaveowners "a great deal of concern." "We dread the future," wrote Mary Pinckney in 1798, "& are fearful that our feelings for the unfortunate [white] inhabitants of the wretched Island of St. Domingo may be our own destruction." As the planters confronted slave insurrection plots and actual violence at the end of the century, they set their government in motion to protect their authority. Jacob Read wrote to Georgia governor James Jackson in 1799 exhorting him to "take such Measures as will secure the State" against "the domestic plan of our artful [French] foes." According to Read, French spies were "actually carrying into effect" a "nefarious Scheme of raising the Slaves" against their masters.[52] Authorities in South Carolina likewise harbored the concern that foreigners would incite the slaves to rebel. When a British ship carrying African American soldiers unexpectedly arrived in Charleston harbor, Governor John Drayton forced it to anchor under guard at Fort Johnson. Drayton "had reason to believe that some of the Black troops [on board] have been, and probably now are notorious Villains; and, that as French Negroes they have been concerned in some of the mischief in the West Indies." To allay "the anxieties of the citizens" of his state, Drayton decreed that "no Negroes or people of Colour of any description whatever bond or free" would be allowed to enter or to depart from the vessel.[53]

By the end of the century, slaveholders in the Deep South had grown to detest the French Revolution. Georgia resident Cornelia L. Greene, for example, deemed her friend John "a monstrous Jacobin" when in 1800 he confessed his admiration for France. Greene asserted that pro-French sentiment "is so unfashionable that I have not heard or seen a *gentleman* before me for the last age that would dare think of [wearing] a red cap—or even a french cockade"—both symbols of the Revolution. Several months later, Greene condemned another professed supporter of France as "a Democrat of that order which aims openly at the destruction of moral society." "My heart sunk within me in horror," she wrote, "when I saw before me a man of that cast which has brought about in the world the convulsions in France," for "it is Men like him who have struck deep at the roots of all Morals & religion throughout the world."[54] Unfortunately for the slaveholders, the international market had exposed their society to the pernicious influence of egalitarian sentiment. However much they sought to isolate themselves from the dangers of the international furor over democracy, the slaveholders had immersed themselves in the transatlantic plantation economy. And by the onset of the nineteenth century, that economy had spawned financial connections linking the slaveowners' fortunes to those of their slaves and those of the merchants who traded their staples to consumers all over the world.

The pivotal political event of the 1790s, the French Revolution, had turned slave ownership into a dangerous business. But the pivotal economic event—Eli Whitney's perfection of the cotton gin in 1793—ensured that it would be a business that expanding numbers of white southerners wanted very much to enter. Until the late eighteenth century, cultivators of cotton had been forced to clean their crops by hand. The demand created by the burgeoning network of textile factories in England, however, set the stage for technological innovation. Whitney had migrated to the Deep South from Connecticut to reside on the late Nathanael Greene's plantation in Georgia. Much to the local planters' delight, he devised a gin that enabled them to clean large amounts of cotton with only minimal labor. The figures for gross cotton production in the South reveal the monumental impact of Whitney's invention. Between 1791 and 1831, cotton harvests in South Carolina and Georgia increased 7,700 percent, and slavery steadily expanded into the interiors of the states.[55]

Simply put, Whitney developed new technology because of the tremendous fiscal incentives of the international market. The events leading to his breakthrough should remind us that the southern plantations existed within the wider economic and social framework of a global economy. For example, the Greene family had coveted Whitney's service as a tutor because the plantation owners valued cultural achievement as well as fiscal gain; they expected their children to meet the intellectual standards not just of their region but also of the elite community spanning both sides of the Mason-Dixon line. For that matter, Greene himself had been a northerner. The grateful citizens of Georgia had given him a plantation to reward him for his leadership during the Revolution. Although southern slaveowners in the late eighteenth century perceived themselves as isolated and vulnerable, their relationships with residents of other regions provided the foundation for their society and their economy.

White southerners confronted the future through the prism of the expanding market, wondering about the impact of modern technology and ideology. If they feared the radical egalitarianism of the French Revolution, they very much welcomed the advances of the developing plantation economy in the Deep South. If they dreaded confrontation about slavery, they nevertheless viewed their own society as progressive. Abolitionists were attacking slavery at the very moment when the international market for cotton was swelling the ranks of slaveowners. Over the course of the preceding century, technology had enabled the rice planters to conquer the coastal swamps. Now it was allowing the slaveowners in the Deep South to carve new plantations from land that had formerly yielded little profit. Although they fretted over the possibility that their own slaves would murder them in the night, few late-eighteenth-century slaveowners yearned for the past. In fact, most felt no qualms about experimenting with innovative technology such as hot-air balloons—technology that enabled them to reach once unattainable heights.[56] Visiting the home of a respected Georgia physician in 1796, Margaret Cowper epitomized the slaveowners' embrace of the modern technology. After recording her favorable impressions of the house's innovative design, she described the doctor's "Electrical Machine." With no apparent concern, each member of her party intentionally "received an Electrical Shock" from the device and "after spending a pleasant hour & [a] half—& taking some *Porter Bitters*, returned in the same order" in which they had arrived.[57] At the end of the eighteenth century, slaveowners questioned whether modernity would always elicit such desirable sensations. As the number of slaves increased through importation and natural population growth, the planters were left to wonder whether their irrevocable commitment to the international market would present them with happiness or ruin—with riches or the trauma of an early, violent death at the hands of their slaves.

In the decades following the Revolution, southerners watched helplessly as the trend toward individual rights fueled the campaign against slavery. Respect for individual liberties had fostered a refined conception of both household and government authority. Enlightened leaders of families and nations now embraced the principle of reciprocity. Late-eighteenth-century slaveowners faced the disturbing prospect that these new standards for authority would undermine their mastery. As a market society, the Deep South could not isolate itself from the attempts by humanitarian reformers to instill a more egalitarian domestic ethos, particularly because enlightened intellectuals were increasingly making their arguments in print. It was during this period that northern authors such as de Crèvecoeur (and even southern ones such as Jefferson) were drawing attention to the failure by slaveholders to recognize their slaves' humanity. De Crèvecoeur, for example, argued that the slaveowners' "ears by habit are become deaf, their hearts hardened; they neither see, hear, nor feel for the woes of their poor slaves."[58]

And in his *Notes on the State of Virginia*, Jefferson described the "whole commerce between master and slave" as "a perpetual exercise of the most boisterous passions, the most unremitting despotisms on the one part, and degrading submissions on the other"—an exercise that corrupted the white children who witnessed their parents' tyranny.[59]

It is worth noting that Jefferson drafted this particular passage for publication in France, the very region that epitomized southern slaveowners' fears about anarchy unleashed by democratic leveling. Recent scholarship has unveiled the intimate relationship between the democratization of print culture and the radical political events in late-eighteenth-century France. As the planters considered these momentous events in Europe, they could not help but notice that transatlantic market connections were injecting incendiary sentiments into their own intellectual landscape.[60] When the English traveler John Pope visited Georgia in 1791, his "very soul revolt[ed] and sicken[ed] at the Thought" of the "numerous Herds of poor miserable Slaves, whose Powers of Body are worn down amidst Stripes and Insults." Enlightened by new domestic standards, a woman visiting Savannah from Massachusetts in 1793 reported that her "feelings have been much wounded at hearing of the treatment [of those] unfortunate Blacks." Slaveowners, in her opinion, were "destitute of Humanity" because they denied their slaves any opportunity for domestic bliss. Recounting the "unhappy situation of a poor Negro in whom appeared the strongest marks of Conjugal Affection" and who "wished to be [reunited] with his Family," the northern woman "felt so strongly his miserable situation" that she "could not stay in the room" as he pleaded with his master.[61] While this particular visitor recorded her observations in a private diary, abolitionists were beginning to marshal in print their condemnations of slavery as an institution incompatible with domestic morality. In a tract published in 1791, Thomas Cooper established the inhumanity of slavery by pointing to the many instances when "the wife is separated from her husband, or the mother from the son." "If filial, conjugal, and parental affection should detain [those slaves separated by sale] but a moment longer in each others' arms," continued the author, "the lash instantly severs them from their embraces." For Cooper, the idealized vision of a loving family could not coexist with human bondage. By appealing to the domestic sensibility of his enlightened white readers, he hoped to bring them to the same conclusion: "Think, o ye tender mothers, how would you feel, if, when ye should send your little boys and girls to fetch a pitcher or calabash of water from the spring, you should never see them return again."[62]

Try as they might, the slaveholders could not silence their accusers.

Southern congressmen managed to prevent the federal government from acting upon antislavery petitions, but they could do very little about the private correspondence and the broader cultural connections exposing slaveowners to a more enlightened conception of their African American slaves. At times, correspondents outside the South directly invited the planters to adhere to the "cause of Equality" championed by those who were "not debased by slavery."[63] In other cases, private correspondence presented more subtle but no less challenging notions about the slaves' humanity. In 1788, for example, Philadelphia physician Benjamin Rush wrote to South Carolina resident William Alston to announce the death of the slaveowner's wife. After conveying the sad news, Rush informed Alston that his black "Coachman Richard has been a faithful & affectionate Servant to his mistress." Rush also emphasized the loyalty displayed by the slave attending the deceased: "Her fidelity, attention & affection of her mistress made a deep impression upon her [mistress's] heart." "During the last half hour of her life," observed Rush, "the poor Creature was upon her knees at the foot of the Bed praying for her, and when she learned that her good mistress was no more, her lamentations & cries were such as affected me in a manner that I cannot well describe."[64] Although Rush dutifully sent the pair back to South Carolina the following day, he had nevertheless challenged the slaveholding order simply by recognizing the slaves' noble and human qualities.[65]

Two years later, New York resident Benjamin Cornell echoed Rush's tone when describing the conduct of a South Carolina slave belonging to a southern planter's deceased brother-in-law. "His servant paid the greatest respects to him that I ever saw and I hope he will be considered as a true and faithful one," wrote Cornell. He then asserted that he had never seen a "servant so much affected . . . [by] the Loss of his Master," informing the South Carolina slaveowner that the faithful bondservant had selflessly refused to improve his meager wardrobe with his deceased owner's clothing.[66] Both Cornell and Rush seemed to be saying that slaves called into question the morality of slavery by exhibiting feelings far worthier than those associated with the lowly station that they were expected to occupy for life. By attributing to the slaves the enlightened sentiments of fidelity and love, the northern correspondents disputed the slaveowners' long-cherished assumptions about the inherent inferiority of their bondservants. For if the slaves could indeed fulfill the responsibilities of enlightened domesticity, then surely their masters had no right to reject their humanity.

Thus, in the last decade of the eighteenth century, southern slaveowners confronted the argument that African Americans were full-fledged human beings who deserved the same rights as their owners. In the Upper South, a vocal minority of slaveowners accepted this principle and expressed remorse over the region's ongoing commitment to unfree labor. In 1789, for example, Robert Carter of Virginia noted that "the worthies who took an active part in the late Revolution, in their public writings, declare to Europe, & to the world—'That all men are born equal, and by the immutable Laws of Nature, are equally entitled to Liberty.'" And yet, as Carter complained, "notwithstanding the publication of this just idea our State has not as other States have done . . . adopted a Plan of Liberation among us."[67] Such outbursts, however, by no means reflected widespread southern support for emancipation. Even in Virginia, supporters of slavery outnumbered the institution's critics by overwhelming margins. And in the Deep South nervous slaveowners were quick to subordinate lofty ideals to the defense of slavery. During the debates over the constitution, for example, the South Carolina delegates had argued against a bill of rights because "such bills generally begin with declaring that all men are by nature born free." As Charles Cotesworth Pinckney observed, the slaveholders "should make that declaration with a very bad grace, when a large part of our property consists in men who are actually born slaves."[68] Although a few exceptional slaveowners set free their slaves "from Motives of Humanity," southern planters remained nearly unanimous in their steadfast support of unfree labor.[69]

But if the planters of the Deep South maintained their unyielding commitment to slavery, they no longer completely rejected the idea (articulated by northerners such as Cornell and Rush) that the slaves were human beings. In fact, during the final two decades of the eighteenth century a small but increasing number of prominent slaveowners began to redefine the master-slave relationship to reflect the principle of corporate individualism. In 1791, for example, Charleston planter Gabriel Manigault expressed his desire that a sick slave "recover his health." After instructing his wife "not to expose him" to "bad or very cold weather," Manigault reminded her that the slave's "fidelity entitles him to every attention."[70] Other slaveowners displayed a growing sensitivity toward their slaves' feelings even as they perpetuated a master-slave relationship. Arranging to sell his friend's slaves in 1789, Edward Rutledge observed that the deal depended on whether they would "consent to live with" the prospective buyer—a man "too humane, & too good to force" the "dear little people" to enter his possession.[71] Clearly, the "dear little people" could still be forced into the fields to cultivate crops, brutally whipped for disobeying orders, sold away from relatives and loved ones, and subjected to a host of indignities that no sane person would inflict on white acquaintances let alone household members. At stake here was less a revolution in the physical circumstances of slavery than a reconfiguration of the slaveowners' psychological perspective on the circumstances of slavery. This shifting white perspective on human bondage merits study not because it created happier circumstances for the slave but because it ultimately informed the slaveowners' regional political perspective and created the cultural foundation for a uniquely southern sectional identity.

Instead of conceptualizing their slaves as animals, some late-eighteenth-century planters construed them as members of an extended family.[72] In some cases, whites developed significant emotional attachments to the men and women they held in bondage. For instance, in 1787 residents of Georgetown, South Carolina, petitioned Governor Thomas Pinckney on behalf of a slave sentenced "to be executed, for breaking open & Robbing" a store. Although "Sensible of the Justice & propriety of the sentence," the slave's owner contended "that his feelings & those of his Family are exceedingly distress'd at the prospect of having a Servant executed who has been in the Family a considerable time, & [for] whom they entertain a certain degree of Affection." Some sixty members of the community affixed their signatures to the petition, suggesting that a vision of slavery informed by corporate individualism commanded a real measure of community support. After considering the petition, Governor Pinckney agreed "to extend Pardon to the Negro man therein mentioned" on the condition that he be deported.[73]

In an age of egalitarian ideology, many slaveowners could no longer ignore the charges that they were cruelly exploiting their slaves. Instead, they sought to disarm abolitionist criticism by affirming that they too abhorred the ill-treatment of slaves. By contrasting their own concern for the slaves with the insensitivity of less conscientious slaveowners, these planters upheld their capacity to be righteous masters. "When I reflect that you sometimes (it surely must be for the sake of argument) endeavor to prove me an unjust master," wrote Gabriel Manigault to his wife in 1792, "I must conclude in justification of both you & myself that you know but little of Mankind, & I almost wish that you knew more, in order to do me justice."[74] By countering his wife's charges of impropriety with evidence of other men's depravity, Manigault remained convinced that his ownership of human beings was just. Two years later, South Carolina residents Ralph and Alice Izard likewise grappled with criticism against slavery. Journeying through North Carolina, Alice Izard (who happened to be Manigault's mother-in-law) looked with "displeasure" at "the very disagreeable situation in which we find the Black People at most of the Houses we stop at." Izard found it "most provoking to find them so ill used" given that their owners were "comfortable clothed." She then admitted that "if the Quakers travelled this road, I should not wonder at their wishes to put an end to slavery. The abuse is glaring, & wicked, in the greatest degree, & well deserves the attention of the Legislatures of the Southern States."[75] In response, Ralph Izard informed her that the unhappy circumstances experienced by the slaves in North Carolina "made the same impression upon me as upon you, when I passed through that Country in 1781 & 82." At that point in time, Izard had attributed the slaves' degraded condition to the fact that "the Inhabitants were then much distressed on account of the War." "It is much to be lamented," he concluded, "that the evil should still continue." Exposed to the campaign against slavery, the Izards judged the institution by the enlightened standards of the international community. Humanitarian concerns did not lead them to abandon their role as slaveowners. Notwithstanding the failings of their counterparts in North Carolina, Ralph Izard and his wife insisted that planters could and should conform to the highest standards of morality. For example, Alice Izard reported that she was "delighted with the order, & humanity at all" the plantations owned by one of their acquaintances in South Carolina.[76]

In a sense, the slaveowners were disarming the critics whom they could not otherwise escape. Yet the planters were not simply reacting to the swelling moral outrage over slavery; rather, a complex shift had occurred in the relationship between the cultural dynamic that integrated plantation households into a broader intellectual community and the political infrastructure that shaped the planters' attitude toward corporate metaphors for government. During the colonial period, the vast distance between imperial administrators and the southern plantations had encouraged southerners to resist the campaign to ameliorate slavery. But by the late eighteenth century, the principle of reciprocity between the governed and their governors had become embedded in the public conscience.[77] The slaveowners' prominent role in shaping a new federal political identity placed them at the apex of American society, a position that led them to view organic metaphors with growing enthusiasm. Like the imperial administrators during the colonial era, American slaveowners in the early national period realized that the recognition of the social ties binding every element of society together would serve to reinforce their mastery. Occupying the top rung on the social hierarchy, the planters could finally feel comfortable extending their humanitarian rhetoric to encompass their subordinates. That this organic doctrine applied even to the lowliest members of society could be seen in the mounting campaign to mitigate the severity of American penal codes. Authors in the Deep South such as Robert Turnbull of Charleston publicly embraced a movement for prison reform and asserted that appeals to "the mild influence of reason and humanity" (as opposed to brutal repression) were the most effective means of maintaining public order.[78] Embracing the principle that moral authority hinged on reciprocity, the slaveowners could no longer simply ignore the charge that they were tyrants. Rather, the time had come for them to forward a new vision of slaveholding society—one tending to infantilize African Americans instead of reviling them as subhuman. Slaveowners such as the Manigaults and the Izards hoped that, far from being the scene of heartless oppression, their plantations would become places of beauty and order.[79] And far from rejecting this idealized vision of plantation life, southerners (such as Robert Turnbull) who had enthusiastically advocated humanitarian reform embraced a conception of slavery that reconciled the ownership of human beings with the principles of corporate individualism. As we shall see, the cultural infrastructure that transmitted new standards of mastery to the slaveowners in Georgia and South Carolina hinged on two key developments: the expanding network of Christian churches and a proliferating market for printed texts.

Certainly it was no coincidence that southern churches proliferated during the very period in which slaveowners contemplated new ideas about slavery. A half century earlier, Anglican and evangelical ministers had advocated a reform of plantation slavery only to discover that the planters perceived Christianity as a threat to social stability. But in the decades following the Revolution, the political context had shifted; having gained direct control of their own government, the slaveowners could appreciate the benefits of an organic ideological framework. When colonial ministers exalted earthly and heavenly hierarchy, southern planters had feared they were being asked to surrender their autonomy to the higher authority of the British church and state. By contrast, when ministers in the late eighteenth century sermonized that God dispersed his "Blessings to innumerable Creatures in various Ranks and Orders," the slaveowners realized that greater deference to hierarchy would strengthen their control over southern society.[80] As planter opposition to Christianity diminished, churches began to multiply in the South. In 1791, for example, Baptist authorities in South Carolina asserted that "the Interests of our Churches appear on the whole to be advancing." Unlike the evangelicals who had faced persecution from government authorities during the colonial period, Furman could write that "our Liberty, religious as well as civil is unrestrained, and those who have Ability and Worth of every Denomination are eligible to places of civil Trust." Although evangelicalism no doubt continued to appeal to marginal members of society, its promoters also sought the acceptance of those in power. Thus, in 1791, Methodists petitioned Georgia governor Edward Telfair for state recognition of their activities. By 1792, according to historian Donald G. Mathews, southern churches already claimed some 150,000 members. One-quarter of the adult white population, in other words, regularly attended religious services.[81]

As the southern churches expanded their domain, they also reached out to the slaves. That religious authorities could pursue this campaign testifies to the evolution in slaveowner values. The influx of refined humanitarian principles led at least some prominent southerners to accept the notion that every human being carried the potential for redemption. Pierce Butler, for example, argued against narrow sectarian prejudice in 1790: "If the throne of grace is reserved only for christians what is to become of Asia, A[f]rica, part of Europe, and part of America yet nearer[?]" Butler rejected religious conceptions that excluded vast numbers of people from any chance for salvation. "Such tenets," in his opinion, "might have [had] their advocates in the dark ages of Ignorance and superstition, but in the present age must meet with contempt."[82] The ideals hatched by the Revolution had become the hallmark for global compassion. Evangelical denominations hastened to take advantage of such magnanimity. Distancing themselves from their denomination's opposition to human bondage, southern Methodists assured slaveowners that Christianity posed no threat to the southern status quo and, by the 1790s, had recruited some twelve thousand black members. In Charleston, African Americans composed more than half of William Hammet's church.[83] The Baptists achieved a similar success. Writing from Savannah in 1791, Baptist minister Jonathan Clark noted that "everything will be done" to "effect the design of building a place of worship for the black people of our profession."[84] By expanding their holy community to include African Americans, the Baptists sought to conform to Christ's teachings, which beckoned them to a universal salvation. The recognition of every individual's capacity for moral growth occupied a central role in this emerging theology; by embracing this tenet, the slaveowners were adopting a major component of corporate individualism.

Yet, despite the egalitarian implications of this inclusive theology, Christianity advanced primarily because it reinforced the slaveowners' power over their slaves. Black defiance of white authority during the Revolution had reminded slaveholders in the Deep South that their human property retained the power of volition—that however much the slaveholders vied to ensure the obedience of their bondservants, African Americans remained capable of resistance. Christianity offered the slaveholders some relief from this dilemma. Unable to vanquish their slaves' humanity, the planters sought instead to channel it in acceptable directions. Left unchecked by white supervision, black spirituality threatened to become the foundation for resistance against the slaveholding order. By contrast, religious instruction at the hands of white authorities promised to make African Americans more faithful to their owners. For this reason, the city council in Savannah curtailed the activities of free black preachers. "The blacks, it seems," noted Baptist minister M. J. Rhees in 1795, "will not be permitted to assemble together, any longer, unless they have a white preacher." In consequence, Rhees initiated plans "to have a meeting house built, large enough to contain both whites & blacks, that they may unite in one church."[85] By embracing the blacks spiritually, white authorities hoped to clasp them more tightly into a position of deference. Here the second major element of corporate individualism—the need for individual volition to be subordinated to the broader social order—informed the slaveowners' perspective on the relationship between Christianity and mastery.

Both in their private actions and in their public words, southern ministers reconciled the Christian faith with the earthly distinction between master and slave. Leading evangelicals such as Richard Furman and William Hammet themselves owned slaves. Mustering the authority of their pulpits, they attempted to bring the master-slave relationship under the purview of the Lord. Instead of inviting the planters to emancipate their slaves, Furman called for "family prayer" that would minimize the "oppression of servants and dependents."[86] Hammet, for his part, did not "think the [slave] trade justifiable on general principles," but he argued that "in a country where the custom has been handed down from generation to generation, and where free people cannot be hired as servants, it is as innocent to hold as to hire slaves" belonging to others. When a member of his Charleston congregation denounced him for owning slaves, he marshaled evidence from the Bible in defense of human bondage: "And, we see that St. Paul, did not enjoin on *Philemon* to emancipate *Onesimus* who was at the time of his conversion a runaway slave." The Methodist minister concluded that "if slavery under every circumstance was an evil, or a sin, Paul would have enjoined on

Philemon to emancipate: but all he recommends is treatment of a lenient kind, to treat him as a brother, converted and renewed."[87]

As the new century approached, Christians in the Deep South yearned for more conversions among their neighbors and fretted that religion (that had enjoyed an upsurge after 1787) was now suffering from widespread indifference in the late 1790s.[88] By 1798, Charleston resident Thomas Legaré asserted that "this low country needs Missionaries as much as any Heathen land." Two years earlier, Edmund Botsford, a South Carolina Baptist minister, had become so discouraged by his congregation's lack of religious enthusiasm that he contemplated leaving his church. In 1799, his fellow Baptist Richard Furman went so far as to issue the tract "On the Languishing State of Religion in the Southern States."[89] Their frustrations reveal that a significant majority of southerners avoided both Christianity and, more particularly, the idealized Christian notion of the master-slave relationship. During the preceding decade religious authorities had deepened their influence on the slaveholders' values, but they continued to face weighty obstacles on the eve of the new century. While a vanguard of elite planters had already internalized familial conceptions of slavery, most of their fellow slaveholders clung to more traditional notions about the bestial and dangerous qualities of their African American bondservants. Indeed, many planters remained so emotionally and ideologically distant from their slaves that efforts to reclaim runaways were hampered by owners' inability to offer detailed physical descriptions.[90] The decades following the Revolution should therefore be characterized in terms of a profound ideological conflict—one that would determine how southern slaveholders would define themselves and the identity of their society.

Throughout the eighteenth century, any who recognized the slaves' humanity risked the wrath of their fellow southerners. And if more slaveowners were beginning to embrace corporate individualism at the century's close, their efforts still roused the community's suspicions. William Hammet discovered this to be true in 1793, when an irate slaveowner asked the Methodist minister to deny the Sacrament to her disobedient slave. Hammet refused to "judge prematurely in these cases" and wrote the slaveholder a note upholding his "duty to investigate the Subject" so as to "not act improper[ly] in [his] station." Although Hammet by no means opposed slavery, his actions in this case led the community to censure him as an advocate of emancipation. "However well intended my lenity [toward the accused slave] was," observed the unhappy minister, "my name was cast out as evil, and my note handed about thro' the highest circles of the community, and the worst construction put on it, . . . even that I put the Maid & Mistress on a[n equal] footing and of course intended to introduce equality which would overset Slavery."[91]

Hammet managed to explain his position to the slaveowner's satisfaction, but other Charleston slaveholders construed his missionary activities as a harbinger of abolition. That same summer, Hammet described being "met by a Mr. Hart, reputed [to be] the richest *Jew* in this City, who told me that I spoiled his Negroes, by going to church and by partaking of the Sacrament." Hammet responded that "I did not know his Negroes, . . . and if what he said was true he may keep them at home." Hart, however, insisted that Hammet "cause[d] them to come, and encourage[d] them to steal," calling the minister a liar before leaving in disgust. Several months later, Hammet described "a day of trial" in which "some enemies" endeavored "to raise the community against me" with a report "that I gave passes to Negroes to travers[e] the town at any hour of the night." The controversy led to an exchange in the city's newspapers that ended in Hammet's favor. Nonetheless, the incident demonstrated the risks attending any effort to establish human fellowship with the slaves—even when that fellowship was initiated to buttress the institution of slavery.[92]

Author and politician David Ramsay likewise encountered the slaveholding community's hostility when he campaigned for the Senate in 1794. Because Ramsay had expressed reservations about the morality of the slave trade, lowcountry planters such as Charles Cotesworth Pinckney were "apprehensive that Ramsay's prejudices against the African property might prove hurtful to the state." When Pinckney "waited upon him to know what line of conduct he intended to hold in Congress on that business if we voted for him," Ramsay "declared explicitly" that in Congress "he would constantly maintain that no power had a right to interfere with or prevent our importation of these people or at all intermeddle with our domestic regulations." Although Ramsay admitted that "he should always oppose further importation of negroes" when debating the matter with other Carolina slaveowners, he sought to establish his proslavery credentials by claiming that "with regard to emancipation he was both in & out of the state a decided enemy to it." Given the volatility of the slavery issue and the planters' fears about abolition, however, even this proslavery declaration was not enough to secure the community's trust. Pinckney noted that Ramsay had "satisfied many of the low country" but that "many were not able to give their confidence." The planters of the Deep South recognized that slavery was under attack and believed that fatal consequences would attend the slightest wavering in their commitment to the institution of un-free labor.[93]

Scholars who have chronicled the impact of the printed word on Western culture agree that a revolution in the production and dispersion of books and periodicals took place in the late eighteenth and early nineteenth centuries. In his study of rural New England, for example, William J. Gilmore contends that it was during this era that previously isolated families found themselves exposed to a multiplying array of printed matter and that these new sources of information "changed forever the material and cultural bases of daily rural existence" in this region. While the South no doubt lagged behind New England in its development of a community of avid readers, evidence suggests that the slaveholders' culture was dramatically affected by a revolution in print technology and marketing. Although southern planters became increasingly cognizant that a global movement toward democracy threatened their authority over their plantation households, they thirsted for publications emanating from regions of political controversy. At the same moment when Pierce Butler finally began to doubt that the French Revolution was advancing enlightened social interests, he still viewed the country as a valuable source for knowledge. Writing to an acquaintance in 1798, Butler reported his protracted negotiations with a French bookdealer who was offering for sale a "large & valuable collection of books."[94]

By no means did the slaveowners welcome every work published abroad. Mary Wollstonecraft's *Vindication of the Rights of Women* (1794), for example, led white southerners to fear that the modern literary world would encourage the destruction of their patriarchal social order. Yet even Wollstonecraft's radical arguments were considered and discussed before being dismissed by outraged slaveowners. In 1801 Alice Izard wrote that she had "just finished reading [Wollstonecraft's] the rights of Women . . . as much of it as I could read, for I was often obliged to stop, & pass over, & frequently to cough & stammer &c." Izard agreed with her husband when he called "the author a vulgar, impudent Hussy." Of course, it was during this era of drastic social and political transformation that white southern men worried about maintaining their ascendancy not only over their slaves but over white women as well. In 1793, for example, William Hammet complained of "the improper conduct of Sister S.," a member of his Charleston church. Observing that the woman had "opposed me as much as possible in the . . .

management of the [church] classes," Hammet asked himself, "when will women 'learn in silence,' and not go out of their place"? The print culture that exposed southern planters to the ideas of Wollstonecraft shaped the dialogue over gender relations in significant if subtle ways. If white southern women did not aim for gender equality, they had certainly traveled a vast ideological distance from colonial stereotypes that defined a dichotomy between debased, passionate women and refined yet ornamental ladies. The legacy of Republican Motherhood meant that women in the early national period could shape the destiny of their society without claiming the same social station as men. Sharing her reading of Wollstonecraft with her daughter Margaret Izard Manigault, Izard insisted that "it is not by being educated with Boys, or imitating the manners of Men that we shall become more worthy beings. The great author of Nature has stamped a different character on each sex, [and] that character ought to be cultivated in a distinct manner." Far from advocating autonomy for women, Alice Izard insisted that they fulfill unique responsibilities within an organic social order: "The rank of a good Woman in society leaves her little to complain of. She frequently guides, where she does not govern, & acts like a guardian angel."[95] In the end, radical texts such as Wollstonecraft's pushed southerners toward more careful definitions of womanhood—definitions that acknowledged potential female agency even as they rejected a social landscape devoid of gender distinctions.

As abolitionists and the slaves themselves pressed for emancipation, the slaveowners realized that they could employ a similar strategy in defense of their racial privileges. What remained to be seen, however, was the exact manner in which the planters would conceptualize the racial difference between themselves and their slaves. By the end of the eighteenth century, the cultural marketplace had fostered a view of bondservants as perpetual children, who needed the guidance of benevolent masters to become productive (if permanently inferior) members of a humane social order. Such ministers as William Hammet and Richard Furman contended that slaves should become full-fledged members of an interracial holy community. Furman averred in 1793 that true adherents of Christ's teachings "find all that is dear to them comprehended in the interests of his kingdom: 'Where there is neither Greek, nor Jew, circumcision or uncircumcision, barbarian, Scithian, bond nor free; but Christ is all and in all.'"[96] As the market penetrated deeper into the southern backcountry and churches spread across the landscape, this ethos of organic unity would ironically become the hallmark for social refinement and class distinction. Slaveowners consciously evoked the image of Christian stewardship as evidence that they had attained elite status.

Certainly the participation of planters in a market economy and their growing fortunes afforded them access to writings that promulgated an organic bond between master and slave.[97] By the 1790s, authors such as David Ramsay were hoping that their words would provide an ideological framework for a unified republic. In his *History of the American Revolution* published in 1789, Ramsay characterized the master-slave relationship in terms of intimacy and kindness. Although Ramsay believed that slavery hindered the economic development of white society, he declared that "Negroes who have been born and bred in habits of slavery, are so well satisfied with their condition, that several have been known to reject proffered freedom, and as far as circumstances authorize us to judge, emancipation does not appear to be the wish of the generality of them." Much like English missionaries earlier in the century, Ramsay asserted that "the peasantry of few countries enjoy as much of the comforts of life, as the slaves, who belong to good masters. Interest concurs with the finer feelings of human nature, to induce slave-holders to treat with humanity and kindness, those who are subjected to their will and power." Notwithstanding his distaste for certain consequences of slavery, Ramsay reinforced the notion that bondage need not entail oppression. He also linked the new American nation's identity to a social landscape that nurtured the individuality of slave as well as master. Authors such as Ramsay therefore injected the defense of human bondage into the very definition of civic purpose. As increasing numbers of American readers gained access to the world of print, they confronted texts that extolled the virtue of reciprocity between all human beings—reciprocity that made all members of society more comfortable in their particular social stations.[98]

In the ensuing half century, the transatlantic trend toward abolition would transform southern slavery into a "peculiar institution." In the 1790s, however, slaveowners garnered both reassurance and scorn from the international literary community. British author Bryan Edwards, for example, provided masters with a justification for slavery when he published *The History, Civil and Commercial, of the British West Indies* in 1793. Writing just two years after the successful uprising of French slaves on St. Domingue, Edwards offered the increasingly familiar refrain that "if the situation of the slaves in the British West Indies were, in all cases, on a level with their circumstances in regard to food, lodging, and medical assistance, they might be deemed objects of half the peasantry of Europe." Bryan maintained that "the *general* treatment of the Negroes . . . is mild, temperate, and indulgent; that instances of cruelty are not only rare, but always universally reprobated when discovered." Like Ramsay, he argued that "humanity and the sense of reciprocal obligation" persuaded the slaveowners to temper their authority with compassion. Through such authors, the slaveowners learned to equate just mastery with a "legislative authority" that "most humanely and laudably circumscrib[ed] the power of the master."[99] By presenting the principle of restraint—by emphasizing the need to limit even the slaveholders' claims to absolute power—texts such as that by Edwards pushed American slaveholders toward a corporate vision of individualism.

Perhaps better than any other figure, the Anglican minister Mason Locke Weems demonstrated the links between the southern market for print and the rising influence of corporate individualism over the slaveowner persona. As an author, Weems himself presented a corporate social vision that stressed the role of hierarchy in moral society. Alarmed by the rancor between Federalists and Republicans in 1799, he wrote a tract reminding Americans that "we all depend on each other, like the links in a golden chain, which, though not all precisely of the same size, are yet equally essential to the beauty and integrity of the whole." Weems believed that the trend toward egalitarian individualism promised only ruin. "Soho! What the plague have we got here now?" he derisively asked. "All men equal! All men equal!!!" Weems targeted the "host of hungry sans-culottes in full march for desolation, *equaling* all *property*, leveling all distinctions, knocking down kings, clapping up beggars, and waving the tri-coloured flag of anarchy, confusion, and wretchedness, over the ruins of happiness and order. From *such equality*, good Lord, deliver us!" Instead, Weems urged that republican society be based on an equality "of *mutual dependence*, of *civil obligation*, of *social affection*, of *dutiful obedience* to the *laws*." In his opinion, the "great doctrine, 'the natural equality of men,'" was "founded in our *equal* wants and *equal* inability to supply them, without brotherly union and co-operation." We should note that Weems was not only a political theorist but also one of the most effective book peddlers in turn-of-the-century America. Having merged the pursuit of fiscal gain with the dissemination of published texts, the parson helped to develop a literary market that influenced readers all over the country, particularly in the states of Georgia and South Carolina. And his message certainly struck a chord in Charleston, where Christopher Gadsden reprinted Weems's tract to meet popular demand.[100]

By the turn of the century, some slaveowners' attitudes toward their slaves had begun to reflect the system of ideas promoted by the market for texts. In 1797, Pierce Butler instructed the overseer on his rice plantation not to follow the inhumane precedent set by "Mr. Joe Allston of noted memory who had the best dams in So. Carolina [and who] required [his enslaved] ditchers [to dig] 600 cubic feet a day." Instead, Butler expressed his "wish . . . that they should do a reasonable day[']s work and no more." The low-country slaveowner went so far as to claim that "I would rather [my] Island be sunk in the sea than I should cause the death of one Negroe. They are slaves but they are human beings." Butler recognized the individual slave's claim to a life that would not be prematurely ended by unceasing labor, but he also defined a reciprocal master-slave relationship in such a way that his claim over his slaves' pace of labor would be perpetuated. In the same letter in which he instructed his overseer to give the slaves only a "moderate, reasonable day[']s work," he also specified that those "characters" that "wish[ed] to do no work . . . must be made to work." Illustrating that the principles of corporate individualism went hand in hand with a plantation venture oriented toward fiscal profit, Butler detailed specific quotas for his enslaved workers. Self-congratulatory attention to the slaves' humanity was, in Butler's case, quickly extended to the number of stockings knitted by his slave women. Told that free white women in the Pennsylvania countryside "can knit a pair of tolerable stockings in eight days," Butler concluded that "mine ought to do it in ten—They really must be made to do more; if fair means will not [achieve this end], possibly by locking them up in separate houses and not allowing any person to speak to them 'till they finish their task, might produce the [desired] effect." Thus, while corporate individualism enabled masters to cloak themselves in an aura of morality during a period of ideological transition, the system of ideas did very little to improve the lot of the enslaved.[101]

We should also remember that many planters in the late-eighteenth-century Deep South had little patience or use for these doctrines. Weems reminded his readers that Christianity "represents men to each other as children of one parent, as members of one family, journeying together . . . towards a region where all the distinctions of *rich* and *poor*, *high* and *low*, are unknown, and where virtue alone shall be exalted and vice degraded forever."[102] Many slaveowners, however, were too concerned about the possibility of class warfare and slave insurrection to consider how these ideas might reinforce their hegemony. Rather, they continued to conceptualize their bondservants as domestic enemies, who would transform any leniency into an opportunity for revolt. Instead of uniting with African Americans in religious brotherhood, these slaveowners denied that a common bond of humanity linked them to their slaves. In Savannah, the Reverend Jonathan Beck turned to the Bible for evidence that God had placed a "curse" on the African race and had granted Christians the "right to perpetually enslave" them. As opposed to such ministers as Furman, Beck identified blacks as the offspring of Ham, Noah's son whose lineage had been tormented by the Lord in Genesis. From this perspective, the slaves' skin color provided evidence that by "nature" they were unworthy of true Christian community.[103]

At the turn of the nineteenth century, then, planters in the Deep South had arrived at an ideological crossroads. For over a century, Christian missionaries and imperial authorities had sought to establish a master-slave relationship that hinged on the ideal of Christian stewardship. And for over a century, colonial slaveowners had responded to that campaign with hostility. They believed that their lives depended on their ability to maintain absolute control over their bondservants. In the wake of the Revolution, however, growing numbers of planters realized that the organic doctrines they had previously dismissed as unsound actually provided a powerful justification for slavery. As these white southerners struggled toward a different conception of plantation domesticity, they were opposed by many of their fellow elite slaveowners, who remained convinced that slavery could rest only on a clear distinction between moral whites and inherently bestial, dangerous blacks. Far from promising an easy resolution to this tension, the coming century held out the prospect of ruin to those slaveholders unable to secure their mastery over an African American slave population that thirsted for freedom. In an age of idealism and tremendous violence, the development of the planters as a class depended on their ability to establish a solid ideological foundation for their plantation society. If their desire for riches necessitated unyielding commitment to unfree labor, their craving for emotional security required devotion to moral principles justifying their racially stratified world. The slaveowners, in other words, needed to domesticate plantation slavery lest they succumb to the unwavering campaign for freedom waged by African Americans and their advocates.

CHAPTER FOUR

One in Christ

The Genesis of a
Southern Slaveholding
Culture, 1800–1815

In the summer of 1800, slaveowners in Virginia discovered the plan by their bondservants "to rise & massacre the whites indiscriminately." Although state authorities unearthed the conspiracy in time to prevent its execution, news of "Gabriel's rebellion" sparked rumors that slaves in the Deep South were devising similar schemes.[1] Southern planters had always worried that their slaves might one day rise against the plantation order. At the dawn of the new century, however, these fears were magnified by an antislavery movement that was obviously growing in strength. As the northern states outlawed slavery, slaveowners in the Deep South realized that they needed to tighten their grip on their African American bondservants or lose them and, quite possibly, their own lives as well. Only a few slaveowners in the Deep South contemplated the immediate emancipation of their slaves, and almost no planters prescribed it as a course for the region as a whole. Instead, masters in the Deep South debated measures that they believed would ensure the ongoing subordination of their black labor force.

Over the next fifteen years, the slaveowners established an ideological foundation for the defense of slavery—namely, a hierarchical, organic social vision that protected the liberties of white men even while it reinforced the subordination of women and slaves. The slaveholders accomplished this, moreover, at the very time that their market economy was expanding and their relationship with a transatlantic capitalist culture was becoming more consequential. To unravel the paradoxical relationship between these historical trends is to make sense of the slaveholders' growth as a self-conscious master class. The religious and literary sources that disseminated the ideal of corporate individualism to the planters reveal the tension between the content and form of white southern culture—between the slaveowners' thoughts about the world and the manner in which those ideas were expressed. By consuming texts that presented the principles of corporate individualism as a blueprint for moral mastery, the planters internalized the notion that masters should maintain highly personalized, affectionate relations with their slaves.

The concept of "domestication" as the taming of uncivilized creatures, according to the *Oxford English Dictionary*, dated back to the seventeenth century. By the early nineteenth century, the slaveowners were describing their bondservants in such terms.[2] The notion that slaves were members of a plantation household characterized by affection rather than force clearly had been foreign to the vast majority of eighteenth-century planters. Rather, these masters had despised and feared their bondservants—emotions that tended to rule out romantic conceptions of agricultural enterprises built around the institution of human bondage. In contrast, the nineteenth-century plantation provided the focal point around which the slaveowners were constructing not just a financial empire but a world view centering on a vision of plantation domesticity. Indeed, as the century progressed, prominent southern families such as the Izards and Manigaults realized that, to survive as a class, they needed to rally other slaveholders in support of a coherent set of values—a consistent ideology. Although dissenting conceptions about the master-slave relationship persisted, ever increasing numbers of slaveowners were, by 1815, subscribing to the notion that mastery entailed responsibility and morality. Given the wretched conditions on their plantations, one can only marvel at their capacity for self-deception.

Between the 1790s and the 1830s, cotton production in the slave-holding South multiplied exponentially, and the plantation system steadily expanded into the backcountry. Although most household heads remained yeomen—that is to say, property owners who owned few or no slaves—the market for cotton reshaped the southern landscape during the early decades of the nineteenth century. In addition to growing and raising their own food, farmers devoted their fields to cotton, which eventually made its way to textile mills in England and the northeastern states.[3] Eager for profits that they could use to purchase consumer goods manufactured in distant locales, white southerners reoriented their daily economic activity toward the international market. To accomplish this feat, these entrepreneurs needed slaves, African Americans whom they could force to do the dirty work in the fields. For this reason, South Carolina planter William Lenoir described the "Negroe [as] the most valuable property a man can own in this part of the country," contending that the acquisition of more bondservants would enable him "to make in a few years a very easy fortune."[4] Enamored of the transatlantic market, American political economists asserted that "the surest way to wealth and prosperity for any country to pursue, is to promote the industry, knowledge, wealth, and prosperity of any other country also."[5] The institution of southern slavery was growing in tandem with the international economy.

Yet as the century progressed, the planters continued to confront the threat of slave insurrection. South Carolina governor John Drayton received word in 1802 that "french Negro incendiary prisoners" were "about to be landed; & turned loose upon us."[6] The governor immediately took steps to repel the potential invasion by "force of arms," ordering that the black troops be executed instead of being taken prisoner. Drayton eventually conceded that "the alarm appears to have been without foundation," but he maintained that "the ardor of the military has not been the less meritorious." "Safety," he concluded, "is best assured by alertness."[7] The passage of time and the vigilance of white authorities, however, did nothing to quell the slaveholders' worries about the possibility of slave insurrection. Individual slaves substantiated their owners' fears as they periodically resisted and attacked their masters. In October 1800, for example, a colony of runaway slaves assailed their white pursuers in the Carolina backcountry, killing several in the process.[8] From their vantage point as slaveowners, white southerners nervously fixed their gaze on a world of countless threats to their hegemony. The northern states were already making the transition from slavery, and humanitarian reformers were beseeching the South to follow suit. By the early nineteenth century, native northerners who moved to the South were complaining about "sacrificing a land of Liberty for a land of slavery—a land flowing with milk and honey by the industry of the husbandman for a land of luxury, acquired by the hearts blood of the poor ignorant Africans." Confronted by northern abolitionism, southern slave-owners reluctantly added fellow citizens to the list of those who might encourage their bondservants to rebel. "I hope your fears with respect to the Yankeys setting . . . our slaves against us will never be realized," wrote William James Ball to his brother in 1806.[9]

Ironically, the slaveholders' fears that outside agitators would ignite a slave rebellion led them to cooperate with northern congressmen on legislation to outlaw the importation of foreign slaves. Since the colonial period, the planters had attempted to maintain control over the slaves whom they already owned by periodically closing their region's borders to new slaves.[10] At the behest of the Georgia and South Carolina delegations in Philadelphia in 1787, the Constitution forbade federal interference in the slave trade until 1808. But by the time Congress deliberated a federal prohibition against the international slave trade in 1806, southern representatives had acknowledged the wisdom of the stricture.[11] Both Georgia and South Carolina had periodically placed limits on the importation of foreign slaves in order to secure the institution where it already existed. South Carolina had even gone so far as to prohibit the importation of slaves from other southern states from 1792 to 1802. Antislavery activists and conservative southerners, however, made a volatile combination. In the House of Representatives, debate over provisions respecting the fate of illegally imported slaves laid bare the diverging sectional attitudes about slavery. For humanitarian reasons, many northern representatives wanted to grant freedom to those Africans illegally transported to America as slaves. Southern congressmen, on the other hand, opposed any measure that would increase the free black population, which they considered a menace.[12]

The arguments articulated by Georgia representative Peter Early and his allies demonstrated that the antislavery campaign was already affecting southern political strategies. In the early stages of the congressional debate, Early adopted a conciliatory tone toward his northern counterparts. Sounding very much like his forebears at the constitutional convention twenty years earlier, he initially conceded that "slavery is an evil, regretted by every man in the country." He even admitted that it was "cruel and disgraceful to keep [the illegally imported Africans] in slavery." By convincing the antislavery congressmen that he shared their disgust for the institution, Early hoped to gain their trust—to convince them that the southern representatives were reasonable men who merely wanted to protect their society from a free black community of "firebrands that would consume them." "This Committee need not now be told," he lectured, "that wherever people of color are found in a state of freedom—I mean in the States where they are found in considerable numbers—they are considered as the instruments of murder, theft, and conflagration."[13] But as the antislavery congressmen maintained their position and even began to press for the death penalty for convicted importers of African slaves, the southerners abandoned their conciliatory approach. After the debate had dragged on several weeks, Early completely reversed his rhetorical direction and stated that "a large majority of the People in the Southern States do not consider slavery as a crime. They do not believe it immoral to hold human flesh in bondage." Admitting that "reflecting men apprehend, at some future day, evils, incalculable evils, from it," he nevertheless insisted that "few, very few, consider it as a crime." He concluded that "it was best to be candid on this subject. If they considered the holding of men in slavery as a crime, they would necessarily accuse themselves, a thing which human nature revolts at. I will tell the truth. A large majority of people in the Southern States do not consider slavery as even an evil."[14] For the sake of political expediency, Early had conceded the immorality of slavery; however, he soured on this approach when antislavery representatives averred that Congress should champion every human being's right, regardless of skin color, to freedom.

Striking out some of the passages that had offended the slaveholders, Congress finally passed the bill in 1807, but not before a sectional fault line had been etched into the southern political consciousness. Since the first Congress had convened almost two decades earlier, abolitionism had gradually been forcing southern congressmen toward a stronger defense of the righteousness of human bondage. When an antislavery representative urged Congress in 1789 to "wipe off the stigma under which America labored," Congressmen James Jackson of Georgia responded that despite "the fashion of the day," he believed that slavery benefited both blacks and whites.[15] And, as we have seen, the presentation of a Quaker antislavery petition in 1790 likewise prompted southern representatives to defend slavery in positive terms. By 1806, politicians such as John Randolph complained that antislavery activists were turning necessary legislation into "a pretext of universal emancipation." Concerned that northerners would seek to liberate southern slaves, Randolph predicted "that if ever the time of disunion between the States should arrive, the line of severance would be between the slaveholding and the non-slaveholding States."[16]

An idealized conception of the master-slave relationship provided both an answer to antislavery reformers and a refuge from escalating fears of slave rebellion. Yet if these concerns created an immediate political context conducive to alternative, elaborate proslavery perspectives, the process of redefining chattel slavery was initiated as far more than a simple response to political challenges to the institution's morality and prospects in an age of freedom.[17] Evidence from the slaveowners' personal lives illustrates their growing conviction that slavery should and could exert a positive influence on both master and slave. Corresponding with his nephew in 1806, Randolph himself described his affection for a "faithful servant" whose "future life will be as easy as I can make it."[18] Of course, even during the colonial period, a few individual slaveowners (such as Henry Laurens) had adopted the role of caretaker of their slaves' welfare. Turn-of-the-century planters, however, departed from previously established patterns by asserting, for the first time, that southern masters as a class were fulfilling the mandates of corporate individualism. "In the part of the country where I live," contended South Carolina planter William Moultrie during this era, "there is great moderation & [i]ndulgence given to the slaves and I believe 'tis [for] the best in the end[.] [Slavery becomes m]ore satisfactory & profitable as what you may think you lose in making small crops you amply make up by the [i]ncrease & long life of your slaves." Unlike colonial reformers such as Laurens, Moultrie contended that a significant number of his slaveowning counterparts shared his concern for the individual slave's circumstances. Whereas Laurens bemoaned the inhumanity of other slaveowners, Moultrie expressed pleasure at seeing "the treatment of the slaves in the country altered so much, for their ease, & happ[i]ness; they are now treated with tenderness, & humanity." As if to reinforce the enlightened attitudes of contemporary masters, Moultrie recalled with disgust an earlier period when slaves had "receive[d] 30, 40 or 50 lashes for not doing what was called their task . . . when perhaps it was impossible for them to do it."[19]

In these early-nineteenth-century manifestations of the ethos of corporate individualism, slaveowners in South Carolina and Georgia typically expressed their fondness for particular slaves, usually houseservants who had served their owners for a number of years. "My poor old Monemia," wrote Carolina slaveowner Jane Ball at the turn of the century, "is very ill which gives me great uneasiness, for she is a valuable & faithful Servant, I look on her in the light of a humble friend."[20] Backcountry planter Samuel Dubose Jr. displayed a similar attachment to a bondservant named Sabey. In March 1803 Dubose informed his brother William that their trusted slave was at "home as well and hearty as ever." Three years later Dubose noted with sorrow that "old age . . . must now very soon take old Sab[e]y from this mortal state." The slaveowner, however, found consolation in the fact that his slave was still industriously "attending his little crop" and contemplating his fate with "a smile." Taking stock of the elderly slave's devotion to his white owners, Dubose observed that "sometimes conversing with him he tells me he is now ready to die, [but] after a pause, 'No!' says he, 'I am not ready but with God's grace [I] will be when once I can see and talk with Mas Billy.'"[21] Whereas Sabey supposedly dreaded death because he had not yet paid his respects to his master, Old Sarah—a slave belonging to Louisa McAllister— shunned African American company because, as her owner observed, "she has always been accustomed to white people & will not be left to the mercy of her own colour."[22] Ironically, McAllister's favorable impression of Old Sarah was reinforcing the more traditional, more negative image of black slaves. Here, slaveowners contended that loyal bondservants shared their masters' contempt for other slaves. Although they transcended, in their owners' opinion, the foibles of their race, slaves such as Sarah also reinforced a racial dichotomy—one that traditionally pitted exasperated whites against shiftless blacks.[23]

Still, there can be no doubt that the slaveowners' warm feelings toward individual slaves softened their attitude toward African Americans in general. Although planters in the Deep South clung to notions about black inferiority, they nevertheless proved willing, with growing frequency, to empathize with their slaves. Scholars such as Winthrop Jordan and George Fredrickson have demonstrated that white Americans tended to conceptualize African Americans as less than human, as savages whose bestial qualities threatened civilized society.[24] But images of domesticated animals were also gaining currency exactly during this period in the early nineteenth century—images that mediated between the alienating metaphor of the dangerous black beast and a warmer, unthreatening conception of a loving, household pet. Given that Jane Ball could sympathize with "two poor Does" killed by her family's hunting party in 1802, it should come as no surprise that many slaveowners were gradually anthropomorphizing the bestial conception of their black slaves. In 1811, for example, South Carolina slaveowner Margaret Izard Manigault characterized her slaves Robert and Toby as "the most amiable ourang outangs that man ever tamed." Several months later her daughter Henrietta confirmed the metaphor's significance by applying it to yet another slave: "We had for our footman a little *Ourang-outang* who my brother brought from the country; it was the first of his attempts [at domestic service] & he caused us a great deal of laughter. At the first house we stopped at he did not know how to knock & that puzzled us a great deal; at the next he wanted to let us out on the side towards the street, & at the third as soon as he had rang the bell, he scampered down the steps as hard as he could (which is not very hard for he has not learned that accomplishment yet) and placed himself behind the carriage."[25] Such accounts emphasized the slaves' bumbling inferiority and subhuman qualities but in decidedly unmenacing terms. Paradoxically, the slaveowners' desire to escape their worries about slave insurrection brought them closer to the very people whom they feared the most. By embracing their slaves as "amiable" and earnest creatures, the planters were unconsciously declawing the black beast that otherwise threatened to consume them.

Some early-nineteenth-century slaveowners went so far as to acknowledge that African American slaves were full-fledged human beings. When North Carolina planter Thomas Amis declared in 1802 that "I can now say that negroes are men," he articulated a sentiment that was resonating with increasing force among antebellum masters.[26] Many of these owners still blamed their slaves' shortcomings on the alleged biological disadvantages of their race; such notions, however, could cultivate the planters' sympathies as well as their contempt. After a favored slave became sick in 1810, Margaret Izard Manigault complained with remorse that "these *unfortunate beings* have a long convalescence."[27] In any event, racial concepts continued to play a crucial role in the newly emerging ideology of slavery that coalesced as a coherent world view only insofar as it provided a powerful resource for the defense of human bondage. Far from eroding support for unfree labor, the assumption that African Americans lacked the capacity to care properly for themselves led ineluctably to the conclusion that they required the guidance of benevolent white masters. Thomas Jefferson demonstrated that this logic could sway even longtime opponents of human bondage. Responding in 1814 to a young critic of slaveholding society, Jefferson opined that "until more can be done for them, we should endeavor, with those whom fortune has thrown on our hands, to feed and clothe them well, protect them from all ill usage, require such reasonable labor only as is performed voluntarily by freemen, & be led by no repugnancies to abdicate them, and our duties to them." Although the former president still championed emancipation as an abstract goal, his desire to end slavery collided with his belief that slaves "are by their habits rendered as incapable as children of taking care of themselves, and are extinguished promptly wherever industry is necessary for raising young."[28] The corporate ties that supposedly restrained the actions of the slaveowners could now be invoked to justify a never-ending delay of emancipation. Remarkably, owners such as Jefferson convinced themselves that they had arrived at this position because they cared so much for their slaves' individual welfare.

Given their commitment to slavery and their growing assumption that African Americans were human beings, owners steadily gravitated toward the notion that slaves were perpetual children. Imagery of the black bondservant as a sometimes wayward but potentially loving child permitted the slaveowners to broaden the boundaries of plantation domesticity. Away from home in 1804, South Carolina slaveowner Mary McDonald sent her "love" to both her own children and to "the little blacks — poor things, the Lord instruct them for the Kingdom of Heaven." In this emerging family dynamic, the slaveowners drew satisfaction from the notion that their slaves were emotionally invested in their relationships with various white family members. Esther Cox informed her daughter in 1811 that "whenever my Servants see me receive a letter they run to know whether tis from you and how the children do — [the children] will long be remembered by them all." Likewise, North Carolina slaveholder Henry William Harrington noted that news of his son's safe arrival from sea had overjoyed the family's slaves: "All the Negroes came to ask about 'Master Henry,'" wrote Harrington in 1812, "and some of them shed tears."[29]

Because the slaveowners offered these sentiments in private correspondence with family members (instead of presenting them publicly to refute abolitionism), we can assume some measure of sincerity on their part. Yet it should go without saying that slaveowners hearkened to the new world view precisely because it disguised the hideous reality of plantation slavery with the distracting imagery of benevolent intentions. Even the masters most concerned with the humanitarian treatment of their bondpeople fell far short of thinking about their slaves in the same terms reserved for their own white family members. In 1809, Savannah owner William Bulloch offered very different responses to the news that both his slave and his own wife were sick. Told of his "poor" slave's illness, Bulloch hoped that "he will not leave us" and asserted that he "should be sorry to part with him." In the end, however, Bulloch remained emotionally distant enough from his slave to observe with resignation that "these things depend not upon us." Such fatalism was nowhere to be found when he contemplated his wife's condition: "I was deeply affected however," he wrote, "to learn that my dear and beloved Mary had been indisposed."[30] Bulloch's tendency to rationalize the suffering of his "black family" revealed the curious power of corporate individualism over the slaveowners' consciences. A newly professed respect for the slaves' moral capacity and physical needs answered the psychological needs of the owners but did relatively little to improve the lives of the million African American slaves.

The court case of John Slater, a South Carolina man accused of murdering his own slave in 1806, served as a depressing reminder that the organic metaphor for human bondage offered slaves scant protection from their masters' sadistic whims. "You caused your unoffending unresisting slave," wrote Judge Welds in his opinion on the gruesome case, "to be bound hand and foot, and by a refinement of cruelty, compelled his companion, perhaps the friend of his heart, *to chop off his head with an axe*, and to cast his body, yet convulsing with the agonies of death, into the water!" Although Slater had clearly violated the emerging standard for humane mastery, he had nothing to fear from a judicial system that protected, above all else, the masters' prerogatives. Laws limiting the slaveowners' actions had been in place since the colonial period, but such statutes were only very sporadically enforced and seldom called for serious punishment of offending owners. Thus, even though a white jury took the unusual step of convicting Slater for his offense, South Carolina law (as the frustrated judge observed) permitted only "a very slight punishment" for "him who murders a slave." "You have profanely pleaded the law under which you stand convicted as a justification of your crime," observed Welds. "You have held that law in one hand, brandished your bloody axe in the other, impiously contending that the one gave a license to the unrestrained use of the other."[31] Obviously, tormented slaves could expect no justice from the white legal system.

But if the proceedings offered little consolation to the slaves, they did offer tremendous reassurance to the owners—even to those who abhorred Slater's brutal behavior. On one hand, slaveowners could rest assured that no one would interfere with their dominion over their slaves. On the other hand, the planters could draw satisfaction from their own perceived adherence to a higher standard of mastery. In other words, by transgressing against a coalescing sensibility that called for restraint on the part of masters, abusive individuals such as Slater brought into clearer focus white notions about widespread slaveowner benevolence. Thus, Judge Welds could speculate that the legislature's "attention would, long ere this, have been directed to the subject [of more harshly punishing sadistic slaveowners], but, for the honour of human nature, such hardened sinners as [Slater] are rarely found, to distract the repose of society." The episode ultimately provided Welds with an opportunity to reaffirm the organic link between master and slave. According to the judge, Slater deserved special condemnation because he had targeted one of his own household dependents. "Had your murderous arm been raised against your equal," speculated the judge, "whom the law of self defence, and the more efficacious laws of the land unite to protect, your crime would not have been without precedent, and would have seemed less horrid. Your personal risk would at least have proved, that though a murder[er], you are not [a] coward." Welds's contempt for Slater hinged on the logic of organic hierarchy—namely, that social superiors and inferiors should enjoy a personalized, reciprocal bond. Thus the slaveowner should rightfully "shield" the slave "from oppression, or avenge his wrongs."[32] But as the headless corpse of Slater's slave indicated, the owners were paying lip service to the logic of corporate individualism even as they were subjecting their slaves to unthinkable cruelties.

Had the slaveowners focused on the brutal reality of plantation slavery with any measure of objectivity or detachment, they would have recoiled in shame. Instead, they gazed at the master-slave relationship through a prism of romantic, often fictive ideas articulated in novels, travel accounts, histories, and religious tracts. These texts enabled the slaveholders to avoid the horrors that occurred daily on their plantations and to face with a steadfast countenance the political developments that threatened their ascendancy over their slaves. By taking careful measure of selected written words, the slaveowners blinded themselves to the terrible truth of human bondage. "Reading is the best relief from the toils, & cares of life," wrote Alice Izard to her son Henry in 1807. "When you have attended for some hours to Rice thumping &c, &c you will be delighted to dwell on more pleasing themes & be charmed to see, of what the human mind is capable."[33] John Randolph of Roanoke likewise typified the manner in which elite slaveholders submerged themselves into the written world. "If from my life were to be taken the pleasure derived from that faculty [of reading]," he observed in 1817, "very little would remain. Shakespeare, and Milton, and Chaucer, and Spenser, and Plutarch, and the Arabian Nights' Entertainments, and Don Quixote, and Gil Blas, and Robinson Crusoe, and 'the tale of Troy divine,' have made up more than half of my worldly enjoyment."

Mary Huger of Georgia spent the twilight hours when it was still "too early for candles" reminiscing about past experiences not just with the friends whom she loved but with "the books I have read, for amusement in my solitary hours." The South Carolina lowcountry physician John Peyre Thomas literally burned the midnight oil consuming an array of borrowed and purchased texts, complaining when he "had no new books to read." And T. W. Peyre of South Carolina claimed that he was spending his "time very pleasantly" during a journey in 1837 but noted that "the greatest exception is that there are no books."[34]

Other slaveholders revealed a similar penchant for diverse and challenging reading. When Joseph Brevard—a prominent resident of Camden, South Carolina—catalogued his books in 1794, his holdings included works such as Montesquieu's *Spirit of Laws*, Richard Blackmore's *Prince Arthur*, David Hume's *History of England*, Milton's *Paradise Lost*, Timothy Dwight's *Conquest of Canäan*, Tobias Smollett's *Adventures of Sir Launcelot Greaves*, and Adam Smith's *Wealth of Nations*.[35] Baptist minister Richard Furman read Homer as he traveled through the lowcountry in 1809; his relatives surveyed the writings of Samuel Blair and Jonathan Swift.[36] And the Manigault family's voluminous correspondence in the late eighteenth and early nineteenth centuries provided a forum for discussion of numerous works and authors—Cervantes's *Don Quixote*, Stéphanie Félicité comtesse de Genlis's *Les Meres Rivales*, Plutarch, Shakespeare, Fénelon's *Telemachus*, George Walker's *Vagabond*, Edward Gibbon, and Walter Scott. Writing to her mother in 1810, Margaret Manigault referred to the "curious variety" in her family's reading, which began with the Bible and included the work of Maria Edgeworth, David Ramsay, and Lord Chesterfield.[37]

Although the Manigaults expressed appreciation for many of these texts, they and other early-nineteenth-century slaveowners responded with the greatest emotion to novels. When John Peyre Thomas's steady literary supply was interrupted in 1835, he complained that "I can not get Novels enough & my time passes heavily." A Scottish traveler passing through Charleston in 1822 surveyed borrowing practices at the city library and concluded that "the novels were most in use, though Reviews, Travels, and other miscellaneous publications did not appear to be neglected." Surviving circulation records from the Charleston Library Society confirm the accuracy of this traveler's report. A sample drawn from the records for the years 1811–12 indicates that novels accounted for 43 percent of the books checked out of the library by society members; histories and biographies, 12 percent; and travelogues, another 9 percent. The rest of the books were a mixture of religious works, scientific treatises, military memoirs, collections of letters, works of philosophy, periodicals, political tracts, and poetry. Because this sample was drawn from a period predating the maturation of an American canon of fiction, it is hardly surprising that members of the society preferred English authors such as Henry Fielding and Edgeworth as well as writers from the Continent such as Cervantes, Genlis and Madame de Staël.[38]

The slaveowners' fixation with chivalric novels extended beyond their well-documented fascination with the works of Walter Scott. In particular, owners "very much admired" Jane Porter's *Scottish Chiefs*, a work published in 1809. In this narrative about thirteenth-century Scottish knight William Wallace's efforts to liberate Scotland from English tyranny, Porter presented ideal models for mastery in a domestic setting, first establishing her protagonists' heroic characteristics through their tender regard for the rest of humanity. Wallace's grandfather contended that Wallace was "always a noble boy. In infancy, he became the defender of every child he saw oppressed by boys of greater power; he was even the champion of brute creation, and no poor animal was ever attempted to be tortured near him. The old looked on him for comfort, the young for protection." Wallace extended his humanity to enemies as well as to friends, chastising one of his lieutenants for craving the blood of their English opponents. "Offended at such savageness," Wallace asserted that "justice and mercy ever dwell together . . . for universal love is the parent of justice, as well as mercy."[39] This sense of universal love, moreover, restructured the extended household in a manner that empowered subordinate individuals to fulfill their own noble potential. When Wallace's wife, Marion, is brutally attacked by a villainous Englishman, the elderly servant Halbert discovers "a giant's strength" and with "a terrible cry" throws "himself on the bleeding Marion," exposing his own neck to the assailant's merciless weapon. Demonstrating that such resolve was no fluke, Halbert later scrambles down a steep mountainside because this obstacle lay "in the path of duty." Porter's narrative empowered the young, the aged, and those bound to service. A brave youth provided instrumental assistance to Wallace's forces during their first campaign for independence. This boy's feats illustrated that, within the moral framework of Porter's narrative, universal love for subordinate members of society would be rewarded by the positive impact of these individuals who, encouraged by their leader's mercy and confidence, conducted themselves with propriety and courage.[40]

In addition to raising the stature of subordinate individuals and recognizing their capacity for personal growth, Porter's novel also emphasized the intimate relationship between individual restraint and moral conduct. Having conceptualized idealized interpersonal relationships predicated on the principle of universal love, Porter depicted her villains' depravity by establishing their willingness to spill the blood of women and children within the sanctified domestic setting. The English soldiers who attack Scottish women commit such a monstrous transgression against appropriate domestic conduct that even their own followers express outrage and offer assistance to the beleaguered ladies. Porter obviously intended her readers to compare the unrestrained conduct of the English invaders with the sensitivity of Wallace, a man so attuned to the suffering of others that he openly shed tears when he heard a new tale of Scottish suffering. The twin themes of compassion and personal restraint enabled Porter to reconcile organic society with emerging notions of humanity by distinguishing between tyranny and mastery. The English sovereign Edward personified tyranny by exercising his power without restraint to create a dominion of moral anarchy. Wallace, by contrast, defined political liberty as the power to freely dispense his assistance to other members of society. One Scottish hero evoked this theme by declaring, "I am the servant of my fellow creatures," as he rescues a defenseless woman from the clutches of pursuing villains. The organic basis for Porter's narrative became clear when she distinguished between the Scots' just campaign to restore order to their ravished countryside and the "general evil of revolt" waged by levelers who intended to benefit only "a few pennyless wretches." Wallace emerged from the "common ranks of the people," but he was certainly no radical egalitarian reformer. For Porter, individualism clearly had its limits.[41]

With these points in mind, it is not difficult to understand why novelists such as Porter appealed to the slaveowners. Upon reading the *Scottish Chiefs* in 1810, Ralph Izard Jr., son of the prominent South Carolina planter, expressed his affinity for Porter's protagonist: "I . . . am delighted with the character of Sir Wm Wallace. I am constantly wishing that Heaven made me such a man." Izard's family background suggests that he wished to emulate more than Wallace's bravery and prowess in battle. Izard's father had long since embraced the principles of corporate individualism, commenting critically on slaveowners who neglected their slaves and insisting that his own sons "must not be without control, or restraint."[42] The Izard family gravitated toward particular works of fiction that articulated the principles around which they attempted to structure their lives. Alice Izard, for example, shared her son's enthusiasm for Porter's creation and described the character of Wallace as "perfect." Other members of the family also mined popular novels for lessons about how their own society should best proceed amid the political crises of the era. In 1801, Margaret Izard Manigault, Ralph and Alice Izard's daughter, read "a book called 'the Vagabond' which shews what the world would be if Jacobinical principles were to prevail." Manigault recommended the book to her mother, despite its description of "horrid" circumstances, because the work reinforced the Izard family's guiding belief that power must be channeled through responsible agents lest anarchy prevail.[43] For this reason, Manigault treated the novel *Self Control* as far more than a simple work of fiction. "We are reading 'Self Control,' " she reported to her mother in 1811, "& I tell my children we have an opportunity of practising it."[44] Indeed, Manigault was thrilled and "surprised to see" the work for sale at a reasonable price when she was passing through Virginia several months later. Confident of the novel's power to reform the character of its readers, Manigault concluded that "it must have been printed by some benevolent person with the design of dispersing it among the poorer classes"—exactly the people that, in Manigault's opinion, most needed a lesson in restraining their passions.[45]

Amid the expanding market for consumer culture in the early-nineteenth-century South, worldly political concerns and fictive representations of power dynamics became increasingly intertwined. When a production of *Othello* arrived at the Charleston theater in 1809, white authorities insisted that Shakespeare's protagonist be shorn of his Moorish roots. He is, observed Margaret Manigault, "by particular orders to be [played as] a *white man*."[46] The slaveowners' racial doctrines held no place for a black character who commanded respect (not to mention the affections of an attractive, white woman). While this fact should surprise no one, it is striking that the early-nineteenth-century planter community recognized and sought to control the impact of fiction and drama on the slaveowners' political consciousness. As very few (if any) slaves attended theatrical performances, city authorities were obviously worried less that Othello might incite rebellion among their slaves than that Shakespeare's flawed but sympathetic character would ruffle prevailing white ideas about black masculinity—ideas that dismissed African American men as intellectually, physically, and socially inferior. In this charged ideological climate, the Othello that sprang from Shakespeare's fertile genius posed a very real threat to the planters' mastery. As John Randolph declared some years later, "Jealousy might have been pardoned to the noble Moor, certainly by me, had he not been a black man; but the idea to me is so revolting of that connexion, that I never can read that play with any sort of pleasure—see it acted I never could."[47] That black

Othello ruffled the owners' sensibilities suggests how deeply they had invested in an idealized conception of white mastery—a conception that they expected their fictive world to reinforce rather than to challenge.

Tantalized by the possibilities lurking within the realm of fiction, the slaveholders began to frame their own experiences with language and style that was taken straight off the pages of their favorite books. Writing from Riceboro, South Carolina, in 1810, Eliza Maybank informed a Charleston friend of the "romantic" news that two of their acquaintances had begun to court. Insisting that the couple's relationship conform to standards inculcated by contemporary writing, Maybank told the suitor that "he [o]ught to have fal[l]en in love, to have made it quite novel like."[48] Other slaveowners hastened to point out the affinities between themselves and their favorite fictional characters. When Georgia planter T. A. Taylor became "deeply engaged" with Walter Scott's novels in 1823, he noted how "the character of Guy Mannering reminds me of my father." For the Izard-Manigault family, the link between their reading and their aspirations toward an idealized identity as slaveowners manifested itself early in the nineteenth century. After learning of her brother's unhappiness in 1802, Margaret Izard Manigault suggested that he utilize his imagination to increase his satisfaction with his lot in life. George Izard had little difficulty in picking out the literary sources for his sister's advice—namely, the works of Leibniz and Voltaire. Thanking his sister for her "excellent hint about being happy and rich," he noted that "I have always had the highest opinion of the admirable effect of Imagination and have on numerous occasions built [imaginary] castles in various countries." Izard then referred to several historical characters (whom he had certainly encountered through authors such as Christopher Marlowe) to assess the merits of imagination as a psychological coping mechanism. "I have often reasoned with my own mind to ascertain whether Tamerlane or Bajazet were the more happy on the principle of Imagination," admitted Izard. Whereas the former figure possessed an "immense dominion" and was "successful in all his undertakings," the latter "was locked up in a beautiful Iron Cage and transported [to] Asia on the back of an Elephant, fed with the most loathsome viands, dishonored in his family, [and] disgraced in the eyes of mankind." Still, "with the help of Imagination his cage might become a Lord Mayor's coach; his elephant six prancing steeds, . . . the whole world paradise, & the Imprecations of his enemies the music of the spheres." Such feats of transformation reminded Izard that his own financial difficulties, however depressing, were ultimately surmountable. "All this would be little more difficult than to persuade me," he concluded, "that I am rich with 200 L. a year, and happy precisely because in the common course of things I ought to hang myself."[49]

Of course, anyone familiar with Voltaire's writings might rightfully raise an eyebrow at the slaveowners' efforts to draw encouragement from *Candide*. When the Manigaults interpreted the text (which offered passages condemning slavery) as a blueprint for a psychological process through which southerners could transform their surroundings into an ideal social landscape, they demonstrated how owners could twist literary works toward the ideological needs of the master class. Perhaps for this reason, the planters proved willing to read many texts that explicitly challenged the morality of slavery. *The Stranger*, a memoir of Englishman Charles William Janson's residence in America, epitomized a genre that would irritate white southerners for the next half century. Passing through South Carolina, Janson asserted that the slaveowners "regard their slaves, as English farmers do their live stock." Remarking the dangers of the swampy lowcountry environment, the author noted that the slave "must toil all day long in soft mud, ditching and draining the ground [which] to a white person . . . would, in a few days, prove certain death." To make matters worse, observed Janson, the slaves received punishments that were "inflicted with savage ferocity, and frequently at the caprice of a cruel overseer." Although Janson did not "advocate an unqualified emancipation," he anticipated the day when the slaves "would have their condition ameliorated by law." But as long as slaves were auctioned like "beasts in a pen" in Charleston's markets, Janson believed that African Americans would remain vulnerable to the callous whims of their masters. The contradiction between slavery and the American ideal of freedom, in Janson's estimation, promised to destroy southern society: "That this state of things cannot be of long duration, must be evident to the most superficial observer."[50]

Such criticism did not escape the well-read planters of the Deep South. Those who on some level shared his concern for the slaves' welfare acknowledged that a few of his accusations were just. Describing the book to her daughter in October 1807, Alice Izard conceded that Janson "ought to know us" since "he lived thirteen years among us," and she admitted that "we should find some truths, & some hints that might lead to our improvement" in his work. Yet Janson's strident denunciation of slaveowning society ultimately alienated even the owners who willingly acknowledged their community's need for moral improvement. Izard, for one, cringed when Janson stated that religion was "at a very low ebb" in the Deep South. "Sundays are there passed in riot and drunkenness; and the negroes indulge uncontrolled in riot and drunkenness," wrote Janson. Charleston residents, he continued, made "some shew of religion on the sabbath, but, perhaps, with as little devotion as in the other parts of the state." This assault on the slaveholders' religious credentials was simply too much for Izard to bear. "What he writes of the state of religion in Carolina," she responded with indignation, "is untrue & disgusting, so that I am not led to form a favorable opinion of him."[51]

Notwithstanding this hostile response, Izard maintained that she still "should like to read his book."[52] Although the slaveowners during this period perceived that specific texts undermined their authority, they exhibited little desire to withdraw from the transatlantic dialogue about republican society's proper course. They abhorred abolitionism but remained hopeful that their perspective on slavery would sway reasonable minds across the globe. Far from isolating themselves from international intellectual trends, the slaveholders fully believed that the dissemination of appropriate texts would enable them to survive as an elite—that certain texts would mold their offspring and their less cultured backcountry counterparts into a self-conscious master class. If Janson denounced the slaveholders, other authors extolled the virtues of southern planters. During this period, for example, Virginia planter John Taylor defended the plantation system from the criticism of another British traveler. In a series of published essays, Taylor championed the idea that slavery benefited not only the slaveowners but also their slaves and society as a whole. Denying Jefferson's description of human bondage as "a perpetual exercise of the most boisterous passions," he insisted that "slavery was carried farther among the Greeks and Romans than among ourselves, and yet these two nations produced more great and good patriots and citizens, than, probably, all the rest of the world." In his estimation, slaves were "docile, useful and happy, if they are well managed."[53] Cognizant that such conservative, organic arguments were being offered in print, slaveowners such as Alice Izard were amused rather than disturbed that books were finding their way across the South. In a letter to her sister, she noted that she had "met with several new things" en route through Fredericksburg, Virginia—a locale that she considered a cultural backwater. "Is it not droll," she asked, "to find new novels in such a little out of the way spot?"[54]

As scholars such as David S. Reynolds have demonstrated, early-nineteenth-century American readers were especially fond of religious works. In the Deep South, Christian authorities who considered the relationship between slavery and enlightened religion saw nothing wrong with presenting their perspectives as fictive narratives, and many slaveowners found such tracts to be diverting as well as didactic. Discussing the Charleston book market in 1814, Richard Furman observed that one retailer "has sold a considerable Number (I think he said *great*)" of *Sambo and Toney*, a religious tract authored by the Baptist minister Edmund Botsford.[55] The work presented three conversations between Sambo and Toney, fictional slaves who resided in the South Carolina lowcountry—the region in which Botsford preached. Over the course of the tract the appropriately named Sambo sermonized to Toney about Christianity's benefits, warning him that "'twill be dreadful if you die in your sins" without repentance. Toney initially scorned his friend's advice because he believed that "this religion [is] for white men, not for negro[s]." As evidence, he pointed to his overseer who said that "all black people will go to the devil."[56] Sambo, however, insisted that the church extended its mercy to blacks as well as whites. "The minister preach to every body," argued Sambo. "The word of the Lord speak to every body alike, white people, black people, rich man, poor man, old man, and young man, and it say, repent every one of you."[57] Ultimately persuaded by this argument, Toney renounced his sinful ways and emulated Sambo's behavior as a model slave who neither cursed nor stole from whites.

Botsford's image of plantation domesticity merits analysis because it presents African Americans as spiritually empowered individuals who demonstrated a capacity to give and to receive love. Sambo and Toney constantly refer to white authorities, and a white minister makes a brief appearance at the end of the work, but the entire narrative is related from the perspective of African Americans—a sure sign of the author's respect for slave individuality. Botsford also emphasized that, by opening their hearts to Christian teachings, religious education increased the ability of slaves to love their relations within the plantation family. The third section of the tract was set in Toney's cabin, where Sambo met Fanny, Toney's wife. Prior to his conversion, Toney had not allowed Fanny to attend church, indicating that their religious differences had caused some tension in their relationship. Once Toney experienced his spiritual awakening, this tension dissolved and the affective bond between slave husband and wife was strengthened. "I always loved my wife, and now I been love her more than ever," exclaimed Toney to Sambo. By this period, antislavery authors were already referring to black emotional capacity to condemn human bondage as a terrible sin. Here, by contrast, a southern minister tapped into romantic imagery of the slaves' family intercourse to argue that such relationships could flourish under Christianized plantation slavery. Moreover, beyond its positive effect on African American family relations, Christianity—as defined by Botsford— also promised to "make [the slaves] feel good" in a way that encouraged them to "love master." Although this domestic paradigm reinforced black subordination to whites, it did not simply reduce the slaves to the role of ignorant children. By acknowledging the slaves' individual capacity to wrestle with difficult spiritual questions and temptations, Botsford's tract placed them on the cusp of moral responsibility. Knowledgeable whites in this narrative could embrace the wisdom and faith of Christian slaves because these qualities promised a harmonious future for the sentimentalized plantation home. Religion supposedly enabled slaves to improve just enough to appreciate and to love their masters but not enough to covet autonomy or equality.[58]

That this work sold well in Charleston indicates the growing influence that notions of corporate individualism exerted over slaveowners in the Deep South. After all, Botsford's literary creation centered on the spiritual awakening of African slaves—hardly a topic that had evoked the owners' approval during the previous century. Furthermore, *Sambo and Toney* offered the implicit message that white masters should humble themselves before God's authority. Far from being infallible and omnipotent, the slaveowners in *Sambo and Toney* at least occasionally misjudged their slaves. In one passage, an overseer mistakenly punishes a faithful Christian who had been framed by another slave. The tract clearly would have offended eighteenth-century planters. Its theme of Christianizing slavery paralleled the message that had been offered by George Whitefield and Alexander Garden—a message that local whites had soundly rejected. But in the early-nineteenth-century Deep South, slaveowners were learning to recognize that acknowledgment of their bondservants' humanity need not undermine their claim to mastery. They agreed that they should implement their authority in accordance with God's laws because they believed that the Bible justified their right to command their bondservants. Secure in the righteousness of his authority, Botsford's ideal master could treat his slaves with mercy, forgiving their errors when appropriate and exhorting them toward spiritual improvement.[59] By the 1830s, this message had captivated a sufficiently large number of readers for publishers to issue a third edition of the work.

Although the narrative of *Sambo and Toney* ostensibly addressed the

slaves, Botsford was really lecturing to an audience of masters. By presenting in print the organic reciprocity of Christian slavery, he hoped to convince the white South that religion would buttress the institution of slavery.
Because this religious tract formulated an idealized hierarchical society that
affected the owners' conception of their role as masters, it had much in
common with the novels cherished by white southerners. Both genres encouraged the planters to equate written scenes with real-life experiences. In
Sambo and Toney, Christianity had narrowed the emotional distance between blacks and whites to the point that faithful slaves earnestly prayed for
their masters' welfare.[60] The same theme reverberated through the diary of
South Carolina slaveholder Eliza Clitherall, in her account of a near brush
with death. "The House & entry was crowded with the poor field hands
who heard that my measure was to be taken & came to request a last look,"
she recorded. Her husband then "called them all to prayer—'Pray for our
Good Mistress, let us pray that the Lord will spare her.'" Clitherall fully believed that her slaves' supplication to God resulted in her subsequent recov-
ery: "Rude as they were in speech, common in expression yet from these
poor unletter'd servants, as incense from grateful, and loving, hearts these
prayers ascended—a faith presented them to the Majesty on high, & they
were heard,—& answered."[61] Clitherall's very act of constructing a dramatic
narrative of this scene demonstrates how published texts pushed the slaveowners toward a new vocabulary with which to express their enlightened
perspective on the master-slave relationship. Moved by the written accounts
that they avidly consumed, the slaveowners recast their own experiences to
conform to the moral code articulated by leading authors. Corporate individualism had become a marketable commodity in the South, one that simultaneously appealed to and reinforced a new standard for mastery.

Even in the nineteenth century, however, some slaveholders continued to
associate Christian teachings with an increased possibility for slave insurrection. Jacob Read complained to South Carolina governor Charles Pinckney in 1807 that "there are every where through the State religious and other
Enthusiasts who are preaching very dangerous Doctrines and exciting in
our black populations Sentiments that must lead to fatal results."[62] Likewise,
Isaac Ball's overseer bragged in 1814 that "by putting a stop to this pretended
religion the negrows gits theare rest at nights & dont give half the trouble in
lying up pretending to be sick when nothing but the want of rest was the
mater."[63] For these white southerners, the prospect of extending Christian
fellowship to the slaves remained dangerous. Ministers such as Furman and
Botsford could preach until they were blue in the face and still not manage

to convince every slaveholder that a Christian slave population would be more easily controlled. But, then again, religious reformers did not have to persuade each master in the Deep South—only the most powerful ones. And evidence suggests that during the first two decades of the nineteenth century, those seeking to Christianize plantation slavery were gaining the upper hand in this century-old debate.[64]

The shifting stance of evangelical churches respecting slavery played a crucial role in their ultimate success in the Deep South.[65] Although individual evangelical preachers such as George Whitefield had condoned slavery, the figures wielding formal power over the Methodist and Baptist Churches traditionally maintained a more critical perspective. In the eighteenth century New Light Baptists had preached without obtaining permission from the appropriate southern authorities—a slight that earned the Baptists a reputation as radical levelers.[66] The Methodists, for their part, had little hope of garnering widespread southern support as long as they remained associated with founder John Wesley's denunciation of slavery. The church condemned slavery as a sin in 1780, and Francis Asbury—the man most responsible for the early growth of Methodism—sought to purge the institution from the ranks of the faithful.[67] In the Deep South, these measures met with a predictably negative reaction on the part of the slaveholders. When Methodists printed pamphlets denouncing slavery "as repugnant to the unalienable rights of mankind, and to the spirit of Christian religion" in 1800, Charleston residents set them on fire to prevent their distribution. For good measure, a mob then carried a Methodist preacher through the city before attempting to drown him.[68]

At the turn of the nineteenth century, however, resident southerners were exerting sufficient pressure on the national conference to gain leeway on the question of slavery. By excepting Methodists in Georgia, South Carolina, North Carolina, and Tennessee from antislavery rules in 1804, the church opened the door to greater acceptance in plantation society.[69] In 1792 the Methodists could claim some 38,000 white and 12,000 black members in the South. Just a quarter-century later, those numbers had exploded to 172,000 whites and 42,500 blacks.[70] Realizing that he was fighting a losing battle, Francis Asbury concentrated his efforts on converting the slaves rather than emancipating them. By 1805, he was contemplating with joy the notion that the "Slaves of our Brethren" would "augment" the church's numbers. Although he continued to discourage the buying and selling of slaves, he had abandoned the radical position that required all church members to emancipate their slaves immediately.[71]

By 1808, some evangelical authorities observed with consternation that slaves were providing the lion's share of new church members.[72] Although the mission to the slaves would not gain widespread attention until the 1820s, Baptist and Methodist ministers were achieving spectacular success in the early nineteenth century. Indeed, some evangelicals felt compelled to reassure themselves that their missionary zeal had not resulted in too much of a good thing. "Dr F[urman] always writes me of the numbers added," noted his mother-in-law, Mary McDonald, in 1813. "Though great part of them are negroes, ought not our hearts to rejoice at the fulfillment of the Scripture, 'And Ethiopia shall stretch her hands unto God'?" When the New England academic Ebenezer Kellog visited Savannah in 1818, he observed that "the duty of masters to their servants very much engages the attention of people in this country. Some question belonging to that general subject is often discussed by a Library Society, consisting of the most intelligent and sober men in the place." According to Kellog, many slaveowners were contemplating a "scheme for regular reading of the Scriptures to their servants in family and larger collections, instead of attempting to learn them to read" independently. Although Kellog noted that slaves preferred to distance themselves from their masters' scrutiny by working in the fields instead of in the house, he nevertheless viewed the slaveholders' religious schemes as evidence that "a great number of the planters here treat their slaves with much kindness."[73]

Having become safe on the question of slavery, evangelicals in the Deep South set about becoming respectable. Ministers such as Hugh Fraser did more than simply condone the ownership of African American bondservants; they acquired substantial numbers of their own and asked their churches to support their enterprise in the field. Because Richard Furman construed his own mastery through the prism of Christian stewardship, he felt no pang of conscience when he "ran in Debt in the purchase of Negroes to increase my Planting Interest." Reserving the term "oppressive" for the Charleston merchants who charged unduly high prices, Furman hoped "through the Goodness of God" that he would "be enabled to surmount these Difficulties" of financing plantation living — difficulties that included no discernible reservations about the morality of slavery.[74] Sensing they had nothing to fear from this slaveholding ministry, growing numbers of owners began to push their bondservants toward the church. Instead of waiting for religious reformers to convince him that Christianity would reaffirm his authority, South Carolina slaveholder Josiah Rivers attempted to bring his bondservants into a community of faith. "I took the Liberty of writing a few

Lines to you Concerning my Servant Toby who has I Believe a Grate desire of Being Baptise[d]," wrote Rivers to Furman in 1807. "Concerning his C[h]aracter, He is very Sober, Honest and Industrious and I Believe [is] a very good Inclined Person."[75]

Because they had disavowed their radical roots, the evangelical churches gained adherents not only in the slave quarters but in the wealthiest segments of white society as well. Edward Hooker noticed in 1807 that the Methodists in Columbia, South Carolina, "appear pretty zealous and have considerably increased their church. Two of our most respectable citizens have lately joined them." This is not to say that old prejudices disappeared overnight. In 1805 Joseph Lowry, a Presbyterian, considered Columbia residents "pol[l]uted with Arm[i]nian poison and methodistical delusion" to be just as irreligious as those who were openly "destitute of the form of religion" and "mockers of morality."[76] And rambunctious South Carolina College students "turn[ed] a methodist congregation out of the church and fill[ed] it with goats" in 1810.[77] Nevertheless, by reformulating their policies respecting slavery, the evangelical churches effectively blurred the line of respectability that had once set their denominations apart from the Episcopalian and Presbyterian churches esteemed by elite southerners. "I suppose you will be surprised to hear that Susan & myself belong to different Churches, she to that of pres[byte]rian and I to the Bapt[i]st, but one in Christ," wrote South Carolina resident Eliza Maybank to her cousin in 1810.[78] By the early nineteenth century, Baptists such as Furman gleefully observed how the more conservative denominations were mimicking evangelical modes of worship. "The Revival, or religious Stir, in N. Carolina," wrote Furman in 1802, "is chiefly among the Presbyterians, who have been wont heretofore to ridicule the disorderly Baptists."[79]

As the ministers carried the gospel along the coast and into the backcountry, and as revivals swept across the southern landscape beginning in 1800, Christianity contributed mightily to the homogenization of slaveowner culture.[80] Church life counteracted the sectional mentality that had traditionally separated the tidewater regions from the backcountry. Because the coastal planters believed that Christian values were replacing the dissipation that had previously characterized backcountry life, they awarded backcountry voters increasing political power. "When Men of property, & education are distributed through all parts of the State," Ralph Izard accurately predicted in 1795, the manner of apportioning representatives to the South Carolina legislature "will be of much less importance than it is at present." Eyeing the Carolina backcountry some two decades later, his daughter insisted that society there could be made to resemble the refined lowcountry. Despite her belief that the backcountry residents were "a strange, forward, foolish, prying set of beings," she "could not help thinking though that with patience, & perseverance, & with an active as well as benevolent disposition, it would not be impracticable to civilize them."[81] Sounding the same theme, South Carolina author and historian David Ramsay contended in 1808 that the "zeal and activity" displayed by the Baptists and Methodists "have been followed with correspondent success in civilizing and evangelizing remote and destitute settlements."[82] The extension of the plantation economy and the attendant proliferation of Christianity were laying the foundation for a slaveowner identity that superseded geographic boundaries.

Without claiming that the market caused the Christian revivals of the nineteenth century, one can still observe that the new religious order made headway in the South because, on a number of levels, the churches worked in concert with an expanding commercial economy. The explosive growth in cotton production at the turn of the century resulted in an influx of capital into backcountry regions that the coastal elite had once dismissed as a savage, Godless realm. Not only did ministers have an easier time reaching these developing plantation zones, but they also could solicit some of the settlers' accumulating wealth for the maintenance of the churches. The resulting infrastructure of new churches provided a crucial foundation for revivals that, at first glance, might have appeared informal and almost spontaneous. The evangelical churches that emerged from this dynamic were notable for a reciprocal flow of respectability between wealthier members of the laity and the denominations they had joined. When such ministers as Furman courted the slaveowners and acquired slaves themselves, they demonstrated once and for all that their churches posed no threat to slavery. Conversely, when slaveowners in new settlements embraced the principles of corporate individualism articulated by Christian preachers and authors, they were laying claim to the moral authority formerly wielded only by the wealthiest segment of the planter elite. Owners who conducted themselves according to the new standard for mastery were, in effect, staking their claims to the first rank in slaveholding society. Both church and slaveowner obviously stood to gain from the alliance between God and master.

The colleges and academies that sprouted in the backcountry provided additional resources with which backcountry slaveholders could lift themselves into the exalted role of the enlightened planter. The founders of South

Carolina College had intentionally located the institution in Columbia to reconcile tensions between the backcountry and the coast.[83] South Carolina governor John Drayton therefore applauded its establishment because the college promised to facilitate "the general diffusion of knowledge." Committed to a system of public education, Drayton anticipated the day when "youth from all parts [of the state] will be connected in friendship, & be prepared to enter on those duties, which their education & abilities will enable them to perform."[84] Although Drayton's dream of widespread public education never came to pass, a host of private academies did bring together the children of slaveowning families from all over the South.

As befitted Christianity's central role in the new regional culture, ministers founded and managed many of these schools. Presbyterian minister Moses Waddel, for example, educated an entire generation of prominent slaveowners at his backcountry academy, administering a dose of religion strong enough to elicit the complaints of some of his students. "Dr Waddell now preaches once a fortnight and imposed the double punishment of two sermons every time," wrote James Edward Calhoun in 1814. "As for my part I'd rather have two hundred lashes. . . . These Pharisees pursue me to my very home & I'm obliged to attend daily to four prayers and six graces, in consequence of which my knees have become as thick and as callous[ed] as a negro's heel and my pantaloons are all worn out."[85] Much to young Calhoun's dismay, the word of God had traveled from the pulpit into the private lives of the slaveowners. Even skeptics such as Thomas Cooper appreciated the manner in which Christianity reinforced the white social order. Cooper, the future president of South Carolina College, informed Thomas Jefferson in 1814 that he had "not yet made up my mind, whether it be not in the order . . . of Providence, that for some centuries to come, men should be deceived by [religious] frauds and lies: and whether these be not necessary to keep them in good order, and whether a sudden blaze of truth would not do as much harm to the mass of mankind, as a sudden emancipation to the negroes."[86] Whether or not they liked it, the slaveowners' authority had become rooted in Christian teaching.

Thanks to the growth of this Christian consumer culture, early-nineteenth-century planters were refining their understanding of domestic relations. But their insistence that household authority be exercised according to Christian principle by no means implied their acceptance of egalitarian democracy. Although growing numbers of slaveowners embraced their bondservants in Christian fellowship, the plantation household continued to revolve around a starkly delineated hierarchy—one that relegated women and slaves to more carefully defined but obviously subordinate social roles.

Let there be no mistake. Slavery remained brutal; masters in the Christian early republic inflicted enormities on their slaves just as their colonial predecessors had done. One witness gave "an account of a [slave] man being gibbeted alive in South Carolina" and contended that "the buzzards came and picked out his eyes. Another was burnt to death at a stake in Charleston, surrounded by a multitude of spectators, some of whom were people of the first rank; . . . and the poor object was heard to cry as long as he could breathe, 'not guilty, not guilty.'"[87] Notwithstanding the growth of religious sentiment, many slaveowners "repented" the "indulgence given . . . to the Negroes," vowing to inflict "Severe and continued punishment on the offend[ing bondservants]."[88] Slaveowners quickly learned to reconcile the role of Christian steward with the discipline of recalcitrant slaves.

Within the schema of corporate individualism, racial distinctions between supposedly benevolent planters and supposedly needy, grateful slaves became more important than ever before. Lacking an organic domestic sensibility, eighteenth-century male slaveowners in the Deep South had pursued their slaves sexually without having to fear a backlash from polite society.[89] Evidence from the nineteenth century, however, suggests that notions of refined slave ownership and stewardship were beginning to deter open sexual relationships with slaves. South Carolina planter Samuel Dubose Jr. demonstrated how ideas about restrained (and therefore moral) mastery could foster the condemnation of interracial liaisons. Pointing to the notorious example of Charles Sinkler, who had "formed a connection" and eventually fathered children with a slave "wench," Dubose asserted that the "practice has become notorious here among young men of property" and that there were "more instances of it than there are to the contrary." Still, Dubose's disapproval of slaveowners who engaged in these sinful pleasures signaled the genesis of a new standard for mastery. Adopting a righteous tone, he declared that Sinkler's "character is gone, respect he possesses none, and as for showing himself in [his home town] he does not [dare]." Henceforth the slaveowning libertine would be "mentioned only as one who is traveling that road which [parents] earnestly pray one of [their children] may never enter upon."[90] Although many slaveowners continued to seek sexual contact with their bondservants, idealized conceptions of the plantation household pushed this behavior into an illicit realm. While this development did not protect slaves from white sexual predators, it strengthened the planters' confidence in the morality of their "family" relations.

In addition to reinforcing the boundaries between whites and blacks, the planters were also redefining gender roles to clarify the distinct responsibilities of slaveowning men and women. Elite planters' wives and daughters shunned radical feminism for the same reason that they abhorred the leveling principles of the French Revolution. A society that rested on a foundation of unfree labor had little room for egalitarian philosophies—whether they sought to grant equal rights to African American slaves or to white women. As we have seen, feminists such as Mary Wollstonecraft tended to alienate white southern women like Alice Izard and Margaret Manigault, who believed instead that "submission is the duty of women." Elite southern women who appeared to pursue their own individual desires at the expense of the needs of their relations were quickly reminded (as was Savannah resident Eliza Mackay in 1813) that "you dont belong to yourself but to your family."[91]

As plantations proliferated across the southern landscape, the realm of activities that women could acceptably perform began to shrink. Chivalry gained currency, meaning that heavy labor performed by white women signaled an uncivilized society that had yet to be refined by the appropriate mores. In 1800, Irishman Michael Gaffney condemned the backcountry region northwest of Charleston because "the women in this country live the poorest lives of any people in the world. It is directly opposite to [the gender convention in] Charleston; here they must do everything from cooking to planting and after that they have no more life in them than Indian squaws."[92] Over the ensuing years, however, the spread of slavery into the backcountry altered the responsibilities of many white women. Although they remained subordinate to their husbands and fathers, they gained authority over a captive African American labor force. No longer having to toil in the fields to feed their families, these women were instead expected to reinforce the carefully orchestrated hierarchy of race and gender that kept potentially rebellious slaves in their place. White women, in other words, were moving from the realm of production into a domestic sphere that separated them from the corruption and dangers of the world at large. By 1809, South Carolina governor John Drayton reacted with horror to the discovery that "the person who has the command of the gaol" in Coosawhatchie "*is a Woman*." Within the emerging framework of household relations, women buttressed the social order through moral influence, not by forcefully holding criminals in submission. Drayton therefore did "not admit the propriety of appointing a Woman to such an office" as jailer and requested that the woman in question be replaced.[93]

In nineteenth-century slaveowning society, refined ladies negotiated a treacherous tightrope. On one hand, plantation mistresses such as Alice Izard believed that the "more retired life is, in general, better suited to the female character."[94] On the other hand, since the Revolution, women had gained some stake in national as well as domestic virtue—in republican motherhood and in personal family relationships. For this reason, parents such as John P. Richardson demanded that their daughters prepare themselves for future responsibilities that transcended the "ornamental" realm. Writing to his daughter Elizabeth in 1808, Richardson supported her "exertions to attain [the] Elegant accomplishment" of being named the first lady of a Charleston ball. But he also hoped that "no means are neglected for the acquirement of other [accomplishments] equally ornamental and more usefull to the well bred Lady." Richardson concluded with his wish that she have a "conviction of [the] importance" of her time, keeping herself "usefully employed."[95] Written works such as Porter's *Scottish Chiefs* reinforced this principle. Heroic female characters in the novel devote themselves to their national cause, insisting that "sex could not have altered [their] sense of duty." One Scottish mother instructed Wallace to "look on my son . . . for the first word he speaks shall be Wallace; the second liberty. Every drop of milk he draws from my bosom, shall be turned into blood to nerve a conquering arm, or to flow for his country."[96]

White southern women's identities as women now hinged on service to their families and communities. They needed to fulfill that responsibility, however, without transgressing standards for womanly conduct. Here lay a tension that pushed women—even the most accomplished and prominent women—in conflicting directions. "I may as well be silent, for I am really ignorant in all political matters," wrote Alice Izard in 1808. Several months later her daughter criticized the author Jane West for being "so rugged in her language." "One would not take her style for that of a woman," continued Manigault, before expressing her desire to "avoid all confrontational subjects" and "to be preserved from all perplexing thoughts." Yet these same women insisted that womanhood required an active role in social and political conflicts that potentially threatened to undermine the ideals of the region. "Did I write that I thought *to be good* was all that was necessary for Women," asked Izard in 1801. "I did not do justice to my sentiments if I did. I would have goodness to be the ground work; but as many accomplishments and [pleasures] as possible in the superstructure."[97] By the same token, Izard found herself unable to keep silent—despite her professed "ig-norance on political matters"—when she heard conversations that violated her own ideas about government proceedings. "I have been obliged several times to exert myself," she confessed in 1808, "& speak in a more decided tone on politics than I ever wish to do, because I found those in company were forgetting themselves." In the end, the slaveowning woman confronted the challenge of "guid[ing], where she does not govern, & act[ing] like a guardian angel by preventing the effects of evil desires, & strong passions, & leading [men] to worthy pursuits."[98]

Although white women coveted a role drastically different from the one assigned to southern slaves, the emerging gender dynamic paral-leled the development of the new model for racial interaction. In both cases, the maturing southern marketplace was transmitting ideas that criticized an impersonal and therefore immoral society. Herein rested the irony of a distinct southern identity: the organic ideal was nurtured by a capitalistic cultural form in which concepts about race and gender were packaged as commodities and marketed for profit across vast areas of the Western world. The slaveowners who aspired to become William Wallace built their idealized identity around the themes presented by novels and religious tracts, but the planters encountered these works only because their econ-omy was expanding, they were cultivating ever larger cotton harvests, and they were purchasing ever increasing numbers of slaves. Plantation mis-tresses insisted that womanly duty entailed the rejection of selfish pleasures, but these women reflected on such matters during the leisure time afforded them by their bondservants' misery in the fields.

Some historians have speculated that paternalistic slaveowner ideology was the product of intimate contact between African American slaves and resident southern slaveowners and was "enormously reinforced" by the de-cision to close the international slave trade. According to this logic, south-ern masters realized they could no longer renew their supply of slaves with fresh imports and therefore adopted more humane management tactics to ensure a naturally increasing slave population.[99] The argument is not with-out merit, particularly because it helps to explain how the slaveowners' pa-ternalistic posturing came into vogue at the exact historical moment when the cotton economy exploded into the southern backcountry. Paternalism made economic sense. Although the organic slaveowning philosophy con-tradicted the buying and selling of human property, it did promise to perpetuate a manageable labor supply without which the plantation system would have folded.

The commodification of Christian stewardship, however, preceded the ban on African slave importation in 1808 and was already swaying the planters by the turn of the century. And as we have seen, organic notions about human bondage proliferated through the cultural channels engendered by the slaveowners' market society. Thus, paradoxically, the organic slaveowning ideal originated far away from the plantations and was gathering momentum exactly because southern markets were becoming more adept at speeding resources—both cultural and economic—between the plantations and the rest of the world. That these markets required the slaves' exploitation could be overlooked by owners who interpreted plantation life through a prism of romantic ideas about domesticity. Curiously enough, the planters who had most thoroughly integrated themselves into transatlantic intellectual debates proved to be the most powerful advocates of the organic world view. Such had been the case during the colonial period, when exceptionally well-read and well-traveled slaveowners such as Henry Laurens waged a preliminary, unsuccessful campaign to reform slavery. In the nineteenth century, the growth of market society exposed increasing numbers of slaveowners to the principles of corporate individualism. Although the new conception of plantation domesticity was predicated on the highly personal bond between master and slave, parent and child, its growth as an ideology hinged on the erosion of provincial attitudes toward slavery. Ironically, the slaveowners who were least intellectually rooted to their plantations were most easily seduced by the organic slaveowning ideal.

The experience of slaveholders who had lived in the North demonstrated the manner in which this bizarre sequence could unfold. Many prominent Carolina and Georgia families (including the Butlers, the Alstons, the Coxes, the Reads, the Izards, and the Manigaults) spent considerable time in northern cities where emancipation was progressing rapidly. These slaveowners were not impervious to arguments against the brutality and waste engendered by chattel slavery. Nevertheless, their desire to protect their families' elite status ultimately led them to reject the ideological trend toward emancipation in favor of an organic, hierarchical social vision. In the end, they feared that an egalitarian, democratic polity would reduce their families to a state of miserable destitution. Their story reveals how an ideology that hinged on the principles of Christian stewardship could gain adherents who profited from a workforce held in captivity hundreds of miles away.

For Gabriel and Margaret Manigault, exposure to northern society initially kindled their uncertainty about slavery's viability in an age of freedom. Relocating to Philadelphia in 1807, they failed to inquire about Pennsylvania statutes mandating the release of slaves kept in the state for longer than six months. "Manigault is in . . . troubles on account of his servants—he will probably lose every one of them," noted George Izard, Manigault's brother-in-law.[100] Because they claimed their freedom, slaves whom the Manigaults had previously described as "always in good humor" became, in the Manigaults' opinion, "so vile, so treacherous, so ungrateful, & so perfectly unfeeling."[101] Margaret Izard Manigault confessed in October 1807 that "there is no knowing what effect this new state of existence [in Philadelphia] may have upon [their African American servants]." Gabriel Manigault, she asserted two months later, "has been so tormented with the rudeness of our Servants, that he had not time to think of anything [else]." Noting that their slaves "were all free by the new, & to us unknown laws of the States of N[ew York] & P[ennsylvania]," Margaret Manigault bemoaned the "machinations" of the men and women whom they had formerly held in perpetual servitude. Soon afterward, the Manigaults were referring to their former slaves as "animals."[102]

Abandoned by their bondservants, both Alice Izard and Margaret Izard Manigault announced a preference for free white labor as opposed to "ungrateful domestic" slaves.[103] "I am glad to hear that you are pleased with your hired Women," wrote Izard to her daughter in Philadelphia. "I like them ten thousand times better than Slaves," she observed in 1807, before admitting that "I have never suffered myself to talk on the subject [of slavery]; but it has always been offensive to me."[104] Margaret Izard Manigault echoed this sentiment four years later when she lamented the difficulties of her brother-in-law in Charleston. Observing that the man was "greatly imposed upon by his Negroes," Manigault trumpeted the virtues of a wage economy: "I should think that the northern system would suit him better than [slavery]. There, [as opposed to in the South,] if you hire a man to work, he does what he engages to do in the day." Manigault and Izard noticed and sympathized with their white servants' virulent antipathy toward African American company. "We have a White Cook, Nursery Maid, & Coachman," wrote Manigault in 1808, "all decent, orderly people," who "never eat with the blacks."[105]

Contrasting the free North with the slaveowning South, Manigault and her mother drew attention to the exploitative and squalid aspects of slave society. As she traveled toward Charleston in 1801, Manigault complained about losing "the pleasant prospects, neat cottages, cheerful faces, & all the comforts, & charms of the northern States—& nothing can be more gloomy, more frightful, more odious & contemptable than the appearance" of the South. Residence in northern society made it possible for these women finally to express their reservations about slavery. Izard confessed in 1807 that because her "lot [had been] cast among" her family's slaves, she "thought it my duty to acquiesce, & not hazard the happiness of your Father, by indulging my own sentiments" against slavery.[106] Emotional and social distance from plantation society in the Deep South, however, enabled Izard to comment at last on the practical and ethical limitations of slavery— limitations that had been troubling her for decades. Her candor illustrated the growing momentum of antislavery sentiment in the new nation. And if we were to freeze the Manigault family's history at this point in the early nineteenth century, their story would demonstrate the manner in which Americans from all regions were being swayed by egalitarian principles.

But the Manigaults and Izards did not take the final step toward emancipation. However sincere their doubts about the morality and efficacy of unfree labor, this family did not divest itself of slaves. In fact, at the end of the antebellum period, Margaret Izard Manigault's son Charles and her grandson Louis made their home on several large rice plantations in Georgia and South Carolina, where they were surrounded by hundreds of African American bondservants. Some seventy years after Alice Izard first confronted the prospect of abolition, her grandson and great-grandson were clinging to their roles as masters.[107] We cannot, moreover, make sense of this seeming incongruity by drawing a clean distinction between Alice Izard's views toward slavery and those of succeeding generations of the Manigault family. Although Izard and her daughter expressed doubts about unfree labor during the early nineteenth century, they participated in a cultural dynamic that made it difficult, if not impossible, for them to accept egalitarian democracy.

As members of an entrenched elite, both Manigault and her mother viewed their bloodline as a source for morality and republicanism—crucial qualities in an increasingly uncertain and immoral age. In 1811 Izard observed that she had "secluded myself" from "the present riotous, boisterous manners" because "I can not reconcile myself to them." Horrified that the unwashed masses were undermining standards of proper conduct, Izard insisted that "our well bred Gentleman must set the example, & so must our well educated Ladies. They are the reformers of the World. To them society has always been indebted for elegance, & refinement."[108] Of course, Izard included her own acquaintances and family in the ranks of those well bred. "It is very pleasant to find that the most agreeable members of society are in our own circle, & among our particular friends," she wrote in 1812. Izard, however, asserted that her daughter's resettlement in Philadelphia had lessened the ability of Manigault's family to reform society. "Were you more stationary than you are," lectured Izard to Manigault, "your well regulated family, & your amiable daughters might do a great deal."[109] If relocation to the North had fostered the Manigaults' antislavery sensibility, it also reinforced their sense of purpose as a family. Uprooted from plantation society, the Manigaults perceived their mandate of noblesse oblige with renewed clarity.

Simply put, emancipation challenged the Manigaults' identity as leading members of society. Although Alice Izard and Margaret Manigault claimed to prefer servants to slaves, free labor proved to be an exasperating alternative to permanent bondage. Alice Izard's numerous problems with her household staff prompted her daughter to observe in 1811 that "your servants, & their ridiculous behavior are too provoking." Without the institutional framework of brutal punishment and coercion available to slaveowners, both mother and daughter found it difficult to maintain a dependable staff of servants. Launching into a typical diatribe against their employees' unreliability, Manigault predicted in 1812 that one of her mother's free black housemaids "would avail herself of every advantage [to] leave you in the lurch."[110] The Manigaults fared no better with white wage laborers. Relatives who had once ruled out black household workers eventually complained that they were "tormented by their white servants."[111] Alice Izard acknowledged that "much of our happiness depends on Servants"; unfortunately for her and her daughter, she perceived that "that class of people [was] grow[ing] every day more insolent in" Pennsylvania.[112] As the century progressed, the Manigaults feared that the movement toward democracy and freedom would degenerate into anarchy.

Alice Izard and Margaret Izard Manigault believed that, given too much freedom, both whites and blacks could easily annihilate moral society. The successful uprising of slaves on St. Domingue and their establishment of the Haitian republic reminded American slaveowners that African Americans might exact a bloody revenge if they could liberate themselves from white control.[113] Back in South Carolina, the campaign to redress the political imbalance between lowcountry planters and upcountry yeomen disturbed Alice Izard. She asserted that awarding greater political power to upcountry whites might result in "Anarchy, & Misrule."[114] By 1814, Margaret Manigault had concluded that the liberation of African American slaves promised disaster for elite residents of Philadelphia. She complained to her sister that a mob of "good Philadelphia idlers" had broken "open our poor innocent little mansion—forcing open the side boards with cleavers & choppers." She considered it an "alarming point" that the city had been left "almost in the hands of those lawless *Maroons* who think because they have been taught to run away from their masters, that they are at liberty to help themselves to whatever they want whenever they can in the houses of the defenceless."[115] By severing the ties between master and slave, northern emancipation threatened to unravel the entire social fabric of law and order.

Marshaling their courage against this grim possibility, the Manigaults found refuge in idealized conceptions of the plantation order. In 1810, Margaret Manigault reported that the slaves on their South Carolina plantation "love[d] their Massa" and complained only that "he never comes to see them." Several years earlier she had surmised that "one may be happy as a Planter by residing among one's people, & endeavoring to make them happy."[116] Such thoughts suggest that the Manigaults could conceptualize slavery in ideal terms exactly because they were experiencing northern emancipation firsthand. As life with free black and white servants became more and more unsatisfactory, the Deep South gained considerable charm. Manigault attempted to convince herself in 1814 that her troubles with her Philadelphia servants were "light" compared with those she experienced with her slaves in South Carolina; but she could not quench the romantic allure that plantation life held for the rest of her family.[117] Although she remained with her husband in Philadelphia, her relatives chose a different path, leaving her feeling "lost & unhinged, & a stranger in the land."[118]

From her plantation residence outside Charleston, Alice Izard reaffirmed her dislike for "the system of Slavery" but vowed to "make the best" of an institution she now characterized as "unavoidable." Two years later in 1816, her affection for slaveowning society was growing. "I must acknowledge that I have seen only one beggar in Charleston," she wrote, "& that I believe the system with regard to our Negroes is much [a]meliorated."[119] As the Manigault family came once again to appreciate the "beautiful" and "enchanting" qualities of plantation life, their disappointment with emancipation became more pronounced.[120] Contemplating another journey northward, Alice Izard noted that Pennsylvania's "new & stricter regulations made with regard to Slaves . . . [fall] particularly hard on me." "There will be something peculiarly rigorous in my fate," she asserted, "if I should be deprived altogether . . . of the services" of "useful" slaves.[121] Having considered the prospects and effects of emancipation for over two decades, Alice Izard was ultimately disgusted by the humanitarian campaign to free African American slaves. "I have long been impressed with the opinion that mistaken philanthropy is the source of great evils," she concluded in 1819.[122] Slavery had weathered a powerful ideological assault. The ideal of resident slaveowners lovingly caring for their grateful bondservants had gained currency among the very planters whose travels ensured the least contact with their human property. A full generation before the 1830s—the decade in which many scholars have located the rise of the defense of slavery as a positive good—elite slaveowners had already staked their identities on the moral foundation of corporate individualism. By 1803, the overseer Roswell King could justify his reluctance to punish an unproductive slave by appealing to the standard for mastery that he claimed to share with his employer, Pierce Butler. "I had rather you to be Cheated out of a little work," wrote the overseer (who himself owned a number of slaves), "than me to have the name of being Cruel & Unjust." When Roswell King Jr. replaced his father as Butler's overseer, Butler took care to remind the young man that recognition of the slaves' humanity constituted a principal element in the planter identity. "Kind management to my People," wrote Butler in 1821, played a key role in his ongoing "effort to exceed other planters in method."[123]

Whether the idealized conception of slavery would dictate to the slaveholders a particular political course had yet to be determined. Certainly the accelerating campaign against human bondage was pushing white southerners in Georgia and South Carolina toward a sectional identity. Their region's peculiar vulnerability was evident during the War of 1812, when the slaveowners fruitlessly attempted to track down slaves who had taken refuge behind British lines and had made their way to Canada. The slaveowners had hoped that the escaped "Negroes would return into our Eastern States, to mingle in the Black Population." The southerners attempted to paint the runaways as traitors to the United States—a strategy that the slaveowners (with unfounded optimism) believed might prompt free blacks in the North to provide assistance "in obtaining some of them." Instead, the former bondservants "formed connections" with the free African American communities, making "the discovery of them difficult, and the apprehension of them still more so."[124] The episode reinforced the slaveowners' suspicion that their system of labor was under attack, leading them to question whether their national institutions could be enlisted in the defense of slavery. Southern politicians had periodically raised these fears since the establishment of the republic and, in defending the principle of state sovereignty, made clear that their own participation in the Union assumed that the central government would respect southern political liberties. In 1798, amid the controversy over the Federalist Alien and Sedition Acts, southern Republicans had gone so far as to issue the Kentucky and Virginia Resolutions, which opened the door to unilateral state rejection of obnoxious federal legislation.

Still, early-nineteenth-century planters remained very much vested in a mainstream American identity. It was the slaveowners who routinely denounced northerners for threatening to secede. As early as 1796, Pierce Butler expressed fears that northern politicians were plotting to shatter the union. Butler reported that he had dined with a company of New York statesmen "who, say they, will no longer submit to a majority composed of a black representation, alluding to the allowance in the representation for Negroes . . . & Civil War was spoken of with a sans froid that wou'd shock the feelings of a Nero or Caligula. I think I perceive in certain characters an infatuated determination to risk every thing rather than lose sight of their object—Idle, deluded Men!" Ten years later, the Aaron Burr Conspiracy had sparked rumors that New York had "declared for a disunion."[125] Although these fears never came to pass, Jefferson's Embargo Act of 1807 antagonized the northeastern communities that depended on commerce with England, raising the possibility of a huge "northern insurrection"—one that even "10,000 Virginians would not be able to quell." Needless to say, the War of 1812 hardened northern Federalist sentiment against the Republican administration's policies. By 1814, southerners who corresponded with acquaintances in Connecticut were articulating the fear that "discontents in the East will drive you to the desperate measure of a dissolution of the union which would seal the ruin of our country."[126] Notwithstanding their alarm about northern advocates of abolition, the slaveowners fretted over the possibility that regional politics might somehow unravel the cords binding the states. Although they were already struggling to protect their prerogatives as masters, the southerners continued to consider the Union their own.

This made perfect sense given that southern masters defended slavery with ideas obtained through a market that connected the plantations to a broader culture. Colonial slaveholders had rejected organic social philosophy because it undermined their authority in favor of opinions offered by imperial administrators and religious reformers. Because they had actively participated in the construction of the new federal government and had obtained ultimate authority over their own lives, post-Revolutionary slave-holders had every reason to embrace well-regulated hierarchy as the defining principle of moral society. As long as they maintained final say on the regulation of the master-slave relationship, the planters would stay fiercely committed to the national political infrastructure. What remained to be seen was how long the enemies of slavery could be kept at bay in Congress. The southerners' integration into a wider literary market and religious community had made possible their development of an ethos of corporate individualism. Owners such as Alice Izard therefore anticipated with excitement the resumption of commercial exchange with England following the War of 1812. "It will be very agreeable to have the two Countries on a pleasing footing of intimacy with each other," she remarked in 1815. "They abound in things which will be useful to us, particularly books."[127] Nevertheless, the themes that the slaveowners lifted out of Christian and secular texts were already providing the foundation for a decidedly regional slave-owning culture—one that increased the likelihood of disunion by providing a framework for a separate political identity.

*We have been
emancipated from a
dependence on Great
Britain, but as if destined
to pass our lives in a State
of Mental Slavery, we have
merely exchanged the
chains of Old England, for
those of New England.*

ROBERT Y. HAYNE,
1827

CHAPTER FIVE

A Storm Portending

The Politics of the
"Peculiar" Deep South,
1816–1829

During the fifteen years following the War of 1812, the slaveholders
began to perceive themselves as an embattled minority within the Union
they had fought to establish. In Congress and at home in slaveowning society, southern ideologues drew increasingly favorable comparisons between
their system of unfree labor and the wage economy developing in the northern United States. Historians have traditionally discounted the cultural significance of these "early," publicly presented defenses of slavery, depicting
them as isolated statements that were disconnected from mainstream
southern opinion. Such scholarship has downplayed the possibility that the
period's political confrontations over slavery sprang from profound cultural differences between northerners and southerners. Approached from
this perspective, those southern politicians beating the sectional drum appeared to be completely out of rhythm with their constituents.[1]

Such interpretation, however, overlooks the fact that a positive conception of human bondage was already affecting the plantation household by the turn of the nineteenth century. A slaveowning culture, in other words, preceded (and to a certain extent made necessary) public expressions of a sectional political philosophy rooted in the defense of slavery. By formally presenting the precepts of corporate individualism as the moral standards of southern society, ideologues and politicians were widening the appeal of a message that they had most certainly not invented.[2] Thus, even before Thomas Dew of Virginia presented his influential defense of slavery in 1832, a proslavery orthodoxy was emerging—one turning on organic assumptions about slave individuality and slaveowner restraint that historians have mistakenly associated exclusively with the late antebellum period. The continually expanding southern market for consumer culture ensured that growing numbers of slaveowners would eventually internalize idealized conceptions of their own mastery. By the end of the decade, the slaveowners themselves had perceived the connection between an emerging mass media and their own political stance as a ruling elite.

Southern economic woes after the War of 1812 provided a gloomy atmosphere in which the slaveowners discussed the future of their region and their nation. Commentators in Charleston noted in 1816 that "our Planters both of rice & cotton suffer great Depression at present."[3] Although the country soon experienced a financial upturn, the good times came to a jarring end in 1819, when a panic sent shock waves through the international banking system. As creditors pressed for repayment, the market for staple crops collapsed, leaving the planters in a desperate situation.[4] The supply of specie, which had never been abundant, dried up completely. "The great depression of trade," observed Camden resident J. C. Carter in July 1819, "has produced the most extraordinary effect upon the state of property." "Failures are daily taking place amongst the most wealthy merchants," he continued. "The scarcity of money is without a parallel."[5] Southern planters had grown accustomed to periodic downturns in their fortunes, but nothing in their past financial experience prepared them for the sustained depression of the 1820s. "I never expected cotton could have remained so long at such low rates," confessed one British factor to his Savannah client two years later.[6] Equally grim reports echoed through Georgia and South Carolina throughout the decade.[7]

During this period, the western frontier offered an enticing alternative to those men and women daring enough to abandon the familiar culture of the southeastern seaboard.[8] Indeed, so many southerners poured into the West that the frontier sometimes turned out to be a fairly crowded place. North Carolina planter Israel Pickens was "sadly disappointed" with his new residence in Alabama. He observed in 1817 that "no lumber [was] to be had for building [and that] every house publick & private [was] filled, such [wa]s the crowd of strangers & emigrants."[9] Notwithstanding such discouragement, families continued to depart for the Southwest. Writing from Georgia in 1817, Samuel McDonald noted that "the disease prevalent here . . . is termed the 'Alabama Fever'—scarce any of those who are attacked by it ever recover; it sooner or later carries them off to the westward."[10] Criticism of westward migration came from the relatives left behind who complained to distant family members that with "each remove . . . the possibility of seeing you again is rendered so much more uncertain."[11] But while they differed over the personal and economic benefits to be derived from migration, white residents of the Deep South agreed that slaveholders possessed an inalienable constitutional right to transport their human property to new residences in the western territories.

Nineteenth-century opponents of slavery, however, chose to contest the slaveowners on this point exactly as the call of western lands was reshaping southern society. When the House of Representatives considered a bill to grant statehood to Missouri in February 1819, New York congressman James Tallmadge Jr. proposed amendments forbidding slavery from the territory.[12] Because Tallmadge staked his opposition to slavery on moral grounds, northern and southern congressmen initiated a heated debate over the relative virtues of free labor and human bondage. In no uncertain terms, antislavery congressmen denounced unfree labor as "a departure from republican principles" and a violation of the Declaration of Independence—a document that supposedly defined "the principle on which our National and State Constitutions are all professedly founded."[13] With equal fervor, southern statesmen denied that "the owners of slaves [were] less moral or less religious than those who hold none." Both parties realized that "no subject which has agitated the councils of the United States of America, from the formation of our Government down to the present period, has been pregnant with more important consequences than the one now under discussion."[14] When the House passed the Tallmadge Amendments, politicians from both sections contemplated civil war as a dire and very real possibility. "They were kindling a fire," contended Georgia representative Thomas Cobb, "which all the waters of the ocean could not extinguish. It could be extinguished only in blood."[15]

The predictions of impending civil war offered by both sides missed their mark by some forty years. Nevertheless, the Missouri controversy proved to be a watershed in the development of a sectional political style grounded on the issue of slavery. Even before the debate over Missouri, a few southern statesmen had moved beyond the justification of slavery as a "necessary evil."[16] By 1820, politicians from slaveowning states—particularly those hailing from the Deep South—were gravitating toward a more powerful public defense of human bondage as a positive good. Thus when South Carolina senator William Smith emphasized the benefits of slavery and the institution's prominent role in moral societies throughout the ages, he revealed the ever widening ideological boundary demarcating the free North from the slaveowning South.

Addressing the Senate in January 1820, Smith initiated his defense of the slaveholding states on constitutional grounds. Like so many southern statesmen, the South Carolina senator argued for a strict construction of federal powers—a constitutional reading that naturally precluded federal interference with slavery. Smith, however, did not rest his argument in the realm of "legal principle." Instead, he boldly presented the historical and religious circumstances that mandated and justified human bondage as a permanent feature of civil society. "It had been the lot of man, in this shape or that," asserted Smith, "to serve one another from all time. At least, slavery has prevailed in every country on the globe, ever since the flood."[17] Having noted the role of slavery in the "most enlightened" republics of antiquity, the South Carolina statesman pointed to the Bible for evidence that "Christ himself gave a sanction to slavery" by "admonish[ing] them to be obedient to their masters." Smith contended that southern slaves were "fully sensible that their comforts are as great, and their labor not more arduous, than any other class of laboring people." Indeed, in his opinion, they were "so domesticated, or so kindly treated by their masters, and their situations so improved," that northern abolitionists "cannot excite one among twenty to insurrection."[18] Northern senators immediately expressed "astonishment and surprise" at Smith's willingness to justify "slavery on the broadest principles, without qualification or reserve." Opponents of slavery reminded the Senate that "this was taking entirely new ground" because "heretofore, in discussions upon this subject, slavery had not been considered as a matter of right, but as an evil, a misfortune entailed upon the country, for which no complete remedy could be suggested."[19] Historians such as William Freehling have tended to agree that Smith was breaking into new ideological territory—that "the huge majority of slaveholders, distressed by slavery but seeing no way out, clung stubbornly to the untenable 'necessary evil' position" and "did not widely discuss or accept the 'positive good' thesis" until the following decade.[20]

The organic justification of slavery, however, was already profoundly influencing southern statesmen. Earlier in the Missouri debate, Maryland senator William Pinkney had assailed the Declaration of Independence for venerating the principle that "all men are created equal." Dismissing the notion of natural rights as "absurd and untrue," he insisted that members of society have "no inalienable rights"—that some measure of hierarchy would always remain inevitable in a well-ordered republic.[21] Like William Smith, Georgia senator Freeman Walker had insisted that the "slaveholding States . . . yield to none in the practice of benevolence and humanity." In his estimation, critics of the South had "received erroneous impressions in relation to the treatment of slaves." To counter such misinformation, Walker assured his fellow senators that "these people . . . are far from being in that state of intolerable vassalage which some gentlemen seem to believe." "They are well clothed, well fed, and treated with kindness and humanity," he concluded. "They are cheerful and apparently happy."[22] Senator Nathaniel Macon of North Carolina likewise offered a positive defense of human bondage when he asserted that "the old [slaves] are better taken care of than any poor in the world, and treated with decent respect by all their white acquaintances." Macon invited critics of the institution to "go home with me, or some other Southern member, and witness the meeting between the slaves and the owner, and see the glad faces and the hearty shaking of hands." "The [slave]owner can make more free in conversation with his slave, and be more easy in his company," he continued, "than the rich man . . . with the white hireling who drives his carriage." In his opinion, emancipated slaves "would be as much or more degraded than in their present condition."[23]

This is not to say that southern statesmen had banished the concept of slavery as a "necessary evil" from their political vocabulary. Clearly, many southern congressmen continued to construe it as "an evil we have long deplored but cannot cure."[24] What we should notice amid these conflicting defenses of slavery, however, is the degree to which elements of corporate individualism had seeped into and, to a large degree, undermined the traditional sectional justification of unfree labor as an unfortunate but nevertheless necessary feature of southern society. Kentucky senator Richard Johnson, for example, denied that it was his or any other southern statesman's intention to "justify the abstract principle of slavery, as either religiously, morally, or politically, correct"; he then proceeded to observe that "slavery has existed from the earliest ages of antiquity to the present day . . . without one admonition from Heaven in the whole book of inspiration against it." Even as Johnson explicitly labeled slavery a "necessary evil," he contended that "the condition [of human bondage], in some respects, is in favor of the slave." "Though slavery still must be confessed a bitter draught," lectured Johnson, "the slave often finds less bitterness in the cup of life than most white servants." The evil of human bondage, according to the Kentucky senator, was clearly mitigated by the fact that slaveowners exerted their authority under the restraint of community standards that supposedly protected the slaves' individual welfare: "No man among us can be cruel to his slave without incurring the execration of the whole community. The slave is trained to industry; and he is recompensed by kindness and humanity."[25]

The Missouri controversy ensured that the depiction of slavery as an institution in keeping with the principle of Christian stewardship would gain new political relevance. After all, defenders of slavery as a "necessary evil" would face an uphill battle convincing Congress to permit the institution to spread. Although a few southern statesmen gamely attempted to argue that extending slavery across the western frontier would disperse the evil and improve the slaves' living conditions, the force of their logic faltered against the blistering criticism of their antislavery opponents.[26] As New York representative John W. Taylor delighted in pointing out, the Tallmadge Amendment provided the southerners "with an opportunity of putting their [professed distaste for slavery] into practice; if they have tried slavery and found it a curse; if they desire to dissipate the gloom with which it covers the land," they could easily "exclude it from the Territory in question." By so doing, they would prevent the next generation of Missouri residents from making the familiar complaint, "We regret the existence of this unfortunate population among us; but we found them here . . . it is our misfortune, we must bear it with patience."[27] Given the impact of such reasoning, it should hardly be surprising that the Missouri controversy signaled the downfall of the "negative evil" stance as a viable political strategy. Henceforth, southern statesmen would find it increasingly difficult both to criticize unfree labor and to argue for its extension into the western territories.

Developments at home in slaveowning society reinforced the growing tendency to defend slavery as a positive good. As the decade progressed, the few resident southerners who opposed slavery faced mounting hostility from their neighbors. All sides were rapidly concluding that the opposing ideological camps could no longer coexist. When South Carolina minister

Basil Manly, a proponent of colonization, averred in 1821 that "the period seems fast approaching when . . . the people of this country as a nation must come to a fixed and final determination" about slavery, the slaveowners as a group could only agree. As the public dialogue over slavery continued, white southerners agonized over the possibility that all the discussion about freedom and natural rights would inspire their slaves to seize liberty by force. The southerners knew of what they spoke. Manly captured the prevailing fear when he observed that the slaves were "becoming gradually more and more informed" of the liberties enjoyed by free citizens in an enlightened republic, and that "no law nor custom, no vigilance nor rigor can prevent the diffusion of knowledge among them."[28] Little did Manly realize that soon after he wrote, hundreds of Charleston slaves would plot the destruction of their masters' society.

In one fell swoop, Denmark Vesey nearly drowned the Carolina lowcountry in white blood.[29] After spending his youth enslaved on a ship working the Caribbean trade, the mulatto bought his freedom in 1800. A lottery ticket worth fifteen hundred dollars provided him with the necessary funds, but his subsequent economic rise rested on more than just luck. Through determination and skill, the former slave earned a considerable fortune as a Charleston craftsman. And whereas many freedmen immediately sought to distance themselves from the slave community, Vesey risked everything he had gained by boldly engineering a scheme in which thousands of slaves were to attack their owners on July 14, 1822.[30] After seizing the city arsenal and killing all the white residents, Vesey and his fellow revolutionaries planned to seek assistance from the black republic of Haiti. As befitting someone who had sailed all across the hemisphere and who had read deeply into texts ranging from the Bible to contemporary political tracts, Vesey envisioned his insurrection unfolding on a grand scale.

The vast scope of the plot, however, proved to be its undoing. Slaves who did not share Vesey's optimism about the prospects of rebellion against heavily armed slaveholders betrayed the conspiracy. Charleston authorities began rounding up suspects in May 1822; by August, thirty-five slaves and free blacks had been executed and another thirty-seven banished from the state. Tortured by their white captors, some of the accused conspirators outlined their plans to liquidate Charleston's white population. Many of those convicted were trusted slaves who enjoyed relatively favorable treatment from their owners. A slave belonging to William Hammet, for example, confessed that "his master thought he was a good servant," when in fact he "had been a very bad boy."[31] That such seemingly loyal "Sambos" were silently devising grisly methods of disposing of their white "families" reveals that the southern slave population was anything except docile.

Not surprisingly, the discovery of the Vesey scheme in 1822 raised questions about the practice of trusting slaves. In a tract published on the heels of the plot's uncovering, Edwin C. Holland emphasized that "our NEGROES are truly *Jacobins* of the country . . . the *anarchists* and the *domestic enemy* . . . the barbarians who would, IF THEY COULD, become the DESTROYERS of our race." Other Charleston residents admitted that "the only principle that can maintain slavery" was "the principle of fear."[32] And some southerners who soberly acknowledged that African Americans yearned for freedom quite understandably decided (as did one Camden, South Carolina, resident in 1816) that the time had arrived "for us to leave a Country [in which] we cannot go to bed in safety."[33] To this extent, the discovery that hundreds or thousands of slaves were willing to murder their unsuspecting owners undermined proslavery ideologues such as William Smith, who had only recently assured the Senate that African American bondservants were too content to rebel.

The vast majority of slaveowners, however, had no intention of abandoning the privileges of mastery for the uncertain benefits of life in a free society. Rather than live in constant fear of slave rebellion, planters in the early nineteenth century placed their psychological need for security before their own common sense and embraced with increasing fervor the organic conception of human bondage that had been taking root since the end of the eighteenth century. Thus, even as white authorities were uncovering evidence of the Vesey conspiracy's unprecedented scale, Charleston slaveowners reassured themselves that they had the situation under control. When James Hamilton Jr. asserted in June 1822 that "we have little reason for apprehension," he was voicing the opinion of numerous elite residents of Charleston.[34] Far from vanquishing the slaveowning ideal of corporate individualism, nineteenth-century revelations about impending slave revolts pushed the slaveowners more deeply into a fantastic world of their own making—into a romantic realm where loyal slaves loved and honored their masters.

Ministers who had long attempted to reconcile plantation slavery with the principles of Christian stewardship likewise maintained their unwavering faith that, under the proper circumstances, black slaves would enthusiastically and gratefully fulfill their duties as bondservants. In a letter to South Carolina governor Thomas Bennett, Richard Furman described his apprehension that "in consequence of the late projected Insurrection, & the claims laid to a religious Character by several of those who ranked as Leaders in the nefarious scheme, Ideas have been produced in the Minds of many Citizens unfavorable to the use of the Bible among the Negroes, and that Attempts will, probably, be made to obtain legislative Interference, to prevent their learning to read it, or to use it freely." To keep this from happening, Furman reminded Bennett that the "lawfulness" of slavery "is positively stated in the Old Testament, & is clearly re[c]ognised in the New." Sounding the same theme articulated by missionaries in the South since the early eighteenth century, Furman contended that far from "encouraging Slaves to engage in [revolutionary] Schemes," proper religious instruction produced "happy Effects in favour, not only of Piety & Devotion, but of willing Subordination to lawful Authority & Conformity to the Principles of Truth, Justice, good order, Peace & Benevolence." Vesey's conspirators had been "Members of an irregular Association, which called itself the African Church, & was intimately connected with a similar body in Philadelphia, from which their Sentiments & Directions in Matters of Religion chiefly derived." By contrast, according to Furman, "very few, indeed, of the religious Negroes, in regular Churches among us, were drawn into the Plot." "One of the best Securities we have to the domestic Peace & Safety of the State," he concluded, "is found in the Sentiments & correspondent Dispositions of the religious Negroes, which they derive from the Bible."[35] For religious reformers such as Furman, the Vesey episode underscored the need for closer white supervision of black spirituality.

Furman drew his corporate ideas about slavery from over thirty years of experience administering to the slaves' spiritual needs. In previous decades, he had personally wielded his Christian faith as a weapon against potential slave resistance. "A faithful Servant, a poor Negro that is honest & faithful to his master, diligent in his business & who lives peacabl[y] with his fellow servants," he sermonized in 1818, "will enjoy more real happiness in this world than the rich who are wicked [and] will be respect[ed] while he lives & when he dies, he will have done with all his labour and sorrow & pain & enter into the joy of his Lord." After exposing the slaves to his conservative reading of the Gospel, Furman expressed to them his "sincer[e] wish [that] many of you may have such a tale told of you."[36] Here, Christianity was so obviously serving the interests of the master class that one is tempted to apply Marx's crude formulation of religion as "the opiate of the masses." Before doing so, however, one must be careful to differentiate between the slaveowners of the early national period and their colonial forerunners.

If Furman echoed the pleas of colonial religious activists ranging from Anglicans such as Francis Le Jau and Alexander Garden to such dissenters as George Whitefield, early-nineteenth-century white authorities constituted a decidedly more receptive audience than were their eighteenth-century predecessors. Eighty years earlier when Charleston residents confronted the Stono slave insurrection, they responded by denouncing Christian missions to the slaves and arresting Whitefield and Hugh Bryan. In the wake of the Vesey controversy, however, prominent southerners rallied behind Furman's message that organic Christian principles would strengthen their standing as masters. When the Baptist minister wrote his *Exposition of the Views of the Baptists, Relative to the Coloured Population of the United States* in 1823, no less an authority than South Carolina governor John L. Wilson endorsed Furman's organic portrayal of the master-slave relationship. "There can be no doubt that such doctrines, from such a source will produce the best of consequences in our [racially] mixed population, and tend to make our servants not only more contented with their lot, but more useful to their owners," wrote Wilson.[37] Far from dismissing the ideal of Christian stewardship as a danger to slaveowning society, nineteenth-century planters embraced it as the key to their earthly as well as heavenly deliverance.[38]

To defend their section from the antislavery movement, white southerners sought to close their regional borders to pernicious antislavery influences. In 1822, their efforts resulted in the passage of the Negro Seamen Acts, which required the incarceration of free black sailors whose ships visited South Carolina ports—a measure that Supreme Court justice William Johnson rejected as unconstitutional the following year. The controversy reinforced the slaveowners' fears that the Constitution would be turned against their sectional interests. In fact, residents of Charleston had become so morbidly sensitive about the wrong kind of public conversation concerning slavery that local newspapers initially declined to publish Johnson's decision. But white southerners quickly learned that issues this significant would find their way into the public arena. Within weeks, Johnson's decision was published as a pamphlet, and debate over the acts filled the pages of the local and national press.[39]

Because the slaveowners blamed the Vesey plot on public debate over slavery, they perceived the need to force public discussion of slavery to move in a more acceptable direction.[40] When southern ideologues formally presented organic proslavery doctrines that had already taken root within many plantation households, they were recasting the dialogue about the potential dangers of human bondage into a discussion of the institution's merits. In addition to Furman, South Carolina writers such as Frederick Dalcho and Edward Brown published tracts that characterized slavery in terms of a reciprocal relationship between needy, grateful slaves and caring white masters. In *Practical Considerations Founded on the Scriptures, Relative to the Slave Population of South-Carolina* (1823), Dalcho—an Episcopalian minister—endeavored to "show from . . . the Old and New Testament, that Slavery is not forbidden by the Divine Law, and, at the same time, to prove, the necessity of giving religious instruction to our Negroes." Like Furman, Dalcho wanted to control the Christian message presented to African Americans to prevent them from deriving any revolutionary meaning from the Bible. He had little doubt that with the proper dose of Christianity "masters will become more kind, and slaves more obedient."[41] Indeed, the master could supposedly invoke the same moral authority that enabled God, statesmen, and fathers to govern their charges in a manner benefiting society at large. "God is the moral Governor of the universe," noted Dalcho, "and the rulers of nations and communities, the fathers of families, and the owners of slaves, are, each in their respective spheres, the head of a moral government, in subjection to God, for the good of society, the happiness of the people, and the glory and honour of God's name."[42]

Three years later, Charleston author Edward Brown defended slavery with even greater enthusiasm. Like Furman, Dalcho and William Smith before him, Brown argued that "slavery has ever been the step-ladder by which civilized countries have passed from barbarism to civilization."[43] And like his predecessors, he pointed to biblical passages that demonstrated slavery's place in God's world. Brown, however, extended his positive defense of slavery into an attack on free society. To the argument that slavery played a moral and necessary role in southern society, he added a bold corollary: free labor, by definition, promised chaos, whether in societies where labor was cheap or dear. In the first instance, the miserable circumstances of "free" workers would result in their moral degradation. "If a man . . . is placed so low in the scale of society, that he has no hope of rising in it, he will have no incentive to virtuous conduct . . . and nothing keeps him from committing atrocious crimes, but the fear of a jail or corporal punishment; he would as soon be found drunk in a gutter as in an honest employment."[44] And "where the wages of labour are excessively high," continued Brown, "the labouring classes would . . . raise themselves to the level of those who employ them; and the state of dependence which tended to keep them sober and honest, no longer existing, they will rush headlong to the gratification of their passions," ending in "a state of general insubordination and immorality." In other words, free labor, no matter what the level of wages offered to the worker, nurtured iniquity. "Hence, the division of mankind into grades, and the mutual dependence and relations which result from them," concluded Brown, "constitute the very seal of civilization."[45] Demonstrating the centrality of this concept to his work, he offered lines from Shakespeare's *Troilus and Cressida* as his book's epigraph: "Take but degree away, untune that string, and hark! What discord follows."

These publications signify the increasing degree to which a positive, organic conception of slavery was affecting southern ideologues in the 1820s. As had been the case during the congressional debates over Missouri, white southerners were construing slavery more and more in terms of its positive role in a humane hierarchy that ostensibly respected the individuality of every member of society. The conception of the institution as a necessary evil was becoming less and less useful. If an author such as Edwin C. Holland conceded in one breath that Negroes threatened to destroy the white race, he spent the next twenty gasping for a less ominous conception of black chattel slavery. Like Furman, Dalcho, and Brown, Holland eventually espoused the familiar argument that the condition of the southern slave was "in every respect preferable to that of the poor laboring class of people of any Government on earth, and that if it were not for foreign, subsidiary causes [such as the meddling of antislavery activists], he would remain perfectly satisfied with his lot."[46] Indeed, Holland devoted pages of his book to the testimony of self-professed humanitarian slaveowners. He quoted George Edwards, who depicted his bondservants as "perfectly happy and contented with their situation." He presented Benjamin Roper's argument that "an *inhumane* master, is a very rare character; *such would be held in contempt and abhorrence.*" And Holland referred to Elias Horry's contention that southern slaves "enjoy a greater share of the blessings of life than falls to the lot of the laboring poor of most countries."[47]

A defense of slavery grounded in the recognition of slave individuality and humanity was slowly but perceptibly emerging as orthodoxy in the Deep South. When South Carolina planter Charles Cotesworth Pinckney— a nephew of his revered namesake—addressed the Agricultural Society of South Carolina in 1829 and pronounced that the "situation of the slave of America will not suffer by comparison with that of the labouring classes of Europe, or perhaps our own favored land," he was merely repeating a hackneyed message. By this time, his slaveowning audience doubtless expected him to dwell on the supposedly happy conditions that the slave enjoyed on southern plantations and to draw on the Bible for evidence of the South's moral standing. They were not disappointed.[48]

By the end of the decade, arguments such as these had become so entrenched in southern society that they affected even the intellectuals who prided themselves on free thinking. The shift in Thomas Cooper's public utterances on slavery serve as a dramatic case in point. Born and educated in England, Cooper entered the public debate over human bondage in 1791 as a fierce critic of the institution. His pamphlet *Remarkable Extracts and Observations on the Slave Trade* depicted the slaveholders as inhumane monsters who routinely tore children from their anguished parents.[49] Arriving in the United States in 1793, his aversion to slavery remained strong enough to steer him away from the South. In 1820, however, he relocated to Columbia, South Carolina, to accept a position as professor of chemistry at South Carolina College. Within a few years of his arrival, he had accepted the local wisdom concerning the righteousness of slavery. In his work *On the Constitution of the United States* (1826), Cooper noted that throughout history societies had relied on unfree labor and that the Bible sanctioned it. The southern slave, he now insisted, enjoyed better conditions than did free workers in industrial England. The man who had once struggled to defend African liberties from European depredations now argued that emancipation would transform blacks into "idle and useless vagabonds and thieves." Swayed by the proslavery mentality, Cooper committed his considerable intellectual energy to the southern cause and emerged as a leading spokesman for the states' rights philosophy.[50]

As those southerners commenting publicly on slavery endlessly parroted one another's pronouncements, they elevated the proslavery ideal into a defining creed that displaced more conventional emblems of southern virtue that antislavery reformers had learned to co-opt. Controversy over Thomas Jefferson's philosophical legacy revealed the extent to which the southern authors and speakers would jettison the past to place themselves on more secure ideological footing. Confronted by the Declaration of Independence and Jefferson's assertion (in his *Notes on the State of Virginia*) that "the whole commerce between master and slave is . . . despotism," South Carolina senator William Smith contradicted Jefferson "on the most unequivocal terms" by arguing that "the whole commerce between master and slave is patriarchal."[51] This disavowal of Jefferson was admired and repeated by authors such as Holland and Brown. Senator William Pinkney's vehement denial that all men were created equal likewise made its way into the southern political vocabulary.[52] To rally the South around a coherent rationale for unfree labor, proslavery ideologues proved willing to repudiate even the most cherished symbols of the Revolutionary era.

Only a fool would accept at face value the owners' professions about the relatively easy and enviable lives of their slaves. Demographic and archaeological evidence from the nineteenth century shows that conditions on Georgia and South Carolina plantations remained grim—particularly on lowcountry properties, where mortality rates approached those experienced in Europe during the Black Death.[53] However, one should not assume hypocrisy on the part of the planters because they idealized slavery while inflicting tremendous suffering on their slaves. To be sure, the slaveowners were avoiding the terrible truth about slavery by embracing the fiction that bondage was bestowing great benefits on the slave. But, in their case, the distinction between hypocrisy and denial is significant. The slaveowners were in deep denial about the actual conditions on their plantations—so much so that many southern masters were sincere when they pontificated about the degree to which their labor system served the slaves' interests as well as their own. To miss this point is to misunderstand how their regional political stance rested on a firmly established culture of corporate individualism. Surveying their private correspondence, one sees that by the 1820s, many slaveowners were struggling to maintain an identity as benevolent masters. And although practically every slaveholder abandoned this role when temper or financial needs required a brutal disregard for the slave's humanity, they eventually returned to their benevolent posturing to convince themselves (not to mention the increasingly critical world outside the South) of their own admirable intentions.

The owners considered their slaves' welfare in ways that transcended the purely economic principle of protecting a large investment. In a will written in 1823, one planter from coastal Georgia specifically requested that "old Negroes" (who returned only a minimal profit to their owners) "be treated with all the humanity & kindness necessary to their comfort." The powerful Georgia planter Edward Harden enjoyed "a close room and a good fire" in 1816, confessing to his wife that his own comfort "admonishes me that the negroes want shoes."[54] Such statements captured the manner in which the proslavery ethos operated. As improperly clothed slaves shivered in the November cold, their owners basked in the satisfying glow that emanated from their professed intention to take better care of their slaves in the future.

Hence Georgia slaveowner Howell Cobb—the namesake of his better-known nephew—could assert in 1817 that he was doing his slaves a favor by not emancipating them: "Such is the present existing state of society that by [freeing them] I may act improperly, and it is by no means improbable that it would be no real or lasting advantage to them, and I presume that their present condition, under the care and protection of generous & humane masters will be much better for them than a state of freedom." The English Parliament's debate over emancipation in the British West Indies prompted other slaveholders to assert that southern slaves "are better off than the majority of the poor of [England] who are obliged to work hard to maintain large families [and] who live in misery and poverty."[55]

As had been the case since the turn of the century, carefully orchestrated Christian missions ensured that the slaveholders would predicate their world view on the concept of enlightened stewardship. By the 1820s, these rapidly expanding religious enterprises were encouraging growing numbers of slaveowners to develop identities as benevolent masters. A Scottish visitor passing through Charleston in 1822 noted that "religion is rapidly progressing in this state and city." In his experience, "the people are too much refined to allow open violation of decency. . . . The sabbath is well kept, and Divine Service punctually attended, both by whites, and blacks." Indeed, Christian churches were multiplying so rapidly that when Juliana Margaret Conner passed through the South Carolina backcountry in 1827, she considered it "remarkable" to encounter "a poor looking" locale that lacked a place of worship.[56] And since ministers ranging from the Baptist Furman to the Episcopalian Dalcho were offering the same wisdom respecting the master-slave relationship, churches jointly played a crucial role in orienting the slaveholders toward a conservative, corporate ideology.

A culture built around the market for the printed word also continued to push the slaveholders toward a value system of corporate individualism. Despite the antebellum South's reputation as a region remarkably inhospitable to intellectual pastimes, renowned thinkers such as Hugh S. Legaré of Charleston bragged that "we have in this city the remnants of a state of improvement and elegance in society and all its accomplishments, such as exist nowhere else. Our scholars disciplined at Eton and Westminster are the only ones this country has ever seen that deserved the names." Legaré characterized Charleston as a haven from the "deep-rooted prejudice against bookish men" that he believed existed "all over the country." During this period of the nineteenth century, moreover, the market that expanded into the southern backcountry transformed books and periodicals into commodities that appealed to far more than just an urban, lowcountry audience of consumers. The sudden appearance of religious periodicals in the early-nineteenth-century South indicated that Christian messages about proper spiritual and domestic conduct could now sustain a readership on a regular weekly or monthly basis. The *Methodist Magazine*, for example, was published in New York but devoted considerable space to material from southern authors (which was only fitting because southerners made up some 40 percent of the American Methodist population and because the largest population of Methodists in any single state resided in South Carolina). In 1818, a North Carolina planter published in this periodical a description of one of his slaves, an elderly man who "had been a member of the Methodist Church near thirty years, and to the day of his death a pious and holy man." Upon the slave's death, his master was moved to renounce Deism and to profess his faith in the religion that, he believed, had guaranteed the slave's entry into heaven. Just as Edmund Botsford had done in *Sambo and Toney*, this slaveowner evoked imagery of faithful Christian slaves who promised, through their exemplary conduct, to effect a positive change in the white religious sensibility. The entire episode turned on an implicit embrace of the individual slave's religious conscience and an acceptance of the slave's innate capacity for moral development.[57]

During this era, the *Methodist Magazine* encouraged its readers to recognize that the corporate individualism nourished by Christianity would benefit individual slaves, individual masters, and society as a whole. Complaining about the widespread resistance that missionaries had encountered in the West Indies, a writer in the magazine took pains to establish in 1818 the existence of a "great number of respectable white inhabitants, owners of slaves, proprietors of estates, or connected with them, who have given great countenance and support to the mission, from their own experience of its beneficial effects upon the negro population." The "salutary effects produced by religious instruction upon their dispositions, morals, general comfort, industry, and contentedness" were especially evident when such qualities were compared with "the gross ignorance and viscious manners of the pagan negro population." Several years later, the South-Carolina Conference urged in the pages of the magazine that this mission be extended to the southern plantations. In making their case, the South Carolina Methodists once again presented slavery as an institution that was lifting blacks into a state of improvement: "We honestly believe that all the circumstances of his condition taken together as they are known to us, the negro in the Carolinas and Georgia, might on no temporal account, envy the peasant of some other Christian countries." These Methodists maintained that "many thousands of [slaves] are both better fed and clothed—and labour less—and are better attended to in sickness, than many of the white population of this, happiest of countries." The religious activists merely wanted to extend these supposedly happy circumstances to the slaves' "spiritual welfare," thereby completing their progression from impoverished savages to comfortable Christians.[58]

By the 1830s, religious periodicals published in the South were suggesting that it was on these grounds that the institution of slavery could best be defended—perhaps only be defended—from abolitionist criticism. The *Southern Christian Herald*, a Presbyterian newspaper published in Columbia, South Carolina, rebuked not only those "who believe slavery to be a curse to the Southern States" but also those who "view the negroes as a race designed only to be Slaves, and incapable of improvement—who hold the system to be the very best, and yet are opposed to Slaves receiving any religious instruction." The *Herald* was clearly upholding the morality of slavery by insisting that slaveowners respect bondservants' capacity for personal growth. "Nothing we believe would so soon terminate the system of Slavery," concluded the *Herald*, "as an unfeeling and unreasonable tyranny that had no regard for the happiness of the slave." At the same time, however, nothing would so quickly terminate the happiness of the slave, the paper suggested, as the abolition of slavery. Pointing to circumstances in Haiti, where slaves had seized their freedom during the French Revolution and had subsequently become "indolent and poor," the *Herald* insisted that abolition was "only another name for extermination" of the slave. The enlightened domesticity of the Christian plantation household promised a way past the twin dangers of a severe bondage that trampled the individual slave's happiness and an unruly freedom that allowed the slaves to lapse into vice and poverty.[59]

Expanding channels for commercial exchange did not merely enable Christian thinkers to spread this message across the region. Rather, the very cultural impulses undergirding market societies ensured that the possibility of progressive change would become a prominent feature of the Christian, slaveowning world view. Amid the transatlantic economic and cultural framework that was materializing in the modern era, the successful exchange of commodities for profit depended increasingly on the appeal to a wide audience of consumers. After all, the broader culture of the market must repeatedly convince consumers that the purchase of a particular item will improve the buyer's quality of life. In the slaveowning South, the pro-

slavery ideology was itself becoming a commodity. To convince white southerners to buy into their value system, religious activists needed to awaken in
these individuals the sense that progressive possibilities abounded—that
spiritual inaction would actually hasten slavery's decline. Evangelical culture in general reached out to segments of the population that had not yet
arrived at the top rungs of society. The path to salvation marked by evangelical rhetoric swayed so many southerners because it enabled them to look
past social conventions that had traditionally marginalized them as uncouth and insignificant, both economically and spiritually. Given this context, one can understand the evangelicals' insistence that slaves too possessed
the capacity for improvement. To reject this possibility was to embrace a
status quo that held no place for social mobility. For upwardly mobile slaveowners and would-be slaveowners, the cultural dynamic of the market enabled them to purchase religious respectability at the same time as they out-
fitted their plantation households with material goods such as clocks, china,
and fashionable clothing. The only price that the slaveholders needed to pay
(in addition to the modest subscription fees for periodicals such as the Herald) was to revise their understanding of human capacity for growth.[60]

As Christian reformers learned to exploit market mechanisms for spreading the gospel, they perceived that certain risks accompanied the proliferating impact of the written word. The turn of the century heralded the arrival
of the age of the novel, a textual form that, according to critics, could injure
the sense of morality of readers. Religious condemnation of such fiction
reveals the early-nineteenth-century American perception that novels
awakened incredibly powerful emotional responses in their readers. The
Southern Christian Herald, for example, blamed the "indulgence in words of
fiction" for "a tendency to give way to the wild play of imagination" and for
"a disruption of the harmony which ought to exist between moral emotions
and conduct." The Herald averred that "in the healthy state of moral feelings
. . . the emotion of sympathy excited by a tale of sorrow ought to be followed
by some efforts for the relief of the sufferer." Novels, however, allegedly produced such emotions "without the corresponding conduct" thereby resulting in a "cold and barren sentimentalism" instead of an "active benevolence." These accusations against popular fiction raised the important point
(sketched out more fully by modern scholars such as Cathy N. Davidson)
that novels could present readers with subversive messages about the existing social order. Still, having learned to encode their own agenda in fictive
narratives, religious reformers could not divorce their movement from a
broader print culture that, as matters turned out, often promoted the same

values as explicitly Christian tracts. In the very same issue of the *Herald* that denounced novels, the editors accepted advertisements for novels from booksellers. While some religious authorities continued to condemn the novel as dangerous and frivolous, the affinity between fiction and moral purpose deepened in the antebellum period. The slaveowning reader could draw equally relevant moral lessons from readings as diverse as religious periodicals and the chivalric novels penned by such authors as Jane Porter and Walter Scott.[61]

Clearly, popular fiction of this era had a powerful impact on white southern thinking. Demonstrating an increasing demand for entertaining texts, southern book peddlers such as Mason Locke Weems informed suppliers that they "could vend a vast many . . . fine sentimental novels." Private correspondence reveals that these works left a deep impression on their readers' perspective on society. When Ann Middleton Izard's carriage broke down in Charleston in 1826, she viewed the scene in literary terms as an unfolding chivalric drama. "Here was an adventure" that she later described to her grandmother: "In this dilemma a knight-errant appeared, and proffered his services." Juliana Conner employed identical imagery as she recounted a young couple's failed elopement in 1827. In her opinion, the suitor "was bound by all the laws of chivalry at least to break a lance" as he defended his love from parental interference. But to Conner's disappointment, "his oath if engraved was forgot[ten] for he relinquished her [to her father] doubtless to perform severe penance for her flight." Significantly, as slaveowners like Robert Mackay immersed themselves in the "beautiful style" of their favorite authors, they attempted to cast their own mastery in a noble light. Immediately after discussing the writings of Lady Mary Wortley Montagu in 1825, Mackay contemplated the fate of a disobedient slave whom he nonetheless wished "to remain in our family." "Let us endeavor," he instructed his relative, to "consign to oblivion his past conduct & anticipate the probability of his future improvement & Let us . . . endeavour to rescue the deluded captive," whom Mackay compared to an "unguarded reptile" who could be "hurried into irretrievable ruin" by a "Russian Despot" before he could "supplicate mercy." Although somewhat incoherent, Mackay's mixture of exotic metaphors reveals with great clarity his belief that power should be tempered by compassion for the weak—a belief that had been nourished by his reading.[62]

There was, of course, a terrible irony to this cultural dynamic. The maturation of the southern domestic market had enabled religious reformers to acquire sufficient capital to construct their churches and had allowed contemporary authors such as Walter Scott to reach an audience of slaveowners who then portrayed their plantations as "enchanting" scenes of tremendous virtue and compassion. But as the slaves themselves never had the luxury of forgetting, the primary economic function of the southern market was the production and sale of rice and cotton as staple crops. The same commercial network that conveyed the latest English novels to Savannah and Charleston encouraged the planters to exploit their slaves with increasing efficiency. In this sense, the mobility of literary ideals was made possible by the most unsavory commerce imaginable: a market for human lives that rightly horrified unaccustomed observers. Witnessing a slave auction in South Carolina in 1822, a Scottish visitor was struck by "a mother of six" offered for sale with only her youngest child: "She was torn from the others, and her husband was a hundred miles distant, sold to another master, never to see her more." The traveler then "shrunk with horror as she was dragged away weeping and clasping the child to her breast."[63]

More recent scholarship has demonstrated that the southern slaveholders committed such atrocities on a scale far larger than historians had previously imagined.[64] Yet in spite of these enormities—or perhaps because of them—the slaveowners continued to view their actions through the warped prism of their proslavery dogma. On occasion individual planters expressed a reluctance to "separate families" of slaves.[65] William R. Davie of Landsford, South Carolina, reunited one slave husband with his wife because Davie "could not [bear to see] the poor creature torn from all that ought or does interest him."[66] But even the masters who demonstrated compassion for their slaves would seldom censure their less scrupulous fellow planters, let alone criticize the institution of slavery as a whole. Instead, the slaveholders of this period collectively generated the myth that they could segregate mercenary concerns from the master-slave relationship.

Enough planters subscribed to this deluded notion of slavery that they managed to convince visitors—sometimes hostile ones—that their slaves benefited from bondage. After moving from Connecticut to Charleston in 1821, T. S. Mills confessed that while he had "always believed that [the slaves] were most cruelly used," he discovered that "the Slaves in this place are much happier than a large number of poor people that I could mention in Colebrook," his hometown. The white working class in the North, he opined, had "hard and cruel masters" of their own, "and altho the people are free in N[ew] E[gland] yet they are frequently more pres[sed] by the rich, than the slaves are by their masters."[67] After spending several months among the slaveowners, the Scottish traveler who had been appalled by the slave auction revised his opinion of his southern hosts. Notwithstanding his poignant encounter with the slave mother crying as she was torn from her family, the Scot contended that Charleston slaves were "apparently the happiest of creatures. Grief, despondency, melancholy, or even serious reflection fled their presence [and] . . . care seemed to belong to the white man."[68] Following his lengthy exposure to the slaveowners' humanitarian pretensions, he fully believed that "a white man in the eastern states does more than five of these blacks"—that "free" whites in the North actually led a more grueling existence than bondservants in the South.[69]

The slaveowners, moreover, believed their own act. In previous decades, they had extended their conception of family to include their "domesticated" slaves. By the 1820s, many slaveowners spoke of their slaves as their own children who needed and deserved their masters' care. Richard Furman captured the essence of this new standard for mastery in the tract that he published in the wake of the Vesey conspiracy: "A master may, in an important sense, be the guardian and even father of his slaves. They become a part of his family, (the whole, forming under him a little community) and the care of ordering it, and of providing for its welfare, devolves on him." Far from being empty propaganda in the campaign against northern critics, this defense of slavery was already deeply embedded in the slaveowners' world view. Charges of cruelty toward slaves offended planters such as J. R. Prosser, who by this time staked their reputations as gentlemen on their concern for their dependents.[70]

In some plantation households, the organic standard for master-slave relations was powerful enough to breed contention between slaveowners and the overseers responsible for keeping the slaves under control. When slaves belonging to the Pinckney family violently resisted their instructions in 1824, their overseer's desire for revenge conflicted with his employer's insistence that he had been placed on their property "to protect my Negroes, not to kill them." Seeking to justify his conduct, the overseer intimated the need for a less lenient approach to plantation management. In his opinion, the "near 30 armed men" who had helped him to restore order following the incident had "sc[ared] them very muc[h]" by "giv[ing] them a threatening reprimand." He contended that, as a result, they "appear[ed] to be more obedient than they have been since I have been on the [job]." The Pinckneys subsequently replaced this man with an overseer who attempted to reconcile a regard for the slaves' individual welfare with an unyielding management philosophy. "As you requested," wrote their new employee in 1827, "I will endeavour to treat [the slaves] with humanity as far as my calling will admit." At the same time, however, he "thought it advisable to observe such rules as would bring them to a sense of their duties"—an approach that he believed "would prevent as much as possible the necessity of punishment." When he concluded that "they now appear to know their place & seem very cheerful in the discharge of their duty," the overseer was tying his authority to the notion that well-established social hierarchy served the needs of slaves as well as masters.[71]

If the expectation that household authority be administered with humanity and restraint complicated the relationship between planter and overseer, it also occasionally became a source of tensions between white parents and children. Writing to his father in 1828, South Carolina resident John Bones expressed concern for his brother who he believed had been mistreated "at home." "You are much more harsh with him," he lectured his father, "than you are with any of your negroes."[72] Slaveowning fathers could also express reservations to their children about the potential impact of organic doctrine on the master-slave relationship. In 1825, South Carolina planter James B. Richardson confronted the anguish of his son, William, who blamed himself for the ailment of a favorite slave. The slave in question had traveled to Columbia to attend to William, only to fall ill upon his arrival. "But from all this," James Richardson reminded his son, "it does not follow that you or any person whatever could be correctly [blamed]." "Why then, My Son, give yourself such uneasiness," he continued, "more than what would naturally result from feeling for a fellow creature, a valuable servant, & one extremely fond of you, & warmly attach'd to you & all that you are interested in?"[73] In this case, a father was attempting to teach his son to channel concern for the slaves in an appropriate direction. First and foremost, conceptions of corporate individualism were intended to comfort the slaveowner, not the slave. Under no circumstance did most slaveowners believe that they should feel guilty for the suffering of their bondservants. Although the planters eagerly suppressed the slaves' autonomy, they avoided blame for any anguish experienced by their black "children."

Of all the slaveholders in the Deep South, the rice planters along the Georgia and South Carolina coast proved most adept at rationalizing their slaves' misery simply because there was so much of it on their tidewater properties. Since the colonial era, planters had acknowledged the dangers of the lowcountry. Devastated by disease, early settlers in the coastal Deep South quickly discerned the perils of their new environment.[74]

By the mid-1700s wealthy tidewater landowners in South Carolina had learned to avoid their plantations in the summer, when sickness was rampant.[75] Tidewater planters continued to note the prevalence of disease in the nineteenth century. Frederick Dalcho observed in 1820 that "few of the [lowcountry] Planters now reside on their plantations during the sickly months." Before purchasing property in the Savannah lowcountry in 1830, Langdon Cheves was warned that "the mortality on the river is . . . a sad drawback to the otherwise certain profit of our fine and fertile lands."[76] Charleston itself endured its share of disease, earning the epithet "city of disasters." But for the tidewater plantation owners, it served as a veritable haven from the risks of life on their coastal property.[77]

Time and time again, the region's inhabitants commented on the poor health of the lowcountry. According to one contemporary observer, "so awfully dreadful was the yellow & billious fever" in 1817 that "one sixth of the population of whites died this year" in Beaufort, South Carolina, as well as the "900 persons [who] died in Savannah [the preceding] October." Three years later, Savannah resident William Bulloch faced the "harrowing task [of] recount[ing] the afflictions of our devoted and ill-fated city." "The inquiry," in his opinion, "will not be Who have died? But, who have escaped death." In 1834 Savannah River planter John Berkley Grimball stated that "on one plantation *half the workers have died*—on another 40—on another 14—on another 12."[78] Langdon Cheves claimed that the lowcountry was "dotted by like misfortunes." Having "placed on [his] Rice Plantation upwards of 330 negroes & . . . having never sold one," Cheves asserted that "only 230" slaves remained alive.[79]

Despite such powerful and abundant evidence, the slaveowners never acknowledged that they were killing their slaves by forcing them to labor in a patently unhealthy environment. Like many other nineteenth-century Americans, both northern and southern, the tidewater planters believed that victims of disease were somehow to blame for their own illness—that the morally and physically irresponsible brought sickness upon themselves. Medical authorities such as the Savannah physician William Coffee Daniell conceptualized disease as a force alien to the community. Writing in 1826, he attributed a yellow fever epidemic to an influx of Irish families, whose "crowded" households "greatly increased" the city's "filth."[80] By this point in time, inhabitants of the Deep South were viewing the sickness as a "Strangers Fever" that primarily threatened members of the lower classes.[81]

By reducing the pathological threat to a question of "habits," the lowcountry scientific community offered a rationale for slave suffering that could be used by slaveowners across the South.[82] Even the more charitably inclined planters such as the Richardsons had little difficulty blaming sickness and suffering on the poor judgment of slaves, who were deemed intellectually deficient. Richardson reminded his son that the slave who became sick in Savannah had been "so exceedingly desirous to go, & plead hard for the indulgence, & enlisted a warm advocate in his behalf, that I felt measurably compel'd to privilege him."[83] Here, Richardson was intimating that had his own superior judgment prevailed, no tragedy would have ensued. Other slaveowners likewise blamed rampant sickness on their slaves' deficient judgment. One South Carolina overseer informed his employer in 1804 that a number of slaves had died because of their "constant eating of poison Berrys." In the same letter, he also speculated that the slave "mothers['] carelessness" had "killed" a number of babies on the property.[84]

In response, the slaveowners advocated a series of preventative measures that, unfortunately, offered their bondservants scant defense against sickness. Nevertheless, the planters could take pride in "spar[ing] no effort to insure the health of the negroes by establishing comfortable hospitals . . . and by procuring medical advice when required."[85] Masters in the Deep South were looking to the future with unbridled and unjustified optimism—an optimism that hinged on their ongoing campaign to supervise their estates according to the latest scientific and humanitarian principles. Typifying this movement to reform plantation management were the slaveholders of Edgefield, South Carolina, who organized an agricultural society dedicated to "advanc[ing] the agricultural art."[86] Societies of this type offset fears about unhealthy slave populations, declining soil fertility, and the stagnant market for cotton and rice. The reformers argued that if only the slaveowners learned to regulate their property according to scientific principles, both whites and blacks could flourish. Although the owners blamed plantation disease on the slave population's deficiencies, their campaign to solve the problem called for an intimate, mutually beneficial, master-slave relationship.[87] In the long run, they insisted that their population of happy, well-trained slaves would put to rest intimations that bondage entailed oppression.

To appreciate the currency of this idea among nineteenth-century slaveowners, one need only consider diverging white stereotypes of African American and American Indian identities. During the colonial period, imperial officials cultivated alliances with various Native American tribes "to keep our numerous Negroes in some Awe." English commentators such as George Milligen-Johnston considered it a "very lucky Circumstance" that a "natural Dislike and Antipathy" subsisted between their "dangerous [black] Domestics" and their "Indian neighbors." Johnston maintained that "it can never be our Interest to extirpate" the Indians "or to force them from their Lands," because "their Ground would soon be taken up by runaway Negroes from our Settlements, whose Numbers would daily increase."[88] Having negotiated with certain Indians as allies in a racial hierarchy that relegated blacks to the bottom rung, white authorities concluded that "however Savage they may appear," the Indians were "not so destitute of natural Sense, or the knowledge of their own Interests, as not to be Sensible of the Importance they are to the Europeans."[89] The fruitful alliance with some Indians offset prejudicial notions that Native Americans were an inferior, "perfidious" race.[90] Indeed, some scholars have gone so far as to argue that the colonists did not perceive a clear racial difference between themselves and their Native American neighbors.[91]

By the nineteenth century, however, this racial dynamic had shifted dramatically. Having secured control over society (in the form of their own republican government with the military power to defend its borders), the slaveholders no longer required Native American assistance to subordinate their black labor force. On the contrary, the Indians seriously threatened the white social order. Slave flight into their territory in Florida contributed to the federal government's decision to wage a campaign against the Seminoles following the War of 1812.[92] More important, Indian settlements were blocking expansion of the plantation economy into northern Georgia. Given these new political circumstances, white southerners began to conceptualize Native American identity in virulently racist terms. Savannah resident William Bulloch concluded in 1817 that to "civilize the Savage Indian . . . would be a dreadful undertaking." "I scarcely know what ought to be the measure of compensation to the Man of Society and family," he averred, "who would embark in such a task."[93] Although Thomas Jefferson had once applauded the Indians' virtues, by 1818 he considered them "chain[ed] to their present state of barbarism and wretchedness" by "a bigoted veneration for the supposed superlative wisdom of their fathers." And after visiting the United States in 1831, Alexis de Tocqueville wrote that "from whatever angle one regards the destinies of the North American natives, one sees nothing but irremediable ills: if they remain savages, they are driven along before the march of progress; if they try to become civilized, contact with more-civilized people delivers them over to oppression and misery."[94]

Meanwhile, the slaveholders were elevating the character of the black slave as they recast the Native American as a luckless savage destined to be left behind by advancing civilization. Passing through north Georgia Indian territory in 1828, a white traveler compared the degraded character of his slaveowning Indian host with that of his "negro woman much more decent than himself." Whereas the slave had just come "from preaching at a Baptist church," the owner "belonged to no church [and] argued against all religion." Domesticated by white civilization, the slave now demonstrated superiority over the Indian, whom whites referred to (in language previously reserved for slaves) as "a vile beast."[95] This theme emerged with even greater clarity when William Gilmore Simms visited the region in 1831. Struck by the manner in which an Indian slaveowner deferred to his black slave, Simms speculated that "acknowledging, as they do, the superiority of the whites," the Indians "conceive that some portion of those faculties which impart . . . that superiority, must, necessarily, have been acquired by the negroes" through their exposure to white civilization. "Can there be a doubt but that authority of the master alone," suggested slaveowners such as Whitemarsh Seabrook, "prevents his slaves from experiencing the fate of the aborigines of America?"[96]

The degree to which the slave had been raised to a more improved station and the Indian had been left behind became the criteria by which the slaveowners measured the progress of their society. Of course, they were also impressed by the century's advancements in the realm of technology. The slaveowners, after all, had been welcoming such innovations since the colonial period.[97] After inspecting a steamboat in Charleston harbor in 1817, one southerner wrote home to express his pleasure with "how regular everything went on"—with "the ingenuity of man." Two years later, Georgia slaveowner James Barrow traveled to Milledgeville and "took my little son and went to see the steamboat," which he called "a wonder indeed."[98] Ultimately, however, the slaveholders constructed their progressive sensibility around the belief that their mastery was improving the character of society.[99] A prosperous tomorrow, in the planters' opinion, depended not just on improved technology but on superior ideals as well. In this sense, they applauded scientific progress because it promised to reform white and black character as well as outdated machinery and exhausted soil. And they harbored their faith in the future even while their slaves suffered and expired in appallingly high numbers.

As the slaveholders cultivated their exalted notions about the morality of plantation society, their opinion of the northern states plummeted. In 1826 Savannah resident Robert Harden acknowledged the healthful benefits of the northern climate when he visited Philadelphia, but he tempered his enthusiasm with his distaste for its residents. "If I could like the people here I would like to live here altogether," he wrote his sister, "but they are sordid, selfish, and very often mean."[100] The Missouri controversy had confirmed southern suspicions about northern society, and the slaveowners feared that the radical forces they witnessed at work in the North would permeate their own communities. When South Carolina planter Elias Ball journeyed to New York in 1823, he discovered, to his dismay, that "the Black gentry of [the city] have opened a Theatre and tell fine stories about their brethren at the South in the Cotton and Rice fields."[101] The potentially incendiary relationship between northern free blacks and southern slaves was not lost on the planters of the Deep South, who had just uncovered Denmark Vesey's plans for revolt. Concerned slaveowners fretted that "in these times of emancipation, freedom and liberality, [the] Gentlemen freeholders in the Southern States will be in constant apprehension, & terror will keep [them] on the everlasting alert."[102]

In preceding decades, this fear had been counterbalanced by the slaveowners' faith that they could manipulate the federal government to protect their regional interests. And because southern economic and population growth initially appeared to be keeping pace with the North, previous generations of slaveowners had no reason to anticipate a decline in their influence in Washington. During the early national period, it was discontented northerners who threatened to secede from a union that was damaging their regional economy. Whatever their antipathy toward Hamiltonian financial policies that privileged commerce and industry over agriculture, the slaveowners of the early republic mounted no equivalent to the Hartford Convention, which they had savagely criticized for threatening the Union. By the time that Congress turned its attention to the Missouri question, however, many slaveowners perceived that they were becoming a minority within the nation that their forebears had battled so valiantly to establish. Northern representatives noted with satisfaction that "we have the numerical force"—a "majority [that] will increase upon the taking of every census."[103] Proslavery southerners normally saw little merit in the arguments of their political enemies, but on this point they tended to agree. The slaveowners' need to maintain their strength in the Senate (where state population did not affect representation) inspired them to fight with intensity for slavery in the western territories. Henceforth, the slaveowners' sectional mentality would increasingly define their stance on crucial political issues.

The revolutionary generation that had risked lives and fortunes to establish the American nation was fading from view. Into their place came politicians who forged reputations not as champions of national interest but as watchmen for their home state's rights. Prominent figures such as John C. Calhoun of South Carolina personified this transition in political goals. Born in the closing days of the Revolution, Calhoun was educated at Moses Waddel's academy and Yale University before running successfully for Congress in 1810. With other young representatives from the southern and western states, he quickly earned the reputation as a "war hawk" who wanted to strengthen the national government so that it could protect the country's honor from foreign abuse. And, in 1816 he argued in favor of tariffs, reasoning that the "policy of the country required protection of our manufacturing establishments."[104] Unlike John Randolph (who even at this early date was arguing that tariffs were "an immense tax on one portion of the community to put money in the pockets of another"), Calhoun believed that his home region's welfare was intertwined with the rest of the nation's and that southerners were ultimately well served by a thriving New England manufacturing community. Hoping "to bind the republic together" into one prosperous economy, the South Carolina representative also advocated the national bank as well as government support for a "perfect system of roads and canals." Far from jealously guarding the South from a potentially dangerous federal government, Calhoun wanted to "conquer space" that still separated the slave economy from the rest of the nation.[105]

By the later 1820s, however, Calhoun had engineered one of the great political reversals in American history. The tariff that he had once supported had been steadily rising, and the northerners who were served by it were becoming more aggressive in their criticism of slaveholding society. In response, Calhoun began to criticize federal interference with the southern economy even as he served both the John Quincy Adams and Andrew Jackson administrations as vice president. In the fall of 1828, he secretly penned the *South Carolina Exposition*, a tract in which he asserted that sovereignty remained vested in state government instead of in Washington, D.C. Just eight years earlier, Calhoun had denied that "there is a conspiracy against our property" in the South. "Our true system is to look to the country; and to support such measures and such men, without a regard to sections as are best calculated to advance the general interest."[106] But the antipathy generated by the decade's momentous political debates had changed his mind. Although he maintained in his *Exposition* that he would still "desire never to speak of our [southern] country . . . but [of] one great whole, having a

common interest," the injustice of the tariff had compelled him "to adopt
. . . the use of sectional language."[107]

Calhoun's work touched off a political firestorm that resulted in his resignation from the Jackson administration, but despite his reputation as a
radical leader, he was not blazing a trail into uncharted ideological territory.
The sectional fire that consumed Calhoun had already pushed other prominent southerners toward open confrontation with a perceived northern
conspiracy. In 1823, a Georgia newspaper editor warned that sectional fears
threatened "to bury our free governments in irretrievable ruin."[108] Whitemarsh Seabrook, a planter from the South Carolina lowcountry, published
*A Concise View of the Critical Situation, and Future Prospects of the Slave-
Holding States* (1825), in which he warned his fellow southerners that, owing
to the agitation of northern antislavery activists, "the tenure by which we
hold our slaves is daily becoming less secure." When Seabrook addressed the
United Agricultural Society of South Carolina two years later, he drew attention to "the anomalous spectacle of so inconsiderable a party as the
[northern] manufacturers swaying the deliberations of the national councils." Portraying them as "wily in their schemes, and bent on the effectua-
tion of their purpose," Seabrook posited the existence of a sinister northern
plot against the South.[109]

Such sentiment immediately touched a nerve in the Deep South, where
resentful planters readily attributed the hated tariff to an effort on the part
of industrialists and abolitionists to destroy their society. Thomas Cooper
speculated to an assembly of South Carolina planters in 1827 that their
northern enemies' "avowed object now is, by means of a drilled and managed majority in Congress, permanently to force upon us a system, whose
effect will be, to sacrifice the south to the north, by converting us into colonists and tributaries."[110] To disarm their foes, southern statesmen such as
Georgia governor George Troup (who spoke to the state's General Assembly
in 1825) pronounced the wisdom of "strictly confin[ing] the action of the
general government to the sphere marked out and limited by the express
provisions of the constitution."[111] Because they believed that the national
government had become the vehicle for northern schemes, the slaveholders
sought to restrict its influence as much as possible.[112]

As southern ideologues such as Cooper defended the liberties of the
"planting interest," they discerned their need for a more coherent southern
identity around which they could rally the slaveowners. In previous decades,
intercourse between slaveowners and a transatlantic intellectual community had exposed them to the corporate standard that became the founda-

tion for their proslavery philosophy. The political battles of the 1820s ironically underscored the benefits to be derived from a clearly demarcated southern culture. In 1827 South Carolina senator Robert Y. Hayne bemoaned that "we have been emancipated from a dependence on Great Britain, but as if destined to pass our lives in a state of mental slavery, we have merely exchanged the chains of Old England for those of New England." "The Southern states," he continued, "have been long regarded abroad, and have submitted to be so regarded, as incapable of any great literary efforts. We have been content like children to receive such mental food as our Eastern friends thought proper to bestow upon us." The solution, in his opinion, was the "establishment of a *Southern Review* after the plan of the North American and Philadelphia Quarterly Review"—a "species of periodical works" that had "exerted a wonderful control over public opinion both in Europe and America." By addressing "itself to a class of persons who have great influence in giving the tone to the sentiments and opinions of the people," Hayne intended the *Southern Review* to instill "sound southern principles" among the rising generation of slaveholders.[113]

The following year saw the publication of not only the *Southern Review* but also the *Southern Agriculturist* and, in the years to follow, a host of explicitly sectional periodicals. These works affirmed the morality of the slaveholding South even as they attempted to reform it by enlightening the reading public. On the question of slavery, authors in the *Southern Agriculturist* reinforced the by now familiar notion that masters and slaves enjoyed a reciprocal relationship—that they "always pull the same end of the rope."[114] During this period, leading southern authors still paid homage to the virtues of the Union but, with increasing frequency, indicated that they loved their nation because it had served the cause of their "country," a term they reserved for their home state. When in 1827 William Gilmore Simms celebrated Jackson's decade-old victory over England at New Orleans, he pointed to Jackson's southern roots to emphasize that the Union itself could not have survived without the slaveholders' sacrifices.[115]

As the slaveholders self-consciously generated their own regional identity, the cultural institutions that had previously linked the sections together began to weaken under the strain of sectionalism. In 1817 southern Baptists fretted that a dispute over foreign missionaries would shatter their denomination "into Parties."[116] Henry Holcombe, a minister who had risen to prominence in South Carolina and Georgia before moving to Philadelphia's First Baptist Church in 1812, stirred up the controversy when he contested the Philadelphia Baptist Association's decision to send a female missionary to India. Holcombe had long advocated taking measures to protect the welfare of neglected women, establishing the Savannah Female Asylum in 1801. But to place women in the position of missionary was simply too much for the minister, who balanced his compassion for the unfortunate with the biblical imperative that the lower orders of society should give "honor to whom honor is due."[117] The slaveholding South had nurtured this conservative social vision, and not surprisingly, Charleston Baptist authorities took Holcombe's side in the matter. Richard Furman expressed his "fear that at Philadelphia there is a source of Evil, which is likely to spread its powerful Influence far. In fact I fear, that Satan has taken some of our Brethren there in a Snare."[118]

This ideological battle did not separate the Baptists along neat sectional lines. Holcombe's Philadelphia church had precipitated the struggle by withdrawing from that city's Baptist Association. Nevertheless, northern and southern religious authorities had long since adopted very different philosophies concerning the relationship between individual rights and the larger corporate good. And as the debate over slavery intensified in the 1820s, southern Christians formally articulated a defense of human bondage that had been circulating in their communities since the late eighteenth century. By 1820, one Kentucky Baptist was heaping scorn on northern missionaries whose "Female Societies, Cent Societies, Mite Societies, Children Societies, and even Negro Societies" gave off the odor of "the *New England Rat*."[119] And as we have seen, South Carolina Methodists issued a report in 1824 which, in effect, instructed northern critics of slavery to tend to their own considerable social problems rather than interfering with an institution of unfree labor that supposedly protected the slaves' interests.[120] Southern Christians now guarded slavery as their own concern, expressing their perspective not only through sermons but also through the numerous religious periodicals established in the South during the 1820s.[121] As Frederick Dalcho opined, "persons born and educated in all the prejudices of non-slave-holding countries, and mere itinerants here for a few winter months, are unfit for the instruction" of slaves. "We claim the right," he continued, "of managing our own affairs, according to our own discretion."[122]

Over the first fifteen years of the nineteenth century, the market for fiction and Christian writings had nurtured romantic notions of slave ownership in the Deep South. During the ensuing fifteen-year period, the planters' intensifying battle with antislavery forces required them to put those notions to political use. Cognizant that their ongoing dependence on unfree labor was turning them into a "peculiar" society, the slaveowners mounted an aggressive defense of their way of life in the 1820s. In the process, ideologues seeking to defend the South tended to inflate the cultural distance between their moral, slaveholding society and the anarchy that they perceived in the North.

Of course, the slaveowners' ties to a broader transatlantic community had first exposed them to the doctrine of corporate individualism. Unaware or unwilling to acknowledge this fact, leading planters believed that only distinctly southern cultural institutions could instill and protect the organic hierarchy that supposedly constituted the foundation of a virtuous society. The politicians seeking to control southern cultural development fully appreciated the role that the mass media now played in shaping the slaveowners' ideals. "In the present state of society," wrote Robert Hayne in 1827, "it is almost unnecessary to notice [and] it would not be easy to exaggerate the influence of the Press. This instrument of knowledge and of power, once so humble, so insignificant, known only in the closets of the studious . . . has in modern days, in consequence of the wide diffusion of education, been directed to the great mass of society with decided effect, and now exercises an almost despotic control over the opinions of mankind."[123] Turning the mass media toward their own political purposes, the planters hoped to mobilize the entire white South in support of the master class. The diffusion of carefully selected information had become the means by which the planters intended to overcome alternative viewpoints respecting slavery.

> *For the slave*
> *question will be*
> *the real issue—*
> *All others will be*
> *absorbed in it.*
> WILLIAM C. PRESTON,
> 1830

CHAPTER SIX

The Tyranny of the Majority

Slaveholder Identity and Democratic Politics in the 1830s

By the 1830s the slaveholders were employing the language of sectionalism to bring political unity to the white South. Cognizant that an ever widening electorate might turn into an unruly majority, the planters hinged their hopes for future security on their campaign to instill the proper conservative values among their countrymen. That whites as well as blacks required discipline had become apparent when students at South Carolina College—the institution charged with "improving [the] civilization" of the backcountry—periodically rioted against school authority during the 1820s.[1] After one such incident in 1822, just months before the Vesey insurrection scare, college president Thomas Cooper reported that "the Professors were threatened, pistols were snapt at them, guns fired near them, Col. John Taylor (formerly of the Senate from this place) was in company with myself burnt in Effigy, the windows of my bedroom were repeatedly shattered at various hours of the night, & guns fired under my window." Confronted by evidence that their own sons were capable of rebelling against authority, the slaveowners suspected that "Democracy" had "run mad."[2] Any lingering doubts on this question were put to rest in 1829, when a chagrined Hugh Legaré watched the teeming masses "crow[d] into the splendid rooms" of Andrew Jackson's White House "without order or restraint, pell mell, with fair ladies & gentleman."[3]

Strangely enough, the slaveholders tackled the challenge of democracy by offering a hierarchical social philosophy for mass consumption. Disseminating their ideals through the modern media of regional publications and political organizations, they turned social change engendered by market society toward their own end. Elite planters realized that they were vastly outnumbered by a white yeomanry that owned few or no slaves. "On the cause of the yeoman," observed Whitemarsh Seabrook in 1827, "rests the prosperity, and, perhaps, the perpetuity of our domestic institutions."[4] The planters' trick lay in convincing their less fortunate neighbors to support a social order in which families with slaves (who made up only a third of the white population) controlled over 90 percent of the wealth.[5] When South Carolina governor Stephen Miller declared to the legislature in 1829 that "slavery is not a national evil" but "a national benefit," he based his case on the fact that "wealth" supposedly had "no influence at the polls" in slaveholding society.[6]

The appeal to sectional spirit and the promise of social mobility enabled the slaveowners to democratize their region on decidedly inegalitarian terms. Ironically, the rapid maturation of southern consumer culture strengthened the reactionary hand of an outnumbered ruling elite that, under different circumstances, would have surrendered its power. Radical southern politicians offered more than empty rhetoric. They argued for regional unity with language than appealed to the slaveowners' central values—with words crafted and marketed with the savvy of the century's most clever businesspeople. Notwithstanding the slaveowners' heated political conflict over how best to respond to the tariff, they increasingly agreed about the principles that defined their world view even while they argued about which political course would best secure their goals. Chivalric fantasies about enlightened mastery had taken center stage in the Deep South and would provide the context for all subsequent discussion about the slaveholders' future within or without the Union.

As their influence within the federal government declined, the slaveowners rejected fiscal policies that they had formerly supported for the good of the nation. First among these was the tariff, a tax on imported consumer goods that enabled northern manufacturers to compete against lower-priced European textiles. In 1820, southern congressmen mustered enough votes to prevent an increase in the tariff that they believed damaged their plantation economy. By 1824, however, they no longer possessed sufficient congressional power to block national revenue schemes. Four years later, the southern congressmen seeking to dismantle the tariff resorted to parliamentary tricks that ultimately blew up in their faces. Rather than pressing for lower duties, the slaveowners sought to increase the tariff on imported raw materials required by some northern manufacturers. Driving a wedge between these industrialists and their counterparts who stood to benefit from a high tariff, the southerners hoped to acquire the necessary votes to sink the bill. But to their chagrin, northern congressmen remained committed to the legislation, and the Tariff of Abominations (as the southerners referred to it) became law.[7]

Although South Carolina statesmen such as John C. Calhoun complained about the "tyranny" of the northern congressional majority, they had not yet lost hope in national politics. Through the election in 1828 of Andrew Jackson, himself a slaveowner born in South Carolina, the planters hoped to obtain redress in Washington, D.C. Jackson had already secured the plurality of the popular vote in the presidential campaign of 1824, but because he had not obtained a majority within the electoral college, the decision landed in the House of Representatives. There, Kentucky presidential candidate Henry Clay threw his support behind John Quincy Adams, enabling the Massachusetts statesman to gain the White House. Empowered by an expanding franchise and appalled by the "corrupt bargain" that had thwarted the voters' will, three times as many voters turned out in 1828, ensuring a landslide victory for Jackson.[8]

The South was now rid of the hated John Quincy Adams.[9] And in the weeks preceding Jackson's inauguration, Thomas Cooper thanked God that he had "been not a little instrumental in turning out" the "yankee" president in favor of Jackson. Although Cooper considered him "ill-informed" on the question of the tariff, radical southern politicians looked to him as "a Pacificator" capable of resolving the "difficulties which the [Adams] administration have created."[10] Eager to give the new president a chance to lobby Congress for a reduced tariff, Cooper anticipated "the Tariff question [being] brought on, not in the present Congress, but the next, when all the turning outs & putting ins, as to office, will be fixed and settled." And since Cooper was one of the most radical figures in South Carolina politics, his willingness to give Jackson a chance spoke volumes about southern prejudice in favor of the new president. Indeed, Cooper was one of very few political activists to threaten disunion, predicting that "if the Tariff of Protection be not repealed, South Carolina & Georgia will secede from the Union toward the close of 1830."[11] Cooper, however, stood practically alone in this sentiment. Disavowing the accusation that southern radicals were already plotting secession, Calhoun asserted in 1829 that "the object of the State is reformation, and not revolution, a reformation essential to the preservation of the Union."[12] Across the Deep South, slaveowners expected Andrew Jackson to assist their efforts to achieve such reform.

Jackson did, in general, adhere to a states' rights philosophy that decried overly broad constructions of federal power—a position that initially provided some solace to antitariff activists. While the president conceded that "provisions for the national defense" necessitated a tariff to ensure domestic "production of those articles which are essential in the emergencies of war," he also characterized tariffs that were too high as "irreconcilable to the objects of the union, and threatening to its peace and tranquillity." Going one step further, Jackson promised to "notice with pleasure an unreserved examination of the measures" of his administration and to "be the last to cry out treason against those who interpret differently from myself the policy, or powers of the government."[13] Although this passage never made it into the much shorter final draft of Jackson's inaugural address, it signaled his desire to redress the southern radicals' grievances, rather than to force them into submission.[14]

Despite this promising beginning, the relationship between the White House and antitariff forces in South Carolina soon soured. By the summer of 1829, radical statesmen were growing increasingly concerned over Calhoun's limited (and ever diminishing) influence within the Jackson administration. Jackson, according to one of the vice president's correspondents, was liable "to yield to the solicitation of [untrustworthy] friends & to be governed too much by his personal feelings"—a prediction that was seemingly confirmed when a number of circumstances drove a wedge between Jackson and his vice president.[15] The ideological and personal gulf that had opened between the two men came into full public view in 1830, when prominent statesmen assembled at a dinner celebrating Thomas Jefferson's birthday. There, the president had glared at Calhoun while lifting a glass to the preservation of the Union—a toast that prompted Calhoun's retort that only next to "our liberties" was the Union "most dear." The exchange verified the slaveholders' fears that Jackson would now "act in opposition to the principles, on which he ha[d] been promoted" in South Carolina during the election two years earlier.[16] In their opinion, "the President's principles [were no longer] such as to afford much hope of relief."[17]

Realizing that the Jackson administration would not come to their aid, radical South Carolina statesmen broke with convention and directly entreated the people to support nullification. Elite southerners had long subscribed to the notion that politicians should lead according to the dictates of their conscience rather than by the voting public's whimsical desires. Like Landon Carter, they traditionally reserved special contempt for any politician who "merely kissed the arses of the people," and they viewed "Popularity" as "an adultress of the first order, for at any time let her be most sacredly wedded to one man [yet] she will [still] be grogged by her gallant over his shoulder."[18] By the 1820s, however, members of the recently formed Charleston Forensic Society were debating whether a representative should "be governed by the will of his Constituents."[19] The society decided the question in the negative, but its eagerness to consider the issue as one of its first topics of debate signified that classical ideas about moral republican leadership were beginning to give way in the nineteenth century. By the time that Georgia voters first exercised their right to vote for president in 1828, it had become clear that "the polite and more considerate part" of society revered by elite planters such as Carter was surrendering power to a voting public that demanded more responsive candidates.[20]

As befitting South Carolina's aristocratic heritage, the state legislature, rather than the general public, continued to select presidential electors during the antebellum period. But if elite Carolina planters sought to protect their privilege from the masses, they also struggled to defend their state's sovereignty from federal encroachment. To achieve this end, leaders of the nullification movement were willing to entreat the people for support. This was a campaign over which the nullifiers intended to maintain careful control. Nevertheless, by inviting the people to participate directly in the formation of a new political party, these statesmen were violating the cardinal principle of the state's ruling elite—an elite that had long equated formal political parties with the corruption of their republican tradition.

The radical slaveowners certainly denounced the political maneuvering of their northern enemies and, at every opportunity, blamed shrewd rivals such as Martin Van Buren for the "universal discontent, distraction, and corruption" that seemed "to be taking possession of the country."[21] But nullifiers such as William Preston and James Hamilton Jr. proved remarkably adept at manipulating public opinion and inviting widespread participation in the campaign to nullify the tariff. Observing in 1830 that "the people are not yet much excited," Preston predicted that "they will gradually take fire from the news-paper-readers," who would be exposed to the nullifiers' artfully presented pitch to sectional sympathies.[22] Hamilton, descendant of one of the state's most prominent tidewater families, devised the strategies that ushered into existence the first political party organized around discrete issues, as opposed to the personal alliances and antipathies that had previously structured the Carolina political scene.[23] Through activities ranging from casual barbecues to formal associations and, ultimately, statewide conventions, he coordinated a coherent party platform that nullifying candidates pledged to support in return for the people's votes. By broadening their political sensibility, the nullifiers gained control of the state legislature by the end of 1830. Although they failed to secure the two-thirds majority required to convene a state convention on nullification, their success signified a turning point in sectional politics.

Radicals such as Hamilton, Cooper, and Preston were able to make inroads into a less privileged voting population by suggesting that their impoverished countrymen might one day join in the privileges of power. For this reason, the accusation that their agenda undermined the standing of humbly situated white farmers rankled the nullifiers most of all. In a letter written to a local newspaper in fall 1831, former South Carolina governor Stephen Miller insisted that "so far from suggesting laws oppressive to the poor, it is recommended to pass laws by which their situation would be improved." Realizing that the fortunes of his party hung in the balance, Miller "challenge[d] the most critical investigation of my public conduct for the production of any act in which I have leaned against the poor in favor of the rich, or against the weak in favor of the strong."[24]

In a few cases, men of humble origin did rise quickly to the role of benevolent planter. James Henry Hammond, for example, catapulted himself from poverty into the first ranks of slaveholding society. He did so by mastering the persona of the gentleman planter—a persona that necessitated a confrontational stance against northern aggression. Speaking at a Fourth of July celebration in Columbia in 1829, Hammond told his audience that "the people of the North have been overbearing and the people of the South have become chafed. . . . We should be warned of the danger of permitting the first approaches of usurpation to pass unnoticed." Powerful politicians such as Hamilton and Calhoun noticed Hammond's eloquent pleas for the southern cause and rewarded him with patronage. Hammond eventually served his state as governor, congressman, and senator, while he amassed a fortune in land and slaves. That most white southerners had little chance of following suit mattered less than their willingness to believe that they too might one day become powerful planters. The white social order held together precisely because poorer whites did not know their place.[25]

After presenting their vision of a white polity undivided by class, the nullifiers warned their countrymen about northern industrialists who were supposedly conspiring to reduce southerners to a state of unmanly dependence. Couching their grievances in the language of agrarian independence, radical South Carolina politicians demonized an overly powerful federal government for undermining the free citizenry and pitted the virtues of independent farmers against the corrupt inclinations of wealthy manufacturers who sought to turn the federal government toward their own selfish purposes. Thus, in his celebrated contest with Massachusetts senator Daniel Webster in 1830, South Carolina stalwart Robert Hayne pronounced that "one of the greatest safeguards of liberty is a jealous watchfulness on the part of the people, over the collection and expenditure of the public money." The tariff, in his opinion, had "done much to weaken the responsibility of our federal rulers to the people" and, even worse, had "made them, in some measure, careless of their rights." Northeastern politicians, insisted Hayne, wanted nothing less than "to regulate the industry of man" so as to "create a manufactory of paupers, in order to enable the rich proprietors of woolen and cotton factories to amass wealth." The nullifiers hoped that the farmers of South Carolina—the yeomen and slaveholders with modest holdings as well as the big planters—would rally to the cause of states' rights and prevent this distressing vision from becoming a reality. Hayne was speaking not just to the Senate but to his own constituents when he observed that "the people of America are, and ought to be for a century to come, essentially an agricultural people."[26] Elite planters hoped that, sharing a tie to the land, an antipathy toward hostile northerners, and a self-professed superiority over their household dependents, white southerners would unite in support of the master class.

Notwithstanding the nullifiers' desires for a unified state, a substantial minority of unionists (or "submissionists," as the nullifiers derisively referred to them) rejected their efforts at every turn. Amid the intensifying rivalry between these groups, the dialogue over the merits of state interposition degenerated into a smoldering silence marked by resentment, intimidation, and sporadic violence. The prevailing sentiment against nullification in Lancaster, South Carolina, drove James D. Cocke out of the newspaper business in 1830. Making plans to "leave the printing office behind," the frustrated nullifier asserted that "no place so much needs an independent press as Lancaster." Unionist antipathy, in his opinion, had stifled open debate.[27] A similar scenario played out in Charleston, but there the roles between unionists and nullifiers were reversed. In September 1830, an incensed crowd of nullifiers attacked William Gilmore Simms for espousing unionist views in his newspaper, the *City Gazette*. In his own account of the incident, Simms contended that he had been "assailed . . . while standing upon the threshold of his Office, by a mob from two to three hundred persons, armed generally with clubs; three of whom assaulted and collared him, without any provocation whatever on his part; and, but for the few friends, who prevailed upon them to take their departure, he would in all probability have lost his life."[28]

As the elections approached in the fall of 1832, tensions between the parties reached a breaking point in Charleston. "The civil contest has begun I fear," wrote Rebecca Motte Rutledge to her husband in New York, "and God only knows how far it may go." Rutledge reported that after participating in rival political meetings, the "rabble of both sides" got "thoroughly drunk" and "roamed the streets." The combination of political rhetoric and liquor resulted in "a scuffle" in which "one man was trampled to death, and another stabbed."[29] During the exchange, nullifiers pelted prominent unionists Joel Poinsett and William Drayton with bricks.[30] Charleston's finest citizens were now, quite literally, just an arm's length away from the people whom they had once successfully excluded from the political process.

Emerging from the elections with control over three-quarters of the state Senate and four-fifths of the House, the nullifiers called a convention in November 1832 to proclaim the tariff unconstitutional. They ultimately passed a nullifying ordinance that outlawed the collection of federal duties in South Carolina beginning in February 1833.[31] To the unionists' dismay, the radical states' rights politicians also required all holders of state office to pledge their allegiance to the principle of nullification. Incensed by this so-called test oath, unionists organized into militia companies and demonstrated their willingness to shed blood before allowing themselves to be excluded from government. "Things go on wildly in this quarter," observed Simms in January 1833. To Simms's delight, "the Nullies no longer call us the *Submission Party*" because "we now are only thinking of war & vengeance—to the very knife. We are practicing at the broad sword & the thrust—pistols are popping in every direction—sabre cuts & bullets have destroyed nearly all our finest trees, and never did people exhibit a more manful desire in all sorts of warring circumstance." The author speculated that "a slight collision will . . . bring on trouble" and insisted that "though something of jest may appear in the above passage, yet a deep & deadly hostility & hate has been engendered in the bosoms of our party by the odious ordinance of that petty dictatorship" of the nullifiers.[32]

Although Simms was not exaggerating the degree of antipathy between nullifiers and their opponents, the warring political parties actually shared common ideological ground. Despite their radical reformation of the political process, the nullifiers espoused a conservative vision of plantation society. Demonizing a powerful federal government as the enemy of agrarian order, the nullifiers attacked majority rule. National virtue, they reasoned, had long rested with a moral minority, whose right to self-government needed to be protected lest the country sink into corruption. But, for the most part, the unionists who opposed the doctrine of nullification by no means rejected the organic world view of the planter elite. To the contrary, aristocratic opponents of nullification such as James Louis Petigru and Joel Poinsett denounced the nullifiers because their unyielding commitment to states' rights threatened to unleash anarchy on plantation society. And the unionists never doubted that if the social barriers keeping each element in society in its assigned place did crumble, the privileged slaveowners would suffer most of all. Lamenting that "civil war seem[ed] inevitable," unionists observed that "the discipline of liberty" had proven to be "too severe" for South Carolina. They maintained that owing to the nullifiers' self-serving appeal to popular passions, calls for restraint met the same fate as "temperance at a feast."[33]

Conservative unionists realized that, no matter how the nullification controversy was to turn out, the nullifiers' party apparatus had already erased the much needed distinction between the upper echelon of powerful planters and the teeming white masses eager to share the benefits of power. Holding to traditional notions that statesmen should lead rather than follow the people, unionists such as Daniel Huger indignantly rejected the suggestion that constituents had the right to contemplate and to question their elected leaders' decisions. "Think!" exclaimed Huger on one storied occasion, "they will think nothing about it—They expect me to think for them." For such men, modern political campaigns embodied the leveling tendencies of an unrestrained democracy. It disgusted Benjamin Perry, for example, that "many persons have joined the rank of the nullifiers in order to get into a company a little above their accustomed circle. . . . [Particularly] those who were ambitious of belonging to the Chivalry."[34] In keeping with this perspective, Stephen G. Deveaux emphatically denounced "all the great feelings kick'd up in Charleston" by the nullifiers, whom he character-ized as "a few ambitious and disappointed Men, who would run any risk of ruining the Country rather than give up the pleasure of heading a party."[35] As the historian William Freehling has persuasively argued, the unionists' distaste for democratic political campaigns sealed their doom in 1832. At the crucial moment when a well-orchestrated nullification party rallied its sup-porters, the embittered unionist elite could only mumble to themselves about the leveling tendencies of their enemies.[36]

While the unionists charged the nullifiers with erasing class lines between whites, the nullifiers offered the more dramatic accusation that the unionists were being manipulated by northern abolitionists and were there-fore working against the most crucial social distinction of all: the one be-tween enslaved blacks and free whites. The radicals inflicted heavy damage on their unionist opponents in South Carolina by fixating on this issue of slavery. "The slave question," as William C. Preston reminded Waddy Thompson, "will be the real issue—all others will be absorbed in it." To awaken white southerners to the dangers of centralized government, the nullifiers pointed out that the tariff implied "the right of laying duties, not only to raise revenue, but to regulate the industry of the country," a right that could be turned to "any purpose that the majority may think to be for the general welfare," including emancipation. "All the Tariff men," as Thomas Cooper succinctly observed in 1828, "rely on exciting a revolt among our slaves."[37]

One year later, Calhoun delved into the heart of the matter when he wrote his friend that the tariff was "the occasion, rather than the real cause of the present unhappy state of things." "The truth can no longer be dis-guised," he continued, "that the peculiar domestick institution of the Southern States, and the consequent direction, which that and her soil and climate have given to her industry, has placed them . . . in opposite relation to the majority of the Union." Calhoun speculated that "if there be no pro-tective power in the reserved rights of the States" to counter a hostile federal government, "they must be forced to rebel, or submit it to have their most paramount interests sacrificed, their domestick institutions subordinated by Colonization and other schemes, and themselves & children reduced to wretchedness."[38]

Having taken as a starting point the assumption that antipathy toward slavery had motivated northerners to inflict the tariff on the South, nullifiers could only conclude that those southerners who did not support the primacy of state sovereignty were the allies, unwitting or not, of the abolitionists. Harriott Pinckney employed this exact line of thinking when she asked her nephew if he had "not read with indignation, the [antislavery] resolution brought forward... at the [pro-]Tariff meeting in Philadelphia?" "It is these discussions & the fire brands in the shape of [antislavery messages in] pamphlets, Handkerchiefs &c. constantly thrown into the South," she contended, "that make our [black] people unhappy & rebel." Invoking the familiar stereotype of the happy slave—a stereotype that had been bandied about for over a generation in the Deep South—Pinckney recounted how one of her bondservants "said to us the other day, 'Ma'am we are perfectly contented if the Northern people will only let us alone, & not be sending in these Pamphlets.'" Somewhat reluctant to accuse southern unionists of treason on the question of slavery, Pinckney conceded that "many of the submission party have said [to the North], touch this question & we shall be united [with the nullifiers] to a Man." But the larger point in her mind was that opposition to nullification meant the company of those who sought to destroy the slaveowning South. "How do you think [unionists such as] Col. Drayton & Mr. Grimké felt," she asked her nephew, "when they received [the abolitionist newspaper] the Liberator sent by some of their Northern Brethren naturally supposing . . . them so bigoted to the North that they would assist in circulating such papers"?[39]

Although the nullifiers scored points on the slavery issue, leading unionists detested abolitionism—a fact that could readily be seen from William Drayton and Thomas Grimké's decision to turn over the unsolicited copies of the *Liberator* to city authorities. The unionists, however, could never quite escape the dilemma of explaining how they could both support the South's peculiar institution and deny their state's right to nullify obnoxious federal legislation. Hugh Swinton Legaré's strained response to this challenge revealed the extent to which the unionists had been put on the defensive when it came to slavery. Facing the question in 1831, he admitted to once thinking that "the Non-slave-holding states w[ere] so decidedly against us as to lead necessarily in a few years to [their] direct interference between masters & slaves"—a belief that "did excite me to a very high & I now think, an inordinate pitch of jealousy & indignation against them." In the constitutional debate over nullification, however, Legaré insisted that cooler heads should prevail. "Do you seriously hold me bound to *act* via a great fundamental question of sovereignty—at a crisis involving, if it involves anything, the *being* of our institutions—upon such expressions" made "in a past moment of excitement?" he queried one of his foes. Here, Legaré was attempting to divorce the issue of the tariff from broader sectional concerns about slavery, an impossible task even for his prodigious intellect.[40]

Opponents of nullification fared much better when they made the slavery issue their own. Writing from his home in Virginia in 1830, James Monroe berated the nullifiers for risking disunion and civil war, threats best avoided by slaveowners who knew their business. "We to the South," wrote the former president as he attempted to dampen the nullifiers' enthusiasm, "where so large a portion of the population consists of slaves, would by domestic insurrections be most apt to fall the victims."[41] Ever the quick study, Legaré reversed field and embraced this perspective in 1832. Having departed Charleston for Europe, he wrote home to remind his sister of the unhappy lesson of France. That nation's "everlasting revolutions," he claimed, carried with them "fearful and unforseen results—the confusion of all distinctions, the contempt for all authority, the savage rudeness and ferocity of jacobinism on the one hand and the stern necessity, on the other, of controlling and crushing it by the power of the sword." From this unhappy evidence Legaré derived the lesson that "no nation in the world can live perpetually in the midst of civil broils and military adventures without degenerating into a horde of Tartars"—a lesson that turned his mind toward the situation in his home state. "Only see what Governor Hamilton and nullification had done[,] before I left home[,] to degrade and corrupt to the core the admirable society of our sweet little Charleston."[42]

In fact, his home state had become so unsettled that Legaré could no longer even consider it a potential haven for the Caribbean planters displaced by the British Parliament's decision to end slavery in the West Indies. Legaré denounced the impending emancipation of British slaves as "impracticable" but seemed equally distressed about the prospects for life in his beloved Carolina. The complaints of an English slaveowner who had bemoaned "the state of society" after a passing through South Carolina led the Charleston intellectual to confess that the negative report "agreed too well with my own idea of the condition [to which] we are reduced to permit me to question its accuracy."[43] In 1831, he had fruitlessly attempted to divorce the issue of nullification from the threat to slavery. Two years later, he joined other conservative unionists in the accusation that the nullifiers' Jacobin behavior could only destabilize plantation society, which (in their minds) had much in common with the ancien régime.[44]

The political career of William Smith provides the strongest evidence that no genuine ideological differences separated the nullifiers and the unionists on the question of slavery. During the Missouri controversy, Smith had presented the firmest defense of unfree labor as a positive institution yet offered before Congress. Staunchly championing the slaveholders' rights, he had endeavored to protect state business from a meddlesome federal government. From all this one might reasonably expect Smith to have been at the helm of nullification. But South Carolina politics still involved personalities, and Smith despised Calhoun—in no small part because of Calhoun's nationalism during his early years in Congress.[45] Unable to swallow any measure prescribed as necessary by Calhoun, Smith eventually staked his influence against nullification, although he had already alienated Jackson by denouncing the new administration for its failure to protect states' rights.

Jackson, however, was willing to overlook this fact once he perceived a potential friend in Calhoun's enemy and therefore took a sudden interest in Smith's political welfare. Robert Hayne speculated in 1831 that "great anxiety was felt" at the White House during Smith's senatorial campaign the preceding year and "a corresponding mortification at his defeat." This could "be accounted for," opined Hayne, only because Jackson "had identified Judge Smith with the anti-state Rights party of South Carolina and relied on [Smith's] being brought back by the force of circumstance into the Jackson fold."[46] Amid these shifting political partnerships and battles, one could easily lose sight of the fact that on the question of slavery, key figures occupying every position on the political spectrum—from Thomas Cooper to Hugh Swinton Legaré to Andrew Jackson himself—shared the same assumption that the institution of slavery conformed to the principles of corporate individualism.[47] Like two magnets sharing the same charge, nullifiers and unionists repulsed one another because they each believed that their opponents' policies would have disastrous repercussions for slaveowning society.

By 1833, civil war had become a very real and distressing possibility. "The matter is now pretty well settled—[by] it is well settled I mean that the very worst ills, which can be apprehended are to come to pass," complained Charles Petigru in the final weeks of 1832. The South Carolina convention's decision to nullify the tariff led him to conclude that "civil war seems inevitable." Few nullifiers imagined that President Jackson would meet the crisis with anything but resolve. Even in November 1832, several months before Jackson presented the Force Bill expressing his readiness to employ the military against the nullifiers, William C. Preston had noted that "Genl Jackson has certainly declared that he will hang any man who attempts to enforce and act on nullification. . . . He will make a civil war if he can and we must be prepared to meet him." "War if it does come will be a terrible calamity," observed nullifiers such as Rebecca Motte Rutledge in January 1833, "but with all its horrors I do not fear it so much as I do the dissolution of our glorious Union." What dismayed Rutledge most of all was the likelihood that "even if the obnoxious laws should be repealed" and the immediate crisis resolved, "the two sections of the country will never return to their former harmony; end how it may we shall be no longer brothers but rivals."[48]

Contemplating a violent confrontation with the federal government, the nullifiers appealed for the support of other slaveholding states. They realized that they faced an uphill battle given Andrew Jackson's overwhelming popularity, but they also believed that, when push came to shove, the slavery issue would ensure the cooperation of South. "I have never calculated on the co-operation of the other States until we have taken some definitive step," confessed Preston in 1830. "They will not join us until circumstances compel them to take one or the other side, and then they must take ours." He reasoned that even Louisiana—a state that benefited from the tariff because it protected the sugar industry—must eventually "ask herself whether she belongs to the slave holding or anti slave holding states." The South Carolina radical concluded with a question that, in his opinion, had a self-evident answer: "Will Louisiana cling to her sugar and give up her negroes?"[49]

Yet lurking beneath Preston's certainty lay the fear that some southern states did not share South Carolina's commitment to the institution of slavery. In all likelihood it was this fear that led him defiantly to proclaim that whether or not "all the southern states would . . . take their stations at our side, . . . I should not pause a moment for them [because] South Carolina is strong enough by herself to do right."[50] Since the Revolutionary era, the possibility that the Upper South might falter on the question of slavery had vexed planters in South Carolina and Georgia. Thanks to the writings of Thomas Jefferson, George Mason, and James Madison, anyone could see that ambivalence over the morality and practicality of human bondage had surfaced in Virginia to a degree inconceivable in the Lower South. With all their talk about universal equality and human rights, Virginia's Revolutionary statesmen had placed a heavy philosophical burden on the many masters who recoiled from accusations of tyranny and oppression.

By the 1830s, the "positive good" defense of slavery had been making its way into the political consciousness of the Deep South for decades, soothing the slaveowners' minds about the morality of their plantation enterprises. But South Carolina planters such as Robert Marion Deveaux remained on the defensive when traveling through the Upper South, especially when they confronted a "general impression in Virginia that the slaves of South Carolina lead a most wretched life, that they are cruelly treated by their owners & worked very hard." "Indeed the cruel treatment (as they think it) of our slaves," noted Deveaux, "has almost become a proverb" among the state's denizens. Since the young man from South Carolina asserted that "our slaves are certainly less miserable & are worked not one iota harder than they are here" in Virginia, his "many disputes on the subject" with fellow students at the University of Virginia probably did not leave Deveaux struggling with a guilty conscience.[51] These exchanges, however, did reinforce suspicions in the Deep South that Virginia had not yet made its peace with slavery.

Just one year later, Nat Turner would lead his fellow slaves in Southampton, Virginia, into the bloodiest slave insurrection of the nineteenth-century South. In its wake, the Virginia legislature openly debated gradual emancipation as a necessary measure to avoid the racial conflagration that many feared would be kindled by angry slaves.[52] Their deliberations seemed to provide ample evidence that the antislavery movement was gathering momentum across the country and was even gaining adherents south of the Mason-Dixon line. When the nullifiers perceived that little support for their actions existed outside South Carolina, they naturally assumed that the other slaveholding states had been corrupted by perfidious northern ideas. Writing to Edward Harden in August 1832, James Hamilton Jr. blamed opposition to nullification in Georgia on "the Yankee influence among you which has got possession of your press, your pulpits, your Trade & your institutions of education—The truth is that the colonial system has been working so steadily, secretly & powerfully on the South that without being conscious of its progress, we have been so embraced in its folds until all vitality is nearly extinct in our bosoms."[53]

The truth, however, was far more complex than Hamilton was willing to concede. Like the unionists within South Carolina, the vast majority of Georgia planters opposed nullification not because they had been seduced by northern values but because they believed that Andrew Jackson's administration served their plantation society's sectional interest. Although Georgia slaveowners had no love for the tariff, they focused their political energy against Cherokee Indians who were clinging to ancestral lands in the northern part of the state. The planters' ultimately successful effort to banish this Native American population to areas west of the Mississippi illustrated their dedication to the states' rights cause. But if many Georgians shared ideals identical to those of the nullifiers, the specific political alliances generated during the Cherokee removal led Georgia planters to condemn nullification as a rash gesture that damaged southern interests as much as did the tariff itself.

Ever touchy over lectures about universal rights, white Georgians associated supporters of the Cherokees with abolitionists. Wilson Lumpkin, a leading Georgia congressman who was elected governor in 1831, recalled the manner in which congressional opposition to Indian removal had been couched in antislavery terms. It was not just that "the Northern fanatics, male and female, had gone to work and gotten up thousands of petitions, signed by more than a million, of men, women, and children, protesting against the removal of the poor dear Indians," but also that "in these petitions we were denounced as slaveholders." Of course, Lumpkin had clear political reasons for observing that antislavery sentiment and the advocacy of Indian rights were "adroitly blended together" by critics of Georgia's policies. Like the nullifiers, Lumpkin and other Georgians played the slavery card to convince reasonable whites across the South that the state had every right to strip the Cherokees of their land, not to mention the rights explicitly awarded to them through treaties with the United States government.[54]

Indeed, the timing of the Cherokee controversy paralleled that of the nullification crisis in South Carolina almost perfectly.[55] In 1827, just one year before Congress passed the tariff that precipitated the nullification movement, the Cherokees declared themselves a sovereign nation completely removed from the jurisdiction of Georgia's state laws. In 1832, both conflicts involving state sovereignty erupted into crises that occupied national attention. During that year, the Supreme Court reviewed the case (*Worcester v. Georgia*) of two missionaries imprisoned by Georgia for violating a statute that prohibited unauthorized whites from visiting Indian territory—a statute that sprang from the insistence by Georgia lawmakers that their state wielded ultimate authority over Cherokee lands. The Supreme Court, however, decided the matter in favor of the incarcerated missionaries and decreed that Georgia had acted in a manner "repugnant to the Constitution, laws, and treaties of the United States."[56] Georgians, like South Carolinians, immediately feared that civil war might result from federal interference with state policy.[57] Although Georgia statesmen called no formal meetings and issued no explicit statements declaring their intention to disregard the verdict, they openly defied the Court's decision. State authorities sanctioned countless acts of violence against the Cherokees with the goal of dispossessing the Indians from their land and speeding them on their way across the Mississippi. John Ross, the chief of the Cherokees, returned from a lobbying trip to Washington, D.C., in 1835 only to find "himself a stranger in his own house, his family having been, some days before, driven out to seek a new home."[58]

Committed to their own campaign for states' rights, significant numbers of Georgia planters might very well have rallied to the nullifiers' cause had Andrew Jackson not entered into the political equation. As it turned out, the president supported Indian removal in Georgia with as much enthusiasm as he opposed nullification in South Carolina. On the question of Indian rights, Jackson departed from the precedent set by his predecessor in the White House, John Quincy Adams, who had consistently threatened Georgia with military reprisal if it dared to violate federally recognized Indian land titles.[59] Jackson, by contrast, articulated a very different philosophy respecting Native Americans. In his first Annual Message to Congress in 1829, he "informed the Indians inhabiting parts of Georgia and Alabama that their attempt to establish an independent government would not be countenanced by the Executive of the United States, and advised them to emigrate beyond the Mississippi or submit to the laws of those states."[60] Because Jackson shared Georgia planters' contemptuous view of the Supreme Court's *Worcester* decision, the planters could ill afford to associate themselves with Jackson's foes in South Carolina.[61] In the end, Georgia, like every other state offering an official response to nullification, denounced the step as a "mischievous policy" that promised to bring "civil commotion and disunion."[62]

Even the few Georgia statesmen such as George M. Troup who sympathized and communicated with leading nullifiers conceded that "our People are unprepared for a decisive measure which woud be likely to end in abortion & disgrace." Troup made no formal statement on nullification, telling his friends in 1832 that they "would have my opinions freely & fully if they would be of the least public benefit" but noting that "they would be more likely to do harm than good" given prevailing political sentiment in Georgia.[63] By January 1833, the nullifiers realized that "the voice of every other [state] has been raised against the course of S.C. . . . expressed with an unanimity not to be disregarded."[64] Having miscalculated the degree to which the slaveholding South would unite behind their radical political stance, the nullifiers initiated a strategic retreat. They minimized tensions with unionists at home by watering down the most stringent aspects of the test oath that nullifiers had used to exclude unionists from positions in the state government. And when Congress passed a compromise tariff, South Carolina rescinded its nullification ordinance. As Rebecca Rutledge pointed out in March 1833, "We Carolinians are a lucky people—we have had the satisfaction of taking the lead in a most honourable resistance, we have had the satisfaction of displaying great courage to a threatened danger, and we have the still greater [satisfaction] of seeing the danger quietly disappear." If the nullifiers failed to abolish the hated tariff altogether, they had managed to restructure state politics around sectional themes without experiencing the actual bloodshed of civil war. In this sense, they could indeed claim (with Rutledge) "all the triumph of Victory and none of its horrors."[65]

The principles and concerns that had motivated the nullifiers, moreover, also recast traditional party lines in Georgia—despite that state's dramatic rejection of nullification. Before the 1830s, Georgia politics, like those in South Carolina, had revolved around personalities. Because Georgia factions, as one historian has aptly noted, were not parties "in any meaningful sense," it was entirely fitting that they were named after men—George M. Troup and John Clark—rather than issues.[66] By the 1820s, however, these political alignments were beginning to unravel. And as the nullification controversy raged in South Carolina, the Clark and Troup factions realigned themselves according to their stands on a struggle that had come to involve the question of state sovereignty. By the end of 1833, the Troupites had designated themselves the State Rights Party, dedicated to combating the Union Party, which consisted of Clark supporters.[67] The irony of this growing confluence between Georgia and South Carolina party structures was profound, given the nullifiers' inability to mobilize any significant measure of southern support for their policies. According to James L. Petigru, state elections in Georgia in 1834 "turned on Carolina Politics altogether."[68]

Notwithstanding the profound political differences between the emerging political parties and between the states as a whole over the issue of nullification, the influence of a coherent master-class ideology was proliferating. Across the Deep South, issues such as the tariff and the Cherokee lands had become not just economic problems but cultural ones as well. In South Carolina, both unionists and nullifiers insisted that only their particular policies could protect the unique virtues of their slaveholding society. In

Georgia, the nearly unanimous white support for Indian removal hinged on far more than the potential expansion of the plantation economy. Many of the Cherokees responsible for organizing the national constitution of 1827 were themselves slaveowners who, like their white counterparts, forced black bondservants to cultivate staple crops. Ideological considerations aside, white Georgians should have had little problem coexisting with these Cherokees. By the 1830s, however, carefully crafted, racially specific definitions of mastery excluded Native Americans from the respect typically awarded to those at the top of slaveholding society. To be sure, the Cherokees who owned slaves proved to be the ones most willing to negotiate with state authorities. These Native Americans moved west under decidedly better conditions than the Cherokees rounded up at gunpoint and forced to march the "trail of tears" in 1838.[69] Nevertheless, in the end, all Cherokees were tied together by racial designation and forced out of Georgia to make room for white masters and their supposedly domesticated black slaves.

The 1830s were the worst of times for the slaveowners for more reasons than just the controversy over the Cherokees and nullification. Cholera, the great scourge of the nineteenth century, ravaged southern cities and plantations in 1832 and 1834. The antislavery movement published ever more strident critiques of southern society and adopted more confrontational tactics in Congress. The planters, for their part, encountered mounting evidence—most readily apparent following Nat Turner's rebellion in Virginia—that their slaves were plotting to obtain their freedom and, even worse, were receiving assistance from white abolitionists. For the slaveowners, a well-managed plantation household offered a sanctuary from the swirling passions of the outside world. The planters believed that their slaves required careful domestic supervision lest their wild tendencies result in disreputable and even seditious behavior. News that slaves had poisoned owners, set fires, and dismembered white pursuers appeared with alarming frequency.[70] Henry S. Glover probably had such tidings in mind when he wrote to Howell Cobb in 1833 that "the Devil you know is a Black man."[71] Away from watchful white eyes, the slaves (according to their masters) acted "so much like wolves" that their owners could only guess about their whereabouts or intentions.[72] Yet while the slaveowners sometimes repeated the adage that "the Ethiopian could not change his skin nor the Leopard his spots," as a group they remained convinced that slave behavior and character could be corrected.[73] Thus upon learning in 1829 that his family had purchased a slave who was a "drunkard," South Carolina planter John Guignard asked his parents to "send [the slave] here [to his Hopewell plantation] to be reformed" by "heavy work."[74]

Even the revelation that slaves were scheming to rebel did not force the planters to abandon perceptions of their bondservants as childlike, loving individuals capable of loyalty to their owners. Rumors of slave plans for insurrection and actual reports of arson placed the white population of Augusta, Georgia, on the alert in 1829. "Great fear begins to be prevalent that the negroes are about to rise [and] alarms of fire occur daily," reported Susan Hutchison on April 7 of that year. One day later, she admitted that her "nerves are completely unstrung" and that her husband was "busy in loading his guns and pistols in expectation of an alarm of insurrection."[75] Yet when Jenny, a slave known by Hutchison, was accused, convicted, and executed for arson, the slaveowner still referred to her with sympathy as "Poor Jenny."[76] Edward Harden Jr. likewise demonstrated how affectionate conceptions of slaves could persist amid clear evidence that African Americans desired freedom instead of loving relations with their masters. Visiting central Georgia during this period of racial tension, he asked his mother to send his "love" to the slaves at his family's residence in Savannah.[77]

The slaveowners' understanding of "love" did not preclude sometimes brutal punishment of wayward slaves. Like Basil Manly, the planters convinced themselves that strict discipline (including corporal punishment) was "indispensable to preserve [a wayward slave] from ruin."[78] The slaveowners' ability to persuade themselves that their bondservants appreciated the benevolent intentions lurking behind the lash and the treadmill at the Charleston workhouse, however, did illustrate the power of ideology to defy all common sense. Despite the local slaves' rebellious behavior, the Hutchisons' organic vision of mastery continued to blind this slaveowning family to their bondservants' capacity to resist white authority. Susan Hutchison perceived nothing absurd in her report that their slave "Jim ran away . . . fearing a correction" in 1833 after they had "sent him to buy a whip."[79]

Thanks to the ongoing propaganda war between northern and southern ideologues, proslavery thinkers enjoyed growing opportunities to pontificate about the warm human connection between caring master and appreciative slave. Disgusted and frightened by abolitionist pamphlets, Georgia passed a statute in 1829 outlawing slave literacy and forbidding the circulation of incendiary tracts that undermined southern claims about slaveholders' humanity toward their bondservants.[80] Meanwhile, southern authors and speakers repeated ad nauseam the rationales for human bondage that such ideologues as Richard Furman had set in print in the 1820s. In a typical sermon delivered in North Carolina in 1836 and republished the following year in South Carolina, Episcopalian minister George Freeman asserted that "our slaves . . . are *always* members of our families; they are *always* subject to our authority and control; and . . . though ever so far advanced in years, they are, from the very nature of their condition, *always children*" to be cared for by slaveowners acting as "christian parents." This standard for mastery had become so central to the slaveholders' culture that even poorly educated masters possessing marginal holdings now referred to their slaves as sympathetic human beings.[81]

As we have seen, textual sources played a significant role in presenting the slaveowning ideal to a wider spectrum of southern society. By the 1830s, southern novelists such as William Gilmore Simms offered cues for domestic conduct that white southerners could find relevant whether or not they owned slaves. Simms, for example, set the action in *Guy Rivers* (1834) on the Georgia frontier to portray the process of cultural refinement by which characters of modest fortunes lifted themselves into the respectable ranks of polite society. Readers saw the stages of individual moral progress personified by a range of Simms's characters. Amid the humble circumstances of a backcountry inn run by her criminal uncle, Lucy Munro revealed a noble bearing and a perfect sense of womanly conduct that, in the end, raised her into friendship with slaveowners from prominent Carolina families. In the character of Mark Forrester, Simms presented an individual on the cusp of moral progress. Uncouth yet moved by principles of domestic affection, Forrester almost takes advantage of the fluid frontier setting to establish a household of his own before ultimately falling prey to the criminal element. Significantly, Simms established the moral credentials of his aristocratic protagonist Ralph Colleton not with reference to the man's wealth (for indeed his family had fallen on difficult financial times) but with descriptions of his corporate vision of slaveowning society. Colleton predictably enjoyed a warm relationship with his uncle's trusted slave Caesar, while less admirable white characters such as a frontier lawyer abused their bondservants. Slavery, as presented in Simms's novel, fostered admirable qualities in enslaved African Americans who prove willing to brave danger on behalf of their masters. Simms even left it up to Caesar to articulate the supposed moral framework that differentiated slaveowning society from the cold-hearted capitalism of the North. Chastising a Yankee peddler for acting like an insensitive businessman instead of sharing his wares with a "wondering idiot," the slave announced, "Der's a time for *trade*, and a time for *gib*, and you must do genteel t'ing, and nebber consider wha's de 'spense of it, or de profit."[82]

If the antebellum readers of *Guy Rivers* learned how to conduct themselves from such characters, they also received a lesson in what kind of behavior to avoid. Reflecting one of the key elements of corporate individualism, Simms presented his villains as individuals who are unable to control their own passions—to restrain and to sublimate their urges toward the service of society. Guy Rivers, the novel's principal villain, reflects on his moral shortcomings midway through the novel: "My passions, always fretful and excitable, were never satisfied except when I was employed in some way which enabled me to feed and keep alive the irritation which was their and my very breath of life. With such a spirit, how could I be what men style and consider a good man?" Establishing the centrality of family life in determining one's ability (or inability) to control the passions, Rivers counsels one of his partners in crime to reform himself, "to get yourself a fireside and a family of your own" because "these are the things that will keep your heart warm within you." For his own part, Rivers realizes that his upbringing has denied him any chance at such happiness: "I have been schooled otherwise. My mother . . . taught me the love of evil with her milk. . . . She roused my *passions* and not my *principles*." This flat-footed dialogue makes Simms a difficult author to stomach for modern readers, but for his audience in the 1830s the morals were clear and applicable to plantation life. Like the characters in *Guy Rivers*, the planters struggled to stamp out unrestrained passions that threatened to subvert not only their slaves but also their white overseers and even themselves. John Peyre Thomas, for example, claimed in 1829 that he "did not wish to keep" his overseer because the man was "so very passionate" and presumably could not be trusted to enact Thomas's instructions. Thomas Jones, another South Carolina planter, lectured his wife to bear all "trials and troubles" with "firmness & fortitude." "The truly virtuous," in his opinion, "should strive unceasingly to subdue every passion calculated in the least degree to disturb their repose."[83] God had ordained a particular order to society and had assigned every human being a place. To give in to one's personal emotions and whims was to reject the holy structure of a stable moral framework.

Vested with considerable ethical and political responsibilities in the new slaveholding order, white southern women needed to take special care to restrain their passions. As had been the case since the colonial era, elite ladies were expected to steer away from any situations outside the home that might threaten a pristine reputation. Parents routinely policed their daughters' social contacts, instructing them to "withdraw entirely from the acquaintance" of undesirable persons to avoid being "contaminated."[84] The world outside the home threatened the moral standing of white daughters in much the same way that it supposedly corrupted otherwise faithful slaves. "It is highly improper for school girls to be seen too often in the Streets," lectured Richard Singleton to his daughter Marion, "being the common resort of *vulgar and depraved women* and not Ladies."[85] During the eighteenth century, unrestrained women had stained the reputation of their families. By the early nineteenth century, however, the stakes had risen considerably. Writing to her daughter in 1814, Alice Izard claimed that "it is so well established a fact that where female depravity takes deep root it is the signal of the fall of Empires."[86]

During the Revolutionary and Early National periods, white women had moved beyond the ornamental realm to take special responsibility for republican virtue—a responsibility that required rigorous education. "The young Ladies of the present day," asserted Betty Coles in 1825, "are so well educated. . . . The last generation was content with the accomplishments of Music, Drawing, and Dancing, but the present race are aiming to combine great intellectual acquirements with those minor accomplishments." "Many of them," she concluded with excitement, "are well grounded in Latin without losing any of the softness and gentleness which is so essential to the female character."[87] By the antebellum period, the ideal woman had divorced herself from material concerns to focus more intently on protecting the virtue of society at large. For this reason, Alexander Garden inadvertently insulted several women attending one of his parties in 1826 when he sought to compliment them "by applying quotation from Shakespeare . . . to their beauties, but [using] such expression as 'a piece of Eve's flesh' & 'reddening complexion.'" The individual who recounted this episode believed that Garden "should have recollected that the ladies in Shakespeare's time were different from ours—Ours are not made of *flesh & blood*—but are angelic."[88]

The new role assigned to elite women, however, by no means separated them from worldly political concerns. To a considerable extent, expectations about proper womanly behavior contributed to the animosity between Andrew Jackson and John C. Calhoun—a personal split that sparked direct confrontation between South Carolina and the federal government. During Jackson's campaign for the presidency, he had watched helplessly as political opponents maligned the character of his wife, who died shortly before he entered the White House. The new president was understandably concerned when John Eaton, his secretary of war, experienced similar anguish following his marriage to a woman of dubious reputation. Describing Peggy Eaton as "a virtuous and much injured Lady," Jackson insisted his supporters stand by the new couple and became furious when women such as Floride Calhoun disregarded his wishes.[89] In some versions of this story, historians have argued that politics at the highest level were turning on the caprice of spiteful women whose prejudices sealed the fate of their husbands. But southern conceptions of gender were anything but whimsical by this point in time. Floride Calhoun could no more have called on Peggy Eaton in good conscience than she could have visited William Lloyd Garrison. The firm standards for manly and womanly conduct required the clear rejection of people and political measures that threatened the moral underpinning of the plantation household. In this sense, it was entirely fitting that the dispute over Peggy Eaton's character as a woman figured into the larger debate over nullification.

As it turned out, women in South Carolina maintained a surprisingly strong public presence over the course of the nullification controversy. After attending a Free Trade Association meeting in Richland District, South Carolina, in April 1832, John A. Partridge reported that "a splendid Banner was presented to the Society by the Ladies of Columbia."[90] Women also demonstrated fierce enthusiasm for the nullifiers' cause on an individual basis. Mary G. Elliott reported her inability to distance herself from the state's political warfare. "I have really striven this past spring," she wrote in 1831, "to keep my mind from being engrossed by those party feelings and prejudices, so much did I repent of my last summer's career—but it is in vain, and I do heartily wish that I and Mr. Elliott were removed from all the evil influence of this violent . . . division here." Decrying the actions of the Unionist Party, Elliott took satisfaction from the political "beating" that the unionists experienced and could hardly restrain from "clapping herself" when listening to the speeches made by leading nullifiers. By no means was Elliott an isolated or even an extreme case. Rebecca Rutledge described a friend as being "in a perfect ecstasy"—completely unable to "restrain her smiles" over the prospect of nullification. This woman, wrote Rutledge, "will not consent to forgive the poor Union people for the part they have taken, and talks of hanging although but in jest with very unbecoming gout. When talking of our position (and she can talk of nothing else,) with her deliberate and emphatic language, her hand raised, the forefinger extended, and her excited countenance, she looks like the prophetess of some heathen temple."[91] In similar fashion, a resident of Columbia, South Carolina, contended that "politicks are common among the Ladies of this place. . . . Our Females are great soldiers round the fireside."[92]

By 1833, many women had worked themselves into a sectional frenzy. Convinced that loyalty to the South prevented true patriots from venturing past the Mason-Dixon line, female radicals such as Maria Pinckney remained at home despite falling sick from the unhealthy lowcountry climate. "She is recommended however to go away," observed Rebecca Rutledge in June 1833, "but her *patriotism* will not let her travel North of the Potomac." Women who had supported nullification even questioned the loyalty of James Hamilton when he contemplated a similar trip for the sake of his and his family's health. "For this preference of the North to the South," wrote Mitchell King later that year, "some of his female compatriots—for the Ladies you know have been, some of them, most vehement, not to say outrageous Nullifiers—have most acrimoniously condemned him, as having been guilty of inconsistency by exposing his children to be tainted with the opinions & prejudices of the enemies—mark that the *enemies* of South Carolina."[93]

Other women exhibited similar enthusiasm for the unionist cause. For instance, Caroline Hart (according to her relative in 1832) was "so violent that she affronts every Nullifier that comes to the house [and] told one that she despised to see one of them enter the house . . . that if she ever pulled a trigger, it would be at a Nullifier, and rather than their party should succeed, she would prefer seeing their leaders hung."[94] Although slaveowning women were expected to control their passion for selfish pleasure, it was clearly acceptable for them to embrace appropriate political measures with unrestrained intensity. Because their homes were working plantations directly affected by national policies respecting slavery, white southern ladies seeking to exercise a moral influence on their households could not help but enter into the fray over nullification. The interplay between the private sphere of plantation life and the public sphere of southern politics enabled these women to have their say on pressing issues that, in a previous era, had been strictly a masculine concern.

Ironically, white women in the Deep South were actively defending a social framework that explicitly denied them the same rights as men. During the earlier congressional battle over Missouri, Maryland senator William Pinkney had sought to discredit antislavery reformers by asking "if it be true that all the men in a republican Government must help to wield its power, and be equal in rights, I beg leave to ask . . . and why not all the women? Why is it that their exclusion from the power of a popular Government is not destructive of its republican character?"[95] White southern women, however, realized that their assigned social station provided them with a sense of genuine power over plantation society. Although southerners such as Pinkney were obviously "no friend of [any] female government" composed of women voters and representatives, they did approve of female government "which reposes on gentleness, and modesty, and virtue, and feminine grace and delicacy." "How powerful a government that is," concluded Pinkney, "all of us, as I suspect, at some time or other, experienced."[96] Northern women who campaigned for universal rights for slaves and Indians (not to mention themselves) could therefore be despised as whores and "impudent hussies" even while virtuous southern women picked up the banner for their regional causes.

Filtering out the last vestiges of the "necessary evil" explanation for slavery, the planters distilled their ideas about class, race, and gender relations into a politically effective orthodoxy. In the process, they increasingly curtailed free discussion of alternative viewpoints on how southern society should be ordered. Having steadily grown in power since the turn of the century, the major Protestant denominations played a huge role in reducing the range of issues that southerners could openly discuss in the 1830s. Just as the nullifiers made a successful democratic appeal to the people of South Carolina, evangelical denominations gained ground in the nineteenth-century Deep South by appealing to individual conscience—by inviting the individual to assume responsibility for his or her own salvation through an active (and sometimes highly emotional) pledge of faith. But in both politics and religion, new modes of personal interaction that seemingly indicated genuine democratic reform actually masked a conservative ideological underpinning. Quite aside from their theological emphasis on personal conscience, the ranks of the evangelical churches swelled because they offered fellowship to individuals who coveted spiritual and social company. When southerners flocked to the revivals sweeping across the countryside, they formed a community of faith that celebrated rather than undermined social order. Although some conservative critics denounced the frenzied atmosphere of these camp meetings, most revivals actually followed an intricate script—one which ensured that order rather than anarchy would prevail.

Like evangelical preachers, advocates of nullification wanted to rouse the public from its lethargy in order to transform the people into militant defenders of a new party line. And given the similarity of these movements, it made perfect sense that the largest religious revival in antebellum South Carolina burst onto the scene just as the nullification movement was achieving its greatest success.[97] Writing from Savannah in July 1831, Mary Bulloch informed her sister that the religious excitement "which has existed here is beyond anything you can conceive—the heads of the people seem completely turned." Several months later, the evangelical crusade had spread into the Georgia upcountry, igniting a revival that E. B. Cobb called "the most overwhelming . . . that my eyes have ever witnessed."[98]

At least initially, the nullifiers appeared to be working at cross-purposes with evangelical ministers. "The people in this District are so deeply immersed in politics," complained one devout Christian in Crowdery Creek, South Carolina, "that but a very small portion of their time and attention is given to Jesus' cause, and I fear but a very little corner of their hearts is set apart for his Spirit." But as the nullifiers gained full command of their state at the end of 1832, their opponents discerned an affinity between the State Rights Party and the revivals. The "declamation" of the nullifiers, commented a disgusted Joel R. Poinsett in January 1833, "always reminded me of the ravings of Methodist exhorters, equally devoid of sense, equally unconnected & equally exciting."[99] There was more to this observation than the frustration of a defeated unionist. The correspondence of the nullifiers themselves indicated how evangelical fervor could translate into a passion for states' rights. South Carolina resident John W. Buridge not only assured his relatives in New York that the "assistance of our Lord and Saviour Jesus Christ" awaited those "born again . . . in the Spirit of [the] Holy Ghost" but also expressed his willingness to "be discarded by all my [northern] friends" in defense of nullification and South Carolina's sovereignty. His belief that he had "a friend in my God who can never forsake me" inspired his confidence that "the God of Justice will strengthen our cause."[100] Confronted by this militant Christianity, unionists such as James Louis Petigru likewise concluded that "very few of our Religionists have any Charity for those who are blind to the light of Calhoun & McDuffie's revelations."[101]

The marriage between Protestant and sectional doctrine made life exceptionally difficult for southern dissenters of all types.[102] When Edward R. Harden expressed his reservations about religion in 1831, his mother reacted with horror. Writing back to her son, who was studying at the University of Georgia, she urged him to "reflect well . . . upon all subjects before expressing your ideas, but upon religion I would not trust my tongue with utterance until you have read and reflected deeply and even then be modest in the advancement of your sentiments." "These are not times," she reminded him, "in which a youth or even [a man of] age can put his opinions in op- position to the multitude, nor indeed do I know whether those times will ever be, for it seems that the monument [of Christianity] grows stronger with age."[103] The Hardens clearly had not sent their son to the University of Georgia to receive an education in liberal thought.

The controversy over Thomas Cooper's religious views illustrated that slaveholding parents in South Carolina harbored equally conservative ideas about Christianity's place in university life. No one doubted Cooper's loy- alty to his adopted region. A leading radical, the president of South Carolina College had helped to nurture the nullification movement from its incep- tion. At the same time, however, his refusal to treat biblical passages as his- torical truth prompted many planters to view him as a potentially insidious influence on their impressionable sons. In December 1831, the South Caro- lina House of Representatives resolved to "investigate the conduct of Dr. Cooper" to determine whether "his continuance in office defeats the ends and aims of the Institution."[104] Many observers predicted that Cooper would, in fact, "be removed from the Presidency of this College . . . in con- sequence of inculcating religious tenets which are considered dangerous doctrines to imbibe on the minds of the youth of this state."[105] During pro- ceedings that dragged out over the next year, enough nullifiers rallied to the cause of their political ally to acquit Cooper of all charges. But the arduous struggle had taken its toll, and in November 1833, he resigned his office.[106] Although his departure had been voluntary, Cooper characterized it as a de- feat before the forces of religion: "The fanatics have succeeded at last in get- ting rid of me . . . [and] I feel somewhat melancholy at this College being degraded into a sectarian presbyterian institution, in which the Boy will learn nothing that the Man ought not to forget."[107]

Lacking Cooper's impeccable political credentials, most religious dis- senters who sought to educate the planter youth found themselves far more vulnerable to community censure. In 1835, John England reflected bitterly on the religious discrimination that he had received as the Catholic bishop of Charleston. Insisting that "Carolina has not a son more attached to her than I have been," England still "found that my religion was never to be for- given." His efforts to open a school ended disastrously owing to community opposition: "In my effort to create a respectable school in which literature alone was to be attended to, and each child's religious instruction left to his parents, . . . I was the victim of a conspiracy of the clergy [and] some of [the city's] principal lay gentlemen [who] succeeded in withdrawing nearly all the pupils."[108]

Given that Christian authorities had played a formative role in crafting the organic defense of slavery, their ascendancy naturally spelled disaster for anyone foolish enough to question the morality of human bondage in the Deep South. By the 1830s, native southerners harboring antislavery views such as Angelina Grimké were giving up all hope of reforming plantation society and were making plans, instead, to relocate to the North. Writing to her sister from Charleston in 1829, Grimké admitted feeling "like an exile, a stranger in the place of her nativity," and emphasized that she knew of no greater potential "earthly blessing than a release from this land of slavery."[109] Critics of slavery who remained behind in Charleston realized the perils of revealing their views to their slaveowning neighbors. In 1835 (after relocating to Philadelphia) Angelina Grimké received a detailed survey of the vicious punishments inflicted on slaves in the Charleston workhouse. The author of the report, however, wisely refused to sign her name, observing that "should it by accident fall into the hands of a Carolinian, it might produce a strong prejudice against me." This antislavery spy considered it her "misfortune to be obliged to reside there."[110]

That white, southern opponents of human bondage feared recrimination from their neighbors was hardly surprising. By the mid-1830s, however, the positive defense of slavery as an organic institution of unquestionable morality had become deeply embedded in the southern political consciousness, leaving little doubt which justifications for slavery prevailed among leading slaveowners. Southerners such as Charleston resident Henry Dickson who continued to deny the slave's human ties with the white population acknowledged that they harbored "heterodox opinions." "When they show me—les Amis des Noir—a picture of a flat nosed thick-lipped wooly head from whose wide mouth issues a label with the sentimental question 'Am I not a man & a Brother,'" contended Dickson in 1838, "I reply you may be of the genus Homo . . . but I decline the honour of any near relationship." Noting that "the Bat & the Whale belong with me in the Mammalia tribe," he denied that biological affinities implied "common parentage." But if Dickson sought to discredit human conceptions of slaves by associating them with abolitionists, he still felt compelled to grapple with the rising tide of Christian proslavery tracts that explicitly acknowledged the master's responsibilities to respect the slave's humanity. Realizing that these authorities contradicted his understanding of the master-slave relationship, he defended his position by observing that "the Bible evidently contains the history [only] of the Caucasian or White race."[111] Dickson, however, was fighting a losing battle. Such views continued to find adherents throughout the antebellum period, but a slaveholding ideal based on the principles of corporate individualism had taken center stage in southern politics and culture.

The need for a unified stance on slavery had begun to outweigh the individual southerner's right to express his or her own political opinions. As the career of Henry Laurens Pinckney makes clear, those slaveowners who deviated even slightly from conventional wisdom about slavery risked being denounced as abolitionists. An avid supporter of nullification, Pinckney repeatedly depicted the struggle over the tariff as an epic battle that would decide the planters' right to hold slaves. In 1831, he had warned that unless South Carolina offered sufficient "opposition to the tariff . . . abolition will become the order of the day."[112] To the disgust of Charleston unionists, Pinckney continued to capitalize on the slavery issue even after the nullification controversy had been resolved. In 1833, according to Mitchell King, Pinckney contended that "the North has entered into a deep conspiracy against the peculiar interests of the South." This appeal to the slaveholders' fears led King to observe that "now they have accepted the compromise and can no longer excite the people by declamations on the tariff," the nullifiers "have taken up a subject on which we have always been exceedingly sensitive in the hope of finding it a better engine for effecting their unholy purposes."[113]

But if the question of slavery catapulted Pinckney into political prominence, it also proved to be his undoing. Elected to represent Charleston in the House of Representatives, Pinckney ran afoul of his constituents when he formulated a response to the influx of abolitionist petitions presented to Congress in 1835 and 1836. Whereas John C. Calhoun and James Henry Hammond indignantly demanded that Congress refuse altogether to accept the antislavery petitions, Pinckney helped to engineer a policy that became known as the "gag rule." Congress would receive the petitions and immediately send them to a select committee (which, under no circumstances, would ever allow them to see the light of day). Although many northerners denounced the gag rule as evidence of a slave power conspiracy against the liberties of free citizens, Pinckney received no accolades in the Deep South.[114]

To the contrary, because he had acknowledged the abstract right of antislavery activists to petition Congress and had implied that Congress had the power—which he hastened to make clear should never be used—to end slavery in the District of Columbia, Pinckney was reviled as an abolitionist. Pinckney's conduct, wrote James Hemphill in March 1836, "is generally disapproved of in the Southern States, and especially by his former friends in the State Rights Party." That same month, Francis W. Pickens expressed his anxiety "to know how the people of old Abbeville, [South Carolina], could bear this betrayal of their dearest rights by a traitor and a dastard." Dismayed southerners such as Sam Warren claimed that they "would not be surprised to see Pinckney support Emancipation."[115] The disgraced congressman attempted to answer his critics in a published address to his constituents. In it, he affirmed his feeling that "the question of slavery should not be discussed in Congress, if it could possibly be avoided," and he "heartily concurred in the desire to reject those petitions at the threshold, or, in other words, 'to kick them out of the halls of Congress.'" Insisting that his measures had effectively undermined the abolitionists, Pinckney made a point of addressing Charleston voters "*as slaveholders.*"[116]

Charleston's planters, however, refused to forgive his heterodoxy. "Mr. Pinckney came out in [a] long piece in vindication of himself," wrote T. W. Peyre from Columbia, "but the people did not wait for him to finish before they commenced to tear it & him to atoms." Pinckney's "very fluent & handsomely written" defense revealed, in Peyre's opinion, "that conscious guilt which is so apt to leak from, & betray vitiated & corrupt minds. His doom, I think, is fixed."[117] Incensed by Pinckney's deviation from the strategy engineered by Calhoun and Hammond, the planters replaced him in Congress with Hugh Swinton Legaré. Pinckney was left with the reputation of "an Abolitionist in heart & soul."[118] Other South Carolina statesmen who dared to pilot their own legislative course in Congress agonized that they might meet the same terrible fate.[119] Notwithstanding the lunacy of his being accused of abolitionism, Pinckney deserved his disgrace. During the nullification crisis, he and his allies had whipped the white southern population into a frenzy over northern plots against their plantation society. Condemning the tyranny of the national majority, the nullifiers had urged the slaveholders to stamp out dissent at home to form a unified electorate capable of protecting slavery. And when the tyranny of this white southern majority manifested itself against South Carolina unionists, men like Pinckney cheered. Certainly it was only fitting that he be consumed by the sectional flames that he had so effectively fanned.

The manic proslavery atmosphere of the 1830s encouraged southerners to police one another's ideas about slavery not just in public but within domestic circles as well. Thus, in 1833, South Carolina resident John Hemphill chastised his brother, who was attending college in Pennsylvania, for embracing antislavery doctrine. "Your mind appears to affected with the cant and sickly sentiment on the subject of slavery," wrote Hemphill, before asserting that nothing could be done about slavery "without convulsing society" and effecting "indescribable horrors." Slaves, he lectured his brother, enjoyed happier circumstances than "misnamed" free laborers, and emancipation served only the interests of employers who could more effectively exploit a wage labor force than an enslaved one.[120] In private conversations between family members, southern slaveowners now sounded exactly like their own proslavery tracts—a development that was only fitting because proslavery authors had tapped into a culture of corporate individualism that had become the standard for plantation domesticity long before the explosion in printed defenses of southern slavery. Perceiving where this confluence between culture and politics might lead, some residents of Carolina predicted that the slaveowners would eventually march together, in perfectly coordinated lockstep, to a glorious doom. "Those wild [antislavery] fanatics are involving us again in new difficulties," wrote Beaufort Taylor Watts in 1836, "& the whole South must be indivisible." "Our population of all parties," he continued, "are very much excited, & *separation* we look to as a *duty*, & . . . should immolation follow, we will go down unto death, befitting men, who disregard death, when their rights are assailed." Watts himself harbored unorthodox views about African American capacity for freedom, but in keeping with the climate of the times, he maintained that "it is ill timed to discuss" the "philosophy of the question of slavery."[121]

Luckily for the union, the emerging two-party system managed to diffuse sectional tensions for the next quarter century.[122] Because both Whigs and Democrats crafted a proslavery message to win southern votes, the slaveholders remained vested in national political institutions. Nevertheless, by the mid-1830s, a distinctly southern cultural sensibility had provided the foundation for a politically self-conscious master class. And central to the planters' world view was their mounting hostility toward wage labor. Charleston resident Andrew Johnston, for example, recounted a South Carolina woman's unhappy experience with free labor when visiting Paris in 1829: "Mrs. Ramsay says . . . the servants about the house . . . are taking every advantage of them by cheating her whenever she wishes anything bought, making her pay five times the value of it & stealing everything they can lay their hands on."[123] Hugh Swinton Legaré offered similar complaints from Europe in 1833, contending that his servants consistently lingered over their own meals instead of tending to his needs. "If the domestics of all the houses of fashion in Brussels carry on the war [against their employers] as mine do," wrote Legaré, "their masters live only for them."[124] Back in the Deep South, the planter John Sherwood Thomas expressed his preference for slave labor to a friend in Georgia: "I very much hope never to be pestered with a gang of drunken, impudent & wrangling whitemen."[125] In short, as northerners internalized the assumption that slave labor could be used only in a "wasteful manner," white southerners were taking note of how their own experiments with free labor "failed entirely."[126]

With increasing frequency and confidence, the planters claimed that their society would triumph because slavery, as practiced in the South, inculcated values that ensured moral progress. The congressional debate over antislavery petitions provided James Henry Hammond with the opportunity to wax poetic about slavery's virtues. Human bondage, he declared in February 1836, was "no evil." "On the contrary," Hammond believed "it to be the greatest of all the great blessings which a kind Providence has bestowed upon our glorious region." "Our slaves," he continued in predictable fashion, "are a peaceful, kind hearted and affectionate race, satisfied with their lot, happy in their comforts, and devoted to their masters." Placing the question of ethics at the heart of their political defense, white southerners such as Francis Pickens readily acknowledged that "moral power has now a high ascendancy in human affairs." Slaveholders from other eras, argued Rebecca Rutledge, had ruled by "brute force"; their "pride and cruelty" had resulted in their fall from power and the emancipation of their slaves. The southern planters, on the other hand, would "keep ourselves unstained by the crimes" of evil masters such as "the french of St. Domingo," thereby ensuring that the South "shall . . . be free from their punishment."[127] Although abolitionists believed that slavery ensured the "declining state" of the South, the planters insisted that their society was progressing morally.[128] "The days of ignorance, superstition and tyranny," announced Charleston resident Thomas Taylor in 1831, "are fast passing away."[129] That the slaveowners could make such pronouncements amid the crises of the 1830s illustrates their ability to create their own vision of reality—a vision brought into focus by their ideology as a ruling elite.

The planters foresaw impending disaster not for themselves but for the denizens of free societies in Europe and the northern United States. "In no part of the world," declared Hammond, "have men of ordinary firmness less fear of danger from their operatives than we have. The fires which in a few years have desolated Normandy and Anjou, the great machine burning in the heart of England, . . . and the mobs which for some years past have figured in the northern states . . . are very powerful illustrations of the peace and security of a community whose laborers are all free." Above all else, Hammond warned white southerners to beware "the mob—THE SANS-CULOTTES" who claimed "as their watchword that immortal but now prostituted sentiment 'that all men are born free and equal'" and who "rallied to their standard the ignorant, uneducated, semi-barbarous mass." Divesting his regional heritage from the legacy of Thomas Jefferson and the French Revolution, Hammond declared that the slaveowning South would be ready to meet the mob if and when it passed through New England to the planters' borders. They were ready "to roll back the frantic tide to whence it came."[130] The mob's destructive "march has commenced in the North and there is nothing to impede it," declared Nathaniel Beverley Tucker in response to Hammond's speech. Taking measure of the benefits bestowed by slavery, Tucker announced with satisfaction that "there is in the frame of our *society* a controlling power over the brute force of the multitude."[131]

Hammond's fellow congressman from South Carolina, Francis W. Pickens, divided all members of society into capitalists and laborers and observed that "the only contest in the world is between the two systems. If laborers ever obtain the political power of a country, it is in fact in a state of revolution, which must end in substantially transferring property to themselves until they shall become capitalists." What disturbed Pickens most was the realization that the masters of the South had interests very different from those of the "capitalists north of Mason and Dixon's line."[132] Pickens perceived that "the capitalists of the non-slaveholding states" lived by a corrupt banking system and "resort[ed] to corporations by which the whole society may be moved by one man." Southern slaveholders, on the other hand, had "no need to resort to such means" because all their "laws & political institutions are based upon this avowed relation between capitalists and labourers: Every slaveholder upon his plantation in the South is already a corporation" whose laborers' interests were identical to his own. For this reason, southern masters, although technically capitalists controlling the means of production, actually "stand as labourers in society as far as [their] class are interested." Needless to say, it was "precisely the reverse of this with capitalists in the non-slaveholding states," who constantly battled against the interests of their workforce.[133] To the "great class of capitalists in the North," Pickens offered the warning, "Beware that you do not drive us into a separate system."[134]

Although those fire-eaters advocating secession constituted an extremely tiny minority in the 1830s, the notion that the planters' dedication to slavery had isolated their region from the rest of the world had become widespread. Slaveholders visiting the North sent back disturbing reports that the abolitionist "party is a very strong & very rich one—dangerous in a high degree to the safety & liberty of the South."[135] And southern leaders such as Pickens conceded that "the moral power of the world is against us." "Everything proclaims that, sooner or later, we shall have to meet the strong and powerful, and contend over the tombs of our fathers for our consecrated hearthstones and household gods, or abandon our country to become a black colony," he argued in Congress.[136] In response to the hostile incursions of the antislavery culture of Europe and the North, southern writers in the 1830s generated a self-consciously sectional literature. The antislavery bias of foreign periodicals such as the *Westminster Review* and the publications springing from northern churches could no longer be tolerated.[137] Into their place came periodicals such as the *Southern Review* and the *Southern Rose*, as well as a host of novels set in the South and stocked with characters who embodied the heroic chivalry of the planter class.[138]

Although southern authors such as William Gilmore Simms could still, in moments of frustration, portray the southern countryside as a region "incompatible with literary labor," the slaveowners of this era had developed a culture oriented toward literary consumption. Simms himself conceded as much when he noted that the planters whom he criticized because they mostly looked "to hunt, to ride, to lounge, and to sleep" might also take the time "to read a few popular novels conducing to repose."[139] And certainly it was significant that the plot of Simms's first novel, *Guy Rivers*, turned on this very possibility. In this work, the character of the noble young planter, Ralph Colleton, makes sense of his emotions only after reading a novel.[140] As much as Simms appreciated the degree to which a cosmopolitan intellectual community stimulated literary creation, the slaveowners who prided themselves on agrarian values and virtue now constituted the ultimate audience for those authors dwelling on pastoral themes. The romantic formulations of early-nineteenth-century novelists had taken early root in the slaveowners' developing sectional consciousness and, over the next three decades, would profoundly influence white southern perceptions about politics and race.

By 1837, ideological differences over slavery had set the stage for a schism in the Presbyterian Church.[141] Convinced that their institution of slavery conformed to Christian principles, southern church members had been experiencing friction with their northern counterparts for much of the decade. As early as 1830, John Hemphill, a prominent Presbyterian from South Carolina, learned that the synod responsible for the western United States had considered excluding slaveholders from communion.[142] Hemphill's informant later conveyed the news that the slavery issue had been placed on hold and expressed his hope that "time will gradually restore a proper tone of feeling & that brotherly love will prevail in that interesting section of our church." Despite the temporary resolution of this issue, slave-owning Presbyterians viewed it as "a portentous cloud," observing that "there was so much said & written with so much asperity on the slavery question [that] feelings were aroused, which may yet . . . exert an influence very prejudicial to . . . truth & godliness."[143]

The issue continued to concern Hemphill over the ensuing years. Writing to his brother in 1833, he brooded over the possibility that a "breach at some day not far distant" would disturb "our own church on the subject of slavery."[144] By August 1836, events were demonstrating that Hemphill's fears were well founded. His brother William (whom John Hemphill had previously worried was being swayed by abolitionist doctrine) alienated the presbyter in Pennsylvania by preaching in favor of slavery. In response, northern church authorities refused to license him, prompting futile protestations on the part of proslavery Presbyterian ministers.[145] After brewing resentment over episodes such as these, the struggle over slavery flared into open crisis in 1837. Writing from Philadelphia (where the Presbyterians convened in summer of that year), South Carolina minister John Witherspoon accurately predicted that "the slavery question" would be "the most exciting & dividing in our body."[146]

Although the resulting schism did not fall perfectly along sectional lines, there was little doubt that proslavery southerners provided the main force behind the Old School Presbyterians who separated themselves from the rest of the church in an effort to purify it. Simply put, the Presbyterian Church could no longer accommodate the sectional tensions between two conflicting definitions of Christian social relations. Over the next quarter century, the same pattern manifested itself in the Methodist and Baptists Churches and, eventually, in the political structures of the nation as a whole.[147] Although Americans might well have been able to avoid civil war had they made different political decisions in the late antebellum era, an essential precondition for the schism had already been met by the late 1830s. Slaveowners had managed to concoct a regional identity that centered on idealized notions of their own mastery. Unlike the wealthy planters of the colonial and Revolutionary periods, nineteenth-century slaveholders did not feel humbled by a cosmopolitan standard for gentility that frowned on human bondage. Drawing on the themes they had obtained over decades of contact with writers and religious authorities on both sides of the Atlantic and the Mason-Dixon line, planters developed a vocabulary of corporate individualism that enabled them to defend slavery and to present their own society as a unique and superior culture. However greatly the ideology of this master class distorted the reality of plantation life and the actual origins of southern cultural precepts, it ultimately proved more powerful than were the civic institutions that held the nation together.

CONCLUSION

In December 1836, Edisto Island planter Joseph Jenkins visited the circus in Columbia, South Carolina, where he saw "the grandest collections of wild beasts . . . ever known in this country." After observing a rhinoceros and several zebras, Jenkins witnessed an amazing scene. "The keeper of these animals opened a small door of the lions cage and entered into it—he sat himself down on the floor of the cage and made the lioness lay her head in his lap," and then "he played with her, as you would," wrote Jenkins to his daughter, "with a puppy." But this was not all. The performer then "thrust his hand into her mouth and ma[de] her show her teeth and enormous claws," which were "enough to have torn him to pieces in a moment." These feats convinced Jenkins that the "animals are perfectly domesticated . . . for they appeared to fear and love [the animal keeper] as much as a good dog would a kind master." Or, as much (Jenkins might very well have continued) as a loyal slave would fear and love a caring master.[1]

Beginning in the last decade of the eighteenth century, the planters of the Deep South had learned, in their own minds, to domesticate their slaves. By 1836, James Henry Hammond could declare that "there is not a happier, more contented race upon the face of the earth" than the black bondservants who populated the plantations of the Deep South. "Their lives and persons," he maintained, were "protected by the law, all their sufferings alleviated by the kindest and most interested care, and their domestic affections cherished and maintained."[2] After depicting slaves as a savage, unpredictable, and extremely dangerous "domestic enemy" over much of the eighteenth century, the planters now embraced them as members of an intimate domestic circle. South Carolina jurist William Harper captured the essence of this ethos when he announced, in 1837, that "the tendency of Slavery is rather to humanize than to brutalize."[3]

Idealized conceptions of the master-slave relationship enabled the planters to sublimate their fears of slave insurrection. Rather than dwelling on the possibility that they might be unexpectedly poisoned or dismembered in the middle of the night, the slaveowners imagined that African Americans (whom they were exploiting for tremendous profit) were actually loving members of their extended family. Still, at times, a few clearsighted whites took stock of the region's immense slave population and shuddered about the future. Writing from his Georgia plantation in 1836, Presbyterian minister Iveson Brookes described to his wife a chilling but "plausible dream": "The substance is that in some twenty or thirty years a division of the Northern and Southern states will be produced by the Abolitionists and then a war will ensue between the Yankees & Slaveholders—that the army of Yankees will be at once joined by the Negroes who will show more savage cruelty than the blood thirsty Indians." Brookes envisioned that white southerners "with gratitude for having escaped alive will gladly leave their splendid houses & farms to be occupied by those who once served in them." Disturbed by this premonition, the minister declared that "all who act with judicious foresight should within two years sell every half of a negro & land & vest the money in western lands."[4]

But, notwithstanding his prophecy, Brookes had no intention of surrendering his position as master. "I am however acting contrary to those sound suggestions of reason," he concluded to his wife, "for I have today bargained for a farm . . . lying next to my plantation." Instead of divesting himself of slaves, Brookes deepened his commitment to the plantation economy.[5] In the 1850s, he even published his own defenses of slavery, in which he depicted the master-slave relationship in corporate rather than violent and confrontational terms.[6] The organic household ideal enabled slaveowners such as Brookes to rationalize their misgivings—to replace "bloodthirsty" and "savage" blacks with comforting images of domesticated servants.

For the millions of African American slaves kept in bondage by southern planters, however, the nightmare was not one that could be escaped through ideological contortions. Their suffering made a mockery of their owners' pretensions. When the Civil War finally gave them an opportunity to claim their freedom, they wasted little time before disavowing the "benevolent care" of whites, who had cloaked cruel economic practice in the mantle of Christian stewardship. The ideological channels linking masters and slaves in the nineteenth-century South entailed an unprecedented degree of cultural inclusion for African Americans. But inclusion amounted neither to equality nor even to significantly improved living conditions.

This characteristic of the slaveowners' culture—inclusion without equality—extended beyond the immediate confines of master-slave relations and, by the 1830s, had come to define the planters' intercourse with less privileged southern whites and the world at large. When southern statesmen could no longer maintain despotic control over the political process, they allowed poorer whites to participate, but only in a manner that upheld the slaveowners' economic and social hegemony. Focusing political debate on sectional concerns about slavery, the planters transformed the threat against the institution of human bondage into an attack on the values of the entire South. This tactic not only defused potential class conflict between planters and yeomen but also concealed the actual cultural dynamic by which the slaveholders developed their sensibility as masters. The planters had immersed themselves in transatlantic intellectual currents only to pronounce that their culture constituted a civilized and secure island—one which would withstand the rising tide of anarchy that was enveloping the rest of the world. Cultural intimacy had bred profound animosity and alienation.

The slaveholders' sectional culture was not less genuine for having developed in a transregional intellectual context. The political stance that sprang from their world view did isolate the slaveholders from the rest of the nation, and they had good reason to fear for the security of their peculiar institution. But the planters had a great deal more in common with the North by the 1830s than they (and many Yankees) cared to admit. The same sentimental domestic tropes that provided cultural order to plantation households also undergirded family life in the North. Although the southerners were the only ones to construct a coherent political identity around corporate standards for human relations, those values still manifested themselves beyond southern borders and continue to affect American ideas about race, class, and gender to this day. In the end, if we conclude that growing numbers of southern masters loved their slaves, we mean it not as an apology for slavery but as an indictment of their notion of domesticity—a notion that equated love with control. The slaveholders' deeds were monstrous, but they construed their actions in decidedly human terms.

However sickening and self-serving the slaveholders' convictions may have been, they were nevertheless deeply rooted in southern society and therefore historically significant. By the time that Harriet Martineau published her critical account of the South in 1837, the planters had long since developed the cultural and ideological resources with which to mount an effective defense. When William Gilmore Simms denounced Martineau's work, he was merely repeating points that had been articulated time and time again in the writings and speeches of leading eighteenth- and nineteenth-century southern ideologues. Simms's personal belief that he had "broach[ed] some new doctrines which [would] startle" the North can be attributed to an artist's vanity.[7] But the assertion also reveals the strange manner in which southern culture operated. If Simms had traced the literary and religious sources of the argument that he promulgated in the *Southern Literary Messenger*, he would have been forced to confront the South's integration into a transatlantic intellectual community which was supported by an international capitalistic market. For political (as well as professional) reasons, however, the Charleston author dwelled instead on the creative aspects of his work. In an age of crisis, the planters convinced themselves that they were making moral progress over the rest of the world. Far from regurgitating long-standing notions about hierarchical society, the slaveowners insisted that they were turning over a fresh page in the history of enlightened mastery. Their misplaced certainty on this point carried disastrous consequences not only for their enslaved African American workforce but also for the nation that would eventually splinter over the great moral question of slavery.

NOTES

AC   *Annals of Congress*

BPRO   British Public Record Office

BPRO-GA   British Public Record Office documents relating to Georgia, copies in the Georgia Department of Archives and History, Atlanta

BPRO-SC   British Public Record Office documents relating to South Carolina, C. Noel Sainsbury transcripts, South Carolina Department of Archives and History, Columbia

CL   Clements Library, University of Michigan, Ann Arbor

DU   Perkins Library, Duke University, Durham, North Carolina

EU   Woodruff Library, Special Collections, Emory University, Atlanta, Georgia

GDAH   Georgia Department of Archives and History, Atlanta

GHS   Georgia Historical Society, Savannah

HLP   *The Papers of Henry Laurens*, edited by Philip M. Hamer et al.

LC   Manuscripts Division, Library of Congress, Washington, D.C.

LPL   Lambeth Palace Library, London, England

NL   Newberry Library, Chicago, Illinois

NYHS   New-York Historical Society, New York

NYPL   New York Public Library, New York

PHS   Historical Society of Pennsylvania, Philadelphia

PJCC   *The Papers of John C. Calhoun*, edited by Robert L. Meriwether et al.

SCDAH   South Carolina Department of Archives and History, Columbia

SCHS   South Carolina Historical Society, Charleston

SCL   South Caroliniana Library, University of South Carolina, Columbia

SHC   Southern Historical Collection, University of North Carolina at Chapel Hill

SPG   Society for the Propagation of the Gospel in Foreign Parts

UGA   Hargrett Library, University of Georgia, Athens

UVA   University of Virginia Library, Charlottesville

VHS   Virginia Historical Society, Richmond

YU   Beinecke Library, Yale University, New Haven, Connecticut

INTRODUCTION

1. Martineau, *Society in America*, 2:121, 118, 129. For background on Martineau, see G. Thomas, *Harriet Martineau*; Webb, *Harriet Martineau*; Pichanick, *Harriet Mar-*

tineau; Nevill, *Harriet Martineau*; and Wheatley, *Life and Work of Harriet Martineau*.

2. The essay was republished the following year as Simms, *Slavery in America*. On Simms, see McCardell, *Idea of a Southern Nation*, chap. 4; Faust, *Sacred Circle*; Guilds, *Simms*; Dye, "Sociology for the South"; Trent, *William Gilmore Simms*; Wakelyn, *Politics of a Literary Man*; and Wimsatt, *Major Fiction of William Gilmore Simms*.

3. Simms, *Slavery in America*, 29, 37, 38.

4. Ibid., 61, 65, 83, 73, 65.

5. See, for example, the remarkable exchange between David Brion Davis and Thomas L. Haskell: D. B. Davis, *Problem of Slavery in the Age of Revolution*, and Haskell, "Capitalism and the Origins of the Humanitarian Sensibility." Notwithstanding their differences, both scholars agree that, on at least some level, the growth of capitalism made possible the sustained campaign against slavery. As Howard Temperley so memorably contended: "Precisely at a time when capitalist ideas were in the ascendant, and large-scale production of all kinds of goods was beginning, we find this system [of plantation slavery] being dismantled. How could this happen unless 'capitalism' had something to do with it? If our reasoning leads to the conclusion that 'capitalism' had nothing to do with it the chances are that there is something wrong with our reasoning" ("Capitalism, Slavery, and Ideology," 105). See also Drescher, *Capitalism and Antislavery*; Anstey, *Atlantic Slave Trade and British Abolition*; Temperley, "Ideology of Antislavery"; E. Williams, *Capitalism and Slavery*; and Solow and Engerman, *British Capitalism and Caribbean Slavery*.

6. For the transition to capitalism, see Marx, *Capital*; Holton, *Transition from Feudalism to Capitalism*; Kriedte, *Peasants, Landlords, and Merchant Capitalists*; Gutmann, *Toward the Modern Economy*; and Aston and Philpin, *Brenner Debate*. For the political economists' increasing emphasis on individual liberty and their mounting criticism of mercantilism and slavery, see A. Smith, *Wealth of Nations*, vol. 2; Mill, *Elements of Political Economy*; Temperley, "Capitalism, Slavery, and Ideology"; Bain, *James Mill*, 113–14; Ross, *Life of Adam Smith*, chap. 16; West, *Adam Smith*, chap. 6; Buchanan, "Justice of Natural Liberty"; Billet, "Justice, Liberty, and Economy"; and Muller, *Adam Smith in His Time and Ours*.

7. For the influence of classical political economists on Martineau, see G. Thomas, *Harriet Martineau*, chap. 4; David, *Intellectual Women and Victorian Patriarchy*, chaps. 2–3; Webb, *Harriet Martineau*, 116–17; Pichanick, *Harriet Martineau*. Exposure to these authors had already prompted Martineau to condemn slavery in her work *Demarara*.

8. Phillips, *American Negro Slavery*.

9. Stampp, *The Peculiar Institution*. See also Elkins, *Slavery*, in which Elkins emphasized the brutality of slavery in what he characterized as a capitalistic, slaveowning South.

10. For historiographical essays mapping these conflicting interpretations, see Faust, "The Peculiar South Revisited," and Kulikoff, "Transition to Capitalism in Rural America." In these fair-minded and insightful studies, Faust and Kulikoff point to common ground between capitalistic and paternalistic interpretations, but

both authors clearly prefer the paternalistic model for the slaveholders' world view. Faust and Kulikoff argue that neoclassical economists and historians who depict the planters merely as businessmen assume (rather than prove) that market participation resulted in the embrace of individualistic values. See Kulikoff, "Transition to Capitalism in Rural America," 14–24; and Faust, "The Peculiar South Revisited," 85. Although both authors express frustration at the stark division between the two interpretive approaches, neither offers a unifying theoretical framework. Faust states that she has "little faith" that historians can ever agree over such a framework (119); Kulikoff, for all his sensitivity to the merits of the neoclassical scholarship, unabashedly expresses his preference for marxist categories of analysis and presents the slaveowners as "anticapitalist" (18, 7–8). See also Parish, *Slavery*, especially chap. 7, and Egerton, "Markets without a Market Revolution."

11. For example, Eugene D. Genovese—the most influential scholar to emphasize the slaveowners' paternalism—depicted in his early work the "premodern quality of the Southern world." By contrast, in his later writings, he contends that the slaveholders "saw themselves as men who sought an alternate route to modernity" and that they pronounced "the industrial revolution and all its works" to be "self-generating, irreversible, and on the whole good" (*The Political Economy of Slavery*, 3, and *Slaveholders' Dilemma*, 13, 4). Likewise, James Oakes, who in his first book forcefully rejected Genovese's paternalistic paradigm, acknowledges in his second work that "the slave South's relationship to liberal capitalism" was "at once closer and yet far more complicated than most studies [including, one assumes, Oakes's earlier book] have hitherto indicated" (*Ruling Race*, especially xi–xiii, and *Slavery and Freedom*, xiii [quotation]). While it would be foolish to underestimate the considerable ideological and interpretive gulf separating these scholars, we can still observe how Genovese's and Oakes's complimentary citations to each other's more recent books reveal their movement away from the historiographical poles that their own work helped to define. See Genovese, *The Slaveholders' Dilemma*, 9 n. 5, and Oakes, *Slavery and Freedom*, xviii–xix.

12. Olwell, "'A Reckoning of Accounts,'" 35 (quotation), and Boles, *The South Through Time*, 185–86. On this point, see also Morris, *Becoming Southern*, 35–36.

13. For instance, see Dusinberre, *Them Dark Days*. Dusinberre contributes greatly to our understanding of lowcountry demographics, economics, and slave culture, but his argument falls flat when he situates himself within a traditional historiographical context that places capitalism at odds with paternalistic hierarchy. Evidence of the planters' acuity as businessmen leads Dusinberre to reject all possibility that paternalistic notions might have contributed to their world view. But his own careful research has revealed numerous instances in which the slaveowners presented themselves in paternalistic terms. See *Them Dark Days*, 46–47, 182–85, 253–54, 288, 301, 303, 308, 335, and 367. Here, rigid historiographical categories seem to be restricting a scholar's vision to narrower choices than the evidence itself suggests. The critical response to Ashworth, *Commerce and Compromise*, provides another case in point. Ashworth's marxist analysis that categorized the slaveholders' views as "pre-capitalist" (49) antagonized reviewers such as William E. Gienapp (*Journal of Southern History* 63 [August 1997]: 651). I point to Dusinberre and Ashworth's works

not to demean them (since I think they both make valuable contributions) but to demonstrate that the broader debate has reached an intellectual dead end.

14. Like other scholars exploring southern slavery, I employ the term "organic" to evoke the slaveowners' vision of society as a unified body—an organism, of sorts, with elements that needed to work in concert to serve the broad needs of the entire society. For just a few examples of impressive recent studies that have complicated and refined our understanding of capitalism and slavery, see M. Smith, *Mastered by the Clock* and "Old South Time," and Chaplin, *Anxious Pursuit.* It is worth noting that, having pushed past traditional historiographical boundaries between slavery and capitalism, these scholars appear uncertain as to where their work fits in to the existing historiographical terrain. Smith, for example, compliments the work of both Genovese and Laurence Shore, a historian who explicitly sought to overturn Genovese's paternalistic paradigm. Smith, "Old South Time," 1453 n. 60 and 1454 n. 64. Without making sense of the apparent contradiction, Chaplin acknowledges both the possibility of an "aggressively antimodern stance of the antebellum era" and the possibility that "capitalist ideology continued" during this period. *Anxious Pursuit,* 59, 356 n. 1.

The term "ideology" has its own long and contested history. I use it synonymously with "world view" to refer to the system of ideas through which a particular segment of society makes sense of its circumstances. I argue in this book that the ideology of the slaveholders made necessary certain political decisions and, at the same time, enabled the slaveowners to justify (in their own minds) their stance as a benevolent ruling elite. My thinking on ideology has been influenced by J. Thompson, *Ideology and Modern Culture,* and by many productive conversations with Mari-Paz Balibrea-Enríquez.

15. I should make clear that I am neither accusing historians of portraying the slaveowners in monolithic terms nor suggesting that I am the first scholar to appreciate a potentially symbiotic (as opposed to an exclusively antithetical) relationship between capitalism and organic social values. To take one notable example, Lacy K. Ford Jr. pays careful attention to the possibility that paternalistic ideas about social relations could manifest themselves in both free and slave labor societies. See his superb *Origins of Southern Radicalism,* 353–65. What I would suggest, however, is that the current terms of the historiographical debate lead most scholars to emphasize one element of the paternalism-capitalism dichotomy over the other. In Ford's case, greater interpretive weight is given to the extension of market growth into an upcountry region characterized by a decidedly racist but nevertheless egalitarian (for whites) social vision.

16. Phillips, *American Negro Slavery;* Genovese, *Roll, Jordan, Roll.*

17. Fox-Genovese, *Within the Plantation Household;* Fox-Genovese and Genovese, *Fruits of Merchant Capital.* Arguing that the master-slave relationship led to a sectional culture that "was in but not of the capitalist world," Fox-Genovese and Genovese proclaim that the planters "did not have a market society," preferring instead to place the claims of an organic, hierarchical community ahead of the individual pursuit of fiscal gain (*Fruits of Merchant Capital,* 16–17). To their credit, these scholars offer this distinction to offset historical interpretations that have explicitly

equated participation in global commerce with a bourgeois mentality and to underscore the paradox of a paternalistic, anticapitalistic master class coalescing within the broader economic framework of a capitalistic international economy. See, for example, Wallerstein, *The Modern World-System*, and Braudel, *Civilization and Capitalism*. Both authors credit historical shifts in the sphere of exchange (as opposed to the sphere of production or class relations) with responsibility for the creation of a modern capitalistic ethos. For a graceful application of this theoretical model to the slaveholding South, see Coclanis, *The Shadow of a Dream*. Fox-Genovese and Genovese, by contrast, contend that an elite within a "peripheral" zone of production can create a distinct world view, notwithstanding their economic dependence on the broader transatlantic market.

18. Censer, *North Carolina Planters and Their Children*, 152. Censer asserts that the "planters sought to transmit not the values of leisure and disdain for work and material success that Genovese has imputed to them, but the importance of education, hard work, thrift, self-control and achievement." Like Censer, Isaac suggests that modern bourgeois notions increased the cultural distance between master and slave and helped to foster sustained criticism of human bondage on moral grounds (*The Transformation of Virginia*, 274–322). Stowe also asserts that slaves were largely removed from white planters' daily family intercourse even as the slaveowners sought to govern their white families by persuasion rather than force. See *Intimacy and Power in the Old South*, xv–xvii. By contrast, for the argument that the planters extended their new conceptions of family to include their slaves, see Lewis, *The Pursuit of Happiness*, 221–22.

19. Genovese, *Roll, Jordan, Roll*, 661–65; quotation on 661. Fox-Genovese goes so far as to concede that "antebellum southern domestic relations owed much of their companionate tenor to the bourgeois rhetoric of domesticity, including companionate marriage and the modern ideologies of motherhood and childrearing." But she follows this observation with her contention that the slaveowners "applied those ideologies according to their own [distinct] social and gender relations." Thus, in the end, the differences between slaveowners' paternalism and northern bourgeois domestic culture matter most (*Within the Plantation Household*, 64).

20. The modern characteristics of the slaveowners' proslavery thought are explored in a number of trenchant works. See Wyatt-Brown, "Modernizing Southern Slavery"; Chaplin, "Slavery and the Principle of Humanity"; Faust, "The Peculiar South Revisited," 104–6; Faust, "Evangelicalism and the Meaning of the Proslavery Argument," 4–5; Faust, "A Southern Stewardship"; and M. O'Brien, *All Clever Men, Who Make Their Way*, 1–25. As I mentioned above, Genovese himself now emphasizes that the planters embraced rather than rejected "modernity." Nevertheless, despite the efforts of scholars seeking to situate proslavery thought within a thoroughly modern context, an assumed dichotomy between paternalism and bourgeois modernity underlies several widely acclaimed surveys of political and economic trends in the early United States. See especially G. Wood, *The Radicalism of the American Revolution*; Sellers, *The Market Revolution*, particularly 280 n. 15; and Yazawa, *From Colonies to Commonwealth*.

21. The transition toward romantic conceptions of the home as a loving domestic

sanctuary for individual growth took place over centuries. Historians, not surprisingly, have reached no consensus about the specific timing of or reasons behind this new domestic sensibility. One might safely suggest, however, that both the spread of Christianity and the subsequent growth of an international market during the early modern era played major roles in the creation of the affective model for family relations. See Herlihy, *Medieval Households*; Hanawalt, *The Ties That Bound*; DeMause, *The History of Childhood*; J. Lynch, *Godparents and Kinship in Early Medieval Europe*; Fichtenau, *Living in the Tenth Century*; Ullmann, *The Individual and Society in the Middle Ages*; C. Morris, *The Discovery of the Individual*; Stone, *The Family, Sex, and Marriage in England*; Ariès, *Centuries of Childhood*; and Degler, *At Odds*. Schneider argues that the Methodists were particularly effective at promoting a "Victorian" domestic sensibility in the Old Northwest in the nineteenth century. See his *The Way of the Cross Leads Home*. Schneider contrasts this evangelical vision of domesticity with the more traditional patriarchal culture of honor in the South. For this vision of the South, see Wyatt-Brown, *Southern Honor*. I argue in this book that, notwithstanding the traditions identified by Wyatt-Brown, the impact of market growth and evangelicalism fostered new visions of domesticity among increasing numbers of southerners.

22. For a rich analysis of Carter as an emblematic figure in the transition away from traditional patriarchal values, see Morgan, "Three Planters and Their Slaves."

23. Carter, *Diary of Colonel Landon Carter*, 1:295 (entry for May 4, 1766), 1:310 (June 27, 1766).

24. Ibid., 2:780–81 (September 27, 1773), 2:1149 (August 31, 1778), 2:1095 (April 20, 1777), 2:840 (June 27, 1774).

25. For the broad affinity between capitalism, bourgeois property, and individual rights, see Hont and Ignatieff, "Needs and Justice in the *Wealth of Nations*"; MacPherson, *The Political Theory of Possessive Individualism*; and Schlatter, *Private Property*.

26. Simms, *Slavery in America*, 61, and "The Morals of Slavery," 213–14, 272–74. Simms even broached the possibility that at some ("very remote") future date, African Americans might progress as a race to such a degree as to deserve freedom (ibid., 269). Notwithstanding her opposition to slavery, Harriet Martineau noted that "a common question put to me by amiable [white southern] ladies was, 'Do you not find the slaves generally very happy?'" (*Society in America*, 2:121). For an intriguing study that stresses the extent to which slaveowners professed to care for their slaves as individuals, see Greenberg, *Masters and Statesmen*.

27. Furman, *Exposition of the Views of the Baptists*, 10–11, 5. For background on Furman, see Rogers, *Richard Furman*.

28. For example, Aristotle depicted the slave as "a part of the master, a living but separated part of his bodily frame." The slave, contended this philosopher, was "a kind of instrument" who by nature had "no deliberative faculty at all" (*Politics*, 9 [1255b11–12], 5 [1253b30], and 19 [1260a12–13]). To be sure, some southern ideologues quoted Aristotle to defend slavery. See Holmes, "Observations on a Passage in the *Politics* of Aristotle Relative to Slavery," 193–205. Nevertheless, southern slaveowners as a group believed that they treated their bondservants with far greater kindness

than had their predecessors throughout history. See, for example, the speech delivered in 1820 by South Carolina senator William Smith: "The Greeks confined their slaves in cells; the Spartans suffered the Lacedemonian youths to fall upon them, when laboring in the fields, by stratagem, and massacre them in gangs, for the purpose of training their youths to feats in arms; the Romans threw them into the arena, where they cut one another down, for the amusement of their rich masters." Smith asserted that antislavery activists had even less regard for the slaves' welfare than had these ancient masters. Meanwhile, he suggested that "the whole commerce between master and slave [in the South] is patriarchal. . . . The black children are the constant associates of the white children; their affections are often times so strongly formed . . . that in thousands of instances there is nothing but the shadow of slavery left." *AC*, 16th Cong., 1st sess., 268. See also Genovese, "The Southern Slaveholders' View of the Middle Ages"; Greenberg, *Masters and Statesmen*, 92; and Jenkins, *Pro-Slavery Thought in the Old South*, 108–10.

29. For a study of how eighteenth-century America was shaped by concepts of liberty that were "characterized [by] a voluntary submission to a life of righteousness," see Shain, *The Myth of American Individualism*; quotation here is on 4. Shain's work, which draws largely on Protestant sermons given in the North, contrasts such communally oriented notions of liberty with nineteenth-century definitions of the concept—definitions that tended to award the individual with greater personal freedom. For an introduction to the question of whether corporate or individualistic political concepts most influence early American politics, see Rodgers, "Republicanism."

30. For Genovese's definition of planter paternalism as a series of reciprocal responsibilities that tied master and slave together into an organic relationship, see *Roll, Jordan, Roll*. Other reasons exist for why I prefer to move away from paternalism as a defining rubric for slaveowner thought. First, no matter how many times scholars such as Genovese explicitly state that "paternalism" did not entail a benevolent slaveowning regime, the term carries enough heavy cultural baggage in our own society to lead less-than-careful readers into profound confusion about what separates Genovese's work from the racist historical studies of U. B. Phillips. Second, paternalism as a concept casts the master-slave relationship in terms of male authority. While the slaveowners certainly privileged male authority over female authority, their conception of household relations carried plenty of room for female mastery (as Fox-Genovese, among others, has demonstrated in *Within the Plantation Household*). To refer to these slaveowning women as paternalists is awkward and misleading, for they construed their mastery as an extension of their motherly duties within the domestic circle of plantation life.

31. Furman, *Exposition of the Views of the Baptists*, 14.

32. Haskell, "Capitalism and the Origins of the Humanitarian Sensibility."

33. Chaplin, "Slavery and the Principle of Humanity," 300, 303.

34. Tise, *Proslavery*, xvii. Tise marshals considerable evidence to demonstrate that a conservative theological tradition in the northern United States and in England provided intellectual firepower to southern authors writing during the antebellum period. Tise, however, overstates his case when he suggests that no proslavery culture existed in the South prior to the mid-1830s. Indeed, one of the principal pur-

poses of my work is to trace the steady growth of a proslavery culture in Georgia and South Carolina in the half-century following the establishment of the new federal system in 1787–89.

35. Matt. 19:24 Revised English Bible; R. Moore, *Selling God*; Leach, *Land of Desire*, chap. 7 (quotations on 213); Weber, *The Protestant Ethic and the Spirit of Capitalism*. For commentary on Weber's thesis, see Lehmann and Roth, *Weber's Protestant Ethic*, and Poggi, *Calvinism and the Capitalist Spirit*.

36. For a study emphasizing that an American print culture fostered no single national mentality, see Zboray, *A Fictive People*. For the English response to chivalric fiction, see Chandler, *A Dream of Order*.

37. Radway, *Reading the Romance*. See also Machor, *Readers in History*, and Tompkins, *Reader-Response Criticism*.

38. Here, I propose that even brilliant studies of individual southern intellectuals (such as those offered by Drew Faust) cannot tell us enough about the cultural context in which these authors operated. By approaching the issue from the perspective of southern readers, I argue that southern thinkers such as Simms were, notwithstanding their own sense of alienation, more thoroughly in tune with the broad cultural and literary trends of their society than Faust, David Donald, and Louis D. Rubin Jr. have suggested. See Faust, *A Sacred Circle*; Donald, "The Proslavery Argument Reconsidered"; and Rubin, *The Edge of the Swamp*.

39. Indeed, Willie Lee Rose's seminal essay "The Domestication of Domestic Slavery" in *Slavery and Freedom* sparked my interest in this entire topic.

40. For studies illustrating black cultural resistance to the slaveowners' cultural agenda, see Creel, *"A Peculiar People"*; Joyner, *Down by the Riverside*; and Sidbury, *Ploughshares into Swords*. In her study of family and community life in one Virginia county, Brenda E. Stevenson divides her analysis of black and white domestic relations into completely different sections—a decision that attracted the attention of some reviewers. Although I focus on the planters' insistence that blacks and whites occupied an organic domestic space, none of my findings challenge Stevenson's argument that blacks created their own domestic culture. As I will attempt to make clear, the slaveowners' ideology reinforced their position as a ruling elite because it blinded them to evidence that their plantations did not conform to their idealized conceptions of an enlightened interracial household. See Stevenson, *Life in Black and White*, and Jane Turner Censer's review of Stevenson in *Journal of American History* 83 (March 1997): 1373–74.

41. See Ford, *Origins of Southern Radicalism*; Thornton, *Politics and Power in a Slave Society*; and Hahn, *The Roots of Southern Populism*.

CHAPTER ONE

1. For the scale of the international slave trade, see Rawley, *Transatlantic Slave Trade*, 428; Curtin, *Atlantic Slave Trade*; and J. Miller, *Way of Death*.

2. Judith Giton Manigault to unidentified brother, n.d., Manigault Family Papers, SCHS.

3. For the role played by Barbados planters in the founding of South Carolina, see

Sirmans, *Colonial South Carolina*, chap. 2; Dunn, *Sugar and Slaves*, 110–16; J. P. Thomas, "The Barbadians in Early South Carolina"; and Greene, "Colonial South Carolina and the Caribbean Connection." For the roots of the European-controlled plantation system, see Verlinden, *The Beginnings of Modern Colonization*, and D. B. Davis, *Slavery and Human Progress*, 51–82.

4. Littlefield, *Rice and Slaves*. In 1685, colonial authorities did not include rice when they were listing exportable commodities. By 1712, however, the colonists considered rice an important enough component of their economy to petition Parliament to allow rice to be directly shipped to markets outside of England. See "An Act to Ascertain the Prices of Commodityes of the Countrye's Growth," in Cooper and McCord, *Statutes at Large of South Carolina*, 2:37; and "An Act for Appointing an Agent to Solicit the Affairs of this Province in the Kingdom of Great Britain," ibid., 601–2.

5. For superb accounts of the market's influence on early Carolina history, see Coclanis, *Shadow of a Dream*, 48–110, and Chaplin, *Anxious Pursuit*.

6. "An Act for the Encouragement of the Making of Engines for Propagating the Staples of this Collony," in Cooper and McCord, *Statutes at Large of South Carolina*, 2:63.

7. For an exceptionally insightful discussion of tidewater rice cultivation, see Stewart, *"What Nature Suffers to Groe,"* 98–116. Other informative accounts include Chaplin, "Tidal Rice Cultivation"; Gray, *History of Agriculture in the Southern United States to 1860*, 2:721–23; and Phillips, *American Negro Slavery*, 88.

8. Coclanis, *Shadow of a Dream*, 83.

9. Henry Laurens to Richard Grubb, June 23, 1747, *HLP*, 1:8. On the growth of this market for consumer goods in both Europe and America, see McKendrick and Plumb, *The Birth of a Consumer Society*; McCracken, *Culture and Consumption*; and Breen, "'Baubles of Britain,'" "An Empire of Goods," and "Narrative of Commercial Life."

10. Henry Laurens to Gidney Clarke, January 12, 1756, *HLP*, 2:64 (quotation); Laurens to Mayne, Burn, & Mayne, February 24, 1756, ibid., 104–5. On this point, see Glen, *Description of South Carolina*, 43: "There are annually imported into this Province, considerable Quantities of fine *Flanders Laces*, the finest *Dutch Linens*, and *French Cambricks, Chints, Hyson Tea*, and other *East India* Goods, *Silks, Gold*, and *Silver Lace*, &c."

11. Henry Laurens to Richard Grubb, February 19, 1748, *HLP*, 1:114; Laurens to Rawlinson & Davidson, June 28, 1755, *HLP*, 1:277–78. For the initial transfer of knowledge that made indigo cultivation possible in South Carolina, see George Lucas to Charles Pinckney, July 25, 1745, and September 17, 1745, Pinckney Family Papers, box 1, ser. 3, LC; Henry Laurens to James Crokatt, June 24, 1747, *HLP*, 1:11. See also Chaplin, *Anxious Pursuit*, 151–52.

12. Henry Laurens to Foster, Cunliffe & Sons, November 5, 1755, *HLP*, 2:9–10.

13. Coclanis, *Shadow of a Dream*, 38–47; Merrens and Terry, "Dying in Paradise"; and Duffy, "Eighteenth-Century Carolina Health Conditions."

14. P. Wood, *Black Majority*, chap. 5.

15. William Bull to the Duke of Newcastle, May 9, 1739, BPRO-SC, vol. 20. See also Gipson, *The British Isles and the American Colonies*, 131.

16. William Bull to [the Lords of Trade], October 5, 1739, BPRO-SC, vol. 20.

17. *South Carolina Commons House Journal, 1739–41*, November 21, 1739, in Wood, *Black Majority*, 319. For a full account of the insurrection and its aftermath, see ibid., chap. 12, and Hewatt, *Rise and Progress of the Colonies of South Carolina and Georgia*, 2:71–74.

18. Glen, *Description of South Carolina*, 88. On this point, see also Gallay, *Formation of a Planter Elite*, 23–29.

19. Van Horne, *Religious Philanthropy*, 9–16; Stewart, *"What Nature Suffers to Groe,"* chaps. 1–2. For background on the religious activists who helped to organize the colony, see Thompson, *Thomas Bray*, and Pennington, *Thomas Bray's Associates and Their Work among the Negroes*.

20. Candler et al., *Colonial Records of the State of Georgia*, 1:11–26, 50–52, and Martyn, *Impartial Inquiry*, 166–74.

21. S. Smith, *Sermon Preach'd before the Trustees*, 21–22; Martyn, *Impartial Inquiry*, 169 (quotation).

22. Scots' petition in Candler et al., *Colonial Records of the State of Georgia*, 3:427. B. Wood, *Slavery in Colonial Georgia*, chap. 2; D. B. Davis, *Problem of Slavery in Western Culture*, 144–50; and Scarborough, *Opposition to Slavery in Georgia prior to 1860*. Indeed, proslavery colonists in Georgia claimed that the authors of the antislavery petition had been bribed. See T. Stephens, *Causes That Have Retarded the Progress of the Colony of Georgia in America*, 93: "The people of Darien . . . were bought with a number of cattle, and extensive promises of future rewards, when they signed the petition against negroes."

23. Gordeon, *Peter Gordeon Journal, 1732–35*, 59.

24. Candler et al., *Colonial Records of the State of Georgia*, 1:495.

25. Chesnutt, "South Carolinian Expansion into Colonial Georgia"; Gallay, *Formation of a Planter Elite*, 101.

26. Candler et al., *Colonial Records of the State of Georgia*, 1:530–31. For Georgia's transition to a slave-based plantation economy, consult B. Wood, *Slavery in Colonial Georgia*.

27. Quotation from "Extract from a Journal of Mr. Habersham," June 11, 1751, Habersham Family Papers, DU. Habersham was referring to the Georgia planters' experimentation with the cultivation of silk. For the Trustees' stubborn (and unsuccessful) efforts to force the colonial landscape to conform to their idealized social vision, see Stewart, *"What Nature Suffers to Groe,"* chaps. 1–2.

28. D. B. Davis, *Problem of Slavery in Western Culture*, 94–97.

29. Blickle, *Revolution of 1525*.

30. John Winthrop, "A Model of Christian Charity," in P. Miller, *American Puritans*, 79–84. For evidence that the Puritans embraced African slavery in principle, see Emmanuel Downing to John Winthrop, ca. August 1645, in *Winthrop Papers*, 5:38: "If upon a Just warre the lord should deliver [sufficient American Indian captives] into our hands, wee might easily have men woemen and Children enough to exchange for Moores, which wilbe more gaynefull pilladge for us then wee conceive, for I doe not see how wee can thrive untill wee gett into a stock of slaves suffitient to doe all our busines."

31. Ahlstrom, *Religious History of the American People,* 219–29.

32. Le Jau, *Carolina Chronicle of Dr. Francis Le Jau,* 52–53. For background on Le Jau and his mission, see Pennington, "Le Jau's Work among Indians and Slaves." For a survey of the Anglican Church's expansion into the colony, see Bolton, *Southern Anglicanism.*

33. Le Jau, *Carolina Chronicle of Dr. Francis Le Jau,* 60. This point had been made as early as 1669 when the English philosopher John Locke had written the Fundamental Constitutions of Carolina: "Since charity obliges us to wish well to the souls of all men, and religion ought to alter nothing in any man's civil estate or right, it shall be lawful for slaves as well as others, to enter themselves and be of what church or profession any of them shall think best, and thereof be as fully members as any freeman. But yet no slave shall hereby be exempted from that civil dominion his master hath over him, but be in all things in the same state and condition he was in before" (Cooper and McCord, *Statutes at Large of South Carolina,* 1:55).

34. Le Jau, *Carolina Chronicle of Dr. Francis Le Jau,* 76.

35. For eighteenth-century slaveowners' familiarity with Matt. 19:24 Revised English Bible ("it is easier for a camel to pass through the eye of a needle than for a rich man to enter the kingdom of God"), see Conder and Gibbons, *Living Christ Delineated,* 39.

36. Le Jau, *Carolina Chronicle of Dr. Francis Le Jau,* 18.

37. Ibid., 50.

38. Ibid., 55.

39. Le Jau to Bishop Henry Comptom, May 27, 1712, SPG General Correspondence, Fulham Papers, microfilm reel 2, LPL.

40. Le Jau, *Carolina Chronicle of Dr. Francis Le Jau,* 128–31; "Queries to be Answer'd by Every Minister," April 15, 1724, SPG General Correspondence, Fulham Papers, microfilm reel 2, LPL. For news of Le Jau's death, see Wardens and Vestry of St. James to Bishop Robinson, October 29, 1717, ibid. For other graphic descriptions of the abuse and torture of slaves, see Le Jau, *Carolina Chronicle of Dr. Francis Le Jau,* 108.

41. Ahlstrom, *Religious History of the American People,* 226.

42. Van Horne, "Joseph Solomon Ottolenghe."

43. Joseph Ottolenghe to [Samuel Smith], June 8, 1752, in Van Horne, *Religious Philanthropy,* 108–9.

44. Joseph Ottolenghe to [John Waring], November 19, 1753, ibid., 111–12. Religious authorities argued, of course, that religion would have the opposite effect on slaves. See S. Smith, *Sermon Preach'd before the Trustees,* 20–21, Burton, *Duty and Reward of Propagating Principles of Religion and Virtue,* 8.

45. Van Horne, *Religious Philanthropy,* 6.

46. D. B. Davis, *Problem of Slavery in Western Culture,* 202.

47. McLoughlin and Jordan, "Baptists Face the Barbarities of Slavery in 1710." For background on the Baptists, see Townsend, *South Carolina Baptists.*

48. The distance that missionaries traveled to reach the slaves was interpreted by some American slaves as an indication of the Anglican organization's sincere regard for their welfare. For a northern example, see Ebenezer Miller to Samuel Smith, Sep-

tember 6, 1748, in Van Horne, *Religious Philanthropy*, 98–99: "The poor Creatures seem's much pleased that Gentlemen at so great a Distance, & who could receive no Advantage from them, shou[l]d have such a Concern for their Instruction in Christian Principles." In the slaveowners' eyes, by contrast, this very disinterest in fiscal gain made the religious authorities' agenda suspect because it threatened to curtail profits.

49. Fleetwood, *Relative Duties of Parents and Children, Husbands and Wives, Masters and Servants*, 339 (quotation); Fleetwood, *Sermon Preached before the Society for the Propagation of the Gospel in Foreign Parts*; E. Gibson, *Two Letters of the Lord Bishop of London*; and Hales, *Sermon Preached before the Trustees for Establishing the Colony of Georgia in America*.

50. Smith, *Sermon Preach'd before the Trustees*, 19. See the provocative and intelligent discussion of this issue in Butler, *Awash in a Sea of Faith*, 135, and "Enlarging the Bonds of Christ." Butler, however, provides little evidence for his claim that early-eighteenth-century slaveowners were actually internalizing an organic slaveowning creed. As Leigh Eric Schmidt points out, scholars must distinguish between the "strategies of [religious] producers" and the "responses of consumers." In the case of the early colonial South, slaveowners did not even begin to buy into the religious proslavery message until the transatlantic religious culture of Christian activists was altered by major political and theological shifts in the late eighteenth and early nineteenth centuries. See Schmidt, *Consumer Rites*, 314 n. 20. For the slow pace of religious growth in the colonial South, see Raboteau, *Slave Religion*, 96–150, and Boles, "Evangelical Protestantism in the Old South." On the distribution of Gibson's tract in the colonies, see Dalcho, *Historical Account of the Protestant Episcopal Church*, 103–14.

51. Le Jau to Bishop Compton, May 27, 1712, SPG General Correspondence, Fulham Papers, microfilm reel 2, LPL.

52. Alexander Garden to Bishop Gibson, September 6, 1737, ibid. For background on Garden, see Bolton, *Southern Anglicanism*, chap. 3. Bolton argues (in chap. 5) that only a tiny minority of the Anglican clergy were guilty of such offenses. Of course, negative colonial perceptions of the moral character of the Anglican ministry need not have been based on the conduct of the majority of ministers.

53. John Moore to Bishop Osbaldeston, September 17, 1762, SPG General Correspondence, Fulham Papers, microfilm reel 2, LPL.

54. Kenney, "Alexander Garden and George Whitefield." See also Aldridge, "George Whitefield's Georgia Controversies." On the Charlestown fire, see William Bull to Thomas Penn, November 29, 1740, Charleston Library Society Miscellaneous Manuscripts, SCHS.

55. Garden to unknown correspondent, March 20, 1742[3], transcript in the Alexander Garden Papers (1685–1756), SCL.

56. Garden to Bishop Gibson, April 24, 1740, SPG General Correspondence, Fulham Papers, microfilm reel 2, LPL.

57. Garden to unknown correspondent, March 20, 1742[3], transcript in the Alexander Garden Papers (1685–1756), SCL. This was not the first time that such fears were expressed by authorities in the colony. The *South Carolina Gazette* re-

ported in April 1724 that Baptist preachers were "filling [the slaves'] heads with a parcel of *Cant-Phrases, Trances, Dreams,* Visions and Revelations" (quoted in Sobel, *Trabelin' On,* 102).

58. Stout, *Divine Dramatist,* 177; Lambert, "Subscribing for Profits and Piety," 529; and Lambert, "'Pedlar in Divinity,'" 812. For Whitefield's denunciation of secular printed works such as "Plays and Romances" as "trifling, sinful Compositions," see Reynolds, *Faith in Fiction,* 3.

59. Whitefield, "Great Duty of Family Religion," 451–52.

60. Quoted in M. Lane, *Neither More nor Less Than Men,* vii.

61. Whitefield, *Three Letters from the Reverend Mr. George Whitefield,* 13–16.

62. Ibid., 15. Whitefield explicitly contended that Christianity would not liberate the slaves but would turn them into a more content workforce: "Do you find one Command in the Gospel, that has the least Tendency to make people forget their Relative Duties? Do you not read that Servants, and as many as are under the Yoke of Bondage, are required to be subject, in all lawful Things, to their Masters?" To establish the slaves' capacity for improvement, Whitefield compared them to the slave-owners' own children: "If teaching Slaves Christianity has such a bad Influence upon their Lives, why are you generally desirous of having your Children taught? Think you they are any way better by nature than the Poor Negroes? No, in no w[ays]" (15).

63. Garden, *Six Letters to the Rev. Mr. George Whitefield,* 51–53.

64. Garden had been living in Charlestown for twenty years when he wrote his response to Whitefield. For his arrival in Charlestown, see William Tredwell Bull to Thomas Mangey, May 12, 1720, SPG General Correspondence, Fulham Papers, microfilm reel 2, LPL. Quotations are from Duncan, "Servitude and Slavery," 358.

65. This account of Garden's Charlestown school is drawn from Klingberg, *Appraisal of the Negro in Colonial South Carolina,* 101–22. For the slave insurrection plot associated with Clarke's preaching, see Olwell, *Masters, Slaves, and Subjects,* 136–37.

66. Philem. 16 Revised English Bible.

67. Isa. 58:6, ibid.

68. W. Culpeper to Cornelia Bridges, December 15, 1753, Murdock and Wright Family Papers, SHC.

69. Candler et al., *Colonial Records of the State of Georgia,* 23:231; Duncan, "Servitude and Slavery," 332; and Calhoon, *Evangelicals and Conservatives in the Early South,* 26.

70. Eliza Lucas Pinckney to Mary Bartlett, March 11, 1741/2, in Pinckney, *Letterbook of Eliza Lucas Pinckney,* 30. For background on the Pinckneys, see F. Williams, *Founding Family.*

71. McCrady, *History of South Carolina under the Royal Government,* 241; Duncan, "Servitude and Slavery," 334–35.

72. *South Carolina Gazette,* November 20, 1740. For Whitefield and Bryan's arrest, see Garden to Bishop Gibson, January 28, 1740/1, SPG General Correspondence, Fulham Papers, microfilm reel 2, LPL. For Bryan's apology, see *Journal of the Commons House of Assembly,* 461–62. This episode is also recounted in Schmidt, "'Grand Prophet,' Hugh Bryan." For the development of the ideas of Bryan and his brother

Jonathan about the relationship between religion and slavery, see Gallay, *Formation of a Planter Elite*.

73. For Bryan's impact on slaveholder religious enthusiasm, see Jackson, "Hugh Bryan and the Evangelical Movement."

74. Garden to unknown correspondent, March 20, 1742[3], transcript in the Alexander Garden Papers (1685–1756), SCL.

75. By emphasizing the slaveowners' rejection of Christian missions, regardless of denomination, I depart from analyses that have explored the considerable theological differences and styles of worship separating radical evangelicals such as Whitefield from traditional liberal ministers such as Garden. See Heimert, *Religion and the American Mind*, 35–37. My reading of these events should also be contrasted with studies characterizing this period more in terms of religious expansion. See Gallay, *Formation of a Planter Elite*; Sobel, *Trabelin' On*; Bolton, *Southern Anglicanism*; Olwell, *Masters, Slaves, and Subjects*; and Butler, *Awash in a Sea of Faith*. One should also note that slaveowners in Georgia were likewise affected by fears of slave insurrection plots that were associated with religious reform. In the 1730s and 1740s, for example, Christi Gotlieb Pryber, a radical refugee from France, antagonized both Georgia and South Carolina authorities by pursuing plans for an interracial religious community. See Candler et al., *Colonial Records of the State of Georgia*, 1:218, and Duncan, "Servitude and Slavery," 613–20.

76. S. Smith, *Sermon Preach'd before the Trustees*, 20.

77. Van Horne, *Religious Philanthropy*, 91; [Charles Martyn?], April 11, 1762, SPG General Correspondence, Fullham Papers, microfilm reel 2, LPL. For earlier reports of the missionaries' inability to reach the slaves, see "Queries to be Answer'd by Every Minister," ca. 1724, ibid.

78. N. Bedgegood to George Whitefield, February 8, 1762, George Whitefield Papers, LC.

79. Duncan, "Servitude and Slavery," 358. For another perspective on this issue, see the work of Annette Laing, who demonstrates the need for historians to consider African perspectives on religion as a crucial factor in determining the success or failure of the Anglican mission in the New World ("'After Their Heathen Way'").

80. For the historical context from which mercantilist thought emerged, see Appleby, *Economic Thought and Ideology in Seventeenth-Century England*.

81. William Bull to the Lords Commissioners for Trade and Plantations, May 25, 1738, James Glen Papers, SCL.

82. Glen, *Description of South Carolina*, 87–88.

83. Alexander Garden II to William Shipley, April 5, 1755, Henry Baker Letterbook, YU.

84. Ibid. It is worth noting that a doctrine of efficiency could just as easily be applied in a manner that would make the slaves' burden heavier rather than lighter. The Virginia planter Landon Carter, for example, paid careful attention to his slaves' daily output, taking care to punish those slaves who failed to meet quotas for productivity. See Carter, *Diary of Colonel Landon Carter*, 1:138.

85. Alexander Garden II to Henry Baker, March 25, 1755, Henry Baker Letterbook, YU.

86. Even James Glen, the former royal governor of South Carolina, expressed some reservations about mercantilism because "it retards our Increase both in People and in Wealth" (*Description of South Carolina*, 43–44).

87. Henry Laurens to James Cowles, August 20, 1755, *HLP*, 1:320–21.

88. James Glen to the Lords Commissioners for Trade, April 14, 1756, BPRO-SC, vol. 27. See also William Henry Lyttelton to Henry Fox, August 5, 1756, ibid.

89. "The Petition of the Merchants. . . ," December 21, 1756, *HLP*, 2:378–79.

90. Charles Pinckney to the Lords Commissioners for Trade and Plantations, December 2, 1756, BPRO-SC, vol. 27.

91. See William Henry Lyttelton to the Lords Commissioners of Trade, May 24, 1757, ibid.

92. Gadsden, *Some Observations on the Two Campaigns against the Cherokee Indians*.

93. Waterhouse, *New World Gentry*, chap. 4.

94. Henry Laurens to Elizabeth Laurens, December 16, 1748, *HLP*, 1:181.

95. For England as a source of education, see Henry Laurens to John Knight, June 26, 1755, ibid. 271–72, and Henry Laurens to Matthew Robinson, October 19, 1768, ibid., 6:139–41. For elite Charlestonians' desire for English literary material, see the Charleston Library Society Records, February 5, 1766, SCHS. Several scholars have even suggested that, of all the regions in the world, the southern colonies were the largest importers of English books. See James Gilreath, "American Book Distribution," in Hall and Hench, *Needs and Opportunities in the History of the Book*, 116–21. See also Cohen, "*South Carolina Gazette*," chap. 11. For the Kimber quotation, see "Itinerant Observations in America," 38, quoted in Rozbicki, "Curse of Provincialism," 744.

96. *Merchant of Venice*, 4.1.376–79. For the exposure of colonial planters to Shakespeare, see William Drayton to Peter Manigault, April 4, 1753, Manigault Family Papers, SCL, and Richard Hutson to Isaac Hayne, January 29, 1767, Charles Woodward Hutson Papers, SHC.

97. See Shields, *Civil Tongues and Polite Letters in British America*.

98. Henry Laurens to Richard St. John, July 26, 1747, *HLP*, 1:31–32.

99. Henry Laurens to John Knight, July 24, 1755, *HLP*, 1:299. Colonial authorities had long since realized that overly zealous attempts to collect debts might jeopardize the collective welfare of the colony. In 1721, the colonial assembly beseeched creditors not to execute writs to collect on debts smaller than thirty pounds sterling because "the poorer sort of people" were "continually running in debt much beyond what they are able to pay," leading them to "daily desert the Province—which, if not timely prevented, will expose this frontier colony to the incursion of the Indians, insurrection of Negroes, and make the same an easy prey to the invasion of any foreign enemy." See "An Act for Preventing the Desertion of Insolvent Debtors," in Cooper and McCord, *Statutes at Large of South Carolina*, 3:122.

100. Crouse, "Manigault Family of South Carolina," 296–97; Introduction to *HLP*, 1:xiv–xxii; Deed to Wambaw Plantation, May 11, 1756, ibid., 180; Henry Laurens to Monkhouse Davison, October 15, 1762, ibid., 3:138–40.

101. Henry Laurens to Mathew Robinson, May 30, 1764, ibid., 4:295–96; Henry Laurens to Devonsheir & Reeve, September 12, 1764, ibid., 419.

102. Richard Hutson to Sam Smith, March 12, 1766, Charles Woodward Hutson Papers, SHC. Likewise, the South Carolina merchant John Guerard announced in 1752 that "I have turnd planter" (R. Nash, "Trade and Business in Eighteenth-Century South Carolina," 12).

103. Henry Laurens to Richard Oswald, July 7, 1764, *HLP*, 4:338.

104. On the flow of luxury goods, see Henry Laurens to John Pagan, Alexander Brown & Company, July 6, 1764, ibid., 329–31. For the Ball family's acquisitions, see Elias Ball Junior to Daniel Huger, April 3, 1764, Ball Family Papers, SCL. For the landscapes of Kensington and Hyde Park, see Henry Laurens to Richard Shubrick, October 12, 1756, *HLP*, 2:335. For the degree to which imported English culture provided the standards by which the southern gentry measured its own social advancement, see Weir, *Colonial South Carolina*, chap. 10. For the English influence on elite colonists' sense of fashion, see Gibson, "Costume and Fashion in Charleston."

105. Henry Laurens to John Ettwein, April 7, 1762, *HLP*, 3:92.

106. Fragment from family Bible, ca. 1763, Mackay and Stiles Family Papers, SHC.

107. For Henry Laurens's participation in the Charleston Library Society, see "Members of the Charleston Library Society, April 4, 1759," *HLP*, 3:6. For the society's agenda, see Milligen-Johnston, *Description of the Province of South-Carolina*, 39. More recent scholarship has established how literature contributed to an eighteenth-century conception of the public sphere. Elite colonists measured their stature within this sphere through their participation in the cultural process of dispersing useful knowledge associated with humanitarianism in order to overcome local prejudices. See Warner, *Letters of the Republic*.

108. Demonstrating the planters' dread of isolation, Henry Laurens warned the father of Pennsylvania naturalist William Bartram that his son was experiencing wretched conditions on his Florida plantation: "No colouring can do justice to the forlorn state of poor Billy Bartram. A gentle mild Young Man, no wife, no Friend, no Companion, no Neighbour, No Human inhabitant within nine miles . . . distant 30 long Miles from the Metropolis." Henry Laurens to John Bartram, August 9, 1766, *HLP*, 5:153.

109. "Instructions to Our Trusty and Wellbeloved Chas. Greville Montagu," February 19, 1766, BPRO-SC, vol. 31.

110. James Wright to unidentified correspondent, November 8, 1762, BPRO-GA, C.O. 5/648, 172–73; *Georgia Gazette*, August 11, 1763.

111. William Bull to the Lords Commissioners of Trade and Plantations, August 10, 1770, and November 25, 1770, in BPRO-SC, vol. 32.

112. Habersham to William Knox, November 26, 1770; Habersham to Rev. Thomas Broughton, December 1, 1770; and Habersham to William Knox, February 11, 1772, Habersham, *The Letters of Hon. James Habersham*, 96, 100–101, and 163–64.

113. For evidence of ties between these merchants, see Richard Hutson to Joel Benedict, February 26, 1766, Charles Woodward Hutson Papers, SHC.

114. Richard Hutson to Mr. Croll, August 22, 1767, ibid.

115. Henry Laurens to Robert & John Thompson & Co., April 20, 1757, *HLP*, 2:524.

116. Henry Laurens to Richard Stevens, December 6, 1762, ibid., 3:183.

117. Henry Laurens to James Lawrence, January 7, 1763, ibid., 205.

118. Henry Laurens to James Lawrence, February 12, 1763, ibid., 248.

119. Henry Laurens to James Brenard, November 16, 1764, ibid., 4:503.

120. Henry Laurens to John Haslin, November 19, 1764, ibid., 507; Henry Laurens to Lloyd & Borton, December 24, 1764, ibid., 5:558–59; Henry Laurens to Abraham Schad, August 23, 1765, ibid., 4:666.

121. Henry Laurens to Elias Ball, April 1, 1765, ibid., 4:595–96.

122. Gallay, *Formation of a Planter Elite*, 30–54; Olwell, "'Reckoning of Accounts,'" 33–52; and Chaplin, *Anxious Pursuit*, 23–65. For an argument locating planter paternalism in the early eighteenth century, see Butler, *Awash in a Sea of Faith*, 129–63.

123. See, for example, "An Act to Prevent the Stealing and Taking Away of Boats and Canoes," 1696, in Cooper and McCord, *South Carolina Statutes*, 2:105. For the long-standing English tendency toward racial prejudice, see Jordan, *White over Black*.

124. Wesley, *Journal of the Rev. Charles Wesley*, entry for August 2, 1736, 1:36–37.

125. For slave branding, see Alexander Wylly's advertisement for a runaway slave, *Georgia Gazette*, February 5, 1765. For the severed heads of convicted slaves, see *Georgia Gazette*, June 6, 1765. For the castration and immolation of slaves, see *South Carolina Gazette and Country Journal*, January 26, 1768, and *Pennsylvania Gazette*, August 14, 1761, quoted in Duncan, "Servitude and Slavery," 515–16, 289, respectively.

126. Dalcho, *Historical Account of the Protestant Episcopal Church*, 361–62; Oliver Hart Diary, December 1, 1769, Oliver Hart Papers (typed transcripts), SCL.

127. Henry Laurens to John Ettwein, March 19, 1763, *HLP*, 3:374. Laurens was responding to Ettwein's observation that "what I saw & heard of the Negroes made me very uneasy. If some care was taken of their Souls their Servitude might be a Blessing unto them but I [could] hear nothing of that and even of no Prospect for such a Thing." Draft of letter from Ettwein to Laurens, March 3, 1763, ibid., 356–57.

128. Habersham to Willet Taylor, April 2, 1764, *Letters of Hon. James Habersham*, 22–23. For a very different reading of this episode, see Chaplin, *Anxious Pursuit*, 55–56.

129. Henry Laurens to William Fisher, November 9, 1768, *HLP*, 6:149.

130. Henry Laurens to James Grant, January 30, 1767, ibid., 5:227.

131. Henry Laurens to John Knight, December 22, 1764, ibid., 4:556; Henry Laurens to William Fisher, November 9, 1768, ibid., 6:149–50.

132. For example, see Laurens to John Holman, September 8, 1770, ibid., 7:344: "If you send any slaves to this place consign'd to me, you may depend upon it that I shall either sell them myself, or put them into such hands as will do you the most Service in the Sale & the most perfect Justice in every respect." For Laurens's inability to resist the temptation of profits arising from the international slave trade, see Laurens to John Knight, February 14, 1763, ibid., 3:253; Laurens to John Rutherford, April 4, 1763, ibid., 403; Laurens to John Knight, December 22, 1763, ibid., 4:96; Laurens to John Knight, August 24, 1764, ibid., 378–83; Laurens to Smith & Baillies, October 22, 1767, ibid., 5:373–76; Laurens to William MakDougal, November 21, 1767, ibid., 466–67; and Laurens to Smith & Baillies, October 17, 1768, ibid., 6:136–37.

133. For "humane" treatment of French prisoners of war, hostile American Indians, and white criminals, see (respectively) William Henry Lyttelton to Henry Fox,

August 5, 1756, BPRO-SC, vol. 27, 130; J. Price to Patrick Colhoun, April 2, 1765, John Caldwell Calhoun Papers, DU; Richard Cumberland to the Lords Commissioners for Trade and Plantations, received March 14, 1764, BPRO-SC, vol. 30.

134. *Georgia Gazette*, April 7, 1763.

135. Richard Hutson to Joel Benedict, October 30, 1765, Charles Woodward Hutson Papers, SHC; James Wright to the Lords Commissioners of Trade and Plantations, December 2, 1765, BPRO-GA, C.O. 649; James Wright to the Lords Commissioners of Trade and Plantations, February 1, 1766, ibid.; and William Bull to Seymour Conway, February 6, 1766, BPRO-SC, vol. 31.

136. Henry Laurens to John Lewis Gervais, September 1, 1766, *HLP*, 5:184.

137. Henry Laurens to Joseph Brown, October 11, 22, 1765, ibid., 23–25, 26–28.

138. Henry Laurens to James Grant, August 12, 1767, *HLP*, ibid., 277–79.

139. Henry Laurens to Lachlan McIntosh, October 15, 1768, ibid., 6:126–28.

140. Henry Laurens to George Grenville, February 24, 1769, ibid., 386–87.

141. Draft of Royal Instructions to Governor William Campbell of South Carolina, [ca. June 20, 1770], BPRO-SC, vol. 32.

142. William Bull to the Earl of Hillsborough, November 30, 1770, BPRO-SC, vol. 32. Bull even argued that "the state of Slavery is as comfortable in this Province as such a state can be; not but there are monsters of cruelty [who] sometimes appear, who are punished & abhorred. To the mildness of Law and prudent conduct of Masters and Patrols, I attribute our not having had any Insurrection since the year 1739."

143. James Habersham to [Benjamin Franklin], May 19, 1768, *Letters of Hon. James Habersham*, 71–72.

144. James Habersham to Benjamin Franklin, May 23, 1770, ibid., 80.

145. James Wright to Earl of Hillsborough, May 11, 1770, BPRO, C.O. 5/660, fol. 98, in Davies, *Documents of the American Revolution*, 2:91–93.

146. Knox, *Three Tracts Respecting the Conversion and Instruction of the Free Indians, and Negroe Slaves in the Colonies*, 17 (first and second quotations), 26 (third and fourth quotations); Knox, *Controversy between Great Britain and Her Colonies Reviewed*, 83 (fifth quotation). For background on Knox, see Bellot, *William Knox*, and Bellot, "Evangelicals and the Defense of Slavery in Britain's Old Colonial Empire."

147. Thomas Boone to the Lords Commissioners of Trade and Plantations, January 21, 1764, BPRO-SC, vol. 30.

148. Henry Laurens to Christopher Rowe, February 8, 1764, *HLP*, 4:164.

149. William Bull to the Colonial House of Assembly, January 8, 1765, Journal of the Commons House of Assembly, 1765, SCDAH.

150. James Wright to the Lords Commissioners of Trade and Plantations, April 20, 1763, BPRO-GA, C.O. 5/648, 195–97. Abbot, *Royal Governors of Georgia*, 100–102; De Vorsey, *Georgia–South Carolina Boundary*, 23–31.

151. Woodmason, *Carolina Backcountry*, 27–28.

152. "Committee to Consider North Carolina/South Carolina Report," December 11, 1768, enclosed in Charles Montagu to Earl of Hillsborough, April 19, 1769, BPRO-SC, vol. 32.

153. William Bull to Earl of Hillsborough, September 10, 1768, ibid.

154. *Boston Chronicle*, September 26, 1768.

155. William Fyffe to James Fyffe, January 20, 1769, Fyffe Papers, CL. For background on the regulator movement, see Klein, *Unification of a Slave State*, chap. 2, and R. M. Brown, *South Carolina Regulators*. Klein's intelligently argued study makes the crucial point that leading Regulators were men of property—often slaveowners—who merely wanted to establish sufficient cultural stability for them to pursue their own claims to the status of a ruling elite.

156. Charles Woodmason Journal, July 3, 1768, in Woodmason, *Carolina Backcountry*, 49.

157. For colonial planter opposition to Shinner, see Henry Laurens to John Lewis Gervais, September 1, 1766, *HLP*, 5:182–83; Charles Woodmason Journal, December 14, 1766, and April 20, 1767, in Woodmason, *Carolina Backcountry*, 10, 21; Charles Shinner to Charles Montagu, May 2, 1767, BPRO-SC, vol. 31; and Charles Montagu to Earl of Hillsborough, March 25, 1768, BPRO-SC, vol. 32. Not coincidentally, the slaveowners also blamed Shinner for using the powers of his office to undermine the institution of slavery. See the "Report of a Committee of the House of Assembly of South Carolina appointed to enquire into the State of the Courts of Justice," enclosed in Montagu to the Commissioners of Plantations, May 12, 1767, ibid., vol. 31.

158. Henry Laurens to Lachlan McIntosh, October 15, 1768, *HLP*, 6:127.

159. *South Carolina Gazette and Country Journal*, April 4, 1769, in Woodmason, *Carolina Backcountry*, 265.

160. Charles Woodmason to unidentified English friend, March 26, 1771, ibid., 210.

161. Charles Woodmason, "We Are Free-Men—British Subjects—Not Born Slaves," petition read in South Carolina Assembly, November 7, 1767, ibid., 213.

162. Henry Laurens to John Lewis Gervais, January 29, 1766, *HLP*, 5:53–54.

CHAPTER TWO

1. Carter, *Diary of Colonel Landon Carter*, 2:812 (entry for May 20, 1774). Carter previously had expressed contempt for the "broker" who, in Carter's opinion, was "a villain in the very engagements he enters into" because "he must buy and must sell as cheap and as dear as he can" (ibid., 373 [March 23, 1770]).

2. Bailyn, *Ideological Origins of the American Revolution*. Bailyn's pathbreaking work mostly concentrated on the ideological content of republican pamphlets. For the purposes of my own analysis, I would emphasize that the transatlantic structure of this political culture of protest was, in many ways, as significant as the content of the ideas presented by radical pamphleteers. Political controversy with England encouraged the planters to formulate identities that rested on ideas derived through a transatlantic intellectual dialogue. The implications that this political culture carried for the institution of slavery and for American conceptions of family relations are the subject matter of this chapter.

3. [Aesop], *Fables and Stories Moralized*, 63.

4. Yazawa, *From Colonies to Commonwealth*.

5. James Habersham to Joseph Habersham, May 10, 1768, in Habersham, *Letters of Hon. James Habersham*, 68. In similar fashion, Peter Manigault reminded his mother

that "mildness is much apter than harshness to produce affection." Quoted in Zuckerman, "Penmanship Exercises for Saucy Sons," 152–53.

6. Lord Shelburn to Charles Montagu, October 25, 1766, BPRO-SC, vol. 31. Henry Laurens to William Cowles & Co., May 24, 1768, *HLP*, 5:692. Again, it is worth noting that cultural contact with the English metropolis had helped to foster the new familial dynamic in the colonies. Anglican ministers such as Philip Reading, for example, had condemned colonial families as "destitute of common humanity," charging American fathers with a "want of natural affection even to their own flesh and blood" (Philip Reading to Samuel Smith, October 10, 1748, in Van Horne, *Religious Philanthropy*, 99–100). Certainly it was ironic that the increasing internalization of English standards for the appropriate application of power ultimately fueled the colonists' distaste for the British Empire.

7. "A Short Discourse on the Present State of the Colonies with Respect to the Interest of Great Britain," n.d., Ayer Collection, NL; William Bull to Earl of Hillsborough, August 28, 1769, BPRO-SC, vol. 32.

8. For the wealth of the planters, see Leger & Greenwood to Greenwood & Higginson, January 12, 1772, Leger & Greenwood Letterbook, CL.

9. William Bull to the Lords Commissioners for Trade and Plantations, November 3, 1765, BPRO-SC, vol. 30; James Wright to the Lords of Trade, November 9, 1765, BPRO-GA, C.O. 649; Richard Hutson to Joel Benedict, October 30, 1765, Charles Woodward Hutson Papers, SHC. See also James Wright to Lords of Trade, January 15, 1766, and February 1, 1766, both in BPRO-GA, C.O. 649.

10. James Habersham to John Nutt, July 31, 1772, *Letters of Hon. James Habersham*, 197.

11. Philip Vickers Fithian to Andrew Hunter, June 3, 1774, in Fithian, *Journal and Letters*, 150.

12. William Bull to the Earl of Dartmouth, December 24, 1773, BPRO-SC, vol. 33.

13. For the impact of republican ideals on the colonial mentality, see Maier, *From Resistance to Revolution*. For the role of "country ideology" in South Carolina politics, see Weir, "'Harmony We Were Famous For.'"

14. For example, see *Georgia Gazette*, April 7, 1763, and May 26, 1763.

15. Ralph Izard to George Dempster, August 1, 1775, in Izard, *Correspondence of Mr. Ralph Izard*, 112.

16. Laurens, *Appendix to the Extracts from the Proceedings of the High Court of Vice-Admiralty in Charlestown, South-Carolina* (Charleston: Bruce, 1769), 1, *HLP*, 7:7. In 1772 Laurens strongly recommended the writings of Trenchard and Gordon to an acquaintance and asserted that they were "to be found in almost every Gentleman's Library" (Laurens to Mynheer Van Teigham, August 19, 1772, ibid., 8:431). For the episode concerning the council, see South Carolina Governor's Council to the King, September 18, 1773, BPRO-SC, vol. 33.

17. James Habersham to [Benjamin Franklin], May 19, 1768, *Letters of Hon. James Habersham*, 72.

18. Leger & Greenwood to Greenwood & Higginson, January 12, 1772, Leger & Greenwood Letterbook, CL.

19. Levinus Clarkson to unidentified correspondent, n.d. [ca. 1773], Levinus

Clarkson Papers, LC. For Henry Laurens's alarm about the increasing importation of African slaves, see Laurens to Gabriel Manigault, March 8, 1773, *HLP*, 8:600. Twentieth-century scholars offer slightly lower estimates for slave importations in 1773 but nevertheless confirm a dramatic growth in the slave trade during this period. See Duncan, "Servitude and Slavery," 105.

20. *South Carolina Gazette and Country Journal*, February 4, 1772, quoted in Duncan, "Servitude and Slavery," 557.

21. *South Carolina Gazette*, October 31, 1774, and *South Carolina Gazette and Country Journal*, November 15, 1774, both quoted in Duncan, "Servitude and Slavery," 498.

22. *Georgia Gazette*, December 7, 1774, in Phillips, *Plantation and Frontier Documents*, 2:118–19.

23. William Bull to the Earl of Hillsborough, November 30, 1770, BPRO-SC, vol. 32.

24. James Habersham to William Knox, November 26, 1770, *Letters of Hon. James Habersham*, 95. The executors of the minister Bartholomew Zouberbuhler also employed Winter "to instruct" the slaves on Zouberbuhler's plantations. Like Habersham, the executors of this estate contacted the bishop to recommend Winter "for holy Orders" (Executors of Bartholomew Zouberbuhler to Bishop Terrick, November 29, 1770, SPG General Correspondence, Fulham Papers, microfilm reel 1, LPL).

25. James Habersham to Rev. Thomas Broughton, Secretary to the Society for Promoting Christian Knowledge, December 1, 1770, *Letters of Hon. James Habersham*, 100.

26. James Habersham to the Countess of Huntingdon, April 19, 1775, ibid., 241.

27. James Habersham to Robert Keen, May 11, 1775, ibid., 243–44.

28. Samuel Cooke, *Sermon Preached at Cambridge.* . . . (Boston: Edes and Gill, 1770), quoted in Bailyn, *Ideological Origins of the American Revolution*, 239.

29. [Samuel Hopkins], *Dialogue concerning the Slavery of Africans* (Norwich, Conn.: Judah P. Spooner, 1776), quoted in Bailyn, *Ideological Origins of the American Revolution*, 244.

30. Quincy, "Journal of Josiah Quincy, Junior, 1773," 463.

31. Fithian, *Journal and Letters*, 65 (January 4, 1774).

32. Ibid., 111 (March 20, 1774); Carter, *Diary of Colonel Landon Carter*, 2:1103 (April 27, 1777).

33. Milligen-Johnston, *Description of the Province of South-Carolina*, 24–25.

34. Henry Laurens to Martha Laurens, August 18, 1771, *HLP*, 7:556.

35. Jo[seph] Habersham to Bella Habersham, July 5, 1778, Habersham Family Papers, UGA.

36. Fithian, *Journal and Letters*, 148 (May 30, 1774).

37. Alexander Gray to Governor Patrick Tonyn, February 20, 1778, Henry Strachey Papers, CL; *Georgia Gazette*, April 4, 1765.

38. Gadsden, *South Carolina Gazette*, June 22, 1769, in Gadsden, *Writings of Christopher Gadsden*, 83. For background on Gadsden, consult Walsh, *Charleston's Sons of Liberty*, and Godbold and Woody, *Christopher Gadsden and the American Revolution*.

39. [William Tennent] to the Ladies of South Carolina, n.d. [ca. 1774], William

Tennent III Papers, SCL. On the Revolution's impact on conceptions of gender, see Kerber, *Women of the Republic*, and Norton, *Liberty's Daughters*.

40. *Writings of Christopher Gadsden*, 83–84.

41. Eliza Pinckney to Betsy Pinckney, June 18, 1780, Pinckney Family Papers, LC.

42. Mary Clay to Nancy Clay, November 10, 1782, Mary Clay Papers, SHC.

43. Anne Hart to Oliver Hart, July 19, 1781, Oliver Hart Papers, SCL.

44. Samuel Johnson quoted in D. B. Davis, *Problem of Slavery in the Age of Revolution*, 275.

45. Nash and Soderlund, *Freedom by Degrees*; Soderlund, *Quakers and Slavery*; and White, *Somewhat More Independent*.

46. Certificate of Freedom by William Williamson et al., June 18, 1774, Miscellaneous Records, vol. WW, SCDAH, quoted in Duncan, "Servitude and Slavery," 399–400.

47. James Coachman to William Bull, June 6, 1770, William Bull Papers, SCL.

48. Henry Laurens to John Lewis Gervais, May 29, 1772, *HLP*, 8:353. For background on the Somerset case, see D. B. Davis, *Problem of Slavery in the Age of Revolution*, 469–501. Davis emphasizes that Judge Lord Mansfield did not seek to undermine "the power of the master on his servant" but merely mandated that "it must always be regulated by the laws of the place where exercised" (498). When Laurens later characterized the verdict as "suitable to the times," he probably was referring to Mansfield's restraint (Laurens to Alexander Garden, August 20, 1772, *HLP*, 8:435).

49. Henry Laurens to Joseph Clay, September 22, 1772, *HLP*, 8:468 (quotation); Laurens to George Appleby, September 21, 1772, ibid., 464.

50. Henry Laurens to George Appleby, February 28, 1774, ibid., 9:317.

51. On this point, see the superb accounts offered by Frey, *Water from the Rock*, and Olwell, "'Domestick Enemies,'" 21–48.

52. Schaw, *Journal of a Lady of Quality*, 198–99.

53. Henry Cruger to Ralph Izard, March 21, 1775, in Izard, *Correspondence of Mr. Ralph Izard*, 58.

54. James Wright to the Earl of Dartmouth, May 25, 1775, BPRO, C.O. 5/664, fol. 113, in Davies, *Documents of the American Revolution*, 9:144, and also in Candler et al., *Colonial Records of the State of Georgia*, vol. 27, pt. 1: 444.

55. James Habersham to Messieurs Clark and Milligan, April 7, 1775, *Letters of Hon. James Habersham*, 236.

56. James Allen to Ralph Izard, *Correspondence of Mr. Ralph Izard*, 26.

57. Joseph Manigault to Gabriel Manigault, June 4, 1775, Manigault Family Papers, SCL.

58. William Campbell to unidentified lord, August 31, 1775, BPRO-SC, vol. 35.

59. Drayton, *Memoirs of the American Revolution*, 1:231.

60. Henry Laurens to John Laurens, May 15, 1775, *HLP*, 10:118.

61. Ralph Izard to unidentified correspondent, October 27, 1775, *Correspondence of Mr. Ralph Izard*, 135. For Lyttelton's speech, see *Parliamentary History of England*, 17:733.

62. Edward Rutledge to Ralph Izard, December 8, 1775, *Correspondence of Mr. Ralph Izard*, 165.

63. Henry Laurens to William Manning, February 27, 1776, *HLP*, 11:123.

64. South Carolina Constitution, March 26, 1776, in Cooper and McCord, *Statutes at Large of South Carolina*, 1:128.

65. Edward Rutledge to Ralph Izard, December 8, 1775, *Correspondence of Mr. Ralph Izard*, 166.

66. Quoted in Bell, *Major Butler's Legacy*, 33. On this point, see also Gould, "South Carolina and Continental Associations," 30–48.

67. Edward Rutledge to Thomas Pinckney, March 1, 1778, Pinckney Family Papers, LC.

68. Oliver Hart to Joseph Hart, February 16 and July 18, 1779, Oliver Hart Papers, SCL.

69. For evidence of American soldiers who eagerly anticipated "getting more" slaves, see Major John Jones to Polly Jones, October 3, 1779, Seaborn Jones Sr. Papers, DU. Tory slaveholders in Florida complained in 1776 about the "most cruel and wanton manner" in which Georgia revolutionaries pillaged the plantations of slaves and livestock (H. Jackson, *Lachlan McIntosh and the Politics of Revolutionary Georgia*, 43). For slaveholder problems with "horse thieves," see William Ancrum to Messr. Paintor Forbes & Co., May 9, 1778, William Ancrum Letterbook, SCL. See also G. Jones, "Black Hessians"; John Martin to Messrs. Washington & Odingsell, August 13, 1782, in [J. Martin], "Official Letters of Governor John Martin," 318.

70. Nathanael Greene to [John Cox], January 9, 1781, Nathanael Greene Papers, CL.

71. Thomas Pinckney, for example, advised his sister that "if you should hire a clever white Housekeeper I do not think it will be amiss." See Thomas Pinckney to Harriot Horry, August 4, 1776, Pinckney Family Papers, LC. For evidence that white southerners preferred slaves to white servants, see Levinus Clarkson to David Vanhorne, January 31, 1774, Levinus Clarkson Papers, LC.

72. Pinckney to Horry, August 4, 1776.

73. William Ancrum to Marlow Pryor, December 23, 1776, William Ancrum Letterbook, SCL. Likewise, South Carolina slaveowner William Snow insisted that his overseer "have no mercy on these negroes or they will deceive you." See Snow to Mr. Rhoads, September 19, 1781, Francis Marion Papers, NYPL.

74. Hewatt, *Rise and Progress of the Colonies of South Carolina and Georgia*, 2:95.

75. William Campbell to Earl of Dartmouth, August 31, 1775, in Davies, *Documents of the American Revolution*, 11:93–95. This incident is discussed in Olwell, "'Domestick Enemies,'" 38.

76. Even self-professed humane slaveowners such as Henry Laurens were "fully Satisfied that Jerry was guilty of a design & attempt to encourage our Negroes to Rebellion & joining the King's Troops if any had been Sent here" (Laurens to John Laurens, August 20, 1775, *HLP*, 10:321). Georgia's royal governor James Wright likewise sympathized with slaves who suffered under the administration of American revolutionaries. In September 1775 patriots refused landing to a shipment of African slaves—a decision that effectively resulted in "the loss of the lives of numbers of them." "The Poor Creatures are so dispirited at the thoughts of being carried to sea again," observed Wright, "that they are growing sickly and many of them will cer-

tainly dye before they can get into another Port" (Wright to Lord Dartmouth, September 16, 1775, in J. Wright, "Letters from Sir James Wright," 210).

77. John Rutledge to Francis Marion, September 1, 1781, Francis Marion Papers, NYPL.

78. Hewatt, *Rise and Progress of the Colonies of South Carolina and Georgia*, 2:95–96; Ralph Izard to unidentified correspondent, December 21, 1777, Ralph Izard Papers, SCL. Three years earlier, Izard had reminded Henry Laurens to "provide such a stock of negro cloth and blankets, that these poor people may not suffer" (Izard to Laurens, August 22, 1774, *Correspondence of Mr. Ralph Izard*, 16).

79. Gabriel Manigault to Anne Manigault, October 8, 1777, Manigault Family Papers, SCL.

80. Eliza Pinckney to unknown correspondent, September 25, 1780, Pinckney Family Papers, LC; *South Carolina Weekly Gazette*, March 18, 1783.

81. Thomas Jefferson, draft of the Declaration of Independence, June 28, 1776, in Jefferson, *Writings*, 22. This passage also raised the familiar southern belief that the British were encouraging slave insurrections, charging that the king "is now exciting those very [enslaved] people to rise in arms among us, and to purchase that liberty of which he has deprived them, by murdering the people on whom he also obtruded them: thus paying off former crimes committed against the LIBERTIES of one people, with crimes which he urges them to commit against the LIVES of another."

82. Jefferson, *Autobiography*, in Jefferson, *Writings*, 18.

83. Henry Laurens to John Laurens, August 14, 1776, *HLP*, 11:224–25.

84. John Laurens to Henry Laurens, October 26, 1776, ibid., 276.

85. John Laurens to Henry Laurens, February 2, 1778, ibid., 12:392.

86. Henry Laurens to John Laurens, ibid., 412. For a perceptive study of Henry Laurens's and John Laurens's views toward slavery, see Massey, "Limits of Antislavery Thought."

87. For the organic element in Tory thought, see Reid, "Scientific Correspondence of Dr. Alexander Garden." For Johnston's statements, see *Parliamentary History of England*, 18:747.

88. Mr. Burgwin to Eliza Bush, August 10, 1777, transcript in Eliza Carolina Burgwin Clitherall Diary (typed transcript), 1:22, SHC.

89. Ibid.; James Wright to Lord Germain, January 6, 1779, "Letters from Sir James Wright," 249–50.

90. Frey, *Water from the Rock*.

91. James Moncrief to Henry Clinton, March 13, 1782, James Moncrief Papers, CL.

92. Moncrief, however, continued to oppose returning the slaves to their owners. See Christopher Gadsden to Francis Marion, October 21, 1782, *Writings of Christopher Gadsden*, 184.

93. Elias Ball to [Elias Ball Jr.], April 21, 1786, Ball Family Papers, SCL.

94. Elias Ball to [Elias Ball Jr.], June 25, 1787, and June 6, 1785, ibid.

95. See Ralph Izard to Alice Izard, October 7, 1782, Ralph Izard Papers, SCL. For analysis of the ways in which slaves responded and contributed to the wartime disruption of the plantation system, see the masterfully researched and written vol-

umes by Quarles, *Negro in the American Revolution*, and Frey, *Water from the Rock*. See also G. Jones, "Black Hessians."

96. John Berrien to Lachlan McIntosh, June 17, 1785, Major John Berrien Papers, NYHS.

97. Joseph Manigault to Gabriel Manigault, September 10, 1784, Manigault Family Papers, SCL; Clay, *Letters of Joseph Clay*, 194–95.

98. Henry Laurens to Dr. Price, February 1, 1785, Henry Laurens Papers (George Bancroft Transcripts), NYPL.

99. Henry Laurens to Alexander Hamilton, April 19, 1785, ibid.

100. Henry Laurens to Dr. Price, February 1, 1785, ibid.; Henry Laurens to Alexander Hamilton, April 19, 1785, ibid.

101. Bonomi, *Under the Cope of Heaven*. As many as two-thirds of the Anglican ministers in the South fled the country during the Revolution. See Woolverton, *Colonial Anglicanism in North America*, 228–33; Bridenbaugh, *Mitre and Sceptre*; Posey, "Protestant Episcopal Church," 7–9; and Boles, *Great Revival*, 1.

102. Haddon Smith to Bishop Terrick, April 4, 1776, SPG Correspondence, Fulham Papers, microfilm reel 1, LPL; William Tennent, Speech on the Dissenting Petition, January 11, 1777, William Tennent III Papers, SCL.

103. For the assembly's response to the disestablishment petition, see Richard Hutson to Isaac Hayne, January 18, 1777, Charles Woodward Hutson Papers, SHC. For the desire of imperial authorities to promote the Anglican Church in the backcountry, see Royal Instructions to Governor William Campbell, ca. June 20, 1774, BPRO-SC, vol. 34.

104. Oliver Hart to Joseph Hart, September 10, 1778, Oliver Hart Papers, SCL.

105. James Simpson to Lord George Germain, December 31, 1780, BPRO, C.O. 5/178, fol. 75, in Davies, *Documents of the American Revolution*, 18:266.

106. Margaret O'Hear to Hannah Splatt, August 13, 1779, Augustin Louis Taveau Papers, DU.

107. Zubly, *Journal of the Reverend John Joachim Zubly*, 105; Mary McDonald to Anne Hart, July 13, 1784, Elizabeth Furman Talley Papers, SHC.

108. William Bull to the Earl of Hillsborough, November 30, 1770, BPRO-SC, vol. 32.

109. Richard Furman to Oliver Hart, January 26, 1785, Richard Furman Papers, SCL. By contrast, Jon Butler has characterized this period in terms of religious growth; see *Awash in a Sea of Faith*, 207.

110. Charles Woodmason Sermon Book, 1771, in Woodmason, *Carolina Backcountry*, 128–29.

111. Anne Hart to Oliver Hart, July 19, 1781, Oliver Hart Papers, SCL.

112. George Galphin to Benjamin Lincoln, February 16, 1779, George Galphin Papers, NL. Galphin was reflecting a long southern tradition of associating religion—particularly evangelical Christianity—with slave resistance. In 1770, for example, Virginia planter Landon Carter blamed religion for the refusal by one of his slaves to obey Carter's commands: "His first religion that broke out upon him was new light and I believe it is from some inculcated doctrine of those rascals that slaves in this Colony are grown so much worse" (*Diary of Colonel Landon Carter*, 1:378 [March 31, 1770]).

113. Charles Woodmason Sermon Book, 1769, in Woodmason, *Carolina Backcountry*, 314–15; Oliver Hart Diary (typed transcript), August 14, 1775, Oliver Hart Papers, SCL. Tory minister John Joachim Zubly found it easier to pursue his mission to the slaves, whom he deemed "as attentive hearers as I could ever wish to have" (Hawes, *Journal of the Reverend John Joachim Zubly*, 105).

114. William Tennent III, journal fragment, August 14, 1775, William Tennent III papers, SCL.

115. Coleman, *American Revolution in Georgia*, 32–44.

116. James Wright to Lord Dartmouth, October 8, 1777, "Letters from Sir James Wright," 246–47.

117. Thomas Pinckney to George Mathews, September 5, 1787, Pinckney Family Papers, LC.

118. Hugh Hughes to Catherine Greene, January 9, 1781, Nathanael Greene Papers, CL. Hughes might very well have been aware that Catherine Greene had developed a very unladylike wartime reputation. A strong-minded woman who refused to act primly, Greene was viewed by some members of "polite" society as a hussy. See Isaac Briggs to Joseph Thomas, November 23, 1785, in Briggs, "Three Isaac Briggs Letters," 180.

119. Quotations from three letters from Jane Bruce to Mr. Jones, August 17, 20, and October 1, 1786, Jane Bruce Jones Papers, SCL.

120. Florence Cooke to the General Assembly, January 21, 1783, Petition 37, SCDAH, quoted in Kerber, *Women of the Republic*, 128–29. I have profited from Kerber's broader discussion of this issue in chap. 4.

121. Fran Pinckney to her unidentified brother, March 30, 1783, Pinckney Family Papers, LC.

122. [Christopher Gadsden] to Governor Mathews, October 16, 1782, Francis Marion Papers (George Bancroft Transcripts), NYPL.

123. Henry Laurens to Alexander Hamilton, April 19, 1785, Henry Laurens Papers, ibid.; Will of Christopher Gadsden, June 5, 1804, *Writings of Christopher Gadsden*, 311–14.

124. George Walton to Seaborn Jones, Seaborn Jones Sr. Papers, DU; John Laurens to Gabriel Manigault, June 16, 1776, Manigault Family Papers, SCL; Christopher Gadsden to Henry William Harrington, February 10, 1784, Henry William Harrington Papers, SHC; David Ramsay to Jedediah Morse, June 19, 1788, David Ramsay Papers, SCL; and Jefferson, *Writings*, 591–92.

125. Hewatt, *Rise and Progress of the Colonies of South Carolina and Georgia*, 2:100.

126. Henry Laurens to Alexander Hamilton, April 19, 1785, Henry Laurens Papers (George Bancroft Transcripts), NYPL.

127. Edward Telfair to unidentified correspondent, December 6, [1786], Edward Telfair Papers, DU. Telfair expected "a proper abatement" to be "made in the price" of lots of slaves containing less desirable workers who wished to remain with their families.

1. Margaret Izard Manigault to Gabriel Manigault, November 23, 1792, Manigault Family Papers, SCL.

2. Gadsden to Peter Timothy, June 8, 1778, in Gadsden, *Writings of Christopher Gadsden*, 130.

3. [Gadsden], "A Steady and Open Republican," *Gazette of the State of South Carolina*, May 6, 1784, in ibid., 200. Burke's charge to the grand jury was printed in the *South Carolina Weekly Gazette*, June 14, 1783.

4. Charles Pinckney, *Observations on the Plan of Government Submitted to the Federal Convention* (New York, [1787]), quoted in Farrand, *Records of the Federal Convention of 1787*, 3:115.

5. Ibid., 2:221.

6. Ibid., 220.

7. Ibid., 370.

8. Ibid., 371; Rossiter, *1787*, 268.

9. Farrand, *Records of the Federal Convention of 1787*, 2:372.

10. See the U.S. Constitution, art. 1, sec. 2; art. 1, sec. 9; art. 5; and art. 4, sec. 2.

11. Farrand, *Records of the Federal Convention of 1787*, 1:605, 3:254, 2:371.

12. Ibid., 372, 371.

13. Ibid., 223.

14. Ibid., 371.

15. Pierce Butler to John Leckey, February 11, 1791, Butler Family Papers, PHS.

16. Pierce Butler to Roger Saunders, September 8, 1792, ibid. See also Butler to James Seagrove, August 7, 1792, ibid., and Bell, *Major Butler's Legacy*, 48.

17. Quoted in Bailyn, *Debate on the Constitution*, 2:20, 152.

18. Elliot, *Debates in the Several State Conventions*, 4:285–86.

19. James Robertson to Daniel Crawford, August 31, 1787, James Robertson Papers, SCL; James Madison to Thomas Jefferson, October 24, 1787, in Boyd, *Papers of Thomas Jefferson*, 12:284.

20. Rossiter, *1787*, 285.

21. Lowndes quoted in Elliot, *Debates in the Several State Conventions*, 4:272; David Ramsay to Benjamin Lincoln, January 29, 1788, in Bailyn, *Debate on the Constitution*, 2:117–18. See also Weir, "South Carolinians and the Adoption of the U.S. Constitution," 73–89, and Ramsay to Benjamin Rush, April 21, 1788, in Ramsay, "David Ramsay on the Ratification of the Constitution in South Carolina," 553–55.

22. Elliot, *Debates in the Several State Conventions*, 4:286.

23. George Nelson to Samuel Ballamy, September 8, 1788, George Nelson Papers, SHC.

24. Ralph Izard to Thomas Jefferson, April 3, 1789, Ralph Izard Papers, SCL; for detailed study of this issue, see Coclanis, "Distant Thunder." Pierce Butler to Charles Phillips, February 3, 1790, Butler Family Papers, PHS.

25. Pierce Butler to Roger Saunders, May 27, 1790, Pierce Butler Papers, SCL. For Butler's decision to sell some of his slaves, see his letter to Alexander Gillon, April 23, 1790, ibid.

26. Pierce Butler and Ralph Izard to unidentified correspondent, September 8, 1789, Butler Family Papers, PHS.

27. Pierce Butler to Roger Saunders, August 26, 1790, ibid. For the increasing tension between Georgia and the federal government respecting the treatment of Native Americans, see Downes, "Creek-American Relations."

28. Jefferson, *Writings*, 290.

29. J. S. Grimké to H. W. Harrington, January 16, 1789, Henry William Harrington Papers, SHC.

30. Pierce Butler to Archibald McClean, March 3, 1790, Butler Family Papers, PHS.

31. Pierce Butler to George Hooper, January 23, 1791, ibid.

32. Pierce Butler to James Jackson, January 24, 1791, ibid.

33. Pierce Butler to Colonel Anderson, September 18, 1792, ibid.

34. Pierce Butler to Edward Butler, February 3, 1790, ibid.; Pierce Butler to Peter Freneau, November 22, 1792, ibid.; Jefferson, *Writings*, 684.

35. Charles Cotesworth Pinckney to unidentified correspondent, Charles Cotesworth Pinckney Papers, LC. For analysis of the congressional struggle over slavery in 1790, see Ohline, "Slavery, Economics, and Congressional Politics."

36. Governor Thomas Pinckney Letterbook, March 23, 1787, Pinckney Family Papers, LC; Charles Pinckney to Colonel C. Vanderhorst, May 28, 1792, Charles Pinckney Papers, SCL.

37. Josiah Tattinal to Chatham Regiment, October 11, 1793, Mackay and Stiles Family Papers, SHC; Mary Smith to William Hammet, November 29, 1792, William Hammet and Benjamin Hammet Papers, DU.

38. Ralph Izard to Edward Rutledge, September 28, 1792, Ralph Izard Papers, SCL.

39. Margaret Izard Manigault to Gabriel Manigault, November 23, 1792, Manigault Family Papers, SCL; Pierce Butler to John Bee Holmes, November 5, 1793, Butler Family Papers, PHS.

40. Joseph Manigault to Gabriel Manigault, September 8, 1789, Manigault Family Papers, SCL; Pierce Butler to George Mason, July 25, 1790, Butler Family Papers, PHS; Pierce Butler to G. C. Richards, February 5, 1791, ibid.

41. Of course, radical artisans embraced the French cause for exactly the opposite reason. They interpreted it as the manifestation of a democratic, leveling impulse — the very impulse behind the campaign by Charleston mechanics to wrestle greater political power from the planter elite. See Klein, *Unification of a Slave State*, 206–7. Michael L. Kennedy's study of Jacobin clubs in South Carolina suggests that supporters of the French Revolution maintained a conservative position on the question of chattel slavery. See "French Jacobin Club in Charleston," 21.

42. Joseph Manigault to Gabriel Manigault, September 22, 1791, Manigault Family Papers, SCL; Pierce Butler to James Gunn, September 12, 1792, Butler Family Papers, PHS.

43. Margaret Izard Manigault to Gabriel Manigault, November 30, 1792, Manigault Family Papers, SCL. For a conflicting scholarly perspective on the significance of the French Revolution in southern religious and political thought, see Boles, *Great Revival*, 21–22.

44. Elias Ball to Elias Ball Jr., January 19, 1793, Ball Family Papers, SCL; J. B. Petry to Gabriel Manigault, February 3, 1793, Manigault Family Papers, SCL.

45. Richard Furman to Oliver Hart, September 23, 1793, Richard Furman Papers, SCL. Conor Cruise O'Brien's intriguing and provocative study of Thomas Jefferson suggests that some slaveowners maintained their enthusiasm for the French Revolution even during the mid-1790s, long after news of rampant political violence had made its way to America (O'Brien, *Long Affair*). As late as 1798, for example, Pierce Butler was still expressing optimism about the course of events in France. See Butler to General Wilkinson, July 20, 1798, Butler Family Papers, PHS: "You and yourself I find by your last letter, have not exactly the same opinion as to the effect of the French revolution. I will not say I may not have miscalculated on that effect, but I will say that I hope I have not, because if I have not, the great bulk of the European people will have their situation bettered by it. It is on this ground and belief that I have wished success to the french arms." Such views, however, were maintained by an increasingly tiny minority of slaveholders as the decade progressed, and even die-hard supporters such as Butler were expressing occasional doubts. Hence, while O'Brien's point raises important questions about Jefferson's political philosophy, I maintain that the French Revolution left the slaveowners, as a group, yearning for greater stability in the 1790s.

46. James Ladson to Thomas Pinckney, October 27, 1793, Pinckney Family Papers, LC.

47. Matthewson, "Jefferson and Haiti"; Murdoch, "Citizen Mangourit," 530–32.

48. Ralph Izard to Thomas Pinckney, August 12, 1793, Pinckney Family Papers, LC.

49. Ralph Izard to John Parker, June 21, 1794, Ralph Izard Papers, SCL.

50. Ralph Izard to Mathias Hutchinson, November 20, 1794, ibid.

51. Jefferson to John Drayton, December 23, 1793, in Jefferson, *Writings of Thomas Jefferson*, 4:97–98.

52. Mary Pinckney to Margaret Izard Manigault, February 5, 1798, Manigault Family Papers, SCL; Jacob Read to James Jackson, March 23, 1799, Jacob Read Papers, SCL.

53. Governor John Drayton Letterbooks, March 21, 1800, SCDAH.

54. Cornelia L. Greene to Margaret Cowper, May 3, 1800, Mackay and Stiles Family Papers, SHC; Cornelia L. Greene to Margaret Cowper, October 10, 1800, ibid.

55. U.S. Department of Commerce, *Historical Statistics of the United States*, 2:518.

56. See Alexander Wylly to his unidentified sister, October 3, 1790, Habersham Family Papers, DU.

57. Margaret Cowper to Eliza Ann McQueen, July 1, 1796, Mackay and Stiles Family Papers, SHC.

58. Crèvecoeur, *Letters from an American Farmer*, 160.

59. Jefferson, *Notes on the State of Virginia*, in Jefferson, *Writings*, 288.

60. For analysis of print culture during the era of the French Revolution, see Darnton and Roche, *Revolution in Print*. On the growth and impact of the literary embrace of humanitarian sentiment in America, see Brodhead, *Cultures of Letters*, chap. 1. Brodhead takes suggestive note of the trend toward an idealized, fictive domesticity; I will argue, however, that this pattern was already emerging by the late

eighteenth century. And while Brodhead rightly explores how this new genre took aim at plantation slavery, I will emphasize (in this chapter and the following ones) how at least some of these published representations of the affective household penetrated the slaveholders' culture and provided them with a powerful tool with which to defend their mastery.

61. John Pope, *A Tour through the Southern and Western Territories of the United States of North America* (Richmond, 1888), 78, quoted in M. Lane, *Neither More nor Less Than Men*, xiv; Mrs. ———— Smith Journal, March 30 and April 1, 1793, DU.

62. Cooper, *Remarkable Extracts and Observations on the Slave Trade*, 4, 11.

63. These phrases were part of the United Irishmen of Dublin's dedication to Pierce Butler, March 3, 1795, Pierce Butler Papers, SCL.

64. Benjamin Rush to William Alston, August 29, 1789, Benjamin Rush Papers, SCL.

65. For evidence that Rush favored the gradual abolition of slavery and applauded the "humane & laudable prejudices of [the] [Q]uakers . . . upon the Subject of Negro Slavery," see Benjamin Rush to Jeremy Belknap, February 28, 1788, in Bailyn, *Debate on the Constitution*, 256.

66. Benjamin Cornell to John Ball, November 4, 1792, Ball Family Papers, SCL.

67. Robert Carter to Elder John Waller, July 22, 1789, Robert Carter Letters, NYHS.

68. Elliot, *Debates in the Several State Conventions*, 4:315–16.

69. Quotation from the will of Thomas Wadsworth, September 14, 1799, Thomas Wadsworth Papers, SCL.

70. Gabriel Manigault to Margaret Izard Manigault, December 6, 1791, Manigault Family Papers, SCL.

71. Edward Rutledge to unknown correspondent, March 12, 1789, Edward Rutledge Papers, SCL. For a similar example, see Jonah Horry to Thomas Winstanly, December 20, 1791, Preston Davie Papers, SHC. Horry felt obliged to inform a prospective buyer that the slaves were "much averse to a sep[a]ration, or to be removed from the neighborhood."

72. For example, see Carolina planter Thomas Lenoir's reference to his "family of blacks": Thomas Lenoir to William Lenoir, April 3, 1791, Lenoir Family Papers, SHC.

73. Petition dated April 4, 1787, and letter from Thomas Pinckney to unknown correspondent, April 8, 1787, Thomas Pinckney Papers, LC.

74. Gabriel Manigault to Margaret Izard Manigault, December 7, 1792, Manigault Family Papers, SCL.

75. Alice Izard to Ralph Izard, November 21, 1794, Ralph Izard Papers, SCL.

76. Ralph Izard to Alice Izard, December 7, 1794, ibid.; Alice Izard to Ralph Izard, December 4, 1794, ibid.

77. For example, Thomas Jefferson argued in 1782 that "laws, to be just, must give a reciprocation of right: that without this, they are mere arbitrary rules of conduct, founded in force, and not in conscience" (Jefferson, *Writings*, 269).

78. Turnbull quoted in Rothman, *Discovery of the Asylum*, 61.

79. See John Farquharson to Gabriel Manigault, June 24, 1789, Manigault Family Papers, SCL, and Ralph Izard to James Mills, August 19, 1794, Ralph Izard Papers, SCL.

80. Richard Furman, "A Sermon on the Constitution and Order of the Christian Church," 1789, Richard Furman Papers, SCL.

81. Richard Furman to Rev. Mr. Pearce, February 12, 1791, ibid.; Francis Asbury et al. to Edward Telfair, March 10, 1791, Francis Asbury Papers, EU; Mathews, *Religion in the Old South*, 47.

82. Pierce Butler to Rev. Mr. Smith, January 23, 1790, Butler Family Papers, PHS.

83. William Hammet Journal, April 21, 1793, SCL.

84. Jonathan Clark to Richard Furman, May 30, 1791, Richard Furman Papers, SCL.

85. M. J. Rhees to Richard Furman, February 7, 1795, ibid.

86. Richard Furman, "On the Languishing State of Religion in the Southern States," 1799, reprinted in the *Greenville* [South Carolina] *Baptist Courier*, May 3, 1934, Richard Furman Papers, SCL.

87. William Hammet Journal, January 15, 1795, SCL.

88. For the frustrated southern clergy's desire for community-wide spiritual rebirth in the 1790s, see Boles, *Great Revival*, chaps. 1–2.

89. Thomas Legaré to Moses Waddel, March 6, 1798, Moses Waddel Papers, LC. For Botsford's frustration, see Boles, *Great Revival*, 14. For Furman, see his "On the Languishing State of Religion in the Southern States."

90. Prude, "To Look upon the 'Lower Sort.'"

91. William Hammet Journal, May 10, 1793, SCL.

92. Ibid., May 14, 1793, and August 26, 1793.

93. Charles Cotesworth Pinckney to Ralph Izard, December 20, 1794, Charles Cotesworth Pinckney Papers, DU. For Ramsay's sometimes conflicted position respecting slavery, see Shaffer, "Between Two Worlds," and Ramsay, *History of the American Revolution*, 1:xxii n. 17.

94. Gilmore, *Reading Becomes a Necessity of Life*, 1; Pierce Butler to General Wilkinson, May 4, 1798, Butler Family Papers, PHS. For the southern market for books, see Zboray, *Fictive People*, chap. 3, and my discussion in Chapter 4 of this volume.

95. Alice Izard to Margaret Izard Manigault, May 29, 1801, Manigault Family Papers, SCL. William Hammet journal, May 2, 1793, SCL. For discussion of how Wollstonecraft's work was received nationally, see Kerber, *Women of the Republic*, 222–25.

96. Furman, *Unity and Peace*, 19–20.

97. For scholarship exploring the link between turn-of-the-century market growth and advancements in printing technology and distribution, see James Gilreath, "American Book Distribution," in Hall and Hench, *Needs and Opportunities in the History of the Book*, 144–50; William S. Pretzer, "The Quest for Autonomy and Discipline: Labor and Technology in the Book Trades," in ibid., 13–59; and Charvat, *Literary Publishing in America*.

98. Ramsay, *History of the American Revolution*, 1:24. For a study of the eighteenth-century relationship between American print culture and conceptions of public virtue, see Warner, *Letters of the Republic*.

99. Edwards, *History, Civil and Commercial, of the British West Indies*, 2:168, 170, 174.

100. Weems, *Philanthropist*, 17, 4, 15. For background on Weems, see Zboray, *Fic-*

tive People, chap. 3; Hart, Popular Book, 47–50; and Gilreath, "American Book Distribution," 141. For Gadsden's role in publishing Weems's work, see Gadsden, Writings of Christopher Gadsden, xvii.

101. Pierce Butler to William Page, November 15, 1797, Butler Family Papers, PHS.

102. Weems, Philanthropist, 31.

103. Beck's argument was discussed in Henry Holcombe to Richard Furman, July 16, 1800, Richard Furman Papers, SCL.

CHAPTER FOUR

1. William Radford to John Preston, September 14, 1800, Preston Family Papers, VHS; Esther Cox to Mary Cox Chesnut, September 27, 1800, Cox and Chesnut Family Papers, SCL. For detailed studies of this slave insurrection plot and the society in which it took place, see Egerton, Gabriel's Rebellion, and Sidbury, Ploughshares into Swords.

2. See the speech offered by South Carolina senator William Smith in January 1820, AC, 16th Cong., 1st sess., 267. I explore the social and political context of this speech in Chapter 5.

3. McCurry, Masters of Small Worlds, 5–91; Ford, Origins of Southern Radicalism.

4. William T. Lenoir to William Lenoir, December 16, 1810, Lenoir Family Papers, SHC.

5. Thomas Cooper to James Madison, September 14, 1810, Thomas Cooper Papers, SCL.

6. Governor John Drayton Letterbooks, March 21 (quotations) and March 22, 1800, SCDAH; William Read to Jacob Read, March 24, 1800, William Read Papers, SCL.

7. Governor John Drayton Letterbooks, September 9 and October 20, 1802, SCDAH. A similar episode occurred in 1809, when residents in the Deep South expressed fears that French refugees from a Cuban slave insurrection would migrate to South Carolina in the company of dangerous blacks. See Ralph Izard Jr. to Alice Izard, March 30, 1809, Ralph Izard Papers, LC; John Drayton to William Rouse, April 9, 1809, Governor John Drayton Letterbooks, SCDAH; Margaret Izard Manigault to Alice Izard, April 9, 1809, Ralph Izard Papers, LC; and George Izard to Henry Izard, May 16, 1809, Ralph Izard Papers, SCL.

8. Governor John Drayton Letterbooks, October 9, 1800, SCDAH.

9. Susan Blanding to the Blanding Family, December 2, 1808, William Blanding Papers, SCL; William James Ball to Isaac Ball, November 24, 1808, Ball Family Papers, SCL.

10. Concerns about the colony's security had prompted the Georgia Trustees to ban slavery until 1750. South Carolina had also periodically enacted a prohibitive restriction on slave imports during the colonial period. In 1798, Georgia outlawed slave importations. South Carolina, on the other hand, continued to vacillate on the question. It closed its borders to slaves in 1788 but reopened them in 1803 to service the backcountry planters' demands for more slaves (Du Bois, Suppression of the African Slave-Trade).

11. For evidence that slaveholders expressed their desire to have their state legislature curtail slave importations, see Henry W. DeSaussure to Ezekiel Pickens, December 1, 1805, Henry William DeSaussure Papers, SCL, and Joseph Manigault to Gabriel Manigault, December 17, 1805, Manigault Family Papers, SCL. Patrick S. Brady has demonstrated that lowcountry slaveholders generally favored closing the trade, whereas their upcountry counterparts continued to press for importation in order to expand their black workforce; see "Slave Trade and Sectionalism in South Carolina."

12. Wallace, *South Carolina*, 365, and *AC*, 9th Cong., 2d sess., 167–90.

13. *AC*, 9th Cong., 2d sess., 174.

14. Ibid., 238. On a similar note, Virginia representative John Randolph argued that "he considered it no imputation to be a slaveholder, more than to be born in a particular country" (ibid., 626).

15. *AC*, 1st Cong., 1st sess., 336–41, quoted in Du Bois, *Suppression of the African Slave-Trade*, 74.

16. *AC*, 1st Cong., 1st sess., 626.

17. Many historians continue to characterize southern proslavery thought as nothing more than a political reaction to the criticism of slavery offered by northern statesmen and abolitionists in the 1830s. For example, see Ashworth, *Commerce and Compromise*, 197.

18. John Randolph to John S. G. Randolph, September 6, 1806, John Randolph Papers, DU.

19. William Moultrie, undated fragment, William Moultrie Papers, SCL. The piece was definitely written sometime after the Revolution and before his death in 1805. Given that he refers to plantation records that he had been keeping for thirty years, Moultrie probably expressed these thoughts at the turn of the century.

20. Jane Ball to Isaac Ball, n.d., ca. 1803, Ball Family Papers, SCL. For evidence that the Ball family recognized the humanity of slaves, see Schantz, "'Very Serious Business,'" 8, 12.

21. Samuel Dubose Jr. to William Dubose, March 15, 1803, and June 20, 1806, Samuel Dubose Jr. Letters, SHC.

22. [Louisa McAllister] to Sarah Cutler, February 25, 1805, Bulloch Family Papers, SHC.

23. For further evidence of this point, see Peter Horry's Journal, July 19, 1812, Guignard Family Papers, SCL. Horry described in glowing terms his relationship with his slaves Susie and Rachel: "The former acts as a Mother & the Latter as a Sister, at all hours they attend to my calls with Chearfulness & tenderness used towards me." Reflection on the loyalty of these slaves, however, prompted him to observe in the same breath that "few Negroes Possess a Sense of Gratitude."

24. Jordan, *White over Black*; Fredrickson, *Black Image in the White Mind*.

25. Jane Ball to Isaac Ball, June 5, 1802, Ball Family Papers, SCL; Margaret Izard Manigault to Alice Izard, August 26, 1811, Ralph Izard Papers, LC: Henrietta Manigault to Charles Manigault, December 15, 1811, Manigault Family Papers, SCL.

26. Thomas G. Amis to Thomas D. Bennehan, June 10, 1802, Cameron Family Papers, SHC.

27. Margaret Izard Manigault to Alice Izard, December 30, 1810, Ralph Izard Papers, LC.

28. Thomas Jefferson to Edward Coles, August 25, 1814, in Jefferson, *Writings*, 1343–44.

29. Mary McDonald to Ann Martin, November 19, 1804, Elizabeth Furman Talley Papers, SHC; Esther Cox to Mary Cox Chesnut, October 26, 1811, Cox and Chesnut Family Papers, SCL; Henry William Harrington to Henry William Harrington Jr., September 13, 1812, Henry William Harrington Papers, SHC.

30. William B. Bulloch to Mary Bulloch, November 9, 1813, Bulloch Family Papers, SHC.

31. "Sentence of Judge Welds on John Slater," 1806, Joshua Sharpe Papers, SCL.

32. Ibid.

33. Alice Izard to Henry Izard, October 18, 1807, Ralph Izard Papers, SCL. The landmark study of the relationship between fiction and slaveholder identity is Taylor, *Cavalier and Yankee*. In contrast to my own analysis, Taylor contends that novels did not begin to affect southern thinking significantly until the 1830s and never provided a basis for a deeply rooted proslavery culture. Other relevant studies include Tracy, *In the Master's Eye*; Moss, *Domestic Novelists in the Old South*; R. Watson, *Cavalier in Virginia Fiction*; Ward, "Development of the Theme of Chivalry in Nineteenth-Century Southern Literature"; Hubbell, *The South in American Literature*; and Osterweis, *Romanticism and Nationalism in the Old South*. Most of the more recent scholarship dealing with the relationship between the early-nineteenth-century marketplace for literature and American values concentrates primarily on the Northeastern states. See Baym, *Novels, Readers, and Reviewers*; Brodhead, *Cultures of Letters*; Kelley, *Private Woman, Public Stage*; and Tompkins, *Sensational Designs*.

34. Randolph to Theodore Dudley, February 16, 1817, quoted in Kirk, *Randolph of Roanoke*, 10; Mary E. Huger to Eliza Mackay, April 4, 1812, Mackay and Stiles Family Papers, SHC; Dr. John Peyre Thomas Diary, March 1, 1831, Thomas Family Papers, SCL; and T. W. Peyre to Robert Marion Deveaux, October 1, 1837, Singleton Family Papers, LC.

35. Joseph Brevard, "Catalogue of My Books," August 1794, Brevard and McDowell Family Papers, SHC. For evidence of other, equally impressive libraries, see the late-eighteenth-century book list in the Lenoir Family Papers, SHC.

36. Ann McDonald Martin Diary, January 13 and 26, 1809, Elizabeth Furman Talley Papers, SHC.

37. Margaret Manigault to Alice Izard, July 26, 1810, Ralph Izard Papers, LC. The demand for many of these works was considerable. For example, François Fénelon's *Telemachus*, a work underscoring the need for organic reciprocity between rulers and their subjects, was described by Mason Weems as "much much wanted" in post-Revolutionary Virginia. See Hart, *Popular Book*, 33.

38. Dr. John Peyre Thomas diary, June 22, 1835, Thomas Family Papers, SCL; Unidentified Scot's Diary, ca. 1822, 3:1272–73, NYHS. I compiled a sample from the manuscript Circulation Records, Charleston Library Society, Charleston, for the period July 1811 and January 1812. My sample consisted of 241 transactions over several four-day periods. Published listings of the society's holdings enabled me to place

more obscure titles into appropriate categories. See Charleston Library Society, *A Catalogue of Books Belonging to the Charleston Library Society* (1811), and *A Catalogue of the Books Belonging to the Charleston Library Society* (1826).

39. Esther Cox to Mary Cox Chesnut, September 11, 1810, Cox and Chesnut Family Papers, SCL; Porter, *Scottish Chiefs*, 223, 163.

40. Porter, *Scottish Chiefs*, 46, 56. For the brave youth's contributions to Wallace's cause, see chap. 21.

41. Ibid., 105.

42. Ralph Izard Jr. to Alice Izard, October 25, 1810, and Ralph Izard to Mr. Baird, June 25, 1794, Ralph Izard Papers, LC.

43. Alice Izard to Margaret Izard Manigault, February 24, 1811, Manigault Family Papers, SCL; Margaret Izard Manigault to Alice Izard, November 9, 1801, ibid. She was referring to Walker, *Vagabond*.

44. Margaret Izard Manigault to Alice Izard, August 23, 1811, Ralph Izard Papers, LC.

45. Margaret Izard Manigault to Alice Izard, October 30, 1811, ibid. The novel in question is Brunton, *Self-Control*.

46. Manigault to Alice Izard, January 29, 1809, Ralph Izard Papers, LC. For the vibrancy of Charleston's theatrical productions, see Hoole, *Ante-Bellum Charleston Theatre*. See also Patrick, *Savannah's Pioneer Theater*.

47. AC, 19th Cong., 1st sess., March 30, 1826, 399.

48. Eliza G. Maybank to Margaret Smith, February 12, 1810, Augustin Louis Taveau Papers, DU.

49. T. A. Taylor to Harriet A. Polhill, January 19, 1823, Emily Hines Nisbet Polhill Papers, SHC. George Izard to Margaret Izard Manigault, March 9, 1802, Louis Manigault Papers, DU. Izard was well read enough to refer to Leibniz's stance on the role of imagination in human sensation. See, for example, McCrae, "Theory of Knowledge," in Jolley, *Cambridge Companion to Leibniz*, 176–98, and Leibniz, "Letter to Queen Sophie Charlotte of Prussia," 186–92. Izard had likely seen Christopher Marlowe's *Tamburlaine*.

50. Janson, *Stranger in America*, 363–66, xxvi.

51. Alice Izard to Margaret Izard Manigault, October 28, 1807, Manigault Family Papers, SCL; Janson, *Stranger in America*, 101–2.

52. Izard to Manigault, October 28, 1807.

53. J. Taylor, *Arator*, 120, 122, 182. Taylor's irritation with Strickland, *Observations on the Agriculture of the United States*, prompted him to compose the *Arator* essays. We should note that Taylor characterized slavery as "an evil which the United States must look in the face." Taylor's ideal world would not have included human bondage, but he refused to indulge in wishful thinking about emancipation. Perceiving that southerners faced a choice between slavery and racial Armageddon, he concentrated on the benefits stemming from human bondage.

54. Alice Izard to Mrs. Joseph Allen Smith, November 1, 1811, Manigault Family Papers, SCL.

55. Reynolds, *Faith in Fiction*; Furman to Botsford, April 1, 1814, Richard Furman Papers, SCL. My citations to the tract are drawn from a later edition published in 1816.

56. Botsford, *Sambo and Toney*, 5. The name "Sambo" has traditionally conjured up images of docile, childlike slaves who fawned over their masters and obviously preferred slavery to freedom. For discussion of this stereotype see Elkins, *Slavery*, chap. 3; A. Lane, *Debate over "Slavery"*; and Wyatt-Brown, "Mask of Obedience." Botsford's work appears to have been one of the earliest to associate this stereotype with the name "Sambo." See Boskin, *Sambo*.

57. Botsford, *Sambo and Toney*, 8.

58. Ibid., 29, 40. In a curious twist on the theme of empathy between master and slave, Botsford depicts the faithful slaves picturing themselves playing their masters' roles — an exercise that leads the slaves into sympathy for the slaveowners' desire for an obedient, faithful slave population.

59. Ibid., 35, 23–24, 36–37.

60. Ibid., 15.

61. Eliza Carolina Burgwin Clitherall Diary, 4:3, n.d. [ca. 1812], SHC.

62. Jacob Read to Charles Pinckney, June 18, 1807, Charles Pinckney (1757–1824) Papers, SCL.

63. Hugh McCauley to Isaac Ball, June 2, 1814, Ball Family Papers, SCL. Ralph Izard Jr. expressed a similar suspicion that slaves who professed Christian faith expended less labor for their owners. See Izard Jr. to Alice Izard, December 18, 1808, Ralph Izard Papers, LC. For the unhappy story of a slave patrol that whipped slaves attempting to attend religious services, see H. F. Clarkson to Harriet Aston, January 4, 1811, Miss H. F. Clarkson Papers, NYHS.

64. For the early-nineteenth-century extension of Christianity to the slaves, see Frey, *Water from the Rock*, chap. 8, and Wood, *Women's Work, Men's Work*, chap. 8. Evidence that Christianity's influence over the slaveholding South surged in the early nineteenth century can be seen in Inscoe's examination of Carolina slave names ("Carolina Slave Names"). Other scholars have contended that Christianity did not dramatically affect plantation life until the late 1820s (Creel, *"Peculiar People,"* chaps. 6, 7).

65. Other scholars — most notably, John Boles — have emphasized the individualistic orientation of southern evangelicalism and have contended that the "communal thrust" of the revivals "was subordinated to the personal." See Boles, *Great Revival*, chap. 9. While I agree that it was on these terms that many backcountry residents and African Americans were attracted to the churches, I see a definite connection between pronouncements by evangelical churches on a broader Christian social order and the churches' dramatically improved fortunes in the turn-of-the-century South. Such ministers as Furman were no doubt concerned with reaching the individual sinner, but they also insisted that their conversion of many individual sinners would result in a moral social hierarchy that would reinforce the slaveholders' authority. I develop this point more fully in the next chapter.

66. Mathews, *Religion in the Old South*, 23–28.

67. Wesley, *Thoughts upon Slavery*; Mathews, *Slavery and Methodism*, chap. 1.

68. John Harper to [Ezekiel Cooper], [November 1800], Cooper Papers, Garrett Theological Seminary, quoted in Mathews, *Slavery and Methodism*, 22.

69. Ibid., 301.

70. Mathews, *Religion and the Old South*, 47, and *Slavery and Methodism*, 25. For the growth of Methodism in the South during the early nineteenth century, see also Posey, "Advance of Methodism into the Lower Southwest."

71. Francis Asbury to Thomas Coke, April 15, 1805, and William Mc[Kendree] and Francis Asbury, Western Annual Conference Notes, October 7, 1808, both in the Francis Asbury Papers, EU; Mathews, *Slavery and Methodism*, 18–21.

72. Richard Furman observed that thirty-one of thirty-eight new church members were slaves: Furman to Ann McDonald Martin, October 26, 1808, Elizabeth Furman Talley Papers, SHC. See also Furman to Charleston Baptist Association [draft], [October 14, 1811], Richard Furman Papers, SCL.

73. Mary McDonald to Alexander McDonald, October 26, 1813, McDonald and Lawrence Papers, SHC; Ebenezer Kellog Diary, January 5, 1818, in Martin, "New Englander's Impressions of Georgia," 259–61.

74. Hugh Fraser to John Hume, October 13, 1806, Charleston Museum Letters, SCL; Furman to unknown correspondent, April 21, 1805, Elizabeth Furman Talley Papers, SHC. For evidence that Furman considered his slaves to be members of his family, see Furman to William Rogers, April 4, 1802, Richard Furman Papers, SCL.

75. Josiah Rivers to Richard Furman, February 17, 1807, Richard Furman Papers, SCL.

76. Edward Hooker to David Lilly, October 21, 1807, Edward Hooker Diary, SCL; Joseph Lowry to James Hemphill, September 7, 1805, Hemphill Family Papers, DU.

77. Recounting the episode, William C. Preston contended that the students were delighting in breaking "the shackles of collegiate restraint and ris[ing] to the madness of their power." Preston to Samuel McDowell Reid, February 3, 1810, William C. Preston Papers, SCL.

78. Eliza Maybank to Cousin Hannah, March 25, 1810, Augustin Louis Taveau Papers, DU.

79. Furman to William Rogers, April 22, 1802, Richard Furman Papers, SCL. Of course, Furman himself would soon receive critical reports (from fellow Baptist minister Edmund Botsford in 1803) about the emotional excesses present at Methodist camp meetings (Boles, *Great Revival*, 94–95). The bottom line, however, was that evangelical Christian churches were making significant progress in gaining new adherents. If individual ministers occasionally decried the methods by which backcountry settlers were converted, they very much enjoyed the long-term result of an expanding Christian infrastructure.

80. For the impact of the revivals in the early-nineteenth-century Deep South, see Boles, *Great Revival*, chap. 6.

81. Ralph Izard to Charles Pinckney, January 18, 1795, Ralph Izard Papers, SCL; Margaret Izard Manigault to Alice Izard, May 25, 1812, Manigault Family Papers, SCL. This patronizing tone was not missed by many of the less privileged backcountry whites. Suspicion that the mission movements were part of a larger elite campaign to more closely regulate the countryside was a major source for antimission sentiment in the early-nineteenth-century South. See Wyatt-Brown, "Antimission Movement."

82. Ramsay quoted in Boles, *Great Revival*, 188.

83. For the interplay between market growth and evangelical Protestantism, see Ford, *Origins of Southern Radicalism*, chap. 1. See also Heyrman, *Southern Cross*, which chronicles the genesis of a "respectable" southern clergy but offers a different time line. Heyrman maintains that not until the 1830s did evangelicals embrace a cult of domesticity and a positive defense of slavery. For a study suggesting that evangelicals never became completely comfortable with the positive-good argument, see Loveland, *Southern Evangelicals and the Social Order*, especially chaps. 7–8. For the role of colleges and academies, see Klein, *Unification of a Slave State*, 241–42.

84. Drayton to South Carolina Legislature, November 23, 1802, Governor John Drayton Letterbooks, SCDAH.

85. James Edward Calhoun to Floride B. Calhoun, May 4, 1814, James Edward Calhoun Papers, SCL.

86. Cooper to Thomas Jefferson, March 20, 1814, Thomas Cooper Papers, SCL.

87. Parrish, *Remarks on the Slavery of the Black People*, 18–19.

88. John Anderson to John Singleton, November 5, 1800, Singleton-Deveaux Family Papers, SCL; Francis Preston to John Preston, July 27, 1806, Preston Family Papers, VHS.

89. As noted in Chapter 2 above, Josiah Quincy observed in 1773 that "the enjoyment of a negro or mulatto woman is spoken of as quite a common thing: no reluctance, delicacy or shame is made about the matter."

90. Samuel Dubose Jr. to William Dubose, October 14, 1806, Samuel Dubose Jr. Letters, SHC.

91. Alice Izard to Margaret Izard Manigault, May 29, 1801, and A. I. Deas to Margaret Izard Manigault, both in the Manigault Family Papers, SCL; Mr. Carnochen to Eliza Mackay, August 18, 1813, Eliza Anne McQueen Mackay Papers, DU.

92. Michael Gaffney Journal, December 11, 1800, SCL.

93. Drayton to W. M. Hatson, April 14, 1809, Governor John Drayton Letterbooks, SCDAH.

94. Alice Izard to Margaret Izard Manigault, March 7, 1814, Ralph Izard Papers, LC.

95. John P. Richardson to Elizabeth P. Richardson, April 14, 1808, Williams-Chesnut-Manning Family Papers, SCL.

96. Porter, *Scottish Chiefs*, 78, 160.

97. Alice Izard to Henry Izard, February 21, 1808, Ralph Izard Papers, SCL; Margaret Izard Manigault to Alice Izard, March 20, 1808, Ralph Izard Papers, LC. On the general reluctance of even the most politically active women to admit their interest in politics, see, for example, Kerber, *Women of the Republic*, 74. Izard to Manigault, July 9, 1801, Manigault Family Papers, SCL.

98. Alice Izard to Henry Izard, February 9, 1808, Ralph Izard Papers, SCL; Alice Izard to Margaret Izard Manigault, May 29, 1801, Manigault Family Papers, SCL.

99. Genovese, *Roll, Jordan, Roll*, 5; Genovese, *World the Slaveholders Made*, 96–101; Wayne, *Reshaping of Plantation Society*, 24.

100. George Izard to Henry Izard, October 22, 1807, Ralph Izard Papers, LC.

101. Margaret Izard Manigault to Alice Izard, June 11, 1801, Manigault Family Papers, SCL; Margaret Izard Manigault to Alice Izard, October 25, 1807, Ralph Izard Papers, LC.

102. Margaret Izard Manigault to Alice Izard, October 25, 1807, November 2, 1807, November 15, 1807, Ralph Izard Papers, LC.

103. Ibid., November 29, 1807.

104. Alice Izard to Margaret Izard Manigault, November 29, 1807, Manigault Family Papers, SCL.

105. Margaret Izard Manigault to Alice Izard, December 15, 1811, and February 21, 1808, Ralph Izard Papers, LC.

106. Alice Izard to Margaret Izard Manigault, November 24, 1807, Manigault Family Papers, SCL.

107. I explore their story in "Ideology and Death on a Savannah River Rice Plantation." A vast and growing literature exists on the slaveholders' response to emancipation following the Civil War. Among others, consult Roark, *Masters without Slaves*; Wayne, *Reshaping of Plantation Society*; Reidy, *From Slavery to Agrarian Capitalism*; and Bryant, *How Curious a Land*.

108. Alice Izard to Margaret Izard Manigault, March 31, 1811, Manigault Family Papers, SCL.

109. Ibid.

110. Margaret Izard Manigault to Alice Izard, March 10, 1811, Ralph Izard Papers, LC; Margaret Izard Manigault to Alice Izard, May 3, 1812, Manigault Family Papers, SCL.

111. Margaret Izard Manigault to Alice Izard, September 3, 1812, and A. I. Deas to Margaret Izard Manigault, June 11, 1813 (quotation), ibid.

112. Alice Izard to Margaret Izard Manigault, May 20, 1814, Ralph Izard Papers, LC; Alice Izard to Margaret Izard Manigault, March 31, 1811, Manigault Family Papers, SCL.

113. Matthewson, "Jefferson and Haiti," 209–48.

114. Alice Izard to Henry Izard, February 9, 1808, Ralph Izard Papers, SCL. For further consideration of the tension between backcountry and coastal residents of South Carolina, see Klein, *Unification of a Slave State*.

115. Margaret Izard Manigault to Mrs. Joseph Allen Smith, September 11, 1814, Manigault Family Papers, SCL.

116. Margaret Izard Manigault to Alice Izard, December 30, 1810, and March 24, 1805, Ralph Izard Papers, LC.

117. Ibid., January 2, 1814.

118. Margaret Izard Manigault to Mrs. Joseph Allen Smith, November 7, 1813, ibid.

119. Alice Izard to Margaret Izard Manigault, January 9, 1814, ibid.; Alice Izard to Margaret Izard Manigault, April 3, 1816, Manigault Family Papers, SCL.

120. Margaret Izard Manigault to Mrs. Joseph Allen Smith, April 16, 1819, Manigault Family Papers, SCL.

121. Alice Izard to Margaret Izard Manigault, February 3, 1816, ibid.

122. Alice Izard to Margaret Izard Manigault, February 19, 1819, ibid.

123. Roswell King to Pierce Butler, July 8, 1803; and Pierce Butler to Roswell King Jr., January 16, 1821, both in Butler Family Papers, PHS.

124. Thomas Spalding to Thomas Pinckney, February 18, 1815, Pinckney Family

Papers, LC. For the slaveholders' fears of attack by Indians and escaped slaves during the War of 1812, see R. Patrick, *Florida Fiasco.*

125. Pierce Butler to Judge Burke, April 20, 1796, Butler Family Papers, PHS. Alice Izard to Henry Izard, November 7, 1806, Ralph Izard Papers, SCL.

126. George Izard to Henry Izard, October 24, 1808, Ralph Izard Papers, SCL; Alice Izard to Margaret Manigault, November 10, 1808 (first and second quotations), Manigault Family Papers, SCL; Henry W. DeSaussure to Benjamin Silliman, July 5, 1814 (third quotation), Henry William DeSaussure Papers, DU.

127. Alice Izard to Margaret Izard Manigault, March 9, 1815, Manigault Family Papers, SCL.

CHAPTER FIVE

1. See, for example, Ashworth, *Commerce and Compromise*, 192–93, and Tise, *Proslavery.* Many scholars—perhaps a majority—maintain that southern sectionalism which hinged on a militant proslavery argument did not provide a framework for a coherent political stance until the 1830s. See W. Freehling, *Road to Disunion*, 150–61, 213–307; Jordan, *Tumult and Silence at Second Creek,* 65–66; W. Cooper, *The South and the Politics of Slavery*, 58–66; Sparks, *On Jordan's Stormy Banks*, chap. 7; and McCardell, *Idea of a Southern Nation*, 48–51. Conversely, for an account stressing the continuity in southern concepts about liberty and slavery, see Greenberg, "Revolutionary Ideology and the Proslavery Argument."

2. Drew Gilpin Faust takes note of this point in her introduction to *Ideology of Slavery*, 1–20. But as her decision to begin her anthology of proslavery writings in the 1830s suggests, she too perceives a significant shift in the slaveholders' ideological stance beginning in that decade. For scholarship depicting the proslavery authors of the 1820s as ideological trailblazers, see Sellers, *Market Revolution*, 273–81.

3. Richard Furman to Edmund Botsford, October 3, 1816, Richard Furman Papers, SCL.

4. Rothbard, *Panic of 1819*; Reznek, "Depression of 1819–1822"; Sellers, *Market Revolution*, 132–39.

5. J. C. Carter to Benjamin Carter, July 24, 1819, Pope-Carter Family Papers, DU.

6. J. Maury to Edward Harden, August 24, 1821, Edward Harden Papers, DU.

7. Andrew Norris to James Edward Calhoun, May 1, 1823, James Edward Calhoun Papers, SCL; Alex Brevard to Theodore W. Brevard, February 13, 1826, Theodore Washington Brevard Papers, SHC.

8. On migration in the South, see Cashin, *Family Venture*; A. Smith, *Economic Readjustment of an Old Cotton State*; W. Lynch, "Westward Flow of Southern Colonists before 1861"; and Miller, "South by Southwest."

9. Israel Pickens to William Lenoir, January 18, 1817, Lenoir Family Papers, SHC.

10. Samuel McDonald to Ann Brantley, May 27, 1817, Elizabeth Furman Talley Papers, SHC.

11. Richard Furman to Ann Martin, April 23, 1809, ibid. See also Ebenezer Jackson to Ebenezer Jackson Jr., April 15, 1818, Ebenezer Jackson Letterbooks, DU, and Cashin, *Family Venture.*

12. For studies of the Missouri controversy, see G. Moore, *Missouri Controversy*, and Woolsey, "The West Becomes a Problem."

13. *AC*, 15th Cong., 2d sess., 1180.

14. Ibid., 16th Cong., 1st sess., 228, 160.

15. Ibid., 15th Cong., 2d sess., 1437.

16. For example, Farrand, *Records of the Federal Convention*, 2:371; Bailyn, *Debate on the Constitution*, 2:20; and *AC*, 9th Cong., 2d sess., 238, 626.

17. *AC*, 16th Cong., 1st sess., 266.

18. Ibid., 267.

19. Ibid., 279.

20. W. Freehling, *Prelude to Civil War*, 82; likewise see Sellers, *Market Revolution*, 139–40.

21. Pinkney's speech was not recorded. I base my discussion of it on New Hampshire senator Morrill's indignant response in *AC*, 16th Cong., 1st sess., 296.

22. Ibid., 173. Walker refused to concede that the institution was evil. Instead, he reminded his opponents that "the evil, if it be one, already exists. . . . I must contend, then, sir, that whether slavery is really an evil or not, is a matter for the people of Missouri to determine for themselves, and not Congress for them" (ibid., 174).

23. Ibid., 226.

24. Ibid., 15th Cong., 2d sess., 1227.

25. Ibid., 16th Cong., 1st sess., 346, 349, 350.

26. For the theory that slavery would be ameliorated by spreading the slaves across America, see Jenkins, *Pro-Slavery Thought in the Old South*, 70.

27. *AC*, 15th Cong., 2d sess., 1174.

28. Basil Manly, "On the Emancipation of Slaves," April 1821, Basil Manly Papers, SCL.

29. Kennedy and Parker, *Official Report of the Trials of Sundry Negroes*; Hamilton, *Negro Plot*; "Confession of Bacchus," 1822, William Hammet and Benjamin Hammet Papers, DU; Starobin, *Denmark Vesey*; Lofton, *Insurrection in South Carolina*; and W. Freehling, *Prelude to Civil War*, 53–60. For a revisionist account downplaying the number of conspirators, see Wade, "Vesey Plot."

30. For an account of one free black family's struggle to become "respectable" citizens of slaveowning society, see Johnson and Roark, *Black Masters*.

31. "Confession of Bacchus."

32. W. Freehling, *Prelude to Civil War*, 59, 67.

33. Rachel Blanding to Hannah Lewis, July 4, 1816, William Blanding Papers, SCL.

34. James Hamilton Jr. to William Lowndes, June 16, 1822, James Hamilton Jr. Papers, SHC; Alice Izard to Margaret Izard Manigault, July 14, 1822, Manigault Family Papers, SCL; E. M. Starr to Zalmon Wildman, July 19, 1822, Zalmon Wildman Papers, SCL.

35. Richard Furman to Thomas Bennett, September 1, 1822, Richard Furman Papers, SCL.

36. Richard Furman to Edmund Botsford, May 12, 1818, ibid.

37. John L. Wilson to Benjamin Elliott, May 28, 1823, quoted in Furman, *Exposition of the Views of the Baptists*, 2. In her excellent discussion of the transition toward

a Christian slaveowning social order in the early nineteenth century, Sylvia Frey offers a somewhat different analysis of these events. She attributes the ideological shift to "a psychic need for religion" stemming from "social strain caused by changing economies and innovations in politics" and to "the decline of the antislavery movement nationally," which "allay[ed] popular fears that the spread of evangelicalism would disrupt the slave system." In her reading of events, Furman's defense of slavery "went well beyond the limited claims of his predecessors" (Frey, *Water from the Rock*, 250, 265). Obviously, I see greater intellectual continuity between Furman and his colonial predecessors. What was changing so dramatically in the nineteenth century, in my opinion, was the slaveowners' reaction to the organic conception of slavery.

38. Remarkably, churches that expected slaves to remain obedient to their masters still censured those slaves who, by following their owners' orders, had violated Christian teaching. Thus the Baptist Church in Euhaw, South Carolina, excluded "a colored member who in accordance with the wish & command of his owner put away his wife & married another." With curious logic, the church authorities required "implicit obedience from their Servants to their Masters" but nevertheless concluded that "in all cases of [such] doubtful morality the individual should bear his own burden" ("The Committee on Correspondence Report," n.d. [ca. 1830], Iveson L. Brookes Papers, SCL). For an enlightening analysis of church discipline in Mississippi, see Sparks, *On Jordan's Stormy Banks*, chap. 9.

39. Hamer, "Great Britain, the United States, and the Negro Seamen Acts." Despite Johnson's decision, city authorities continued to enforce the law at their own discretion. In 1826, Georgia also passed an act restricting the movement of free black sailors (ibid., 12).

40. For the connection between congressional debate over slavery and the Vesey plot, see Seabrook, *Essay on the Management of Slaves*, 24.

41. Dalcho, *Practical Considerations*, 3, 27.

42. Ibid., 27.

43. Brown, *Notes on the Origin and Necessity of Slavery*, 6.

44. Ibid., 26.

45. Ibid., 30, 26.

46. Holland, *Refutation of Calumnies*, 47.

47. Ibid., 49, 51, 56.

48. Pinckney, *Address Delivered in Charleston before the Agricultural Society of South-Carolina*.

49. See my discussion of this work in Chapter 3.

50. Malone, *Public Life of Thomas Cooper*, 19–22, 76, 284–89 (quotation on 289). In contrast to my interpretation, Malone argues that Cooper's proslavery stance was "yet most uncommon" in South Carolina at this point in time.

51. *AC*, 16th Cong., 1st sess., January 1820.

52. Holland, *Refutation of the Calumnies*, 46–47; Brown, *Notes on the Origin and Necessity of Slavery*, 40–41. For Pinkney, see n. 21 above.

53. Young, "Ideology and Death on a Savannah River Rice Plantation"; Fogel, *Without Consent or Contract*, 127; and Steckel, "Slave Mortality," 106.

54. Charles Harris to J. P. De Villers, February 13, 1823, Schomburg Collection, NYPL; Edward Harden to Marian Harden, November 10, 1816, Edward Harden Papers, DU.

55. Howell Cobb's will, April 15, 1817, Howell Cobb Papers, UGA; John Moultrie to Isaac Ball, October 10, 1823, Ball Family Papers, SCL.

56. Unidentified Scot's Diary, 3:1319–21, NYHS; Juliana Margaret Conner Diary, June 13, 1827, SHC. For a Methodist minister's glowing reports on the spread of religion in South Carolina, see John Wesley Young to James E. Glenn, September 30, 1821; Glenn to Young, October 23, 1821; and Glenn to Young, August 21, 1822, all in John Wesley Young Papers, DU.

57. Hugh S. Legaré to J. Burton Harrison, April 2, 1829, Hugh Swinton Legaré Papers, SCL. For a marvelous study of this important figure, see O'Brien, *Character of Hugh Legaré*. For the rise of religious periodicals in the South, see Stroupe, *Religious Press in the South Atlantic States*. For the efforts of Christian reformers to utilize print as a tool for spreading the gospel, see Nord, "Systematic Benevolence," and Griffin, *Their Brothers' Keepers*. For the population figures for southern Methodists, see *Methodist Magazine*, February 1818, 75. Quotation from *Methodist Magazine*, October 1818, 385–87.

58. *Methodist Magazine*, August 1818, 312–18; ibid., May 1824, 198.

59. *Southern Christian Herald*, December 23, 1834, August 12, 1834.

60. On the connection between the birth of a consumer culture in the early modern period and the trend toward increasing inclusion of subordinate social groups in the market dynamic as well as the embrace of the principle of individual social mobility, see McCracken, *Culture and Consumption*, and McKendrick and Plumb, *Birth of a Consumer Society*. The use by religious reformers of market-oriented strategies to convert unprecedented numbers of people initiated a new mode of religious communication that had a revolutionary impact on perceptions of the moral capacity of subordinate members of society. See Stout, "Religion, Communications, and the Ideological Origins of the American Revolution." For more recent scholarship exploring consumer goods as signifiers of social meaning, see Fox and Lears, *Power of Culture*; Fox and Lears, *Culture of Consumption*; R. Williams, *Dream Worlds*; and Mukerji, *From Graven Images*. For the early-nineteenth-century Christian appeal to those of modest economic backgrounds, see Hatch, *Democratization of American Christianity*. Southern historians used to view evidence of the planters' conspicuous consumption of luxury goods as evidence of their cultural removal from the capitalistic North. By contrast, I maintain that the slaveowners' purchasing habits linked them to a transatlantic market responsible for their exposure to the principles of a corporate ethos. For a review of traditional assumptions about owner consumption, see Pease, "Patterns of Conspicuous Consumption among Seaboard Planters."

61. *Southern Christian Herald*, March 25, 1834; Davidson, *Revolution and the Word*.

62. Hubbell, *The South in American Literature*, 231–32 (Weems quotation); Ann Middleton Izard to Alice Izard, Ralph Izard Papers, SCL; Juliana Margaret Conner Diary, August 12, 1827, SHC; Robert William Mackay to George Chisolm Mackay, March 28, 1825, Mackay Family Papers, SCL. For yet another example, see Elizabeth

Lundie to Eliza Mackay, July 18, 1827, Eliza Anne McQueen Mackay Papers, DU. See also Fox-Genovese, *Within the Plantation Household*, 17–18.

63. Unidentified Scot's Diary, 2:976–78, NYHS.

64. Tadman, *Speculators and Slaves*.

65. Anna J. White, Copy of Will, December 18, 1819, Peter Samuel Bacot Papers, SCL.

66. William R. Davie to unidentified sister, n.d. [ca. 1821–22], William Richardson Davie Papers, SHC.

67. T. S. Mills to William Holabird, January 29, 1821, T. S. Mills Papers, SCL.

68. Unidentified Scot's Diary, 3:1263–66, NYHS.

69. Ibid., 1309.

70. Furman, *Exposition of the Views of the Baptists*, 10–11; J. R. Prosser to Richard Singleton, June 20, 1826, Singleton-Deveaux Family Papers, SCL.

71. John Evans to Charles Cotesworth Pinckney, November 23, 1824; William Robertson to Charles Cotesworth Pinckney, November 24, 1824; J. Dorsey to Charles Cotesworth Pinckney, November 29, 1824; Charles Cotesworth Pinckney to J. Dorsey, December 6, 1824; John E. Pope to Charles Cotesworth Pinckney, December 14, 1824; unidentified correspondent to Charles Cotesworth Pinckney, December 17, 1824; C. C. Pinckney Jr. to Charles Cotesworth Pinckney, December 18, 1824; and John Huey to Elizabeth Pinckney, June 8, 1827, all in the Pinckney Family Papers, LC.

72. John Bones to James Bones, July 24, 1828, Hughes Family Papers, SHC.

73. James B. Richardson to William Richardson, n.d. [ca. 1825–26], James Burchell Richardson Papers, DU.

74. Merrens and Terry, "Dying in Paradise"; Stewart, *"What Nature Suffers to Groe."*

75. P. Wood, *Black Majority*, 73.

76. Dalcho, *Historical Account of the Protestant Episcopal Church*, vi; James Hamilton Jr. to Langdon Cheves, April 14, 1830, quoted in Huff, *Langdon Cheves of South Carolina*, 171–72.

77. Unidentified Scot's Diary, 3:1298–99, NYHS.

78. Alexander James Lawton Journal, April 23, 1817, Alexander Robert Lawton Papers, SHC; William B. Bulloch to David B. Mitchell, September 30, 1820, Bulloch Family Papers, SHC; John Berkley Grimball Diary, September 18, 1834, ser. 2, folder 18, Grimball Papers, SHC.

79. Langdon Cheves to T. P. Huger, December 30, 1846, Langdon Cheves Papers, GHS. See also Stephen Elliott to Dr. Jas. P. MacBride, March 14, 1815, Charleston Museum Letters, SCL; Ralph Izard Jr. to Alice Izard, June 9, 1815, Ralph Izard Papers, SCL.

80. Daniell, *Observations upon the Autumnal Fevers of Savannah*, 23.

81. Charles W. Furman to John W. Mitchell, August 7, 1817, John Wroughton Mitchell Papers, SHC; Thomas Tudor Tucker to Dr. Isaac Chanler, October 9, 1799, Thomas Tudor Tucker Papers, DU; Henry W. DeSaussure to Ezekiel Pickens, August 22, 1804, Henry William DeSaussure Papers, SCL.

82. For example, Savannah doctor Richard D. Arnold maintained that "the deaths that do occur are mostly among the Non-Residents, foreigners, who are victims of intemperance more than climate" (Arnold, *Letters of Richard D. Arnold*, 14).

83. Richardson to William Richardson, n.d. [ca. 1825–26], James Burchell Richardson Papers, DU.

84. John Cummings to Hannah Moultrie, March 9, 1804, William Moultrie Papers, SCL. Antebellum correspondence abounds with similar examples. For a sampling, consult David R. Williams to James Chesnut, May 31, 1829, Williams-Chesnut-Manning Family Papers, SCL; Hugh Swinton Legaré to Mary S. Legaré, September 26, 1832, Hugh Swinton Legaré Papers, SCL; Robert B. Corbin to Frank P. Corbin, June 18, 1833, Francis Porteous Corbin Papers, NYPL; unidentified correspondent to William Moultrie Reid, August 29, 1836, Reid Family Papers, DU; and Stephen G. Deveaux to Robert Marion Deveaux, September 14, 1836, Singleton Family Papers, LC.

85. J. Hamilton Couper to Francis P. Corbin, November 21, 1835, Francis Porteous Corbin Papers, NYPL.

86. Whitefield Brooks to Richard Singleton, November 1, 1825, Richard Singleton Papers, DU.

87. Pinckney, *Address Delivered in Charleston*; Seabrook, *Essay on the Management of Slaves*. On the question of agricultural reform and planter ideology in South Carolina, see the informative study by Steffen, "In Search of the Good Overseer."

88. Charles Montagu to Earl of Hillsborough, April 19, 1769, BPRO-SC, vol. 32; Milligen-Johnston, *Short Description of the Province of South-Carolina*, 25–26.

89. William Bull to the Lords Commissioners for Trade and Plantations, May 25, 1738, James Glen Papers, SCL.

90. The quotation is from William Henry Lyttelton to the Lords Commissioners of Trade, September 15, 1757, BPRO-SC, vol. 27.

91. Alden T. Vaughan asserts that "not until the middle of the eighteenth century did most Anglo-Americans view Indians as significantly different in color from themselves, and not until the nineteenth century did red become the universally accepted color label for American Indians" ("From White Man to Redskin," 918 [quotation]).

92. Eaton, *Life of Major General Andrew Jackson*, 279.

93. William Bulloch to David B. Mitchell, October 29, 1817, Bulloch Family Papers, SHC. See also L. Comprere to A. Lawton, June 2, 1828, Alexander Robert Lawton Papers, SHC.

94. Jefferson, "Report of the Commissioners for the University of Virginia," August 4, 1818, in Jefferson, *Writings*, 461. Three decades earlier, Jefferson had observed that Indians "astonish you with strokes of the most sublime oratory; such as prove their reason and sentiment strong, their imagination glowing and elevated" (*Notes on the State of Virginia*, in ibid., 266). Tocqueville, *Democracy in America*, 338.

95. Anonymous travel diary, August 21, 1828, Theodore Washington Brevard Papers, SHC.

96. Simms in the *Charleston City Gazette*, April 28, 1831, in *Letters of William Gilmore Simms*, 1:28; Seabrook, *Essay on the Management of Slaves*, 7.

97. Chaplin, *Anxious Pursuit*.

98. Unidentified correspondent to Mira Lenoir, May 15, 1817, Lenoir Family Papers, SHC; James Barrow Diary, April 13, 1819, Barrow Family Papers, SHC.

99. Genovese, *Slaveholders' Dilemma.*

100. Robert R. Harden to Mary Ann Harden, January 28, 1816, Edward Harden Papers, DU.

101. He made this observation in the same letter in which he complained about the "bustle and confusion" of the business district. See Elias Ball to Isaac Ball, July 23, 1823, Ball Family Papers, SCL.

102. John Moultrie to Isaac Ball, March 17, 1823, ibid.

103. *AC,* 15th Cong., 2d sess., 1279. For the South's minority status within the nation, see McCardell, *Idea of a Southern Nation,* 22.

104. Wiltse, *John C. Calhoun,* 119; Preyer, "Southern Support of the Tariff of 1816."

105. Wiltse, *John C. Calhoun,* 120, 134.

106. Ibid., 219.

107. *South Carolina Exposition,* in Calhoun, *Union and Liberty,* 315–16. Of course, Calhoun's personal political ambitions also contributed to his shifting stance on constitutional issues. See Capers, "John C. Calhoun's Transition from Nationalism to Nullification."

108. *Milledgeville Georgia Patriot,* February 14, 1823, quoted in Nagel, "Election of 1824," 316. Nagel depicts the considerable impact that sectional concerns had on the presidential campaign of 1823–24.

109. Seabrook, *Concise View of the Critical Situation,* 3, and *Address,* 36.

110. *New York Evening Post,* July 27, 1827. On southern fears that the federal government might assist antislavery activists in the 1820s, see Fladeland, "Compensated Emancipation."

111. Troup's speech extracted in [Mary Harden] to Edward Harden, November 28, 1825, Edward Harden Papers, DU.

112. In 1830, Georgia governor George R. Gilmer made this point with special force. Responding to the controversy that abolitionist pamphlets had incited in Savannah in 1829, Gilmer emphasized that it would be foolish for the slaveholding states to look to the federal government for redress: "The slave-holding states are a minority in the Union. The strongest prejudices are continually excited against us. The exercise of any authority in relation to our slaves, tho its pretense may be to secure us from the danger of servile insurrection might eventually lead to the assumption of legislative control over the whole subject and would most probably end in the loss of our rights of property and the utter destruction of the present state of society." Gilmer to William T. Williams, March 13, 1830, Letter Book of the Governors of Georgia, 1829–1831, p. 98, GDAH, quoted in Eaton, "Dangerous Pamphlet," 327.

113. Robert Y. Hayne to Warren R. Davis, September 25, 1827, Robert Y. Hayne Papers, UVA.

114. Theodore Rosengarten, "The *Southern Agriculturist* in an Age of Reform," in O'Brien and Moltke-Hansen, *Intellectual Life in Antebellum Charleston,* 279–94; quotation on 287.

115. William Gilmore Simms, *Early Lays* (Charleston: A. E. Miller, 1827), iii–viii, referred to in Wakelyn, *Politics of a Literary Man,* 8.

116. Richard Furman to Edmund Botsford, January 24, 1817, Richard Furman Papers, SCL.

117. Holcombe, *Letter to Thomas Gillison*; Holcombe, *Protest against the Proceedings*; and Boles, "Henry Holcombe," 390 (quotation).

118. Richard Furman to Edmund Botsford, January 24, 1817, Richard Furman Papers, SCL.

119. Wyatt-Brown, "Antimission Movement," 510.

120. *Methodist Magazine*, May 1824, 198; Mathews, *Slavery and Methodism*, 42.

121. Sydnor, *Development of Southern Sectionalism*, 56–57.

122. Dalcho, *Practical Considerations*, 4–5.

123. Hayne to Littleton Waller Tazewell, September 27, 1827, Robert Y. Hayne Papers, UVA.

CHAPTER SIX

1. Henry M. DeSaussure to Charles Cotesworth Pinckney, May 17, 1824, Pinckney Family Papers, LC.

2. Thomas Cooper to Thomas Jefferson, February 14, 1822, Thomas Cooper Papers, SCL. For a description of other student riots at the college, see Cooper's notes, March 12, 1827, and untitled notice, February 25, 1831, ibid. The latter document notes Cooper's frustrations with riots "that must ere long prostrate this Institution and gratify every one of [its] numerous northern enemies."

3. Hugh S. Legaré to Mary S. Legaré, March 8, 1829, Hugh Swinton Legaré Papers, SCL.

4. Seabrook, *Address*, 4–5.

5. G. Wright, *Political Economy of the Cotton South*, 15–42.

6. Quoted in Jenkins, *Pro-Slavery Thought in the Old South*, 76–77.

7. W. Freehling, *Prelude to Civil War*, 106–8, 136–40.

8. Sellers, *Market Revolution*, 197–201, 297–300. Jackson himself referred to the deal as a "corrupt bargain." See Remini, *Life of Andrew Jackson*, 155. As early as September 1, 1828, John C. Calhoun observed that "we are so unanimous in the South on the presidential question, that it has ceased to engross publick attention" (Calhoun to John A. Dix, September 1, 1828, *PJCC*, 10:412).

9. For the antipathy toward Adams in South Carolina, see John C. Calhoun to Christopher Vandeventer, September 8, 1828, ibid., 421.

10. Robert Y. Hayne to Jackson, September 3, 1828, in A. Jackson, *Correspondence of Andrew Jackson*, 3:435.

11. Cooper to Joseph Parkes, February 21, 1829, Thomas Cooper Papers, SCL. For the willingness of other nullifiers to grant the Jackson administration some time before enacting their radical campaign, see John C. Calhoun to William Campbell Preston, November 6, 1828, *PJCC*, 10:431–32.

12. John C. Calhoun to William Campbell Preston, January 6, 1829, *PJCC*, 10:545.

13. Draft of First Inaugural Address, March 4, 1829, in A. Jackson, *Correspondence of Andrew Jackson*, 4:12–13.

14. In the inaugural address itself, the new president defended the tariff on very limited terms, arguing that "the spirit of equity, caution, and compromise in which the Constitution was formed requires that the great interests of agriculture, com-

merce, and manufactures should be equally favored, and that perhaps the only exception to this rule should consist in the peculiar encouragement of any products of either of them that may be found essential to our national independence" (J. Hunt, *Inaugural Addresses of the Presidents*, 88–89). For the tension between Jackson's states' rights philosophy and his distaste for nullification, see Latner, "Nullification Crisis and Republican Subversion."

15. Virgil Maxcy to Calhoun, July 4, 1829, *PJCC*, 11:57–58.

16. Calhoun to John McClean, September 22, 1829, ibid., 76. For analysis of this event, see Stenberg, "Jefferson Birthday Dinner."

17. Calhoun to Virgil Maxcy, August 6, 1830, *PJCC*, 11:215. For Calhoun's admission that his own "hope is faint indeed" that Jackson would resolve the controversy, see Calhoun to Maxcy, November 3, 1830, ibid., 259.

18. Carter, *Diary of Colonel Landon Carter*, 2:1008–9 (April 1, 1776).

19. "Proceedings of the Charleston Forensic Society," September 27, 1821, NYHS.

20. For Georgia's transition to popular presidential campaigns, see Carey, *Parties, Slavery, and the Union.*

21. Calhoun to James Henry Hammond, February 16, 1831, *PJCC*, 11:333.

22. Preston to Waddy Thompson, February 14, 1830, William C. Preston Papers, SCL.

23. W. Freehling, *Prelude to Civil War*, 149–52.

24. Stephen D. Miller to unknown correspondent, September 9, 1831, newspaper fragment in Stephen Decatur Miller Papers, SCL.

25. Faust, *James Henry Hammond and the Old South*, 36. For the genuine manifestation of economic and social mobility in the South Carolina upcountry and the subsequent democratic tone in South Carolina politics, see Ford, *Origins of Southern Radicalism.* Because Ford's interpretation of political ideology in nineteenth-century South Carolina is, at first glance, quite different from my own, I should make clear that I do not feel that my analysis is incompatible with his reading of events. Certainly, there were significant numbers of upcountry residents who harbored no ambition to become great planters and who were entirely unwilling to defer to any white man in the realm of politics. As I argue below, however, the slave-owners' political rhetoric enabled them to appeal to such voters on democratic terms even as they hoped to channel the power of more modestly situated whites toward the ends of slaveowning society. Moreover, as Stephanie McCurry argues, even the yeomanry had a vested interest in corporate ideology, invoking patriarchal privileges to justify their authority over the women and children in their households (*Masters of Small Worlds*).

26. *AC*, 21st Cong., 1st sess., January 19, 1830, 33–34.

27. James D. Cocke to Stephen D. Miller, January 10, 1830, Stephen Decatur Miller Papers, DU.

28. *Charleston City Gazette*, September 8, 1830, in Simms, *Letters of William Gilmore Simms*, 1:4.

29. Rebecca Motte Rutledge to Edward Cotesworth Rutledge, September 6, 1832, Rutledge Family Papers, SCL.

30. W. Freehling, *Prelude to Civil War*, 253.

31. Ibid., 254–55, 263.

32. Simms to James Lawson, January 19, 1833, *Letters of William Gilmore Simms*, 1:49–50.

33. Charles Petigru to Hugh Swinton Legaré, December 21, 1832, and unidentified correspondent to Legaré, December 21, 1832, both in Hugh Swinton Legaré Papers, SCL.

34. W. Freehling, *Prelude to Civil War*, 241, 229.

35. Stephen G. Deveaux to Robert Marion Deveaux, August 9, 1831, Singleton Family Papers, LC.

36. W. Freehling, *Prelude to Civil War*, 235–44. Likewise, the impressive quantitative analysis performed by Jane H. Pease and William H. Pease suggests that those Charleston residents "most accustomed to wielding power . . . gravitated to the Unionists, the party of the status quo" ("Economics and Politics of Charleston's Nullification Crisis," 353).

37. Preston to Waddy Thompson, February 14, 1830, William C. Preston Papers, SCL; Cooper to David J. McCord, July 16, 1828, Thomas Cooper Papers, SCL.

38. Calhoun to Virgil Maxcy, September 11, 1830, *PJCC*, 11:229. See also McCardell, *Idea of a Southern Nation*, 36–37.

39. Harriott Pinckney to Edward Rutledge, October 6, 1831, Thomas Pinckney Papers, LC.

40. Legaré to Robert Barnwell Rhett, October 26, 1831, Hugh Swinton Legaré Papers, SCL.

41. James Monroe to Calhoun, February 16, 1830, *PJCC*, 11:123–24.

42. Legaré to unidentified sister, October 13, 1832, Hugh Swinton Legaré Papers, SCL. Even some northerners condemned the nullifiers for adopting a course of action that would lead to "Negroe Insurrections." See Jacob M. Bailey to William M. Bailey, [November] 24, 1832, Charleston Library Society Miscellaneous Manuscripts, SCHS.

43. Legaré to unidentified sister, June 16, 1833, Hugh Swinton Legaré Papers, SCL.

44. On this point, see Taylor, *Cavalier and Yankee*, 55. For evidence of other aristocratic unionist planters who condemned nullification as the first step toward the anarchy already unleashed in Europe, see L. Jones, "William Elliott," 366.

45. Many South Carolina unionists sought to discredit the nullifiers by emphasizing their previously nationalist stance (Ellis, *Union at Risk*, 8–9).

46. Hayne to Stephen D. Miller, January 26, 1831, Robert Y. Hayne Papers, UVA.

47. Malone, *Public Life of Thomas Cooper*, 288; Hugh Swinton Legaré to Mary S. Legaré, June 26, 1835, Hugh Swinton Legaré Papers, SCL; and Andrew Jackson to Andrew Jackson Jr., July 20 and August 19, 1829, *Correspondence of Andrew Jackson*, 4:54, 62. Compare my reading with that in Ellis, *Union at Risk*, 190–98.

48. Petigru to Hugh Swinton Legaré, December 21, 1832, Hugh Swinton Legaré Papers, SCL; Preston to Waddy Thompson, November 8, 1832, William C. Preston Papers, SCL; Rebecca Motte Rutledge to Edward Cotesworth Rutledge, January 30, 1833, Rutledge Family Papers, SCL.

49. Preston to Waddy Thompson, February 14, 1830, William C. Preston Papers, SCL.

50. Ibid.

51. Robert Marion Deveaux to Stephen G. Deveaux, February 12, 1830, Singleton Family Papers, LC.

52. A. Freehling, *Drift toward Dissolution*; W. Freehling, *Road to Disunion*, chaps. 9–10.

53. James Hamilton Jr. to Edward Harden, August 31, 1832, Edward Harden Papers, DU.

54. W. Lumpkin, *Removal of the Cherokee Indians from Georgia*, 1:47, 73. For evidence of other southerners describing advocates of Indian rights as northern fanatics, see *Columbus City Gazette*, April 2, 1831, in *Letters of William Gilmore Simms*, 1:29–31, and Simms, *Slavery in America*, 53.

55. For illuminating comparisons between the two events, see Miles, "After John Marshall's Decision"; W. Freehling, *Prelude to Civil War*, 232–34; and Carey, *Parties, Slavery, and the Union*. See also Coulter, "Nullification Movement in Georgia."

56. *Worcester v. Georgia*, March 1832, in Perdue and Green, *Cherokee Removal*, 7.

57. Susan Davis Nye Hutchison Diary, March 10, 1832, SHC.

58. Perdue, *Slavery and the Evolution of Cherokee Society*, 80.

59. Green, *Politics of Indian Removal*.

60. Jackson, First Annual Message, in Israel, *State of the Union Messages*, 1:309; Ellis, *Union at Risk*, 25–32, 102–22.

61. One local observer who maintained that many southerners outside South Carolina did support nullification still conceded that these individuals were "afraid to say so, for fear of injuring Jackson" (Job Johnston to Francis Bernard Higgins, October 4, 1831, Francis Bernard Higgins Papers, SCL).

62. "Resolves of the Legislature of Georgia," in *State Papers on Nullification*, 274.

63. George M. Troup to Edward Harden, September 20, 1832, Edward Harden Papers, DU.

64. Charles Fraser to Hugh Swinton Legaré, January 30, 1833, James Hamilton Jr. Papers, SHC.

65. Rebecca Rutledge to Edward Cotesworth Rutledge, March 9, 1833, Rutledge Family Papers, SCL.

66. Carey, *Parties, Slavery, and the Union*, 22.

67. See, in particular, the draft of resolutions formally ushering the Georgia State Rights Party into existence, November 13, 1833, Alexander H. Stephens Papers, DU. For an account of this transformation, see Carey, *Parties, Slavery, and the Union*, chap. 1.

68. Petigru to Hugh Swinton Legaré, October 26, 1834, James L. Petigru Papers, SCL.

69. Perdue, *Slavery and the Evolution of Cherokee Society*, 66–69.

70. See, for example, Dr. John Peyre Thomas Diary, March 25, 1829, Thomas Family Papers, SCL; Susan Davis Nye Hutchison Diary, April 10, 1829, SHC; and Sarah Ann Robson to Mrs. Charles Hunt, July 3, 1831, Hughes Family Papers, SHC.

71. Henry S. Glover to Cobb, November 12, 1833, Howell Cobb Papers, UGA.

72. David R. Williams to James Chesnut, May 31, 1829, Williams-Chesnut-Manning Family Papers, SCL.

73. For use of the adage, see Susan Davis Nye Hutchison Diary, September 6, 1829, SHC; Whitefoord Smith to Mrs. Whitefoord Smith, October 27, 1829, Whitefoord Smith Papers, DU.

74. John G. Guignard to James S. Guignard, February 14, 1829, Guignard Family Papers, SCL.

75. Susan Davis Nye Hutchison Diary, April 7 (first quotation), April 8 (second quotation), and April 10 (third quotation), 1829, SHC.

76. Ibid., December 4, 1829.

77. Harden Jr. to Marian Harden, June 28, 1829, Edward Harden Papers, DU.

78. Basil Manly Diary, July 5, 1833, Basil Manly Papers, SCL.

79. Susan Davis Nye Hutchison Diary, March 25, 1833, SHC.

80. Eaton, "Dangerous Pamphlet."

81. Freeman, *Rights and Duties of Slaveholders*, 32. Freeman's position was echoed by the Charleston Episcopalian minister William H. Barnwell. Barnwell asserted in 1836 that white northerners were no more willing than southerners to accept blacks as social equals. He then stated that "the subject is a difficult one, but I believe God will do what is right, and as long as I am doing for my slaves as I would be done by in their situation (and this is ever the subject of my prayers and effort) I feel satisfied that whatever be the result, all shall be well with me. If I can only set my People free from their cruel Master, the Devil, and certainly there is more prospect of doing this while they continue under wholesome restraint, I shall feel satisfied that the hardships that they endure on my account, are no greater than they must have undergone in any other situation" (Barnwell to Edgar B. Day, January 4, 1836, Barnwell Family Papers, SCHS). For other proslavery works published in the 1830s, see Thomas R. Dew, "The Abolition of Negro Slavery," *American Quarterly Review* 12 (1832), and William Harper, *Memoir on Slavery* (Charleston: James S. Burges, 1838), both reprinted in Faust, *Ideology of Slavery*, 21–77 and 78–135, respectively. For a comprehensive bibliography of such works, consult Tise, *Proslavery*, 431–46. For evidence that poorly educated slaveowners were recognizing their slaves as fellow human beings, see Rebecker M. Jones to William L. Miller, August 6, 1836, John Fox Papers, DU. Jones, who was barely literate, made a point of conveying greetings from her slaves to Miller's family. For a rich examination of the impact of organic values on whites of modest background, see McCurry, *Masters of Small Worlds*.

82. Simms, *Guy Rivers*, 120–21, 180, 39, 73, 76, 174–75, 440 (Caesar quotation).

83. Ibid., 217, 403–4; Dr. John Peyre Thomas Diary, November 28, 1829, SCL; Thomas Jones to Emily C. Jones, December 1, 1829, Jones, Watts, Davis Family Papers, SCL.

84. Richard Singleton to Marion Singleton, June 15, 1830, Singleton Family Papers, LC.

85. Ibid., May 8, 1831.

86. Alice Izard to Margaret Manigault, August 24, 1814, Manigault Family Papers, SCL.

87. Betty Coles to Marion Singleton, March 12, 1825, Singleton Family Papers, LC. For other evidence of adults urging young southern women to engage in serious study, see James Henry Hammond to Margaret Williford, May 21, 1827, Emma Maria

Service Papers, SHC, and E. H. Lide to Hannah A. Lide, December 30, 1829, Lide-Coker Family Papers, SCL. Likewise, see Sparks, *On Jordan's Stormy Banks*, 55–59. Linda Kerber also chronicles this trend (although she suggests that the South lagged behind the North in providing new educational opportunities for women); see *Women of the Republic*, chap. 7.

88. I. H. L. to Frederick G. Fraser, July 20, 1826, Frederick Fraser Papers, DU.

89. Jackson to Richard K. Call, July 5, 1829, in Jackson, *Correspondence of Andrew Jackson*, 4:50–53.

90. John A. Partridge to Eliza L. Partridge, April 1, 1832, Benjamin Waring Partridge Papers, DU.

91. Mary G. Elliott to William H. Barnwell, July 7, 1831, Barnwell Family Papers, SCHS; Rebecca Rutledge to Edward Cotesworth Rutledge, November 19, 1832, Rutledge Family Papers, SCL.

92. Unidentified correspondent to Jane G. Barkley, November 20, 1832, Gaston-Crawford Family Papers, SCL. For further evidence on this point, see Mary Ann Taylor to Marion Singleton, January 6, 1833, Singleton Family Papers, LC, and James Hemphill to W. R. Hemphill, November 15, 1833, Hemphill Family Papers, DU.

93. Rebecca Rutledge to Edward Cotesworth Rutledge, June 14, 1833, Rutledge Family Papers, SCL; Mitchell King to Hugh Swinton Legaré, September 14, 1833, James Hamilton Jr. Papers, SHC.

94. Unidentified Hart family member to Sarah Hart, December 22, 1832, Oliver Hart Papers, SCL.

95. *AC*, 16th Cong., 1st sess., 412.

96. Ibid., 414.

97. For evidence and analysis of this point, see McCurry, *Masters of Small Worlds*, 150–69.

98. Mary Bulloch to Anna Louisa Bulloch, July 3, 1831, Bulloch Family Papers, SHC; E. B. Cobb to Howell Cobb, October 5, 1831, Howell Cobb Papers, UGA.

99. Poinsett to George Ticknor, January 9, 1833, Joel R. Poinsett Papers, SCL.

100. John W. Buridge to Clarissa Buridge, January 28, 1833, Rosina Mix Papers, SHC.

101. Petigru to Hugh Swinton Legaré, November 20, 1833, James L. Petigru Papers, SCL. Even in Georgia, ministers included the doctrine of states' rights in their reading of the gospel. See J. B. L. Mallard to Alexander H. Stephens, June 2, 1834, Alexander H. Stephens Papers, DU.

102. On this question see Eaton, *Freedom of Thought in the Old South*.

103. Maryann S. Harden to Edward R. Harden, May 22, 1831, Edward Harden Papers, DU.

104. R. Anderson (Clerk of the S.C. House of Representatives), December 7, 1831, Thomas Cooper Papers, SCL.

105. John Springs to Mary Springs, December 8, 1831, Springs Family Papers, SCL; *New York Gospel Anchor*, February 2, 1833.

106. Malone, *Public Life of Thomas Cooper*, chap. 11. Not surprisingly, his religious foes were delighted (D. Fullerton Rogers to William R. Hemphill, December 19, 1833, Hemphill Family Papers, DU).

107. Cooper to Warren Davis, January 3, 1834, Thomas Cooper Papers, SCL. Controversy flared anew when the college awarded a professorship to Francis Lieber, a German emigrant whose writings demonstrated an antipathy toward slavery. Only after such prominent figures as Robert Hayne and William Harper vouched—wrongly, as it turned out—for his safety on the question of slavery did his opponents cease their attack. For this episode, see Freidel, "Francis Lieber, Charles Sumner, and Slavery."

108. John England to Francis Lieber, October 27, 1835, Francis Lieber Papers, SCL.

109. Angelina Grimké to Sarah Grimké, January 9 and August 5, 1829, Grimké-Weld Papers, CL.

110. Unidentified correspondent to Angelina Grimké, March 30, 1835, ibid.

111. Henry Dickson to Joseph Milligan, December 2, 1838, Milligan Family Papers, SHC.

112. Quoted in W. Freehling, *Prelude to Civil War*, 256.

113. Mitchell King to Hugh Swinton Legaré, September 14, 1833, James Hamilton Jr. Papers, SHC.

114. This story is expertly told by W. C. Miller, *Arguing about Slavery*.

115. James Hemphill to William R. Hemphill, March 17, 1836, Hemphill Family Papers, DU; Francis W. Pickens to Patrick Noble, March 7, 1836, Noble Family Papers, SCL; Sam Warren to John S. Palmer, March 19, 1836, Palmer Family Papers, SCL.

116. H. Pinckney, *Address to the Electors of Charleston District*, 6–7, 10.

117. T. W. Peyre to Robert Marion Deveaux, September 4, 1836, Singleton Family Papers, LC.

118. Unidentified correspondent to John W. Mitchell, August 4, 1838, John Wroughton Mitchell Papers, SHC.

119. See, for example, Louisa Penelope Davis Preston Diary, January 6, 1836, Mrs. William C. Preston Papers, SCL.

120. John Hemphill to William R. Hemphill, July 26, 1833, Hemphill Family Papers, DU.

121. Watts to Henry Hunt, January 8, 1836, Beaufort Taylor Watts Papers, SCL.

122. William J. Cooper Jr. has brilliantly demonstrated how both the Democratic and Whig Parties offered proslavery platforms to southern voters, thereby sublimating sectional tensions even as the slavery issue remained at the center of political discussion. See Cooper, *The South and the Politics of Slavery*; see also Carey, *Parties, Slavery, and the Union*.

123. Andrew Johnston to William Johnston, September 3, 1829, William Johnston Papers, SCL.

124. Legaré to unidentified sister, August 4, 1833, Hugh Swinton Legaré Papers, SCL. See also Legaré to Mary S. Legaré, December 21, 1833, ibid., and James S. Guignard to Peter S. Bacot, December 6, 1833, Peter Samuel Bacot Papers, SCL.

125. John Sherwood Thomas to Carter, March 6, 1830, Farish Carter Papers, SHC.

126. Tim B. Green to John W. Mitchell, December 4, 1832 (first quotation), John Wroughton Mitchell Papers, SHC; Rebecca Rutledge to Edward Cotesworth Rutledge, March 10, 1833 (second quotation), Rutledge Family Papers, SCL.

127. Hammond, *Remarks of Mr. Hammond*, 11–12; Francis Pickens, draft of ora-

tion, July 4, 1831, Pickens Family Papers, SCL; Rebecca Rutledge to Edward Cotesworth Rutledge, December 18, 1832, Rutledge Family Papers, SCL.

128. Angelina Grimké to Thomas Smith Grimké, February 3, 1833 (quotation), Grimké-Weld Papers, CL.

129. Taylor, *Address*, 6.

130. Hammond, *Remarks of Mr. Hammond*, 10, 15–16.

131. Nathaniel Beverley Tucker to Hammond, February 17, 1836, James Henry Hammond Papers, LC. For the progression of this theme in southern writings, see Carsel, "Slaveholders' Indictment of Northern Wage Slavery."

132. F. W. Pickens, *Congressional Globe*, 24th Cong., 1st sess., January 21, 1836, 287. For an examination of antebellum comparisons between wage and slave labor, see Cunliffe, *Chattel Slavery and Wage Slavery*.

133. Pickens to R. Crolle, June 28, 1837, Francis Wilkinson Pickens Papers, DU.

134. *Congressional Globe*, 24th Cong., 1st sess., 290.

135. Robert I. Gage to James M. Gage, August 31, 1835, James McKibbin Gage Papers, SHC.

136. *Congressional Globe*, 24th Cong., 1st sess., 288.

137. For the rejection of the *Westminster Review*, see Condy Raguet to James Edward Calhoun, March 15, 1834, James Edward Calhoun Papers, SCL; for the call for a southern Methodist newspaper to combat the "fanatical spirit of Abolitionism which rages at this time in the North," see Whitefoord Smith's circular, August 10, 1835, Whitefoord Smith Papers, DU.

138. On this point, see Ridgely, *Nineteenth-Century Southern Literature*; Taylor, *Cavalier and Yankee*; and McCardell, *Idea of a Southern Nation*.

139. Simms, "Country Life Incompatible with Literary Labor," 297.

140. Simms, *Guy Rivers*, 28.

141. Snay, *Gospel of Disunion*, and Staiger, "Abolitionism and the Presbyterian Schism." Snay contends that theological differences unrelated to slavery played a considerable role in the split, but he nevertheless places sectional tensions over slavery at the center of his analysis. See also Thompson, *Presbyterians in the South*, 1:377–94; Crocker, *Catastrophe of the Presbyterian Church*, 56–70; Posey, "Slavery Question in the Presbyterian Church"; and DesChamps, "Union or Division?"

142. John T. Keply to John Hemphill, August 30, 1830, Hemphill Family Papers, DU.

143. Ibid., February 16, 1831.

144. John Hemphill to William R. Hemphill, September 3, 1833, ibid.

145. John Pressy to William R. Hemphill, August 11, 1836, ibid.

146. John Witherspoon to Susan McDowall, May 23, 1837, Witherspoon-McDowall Papers, SHC. Witherspoon's response to the slavery issue demonstrated the degree to which positive conceptions of human bondage reigned supreme in the Deep South. In correspondence with his daughter, the minister admitted to doubts about the institution's economic utility, although he did reaffirm his belief that it was "lawful & not Unchristian and that it is better for [the slaves], on the whole, than liberty without a due preparation for the reception of this blessing." Witherspoon even penned a critique of southern slavery in a Charleston newspaper. Cognizant, how-

ever, of the dangers posed by such departure from prevailing ideas about slavery, Witherspoon took care to remain anonymous. When northerners pressed their case against slavery, he did not hesitate to side with the slaveowning South, even pledging his life in its defense. Witherspoon to McDowall, January 14 and 24, and February 18, 1836, ibid.

147. Indeed, Georgia Methodists declared slavery to be a positive moral influence on society in 1837, the same year as the Presbyterian schism (Harwood, "British Evangelical Abolitionism," 295).

CONCLUSION

1. Joseph Jenkins to Martha Jenkins, December 5, 1836, John Hamilton Cornish Papers, SHC.

2. Hammond, *Remarks of Mr. Hammond*, 12.

3. Harper, *Memoir on Slavery*, in Faust, *Ideology of Slavery*, 100.

4. Brookes to Sarah J. Brookes, February 25, 1836, Iveson L. Brookes Papers, DU.

5. Ibid.

6. Brookes, *Defense of the South* and *Defence of Southern Slavery*.

7. Simms to James Lawson, August 30, 1837, in Simms, *Letters of William Gilmore Simms*, 1:114.

BIBLIOGRAPHY

MANUSCRIPTS

Ann Arbor, Michigan
Clements Library, University of
   Michigan
Thomas Flournoy Papers
Fyffe Papers
Nathanael Greene Papers
Grimké-Weld Papers
Leger and Greenwood Letterbook
James Moncrief Papers
Henry Strachey Papers
George Wray Papers

Athens, Georgia
Hargrett Library, University of Georgia
Howell Cobb Papers
Habersham Family Papers
Johnston Family Papers
Jones Family Papers
Lucas Family Papers
Slavery Documents
Turner-Brunswick Papers
Moses Waddel Papers
Willis Family Papers

Atlanta, Georgia
Georgia Department of Archives and
   History
British Public Record Office
   documents relating to Georgia
Daniel S. Buttrick Journal
Woodruff Library, Emory University
James O. Andrew Papers
Francis Asbury Papers
Godfrey Barnsley Papers
Levi Brotherton Papers
William H. Crawford Papers
James Dorris Papers

Tomlinson Fort Papers
Thomas F. Furman Papers
Oliver Family Papers
Charles Pinckney Papers

Chapel Hill, North Carolina
Southern Historical Collection,
   University of North Carolina
Anderson and Thornwell Family
   Papers
Clifford Anderson Papers
Edward Clifford Anderson Papers
George Wayne Anderson Papers
Charles Haynes Andrews Papers
William J. Ball Books
Charles F. Bansemer Papers
Barrow Family Papers
Black Family Papers
James Baylor Blackford Collection
Brevard and McDowell Family
   Papers
Theodore Washington Brevard
   Papers
John Peter Broun Papers
Brumby and Smith Family Papers
James R. Brumby Family Books
Bulloch Family Papers
Mac Hazelhurst Burroughs
   Collection
Cameron Family Papers
Farish Carter Papers
Charles Lyon Chandler Papers
Mary Clay Papers
Eliza Carolina Burgwin Clitherall
   Diary
Juliana Margaret Conner Diary
Thomas Cooper Papers

John Hamilton Cornish Papers
Marianne Bull Cozens Diary
Hardy Bryan Croom Papers
Cudworth Family Papers
Preston Davie Papers
William Richardson Davie Papers
James Dawkins Papers
Dickson Family Papers
Richard Dozier Papers
Samuel Dubose Jr. Letters
C. W. Dudley Reminiscences
Habersham Elliott Papers
Susan Fisher Papers
James McKibbin Gage Papers
Gildersleeve and Cooper Letters
Gordon Family Papers
Graves Family Papers
Gregorie and Elliott Family Papers
John Berkley Grimball Diary
Habersham Family Papers
James Hamilton Jr. Papers
Christopher Happoldt Papers
William Curry Harllee Papers
Henry William Harrington Papers
Hawks Family Papers
William Heriot Papers
John Deberniere Hooper Papers
Hughes Family Papers
Susan Davis Nye Hutchison Diary
Charles Woodward Hutson Papers
William Hall Johnston Papers
Roger Kelsall Letters
John Brevard Kershaw Papers
Caroline Olivia Laurens Diary
Alexander Robert Lawton Papers
Lenoir Family Papers
McBee Family Papers
McDonald and Lawrence Papers
Mackay and Stiles Family Papers
Duncan Malloy Papers
Giles Mebane Papers
Milligan Family Papers
John Wroughton Mitchell Papers
William Letcher Mitchell Papers
Rosina Mix Papers

Murdock and Wright Family Papers
George Nelson Papers
James M. Nelson Papers
Larkin Newby Papers
George F. Palmes Papers
Parish Family Papers
John Parkhill Papers
James W. Patton Papers
James Louis Petigru Papers
Phillips and Myers Family Papers
Pickens-Dugas Family Papers
Emily Hines Nisbet Polhill Papers
Charlotte Porcher Papers
Elizabeth W. Rankin Papers
Courtland Van Rensselaer Papers
David Rivers Papers
Thomas Prichard Rossiter Papers
William Royal Papers
Archibald H. Rutledge Papers
Emma Maria Service Papers
James Shackelford Papers
William Dunlap Simpson Papers
Anne Hinman Broun Singleton
    Papers
Thomas Bog Slade Papers
Josiah Smith Jr. Letterbook
Marcus Cicero Stephens Letters
James Stuart Diary
Elizabeth Furman Talley Papers
Waddy Thompson Papers
Trapier Family Papers
Moses Waddel Letters
James Wilson White Papers
John Blake White Papers
Willie Stewart White Papers
Thomas Whiteside Papers
Aaron Wilbur Papers
William Henry Wills Papers
Witherspoon-McDowall Papers

Charleston, South Carolina
Charleston Library Society
    Circulation Records, 1811–1818
South Carolina Historical Society
    Mary Montcrief Allen Diary

Robert F. W. Allston Papers
Thomas W. Bacot Letterbook
Ball Family Papers
Barnwell Family Papers
Charleston Library Society
  Miscellaneous Manuscripts
Charleston Library Society Records
Langdon Cheves Papers
Grimké Family Papers
Lucas Family Papers
Charles Izard Manigault Papers
Peter Manigault Letterbook
Andrew Pickens Papers
John Rutledge Letters

Charlottesville, Virginia
University of Virginia Library
  Robert Y. Hayne Papers
  Littleton Waller Tazewell Papers

Chicago, Illinois
Newberry Library (Ayer Collection)
  Thomas Browne Papers
  William Henry Drayton Papers
  Nathan Welby Fiske Papers
  George Galphin Papers
  Georgia Governor, 1786 (Edward
    Telfair Papers)
  John Habersham Papers
  "Notes on Indian Slavery"
  Richard Parker Jr. Papers
  Andrew Pickens Papers
  John Ross Papers
  Lewis Ross Papers
  James Seagrove Papers
    "A Short Discourse on the Present
    State of the Colonies with Respect
    to the Interest of Great Britain"
  Snow Wennie Log

Columbia, South Carolina
South Carolina Department of Archives
    and History
  British Public Record Office
    Transcripts (C. Noel Sainsbury)
  Governor John Drayton Letterbooks

South Caroliniana Library, University
    of South Carolina
  William Ancrum Letterbook
  Peter Samuel Bacot Papers
  Ball Family Papers
  John Blair Journal
  James Douglas Blanding Papers
  William Blanding Papers
  Milledge Luke Bonham Papers
  Bookman Family Papers
  Bratton Family Papers
  Iveson L. Brookes Papers
  William Bull Papers
  Pierce Butler Papers
  Pierce Mason Butler Papers
  James Edward Calhoun Papers
  Cantey Family Papers
  Charleston Museum Letters
  Alexander Chesney Papers
  James Chesnut Papers
  Cheves Family Papers
  Langdon Cheves Papers
  John Ewing Colhoun Papers
  Thomas Cooper Papers
  Cox Family Papers
  Cox and Chesnut Family Papers
  Paul Cross Papers
  Anne Manigault Middleton Dehon
    Papers
  Demosthenian Debating Society
    Minutes
  Henry William DeSaussure Papers
  William Ford DeSaussure Papers
  John Drayton Papers
  William H. Drayton Papers
  Godfrey Dreher Journal
  Edgeworth Family Papers
  Morgan Edwards Papers
  Ellis Family Papers
  Andrew Flinn Papers
  Ford Family Papers
  Fouche Family Papers
  John Fox Papers
  Thomas Boone Fraser Papers
  Richard Furman Papers

Christopher Gadsden Papers
Michael Gaffney Journal
Alexander Garden (1685–1756)
 Papers
Alexander Garden (1730–1791)
 Papers
Alexander Garden (1757–1829) Papers
Gaston-Crawford Family Papers
Robert Wilson Gibbes Papers
Samuel Gilman Papers
James Glen Papers
Glover-North Family Papers
John Grimball Papers
John Berkley Grimball Papers
Grimké Family Papers
Guignard Family Papers
James Hamilton Jr. Papers
Paul Hamilton Papers
William Hammet Journal
Edward Spann Hammond Papers
Harllee Family Papers
Robert Young Harper Papers
Henry William Harrington Diary
Harrison Family Papers
Oliver Hart Papers
Robert Henry Papers
Francis Bernard Higgins Papers
Edward Hooker Diary
Mary Hort Journal
Huger Family Papers
Ralph Izard Papers
Jefferies Family Papers
John Jenkins Papers
Jennings Family Papers
David Johnson Papers
William Johnston Papers
Jane Bruce Jones Papers
Jones, Watts, Davis Family Papers
Robert McMillen Kennedy Papers
Kincaid-Anderson Family Papers
Lawton Family Papers
Hugh Swinton Legaré Papers
Tarleton Lewis Papers
Lide-Coker Family Papers
Lide-Coker-Stout Family Papers

Francis Lieber Papers
Davison McDowell Papers
George McDuffie Papers
Mackay Family Papers
Manigault Family Papers
Charles Izard Manigault Papers
Basil Manly Papers
Means-English-Doby Family Papers
Middleton Family Papers
Stephen Decatur Miller Papers
George Milligen-Johnston Papers
T. S. Mills Papers
Morris and Rutherfurd Family
 Papers
William Moultrie Papers
Rapelye Napier Papers
Noble Family Papers
Joseph Jeptah Norton Papers
Palmer Family Papers
Pegues Family Papers
James L. Petigru Papers
Pickens Family Papers
Francis W. Pickens Papers
Charles Pinckney (1757–1824) Papers
Charles Cotesworth Pinckney Papers
Elizabeth Lucas Pinckney Papers
Thomas Pinckney Papers
Joel R. Poinsett Papers
Elizabeth Pratt Papers
Mrs. William C. Preston Papers
William C. Preston Papers
David Ramsay Papers
John Ravenel Papers
Jacob Read Papers
William Read Papers
William Moultrie Reid Papers
John Mitchell Roberts Papers
James Robertson Papers
Benjamin Rush Papers
Rutledge Family Papers
Archibald Rutledge Papers
Edward Rutledge Papers
Henry Middleton Rutledge Papers
John Rutledge Papers
Sams Family Papers

Joshua Sharpe Papers
Singleton Family Papers
Richard Singleton Papers
Singleton-Deveaux Family Papers
Elihu Penquite Smith Papers
Henry J. Smith Papers
William Loughton Smith Papers
Gilbert T. Snowden Papers
Society for the Amelioration of
    Slavery Papers
South Carolina Attorney General
    Papers
South Carolina Regulators Papers
James Spann Papers
James Ritchie Sparkman Papers
Springs Family Papers
John Stapleton Papers
Edwin P. Starr Papers
Clark B. Stewart Papers
William Stokes Papers
Stone Family Papers
Mary Stuart Papers
William Tennent III Papers
Dr. John Peyre Thomas Diary
Thomas Family Papers
Thomas Wadsworth Papers
Thomas Waties Papers
Beaufort Taylor Watts Papers
Zalmon Wildman Papers
Williams-Chesnut-Manning Family
    Papers

Durham, North Carolina
Perkins Library, Duke University
Eli Whitney Bonney Papers
Iveson L. Brookes Papers
Oze Reed Broyles Papers
William Bull Papers
John Caldwell Calhoun Papers
Sir James Carmichael-Smyth Papers
Francis Porteous Corbin Papers
John J. Dearing Papers
Henry William DeSaussure Papers
Robert Marion Deveaux Papers
Sarah Ann Rice Dogan Papers

James Dove Papers
Thomas Rhett Smith Elliott Papers
John Fox Papers
Frederick Fraser Papers
Mary DeSaussure Fraser Papers
James Gadsden Papers
John Gibbons Papers
Robert Newman Gourdin Papers
Francis Calley Gray Diary
Grimké Family Papers
Habersham Family Papers
William Henry Hall Papers
William Hammet and Benjamin
    Hammet Papers
Edward Harden Papers
Paul Hamilton Hayne Papers
Leighton Wilson Hazlehurst Papers
Hemphill Family Papers
Solomon Howe Papers
Jared Irwin Papers
Ralph Izard Papers
Ebenezer Jackson Letterbooks
James Jackson Papers
David Flavel Jamison Papers
Mrs. Christopher C. Jenkins Papers
Thomas Sidney Jesup Papers
Job Johnston Papers
Charles Colcock Jones Jr. Papers
Noble Wimberly Jones Papers
Seaborn Jones Sr. Papers
Sylvanus Keith and Cary Keith
    Papers
Thomas Ellison Keitt Papers
John Basel Lamar Papers
Thomas Legaré Papers
Milo Lewis Papers
Benjamin Lincoln Papers
Major Lines Papers
Ann Heatly Reid Lovell Papers
Hugh McCall Papers
McCullogh-Hutchison Papers
Charles James McDonald Papers
George McDuffie Papers
Alexander McInnis Papers
Lachlan McIntosh Papers

Eliza Anne McQueen Mackay Papers
Louis Manigault Papers
Robert Marion Papers
Virgil Maxcy Papers
Sarah P. Maxwell Papers
John Middleton and Robert
   Middleton Papers
William Joseph Mikell Papers
John Milledge Jr. Papers
Stephen Decatur Miller Papers
Thomas Moore Papers
Arthur A. Morgan Papers
Jacob Rhett Motte Papers
George Henry Muller Papers
Eugenius Aristides Nisbet Papers
Benjamin Waring Partridge Papers
Petigru Family Papers
Ebenezer Pettigrew Papers
Francis Wilkinson Pickens Papers
Charles Cotesworth Pinckney
   Papers
Elizabeth Lucas Pinckney Papers
Pope-Carter Family Papers
Abner Pyles Papers
John Randolph Papers
Allen Rawls Papers
Reid Family Papers
James Burchell Richardson Papers
Jesse Rountree Papers
R. Y. Russell Papers
John Rutledge Jr. Papers
Scarborough Family Papers
Langhorne Scruggs Papers
John Simpson Papers
Richard Singleton Papers
Mrs. ―――― Smith Journal
Whitefoord Smith Papers
William Smith Papers
Thomas Spalding Papers
Charles Steedman Papers
Alexander H. Stephens Papers
Augustin Louis Taveau Papers
Thomas Jerome Taylor Papers
Edward Telfair Papers
George Michael Troup Papers

Nathaniel Beverley Tucker Papers
Thomas Tudor Tucker Papers
John Twiggs Papers
George Walton Papers
James Henry Russell Washington
   Papers
James Moore Wayne Papers
George Whitefield Papers
John Leighton Wilson Papers
Isaac Winslow Journal
Sir James Wright Papers
John Wesley Young Papers
John Joachim Zubly Papers

London, England
Lambeth Palace Library
   Society for the Propagation of the
      Gospel in Foreign Parts General
      Correspondence, Fulham Papers

New Haven, Connecticut
Beinecke Library, Yale University
   Henry Baker Letterbook

New York, New York
New-York Historical Society
   John McPherson Berrien Papers
   Major John Berrien Papers
   Robert Carter Letters
   Charleston Account Book
   Miss H. F. Clarkson Papers
   Mahlon Day Papers
   James De Wolf Papers
   Diary of a Travel from Vermont to
      Alabama
   Joseph Gales Papers
   John Lewis Gervais Papers
   Sarah J. Hale Papers
   Robert Young Hayne Papers
   Isaac Hicks Papers
   James Jackson Papers
   Lachlan McGillivray Papers
   Gabriel Manigault Letter
   William L. Marcy Papers
   Lewis Morris Jr. Papers
   Phillips & Gardner Papers

Prince Family Papers
"Proceedings of the Charleston
  Forensic Society"
Dr. Thomas T. Wickam Papers
Unidentified Scot's Diary
New York Public Library
  Francis Porteous Corbin Papers
  Henry Laurens Papers (George
    Bancroft Transcripts)
  Francis Marion Papers (George
    Bancroft Transcripts)
  David Bradie Mitchell Papers
  William Laurence Poole Letterbook
  Schomburg Collection

Philadelphia, Pennsylvania
Historical Society of Pennsylvania
  Butler Family Papers

Richmond, Virginia
Virginia Historical Society
  Preston Family Papers

Savannah, Georgia
Georgia Historical Society
  Langdon Cheves Papers
  Manigault Family Papers

Washington, D.C.
Library of Congress
  John Chesnutt Papers
  Levinus Clarkson Papers
  Habersham Family Papers
  James Henry Hammond Papers
  George Frederick Holmes Papers
  Robert Howe Papers
  Ralph Izard Papers
  Richard Lathers Papers
  Daniel W. Lord Papers
  William Lowndes Papers

Pinckney Family Papers
  Charles Cotesworth Pinckney
    Papers
  Thomas Pinckney Papers
Singleton Family Papers
  Waddy Thompson Papers
  Moses Waddel Papers
  George Whitefield Papers

OFFICIAL RECORDS

*Annals of Congress: The Debates and
  Proceedings in the Congress of the
  United States.* 42 vols. Washington,
  D.C.: Gales and Seaton, 1834–56.
Congressional Globe. Washington, D.C.:
  Blair and Rives, 1834–.
*The Journal of the Commons House
  of Assembly.* 14 vols. to date. Edited
  by J. H. Easterby et al. Columbia:
  Historical Commission of South
  Carolina, 1951–.
*The Parliamentary History of England
  from the Earliest Period to the Year
  1803.* 36 vols. London: T. C. Hansard,
  1806–20.

NEWSPAPERS AND JOURNALS

Boston Chronicle (1768)
Georgia Gazette (1763–70)
Methodist Magazine (1818–28)
New York Evening Post (1827)
South Carolina Gazette (1740)
South Carolina Weekly Gazette (1783)
Southern Christian Herald (1834)
Southern Literary Journal (1835–37)
Southern Literary Messenger (1834–37)

PUBLISHED SOURCES

[Aesop]. *Fables and Stories Moralized.* Edited by Roger L'Estrange. London:
  D. Brown, 1724.
Aristotle. *Politics.* Edited by Stephen Everson. Cambridge: Cambridge University
  Press, 1988.

Arnold, Richard D. *Letters of Richard D. Arnold, M.D., 1808–1876.* Edited by Richard H. Shryock. Durham: Duke University Press, 1929.

Bailyn, Bernard, ed. *The Debate on the Constitution: Federalist and Antifederalist Speeches, Articles, and Letters during the Struggle over Ratification.* 2 vols. New York: Library of America, 1993.

Bolzius, Johann Martin. "Johann Martin Bolzius Answers a Questionnaire on Carolina and Georgia." Edited by Klaus G. Loewald et al. *William and Mary Quarterly,* 3d ser., 24 (April 1957): 218–61.

Botsford, Edmund. *Sambo and Toney, a Dialogue between Two Africans in South Carolina.* Philadelphia: D. Hogan, 1816.

Boyd, Julian P., et al., eds. *The Papers of Thomas Jefferson.* 27 vols. to date. Princeton: Princeton University Press, 1950–.

Breeden, James O., ed. *Advice among Masters: The Ideal of Slave Management in the Old South.* Westport, Conn.: Greenwood, 1980.

Briggs, Isaac. "Three Isaac Briggs Letters." *Georgia Historical Quarterly* 12 (June 1928): 177–84.

Brookes, Iveson. *A Defence of Southern Slavery against the Attacks of Henry Clay and Alexander Campbell.* Hamburg: Robinson and Carlisle, 1851.

———. *A Defense of the South against the Reproaches and Incroachments of the North: In Which Slavery Is Shown to Be an Institution of God.* Hamburg: Republican Printing Office, 1850.

Brown, Edward. *Notes on the Origin and Necessity of Slavery.* Charleston: A. E. Miller, 1826.

Brunton, Mary. *Self-Control.* 2d ed. London: Walter Scott, 1811.

Burton, John. *The Duty and Reward of Propagating Principles of Religion and Virtue Exemplified in the History of Abraham: A Sermon Preach'd before the Trustees for Establishing the Colony of Georgia in America.* London: J. March, 1733.

Calhoun, John C. *The Papers of John C. Calhoun, 1782–1850.* Edited by Robert L. Meriwether et al. 23 vols to date. Columbia: University of South Carolina Press, 1959–.

———. *Union and Liberty: The Political Philosophy of John C. Calhoun.* Edited by Ross M. Lence. Indianapolis: Liberty Fund, 1992.

Candler, Allen D., et al., eds. *The Colonial Records of the State of Georgia.* 26 vols. Atlanta: Franklin Turner Co., 1904–16. 6 vols. Athens: University of Georgia Press, 1977–89.

Carter, Landon. *The Diary of Colonel Landon Carter of Sabine Hall, 1752–1778.* Edited by Jack P. Greene. 2 vols. Charlottesville: University Press of Virginia, 1965.

Charleston Library Society. *A Catalogue of Books Belonging to the Charleston Library Society.* Charleston: W. P. Young, 1811.

———. *A Catalogue of the Books Belonging to the Charleston Library Society.* Charleston: A. E. Miller, 1826.

Clay, Joseph. *The Letters of Joseph Clay.* Georgia Historical Society Collections, vol. 8. Savannah: Georgia Historical Society, 1913.

Cohen, Hennig. *The "South Carolina Gazette": 1732–1775.* Columbia: University of South Carolina Press, 1953.

Conder, John, and Thomas Gibbons, eds. *Living Christ Delineated, in the Diaries and Letters of Two Eminently Pious Persons*. London: J. Buckland, 1760.

Cooper, Thomas. *Remarkable Extracts and Observations on the Slave Trade. With Some Considerations on the Consumption of West India Produce*. London: Darton and Harvey, 1791.

Cooper, Thomas, and David J. McCord, eds. *The Statutes at Large of South Carolina*. 10 vols. Columbia: Republican Printing, 1872.

Crèvecoeur, Hector St. John de. *Letters from an American Farmer*. 1782. Reprint, London: J. M. Dent, 1926.

Dalcho, Frederick. *Practical Considerations Founded on the Scriptures, Relative to the Slave Population of South-Carolina*. Charleston: A. E. Miller, 1823.

———. *An Historical Account of the Protestant Episcopal Church in South-Carolina*. Charleston: E. Thayer, 1820.

Daniell, W. C. *Observations upon the Autumnal Fevers of Savannah*. Savannah: W. T. Williams, 1826.

Davies, K. G., ed. *Documents of the American Revolution, 1770–1783 (Colonial Office Series)*. 21 vols. Shannon: Irish University Press, 1972–81.

Drayton, John. *Memoirs of the American Revolution, from Its Commencement to the Year 1776, Inclusive; As Relating to the State of South-Carolina*. 2 vols. Charleston: A. E. Miller, 1821.

Eaton, John Henry. *The Life of Major General Andrew Jackson: Comprising a History of the War in the South*. Philadelphia: McCarty and Davis, 1828.

Edwards, Bryan. *The History, Civil and Commercial, of the British West Indies with a Continuation to the Present Time*. 4 vols. 1793. Reprint, New York: AMS Press, 1966.

Elliot, Jonathan, ed. *The Debates in the Several State Conventions on the Adoption of the Federal Constitution*. 2d ed. 5 vols. Philadelphia: J. B. Lippincott, 1876.

Farrand, Max, ed. *The Records of the Federal Convention of 1787*. Rev. ed. 4 vols. New Haven: Yale University Press, 1937.

Faust, Drew Gilpin, ed. *The Ideology of Slavery: Proslavery Thought in the Antebellum South, 1830–1860*. Baton Rouge: Louisiana State University Press, 1981.

Fithian, Philip Vickers. *Journal and Letters of Philip Vickers Fithian, 1773–1774: A Plantation Tutor of the Old Dominion*. Edited by Hunter Dickinson Farish. Williamsburg: Colonial Williamsburg, 1943.

Fleetwood, William. *The Relative Duties of Parents and Children, Husbands and Wives, Masters and Servants*. 1705. Reprint, New York: Garland, 1985.

———. *A Sermon Preached before the Society for the Propagation of the Gospel in Foreign Parts*. London: Joseph Downing, 1711.

Freeman, George W. *The Rights and Duties of Slaveholders*. Charleston: A. E. Miller, 1837.

Furman, Richard. *Exposition of the Views of the Baptists, Relative to the Coloured Population of the United States*. Charleston: A. E. Miller, 1823.

———. *Unity and Peace: A Sermon*. Charleston: Markland, M'Iver and Company, 1794.

Gadsden, Christopher. *Some Observations on the Two Campaigns against the*

Cherokee Indians in 1760 and 1761 in a Second Letter from Philopatrios.
Charleston: Peter Timothy, 1762.

————. *The Writings of Christopher Gadsden, 1746–1805.* Edited by Richard Walsh.
Columbia: University of South Carolina Press, 1966.

Garden, Alexander. *Six Letters to the Rev. Mr. George Whitefield.* Boston: T. Fleet,
1740.

Gibson, Edmund. *Two Letters of the Lord Bishop of London.* London: J. Downing,
1711.

Glen, James. *A Description of South Carolina.* London: R. and J. Dodsley, 1761.

Gordeon, Peter. *Peter Gordeon Journal, 1732–35.* Edited by E. Merton Coulter.
Athens: University of Georgia Press, 1963.

Habersham, James. *The Letters of Hon. James Habersham, 1756–1775.* Georgia
Historical Society Collections, vol. 6. Savannah: Georgia Historical Society, 1904.

Hales, Stephen. *A Sermon Preached before the Trustees for Establishing the Colony of
Georgia in America.* London: T. Woodward, 1734.

Hamilton, James, Jr. *Negro Plot: An Account of the Late Intended Insurrection
among a Portion of the Blacks in the City of Charleston, South Carolina.* Boston:
J. W. Ingraham, 1822.

Hammond, James Henry. *Remarks of Mr. Hammond of South Carolina on the
Question of Receiving Petitions for the Abolition of Slavery.* Washington, D.C.:
Duff Green, 1836.

Hewatt, Alexander. *An Historical Account of the Rise and Progress of the Colonies of
South Carolina and Georgia.* 2 vols. London: A. Donaldson, 1779.

Holcombe, Henry. *A Letter to Thomas Gillison, Esq., of South Carolina, on the
Silence of the Second Annual Report of the Baptist Board of Foreign Missions.*
Philadelphia: John Bioren, 1816.

————. *A Protest against the Proceedings of the Philadelphia Baptist Association.*
Philadelphia: R. Johnsen, 1816.

Holland, Edwin C. *A Refutation of the Calumnies Circulated against the Southern
and Western States.* Charleston: A. E. Miller, 1822.

Holmes, George Frederick. "Observations on a Passage in the *Politics* of Aristotle
Relative to Slavery." *Southern Literary Messenger* 16 (April 1850): 193–205.

House, Albert Virgil, ed. *Planter Management and Capitalism in Ante-Bellum
Georgia: The Journal of Hugh Fraser Grant, Ricegrower.* New York: Columbia
University Press, 1954.

Hunt, John Gabriel, ed. *The Inaugural Addresses of the Presidents.* New York:
Gramercy, 1995.

Israel, Fred L., ed. *The State of the Union Messages of the Presidents.* 3 vols.
New York: Chelsea House, 1966.

Izard, Ralph. *Correspondence of Mr. Ralph Izard, of South Carolina, from the Year
1774 to 1804.* Edited by Anne Izard Deas. 1844. Reprint, New York: AMS Press,
1976.

Jackson, Andrew. *Correspondence of Andrew Jackson.* Edited by John Spencer
Bassett. 7 vols. Washington, D.C.: Carnegie Institute, 1926–35.

Jackson, James. *The Papers of James Jackson, 1781–1798.* Edited by Lilla M. Hawes.

Georgia Historical Society Collections, vol. 11. Savannah: Georgia Historical Society, 1955.

Janson, Charles William. *The Stranger in America*. 1807. Reprint, London: Albion Press, 1935.

Jefferson, Thomas. *Writings*. Edited by Merrill D. Peterson. New York: Library of America, 1984.

———. *The Writings of Thomas Jefferson*. Edited by Henry A. Washington. 9 vols. New York: Taylor and Maury, 1854–57.

Jones, Charles Colcock. *A Catechism, of Scripture Doctrine and Practice, for Families and Sunday Schools, Designed Also for the Oral Instruction of Colored Persons*. Savannah: T. Purse, 1837.

———. *The Religious Instruction of the Negroes*. Princeton: D. Hart, 1832.

Kennedy, Lionel H., and Thomas Parker. *An Official Report of the Trials of Sundry Negroes, Charged with an Attempt to Raise an Insurrection in the State of South Carolina*. Charleston: James R. Schenck, 1822.

Knox, William. *The Controversy between Great Britain and Her Colonies Reviewed*. London: Mein and Fleeming, 1769.

———. *Three Tracts Respecting the Conversion and Instruction of the Free Indians, and Negroe Slaves in the Colonies Addressed to the Venerable Society for Propagation of the Gospel in Foreign Parts*. London: n.p., 1768.

Labaree, Leonard Woods, ed. *Royal Instructions to British Colonial Governors, 1670–1776*. 2 vols. New York: D. Appleton-Century, 1935.

Lane, Mills, ed. *Neither More nor Less Than Men: Slavery in Georgia*. Savannah: Beehive Press, 1993.

Laurens, Henry. *The Papers of Henry Laurens*. Edited by Philip M. Hamer et al. 14 vols. to date. Columbia: University of South Carolina Press, 1968–.

Le Jau, Francis. *The Carolina Chronicle of Dr. Francis Le Jau, 1706–1717*. Edited by Frank J. Klingberg. Berkeley: University of California Press, 1956.

Leibniz, G. W. "Letter to Queen Sophie Charlotte of Prussia, on What Is Independent of Sense and Matter." In *Philosophical Essays, G. W. Leibniz*, edited and translated by Roger Ariew and Daniel Garber, 186–92. Indianapolis: Hackett, 1989.

Lumpkin, Wilson. *The Removal of the Cherokee Indians from Georgia*. 2 vols. Wormsloe: Privately published, 1907.

McIntosh, Lachlan. "The Papers of Lachlan McIntosh, 1774–1799." Edited by Lilla M. Hawes. *Georgia Historical Quarterly* 38 (1954): 148–69, 253–67, 356–68; 39 (1955): 52–68, 172–86, 253–68, 356–75; 40 (1956): 68–88, 152–74.

McLoughlin, William G., and Winthrop D. Jordan, eds. "Baptists Face the Barbarities of Slavery in 1710." *Journal of Southern History* 29 (November 1963): 495–501.

[Martin, John]. "Official Letters of Governor John Martin, 1782–1783." *Georgia Historical Quarterly* 1 (December 1917): 281–346.

Martin, Sidney Walter, ed. "A New Englander's Impressions of Georgia in 1817–1818: Extracts from the Diary of Ebenezer Kellog." *Journal of Southern History* 12 (May 1946): 247–62.

Martineau, Harriet. *Demarara*. London: Charles Fox, 1834.

———. *Society in America*. 2 vols. New York: Saunders and Otley, 1837.

Martyn, Benjamin. *An Impartial Inquiry into the State and Utility of the Province of Georgia*. London: W. Meadows, 1741. In Georgia Historical Society Collections, vol. 1:153–201. Savannah: Georgia Historical Society, 1840.

Mill, James. *Elements of Political Economy*. 3d ed. 1844. Reprint, New York: Augustus M. Kelley, 1963.

Miller, Perry, ed. *The American Puritans: Their Prose and Poetry*. Garden City, N.Y.: Doubleday, 1956.

Milligen-Johnston, George. *A Short Description of the Province of South-Carolina*. London: John Hinton, 1770.

Moultrie, William. *Memoirs of the American Revolution: So Far As It Related to the States of North and South Carolina, and Georgia*. 2 vols. Charleston: D. Longworth, 1802.

O'Brien, Michael, ed. *All Clever Men, Who Make Their Way: Critical Discourse in the Old South*. Athens: University of Georgia Press, 1992.

Parrish, John. *Remarks on the Slavery of the Black People*. Philadelphia: Kimber, Conrad, 1806.

Perdue, Theda, and Michael D. Green, eds. *The Cherokee Removal: A Brief History with Documents*. Boston: Bedford, 1995.

Phillips, Ulrich B., ed. *Plantation and Frontier Documents: 1649–1863, Illustrative of Industrial History in the Colonial and Ante-Bellum South*. 2 vols. Cleveland: Arthur H. Clark, 1909.

Pinckney, Charles Cotesworth. *An Address Delivered in Charleston before the Agricultural Society of South-Carolina*. Charleston: A. E. Miller, 1829.

Pinckney, Eliza Lucas. *The Letterbook of Eliza Lucas Pinckney*. Edited by Elise Pinckney and Marvin R. Zahniser. Chapel Hill: University of North Carolina Press, 1972.

Pinckney, Henry Laurens. *Address to the Electors of Charleston District, South Carolina, on the Subject of the Abolition of Slavery*. Washington, D.C.: n.p., 1836.

Porter, Jane. *The Scottish Chiefs*. Rev. ed. New York: Derby and Jackson, 1857.

Pringle, Robert. *The Letterbook of Robert Pringle*. 2 vols. Edited by Walter B. Edgar. Columbia: University of South Carolina Press, 1972.

Quincy, Josiah, Jr. "Journal of Josiah Quincy, Junior, 1773." Edited by Mark Antony De Wolfe Howe. *Massachusetts Historical Society Proceedings* 49 (1915–16): 424–81.

Ramsay, David. "David Ramsay on the Ratification of the Constitution in South Carolina, 1787–1788." Edited by Robert L. Brunhouse. *Journal of Southern History* 9 (November 1943): 549–55.

———. *History of South-Carolina, from Its First Settlement in 1670 to the Year 1808*. 2 vols. Charleston: D. Longworth, 1809.

———. *The History of the American Revolution*. 2 vols. 1789. Reprint, Indianapolis: Liberty Classics, 1990.

———. *The History of the Revolution of South-Carolina*. Trenton, N.J.: Isaac Collins, 1785.

Schaw, Janet. *Journal of a Lady of Quality. Being the Narrative of a Journey from Scotland to the West Indies, North Carolina, in the Years 1774 to 1776.* Edited by Evangeline Walker Andrews. New Haven: Yale University Press, 1939.

Seabrook, Whitemarsh B. *An Address Delivered at the First Anniversary Meeting of the United Agricultural Society of South-Carolina.* Charleston: A. E. Miller, 1828.

———. *A Concise View of the Critical Situation, and Future Prospects of the Slave-Holding States, in Relation to their Coloured Population.* Charleston: A. E. Miller, 1825.

———. *An Essay on the Management of Slaves, and Especially Their Religious Instruction.* Charleston: A. E. Miller, 1834.

Shryock, Richard H., ed. *Letters of Richard D. Arnold, M.D., 1808–1876.* Papers of the Trinity College Historical Society, vols. 28–29. Durham: Duke University Press, 1929.

Simms, William Gilmore. "Country Life Incompatible with Literary Labor." *Southern Literary Journal* 1 (June 1837): 297–99.

———. *Guy Rivers: A Tale of Georgia.* Edited by John Caldwell Guilds. 1833. Reprint, Fayetteville: University of Arkansas Press, 1993.

———. *Letters of William Gilmore Simms.* Edited by Mary C. Simms Oliphant et al. 6 vols. Columbia: University of South Carolina Press, 1952–82.

———. "The Morals of Slavery." In *The Pro-Slavery Argument, as Maintained by the Most Distinguished Writers of the Southern States,* 175–285. Charleston: Walker, Richards and Company, 1852.

———. *Slavery in America, Being a Brief Review of Miss Martineau on That Subject.* Richmond: White, 1838.

Smith, Adam. *The Wealth of Nations.* 1776. Reprint, New York: Knopf, 1991.

Smith, Samuel. *A Sermon Preach'd before the Trustees for Establishing the Colony of Georgia in America.* London: J. March, 1733.

Starobin, Richard S., ed. *Denmark Vesey: The Slave Conspiracy of 1822.* Englewood Cliffs, N.J.: Prentice Hall, 1970.

State Papers on Nullification: Including the Public Acts of the Convention of the People of South Carolina. Boston: Dutton and Wentworth, 1834.

Stephens, Thomas. *Brief Account of the Causes That Have Retarded the Progress of the Colony of Georgia in America.* London: n.p., 1743.

Stephens, William. *The Journal of William Stephens, 1743–1745.* 2 vols. Edited by E. Merton Coulter. Athens: University of Georgia Press, 1958–59.

Strickland, William. *Observations on the Agriculture of the United States.* London: W. Bulmer, 1801.

Taylor, John. *Arator, Being a Series of Agricultural Essays, Practical and Political.* Edited by M. E. Bradford. 1813. Reprint, Indianapolis: Liberty Classics, 1977.

Taylor, Thomas House. *An Address, Delivered before the Charleston Infant School Society.* Charleston: J. S. Burgess, 1831.

Tocqueville, Alexis de. *Democracy in America.* Edited by J. P. Mayer. Translated by George Lawrence. 1833. Reprint, New York: Harper and Row, 1988.

Van Horne, John C., ed. *Religious Philanthropy and Colonial Slavery: The American*

Correspondence of the Associates of Dr. Bray, 1717–1777. Urbana: University of Illinois Press, 1985.

Ver Steeg, Clarence L., ed. *A True and Historical Narrative of the Colony of Georgia by Pat. Tailfer and Others, with Comments by the Earl of Egmont.* Athens: University of Georgia Press, 1960.

Walker, George. *The Vagabond.* Dublin: D. Graisberry, 1800.

Weems, Mason Locke. *The Philanthropist; or, A Good Twenty-Five Cents Worth of Political Love Powder.* Charleston: n.p., 1799.

Wesley, Charles. *The Journal of the Rev. Charles Wesley.* Edited by Thomas Jackson. 2 vols. London: J. Mason, 1849.

Wesley, John. *Thoughts upon Slavery.* London: R. Hawes, 1744.

Whitefield, George. "The Great Duty of Family Religion." In *Memoirs of Rev. George Whitefield.* Edited by John Gillies. Middletown, Conn.: Hunt and Noyes, 1837.

———. *Three Letters from the Reverend Mr. George Whitefield.* Philadelphia: B. Franklin, 1740.

Winthrop, John. *Winthrop Papers.* 5 vols. Edited by Samuel Eliot Morison et al. [Boston]: Massachusetts Historical Society, 1929–.

Woodmason, Charles. *The Carolina Backcountry on the Eve of the Revolution: The Journal and Other Writings of Charles Woodmason, Anglican Itinerant.* Edited by Richard J. Hooker. Chapel Hill: University of North Carolina Press, 1953.

Wright, James. "Letters from Sir James Wright." Georgia Historical Society Collections, 3:157–375. Savannah: Georgia Historical Society, 1873.

Zubly, John Joachim. *The Journal of the Reverend John Joachim Zubly A.M., D.D., March 5, 1770 through June 22, 1781.* Edited by Lilla Mills Hawes. Georgia Historical Society Collections, vol. 21. Savannah: Georgia Historical Society, 1989.

SECONDARY SOURCES

Abbot, W. W. *The Royal Governors of Georgia, 1754–1775.* Chapel Hill: University of North Carolina Press, 1959.

Abernathy, Thomas P. *The South in the New Nation, 1789–1819.* Baton Rouge: Louisiana State University Press, 1961.

Ahlstrom, Sydney E. *A Religious History of the American People.* New Haven: Yale University Press, 1972.

Alden, John Richard. *John Stuart and the Southern Colonial Frontier: A Study of Indian Relations, War, Trade, and Land Problems in the Southern Wilderness, 1754–1775.* Ann Arbor: University of Michigan Press, 1944.

Aldridge, Alfred O. "George Whitefield's Georgia Controversies." *Journal of Southern History* 9 (August 1943): 357–80.

Anstey, Roger. *The Atlantic Slave Trade and British Abolition, 1760–1810.* London: Macmillan, 1975.

Appleby, Joyce O. *Economic Thought and Ideology in Seventeenth-Century England.* Princeton: Princeton University Press, 1978.

Ariès, Philippe. *Centuries of Childhood: A Social History of Family Life.* Translated by Robert Baldick. New York: Vintage, 1962.

Ashworth, John. *Commerce and Compromise, 1820–1850.* Vol. 1 of *Slavery, Capitalism, and Politics in the Antebellum Republic.* Cambridge: Cambridge University Press, 1995.

Aston, T. H., and C. H. E. Philpin, eds. *The Brenner Debate: Agrarian Class Structure and Economic Development in Pre-Industrial Europe.* Cambridge: Cambridge University Press, 1985.

Bailey, Kenneth K. "Protestantism and Afro-Americans in the Old South: Another Look." *Journal of Southern History* 41 (November 1975): 451–72.

Bailyn, Bernard. *The Ideological Origins of the American Revolution.* Cambridge: Harvard University Press, 1967.

Bain, Alexander. *James Mill.* 1882. Reprint, New York: Augustus M. Kelley, 1966.

Baker, Robert A. *Relations between Northern and Southern Baptists.* Fort Worth: n.p., 1954.

Baym, Nina. *Novels, Readers, and Reviewers: Responses to Fiction in Antebellum America.* Ithaca: Cornell University Press, 1984.

———. *Woman's Fiction.* Ithaca: Cornell University Press, 1978.

Bell, Malcolm, Jr. *Major Butler's Legacy: Five Generations of a Slaveholding Family.* Athens: University of Georgia Press, 1987.

Bellot, Leland J. "Evangelicals and the Defense of Slavery in Britain's Old Colonial Empire." *Journal of Southern History* 37 (February 1971): 19–40.

———. *William Knox: The Life and Thought of an Eighteenth-Century Imperialist.* Austin: University of Texas Press, 1977.

Bercovitch, Sacvan, ed. *Reconstructing American Literary History.* Cambridge: Harvard University Press, 1986.

Berlin, Ira, and Ronald Hoffman, eds. *Slavery and Freedom in the Age of the American Revolution.* Charlottesville: University Press of Virginia, 1983.

Billet, Leonard. "Justice, Liberty, and Economy." In *Adam Smith and the Wealth of Nations: 1776–1976, Bicentennial Essays,* edited by Fred R. Glahe, 83–110. Boulder: Colorado Associated University Press, 1978.

Blickle, Peter. *The Revolution of 1525: The German Peasants' War from a New Perspective.* Translated by Thomas A. Brady Jr. and H. C. Erik Midelfort. Baltimore: Johns Hopkins University Press, 1981.

Boles, John B. "Evangelical Protestantism in the Old South: From Religious Dissent to Cultural Dominance." In *Religion in the South,* edited by Charles Reagan Wilson, 13–34. Jackson: University Press of Mississippi, 1985.

———. *The Great Revival, 1787–1805: The Origins of the Southern Evangelical Mind.* Lexington: University Press of Kentucky, 1972.

———. "Henry Holcombe, a Southern Baptist Reformer in the Age of Jefferson." *Georgia Historical Quarterly* 54 (Fall 1970): 381–407.

———. *The South through Time: A History of an American Region.* Englewood Cliffs, N.J.: Prentice Hall, 1995.

Bolton, S. Charles. *Southern Anglicanism: The Church of England in Colonial South Carolina.* Westport, Conn.: Greenwood, 1982.

Bonomi, Patricia U. *Under the Cope of Heaven: Religion, Society, and Politics in Colonial America.* New York: Oxford University Press, 1986.

Boskin, Joseph. *Sambo: The Rise and Fall of an American Jester.* New York: Oxford University Press, 1986.

Bowes, Frederick P. *The Culture of Early Charleston.* Chapel Hill: University of North Carolina Press, 1942.

Brady, Patrick S. "The Slave Trade and Sectionalism in South Carolina, 1787–1800." *Journal of Southern History* 38 (November 1972): 601–20.

Braudel, Fernand. *Civilization and Capitalism: Fifteenth to Eighteenth Century.* Translated by Sian Reynolds. 3 vols. New York: Harper and Row, 1982.

Breen, T. H. "'Baubles of Britain': The American and Consumer Revolutions of the Eighteenth Century." *Past and Present* 119 (1988): 73–104.

———. "An Empire of Goods: The Anglicization of Colonial America, 1690–1776." *Journal of British Studies* 25 (October 1986): 467–99.

———. "Narrative of Commercial Life: Consumption, Ideology, and Community on the Eve of the American Revolution." *William and Mary Quarterly,* 3d ser., 50 (July 1993): 471–501.

Bridenbaugh, Carl. *Mitre and Sceptre: Transatlantic Faiths, Ideas, Personalities, and Politics, 1689–1775.* New York: Oxford University Press, 1962.

Brinsfield, John Wesley. *Religion and Politics in Colonial South Carolina.* Easley, S.C.: Southern Historical Press, 1983.

Brodhead, Richard H. *Cultures of Letters: Scenes of Reading and Writing in Nineteenth-Century America.* Chicago: University of Chicago Press, 1993.

Brown, Richard D. *Modernization: The Transformation of American Life, 1600–1865.* New York: Hill and Wang, 1976.

Brown, Richard Maxwell. *The South Carolina Regulators.* Cambridge: Harvard University Press, Belknap Press, 1963.

Bruce, Dickson D., Jr. *And They All Sang Hallelujah: Plain-Folk Camp-Meeting Religion, 1800–1845.* Knoxville: University of Tennessee Press, 1974.

———. *The Rhetoric of Conservatism: The Virginia Convention of 1829–30 and the Conservative Tradition in the South.* San Marino, Calif.: Huntington Library, 1982.

Bryant, Jonathan M. *How Curious a Land: Conflict and Change in Greene County, Georgia, 1850–1885.* Chapel Hill: University of North Carolina Press, 1996.

Buchanan, James M. "The Justice of Natural Liberty." In *Adam Smith and Modern Political Economy: Bicentennial Essays on the Wealth of Nations,* edited by Gerald P. O'Driscoll Jr., 117–31. Ames: Iowa State University Press, 1979.

Butler, Jon. *Awash in a Sea of Faith: Christianizing the American People.* Cambridge: Harvard University Press, 1990.

———. "Enlarging the Bonds of Christ: Slavery, Evangelism, and the Christianization of the White South." In *The Evangelical Tradition in America,* edited by Leonard I. Sweet, 87–112. Macon, Ga.: Mercer University Press, 1984.

Calhoon, Robert M. *Evangelicals and Conservatives in the Early South, 1740–1861.* Columbia: University of South Carolina Press, 1988.

Capers, Gerald M. "A Reconsideration of John C. Calhoun's Transition from

Nationalism to Nullification." *Journal of Southern History* 14 (February 1948): 34–48.

Carey, Anthony Gene. *Parties, Slavery, and the Union.* Athens: University of Georgia Press, 1997.

Carsel, Wilfred. "The Slaveholders' Indictment of Northern Wage Slavery." *Journal of Southern History* 6 (November 1940): 504–20.

Cashin, Joan E. *A Family Venture: Men and Women on the Southern Frontier.* Baltimore: Johns Hopkins University Press, 1991.

Censer, Jane Turner. *North Carolina Planters and Their Children, 1800–1860.* Baton Rouge: Louisiana State University Press, 1984.

Chandler, Alice. *A Dream of Order: The Medieval Ideal in Nineteenth-Century English Literature.* Lincoln: University of Nebraska Press, 1970.

Chaplin, Joyce E. *An Anxious Pursuit: Agricultural Innovation and Modernity in the Lower South, 1730–1815.* Chapel Hill: University of North Carolina Press, 1993.

———. "Slavery and the Principle of Humanity in the Early Lower South." *Journal of Social History* 24 (Winter 1990): 299–316.

———. "Tidal Rice Cultivation and the Problem of Slavery in South Carolina and Georgia, 1760–1815." *William and Mary Quarterly,* 3d ser., 49 (January 1992): 29–61.

Charvat, William. *Literary Publishing in America, 1790–1850.* Philadelphia: University of Pennsylvania Press, 1959.

Clarke, Erskine. *Wrestlin' Jacob: A Portrait of Religion in the Old South.* Atlanta: John Knox, 1979.

Clinton, Catherine. *The Plantation Mistress: Woman's World in the Old South.* New York: Pantheon, 1982.

Clowse, Converse D. *Economic Beginnings in Colonial South Carolina, 1670–1730.* Columbia: University of South Carolina Press, 1971.

Coclanis, Peter A. "Distant Thunder: The Creation of a World Market in Rice and the Transformations It Wrought." *American Historical Review* 98 (October 1993): 1050–78.

———. *The Shadow of a Dream: Economic Life and Death in the South Carolina Low Country.* New York: Oxford University Press, 1989.

Coleman, Kenneth. *The American Revolution in Georgia, 1763–1789.* Athens: University of Georgia Press, 1958.

Coleman, Peter J. *Debtors and Greditors in America: Insolvency, Imprisonment for Debt, and Bankruptcy, 1607–1900.* Madison: State Historical Society of Wisconsin, 1974.

Cooper, William J., Jr. *The South and the Politics of Slavery, 1828–1856.* Baton Rouge: Louisiana State University Press, 1978.

Coulter, E. Merton. "The Nullification Movement in Georgia." *Georgia Historical Quarterly* 5 (March 1921): 3–39.

Cox, Joseph W. *Champion of Southern Federalism: Robert Goodloe Harper of South Carolina.* Port Washington, N.Y.: Kennikat Press, 1972.

Creel, Margaret Washington. *"A Peculiar People": Slave Religion and Community Culture among the Gullahs.* New York: New York University Press, 1988.

Crocker, Zebulon. *The Catastrophe of the Presbyterian Church in 1837.* New Haven: B. and W. Noyes, 1938.

Crowley, J. E. *This Sheba, Self: The Conceptualization of Economic Life in Eighteenth-Century America.* Baltimore: Johns Hopkins University Press, 1974.

Cunliffe, Marcus. *Chattel Slavery and Wage Slavery: The Anglo-American Context, 1830–1860.* Athens: University of Georgia Press, 1979.

Curtin, Philip D. *The Atlantic Slave Trade: A Census.* Madison: University of Wisconsin Press, 1969.

Darnton, Robert, and Daniel Roche, eds. *Revolution in Print: The Press in France, 1775–1800.* Berkeley: University of California Press, 1989.

David, Dierdre. *Intellectual Women and Victorian Patriarchy: Harriet Martineau, Elizabeth Barrett Browning, George Eliot.* Ithaca: Cornell University Press, 1987.

Davidson, Cathy N. *The Revolution and the Word: The Rise of the Novel in America.* New York: Oxford University Press, 1986.

Davis, Curtis Carroll. *Chronicler of the Cavaliers: A Life of the Virginia Novelist Dr. William A. Caruthers.* Richmond: Dietz Press, 1953.

———. *That Ambitious Mr. Legaré: The Life of James M. Legaré of South Carolina.* Columbia: University of South Carolina Press, 1971.

Davis, David Brion. *The Problem of Slavery in the Age of Revolution, 1770–1823.* Ithaca: Cornell University Press, 1975.

———. *The Problem of Slavery in Western Culture.* Ithaca: Cornell University Press, 1966.

———. *Slavery and Human Progress.* New York: Oxford University Press, 1984.

Davis, Richard Beale. *A Colonial Southern Bookshelf: Reading in the Eighteenth Century.* Athens: University of Georgia Press, 1979.

———. *Literature and Society in Early Virginia, 1608–1840.* Baton Rouge: Louisiana State University Press, 1973.

Degler, Carl N. *At Odds: Women and Family in America from the Revolution to the Present.* New York: Oxford University Press, 1980.

———. *Place over Time: The Continuity of Southern Distinctiveness.* Baton Rouge: Louisiana State University Press, 1977.

Demaree, Albert Lowther. *The American Agricultural Press, 1819–1860.* New York: Columbia University Press, 1941.

DeMause, Lloyd, ed. *The History of Childhood.* New York: Psychohistory Press, 1974.

DesChamps, Margaret Burr. "Union or Division? South Atlantic Presbyterians and Southern Nationalism, 1820–1861." *Journal of Southern History* 20 (November 1954): 484–98.

De Vorsey, Louis, Jr. *The Georgia–South Carolina Boundary: A Problem in Historical Geography.* Athens: University of Georgia Press, 1982.

Dillon, Merton L. *Slavery Attacked: Southern Slaves and Their Allies, 1619–1865.* Baton Rouge: Louisiana State University Press, 1990.

Dobson, Joanne. "The Hidden Hand: Subversion of Cultural Ideology in Three

Mid-Nineteenth-Century Women's Novels." *American Quarterly* 38 (Summer 1986): 223–42.

Dodd, Donald B., and Wynelle S. Dodd. *Historical Statistics of the South, 1790–1970.* University: University of Alabama Press, 1973.

Donald, David. "The Proslavery Argument Reconsidered." *Journal of Southern History* 37 (February 1971): 3–18.

Dorman, James H., Jr. *Theater in the Ante-Bellum South, 1815–1861.* Chapel Hill: University of North Carolina Press, 1967.

Douglas, Ann. *The Feminization of American Culture.* New York: Knopf, 1977.

Downes, Randolph C. "Creek-American Relations, 1790–1795." *Journal of Southern History* 8 (August 1942): 350–73.

Drescher, Seymour. *Capitalism and Antislavery: British Mobilization in Comparative Perspective.* New York: Oxford University Press, 1987.

Du Bois, W. E. B. *The Suppression of the African Slave-Trade to the United States, 1638–1870.* 1896. Reprint, New York: Social Science Press, 1954.

Duffy, John. "Eighteenth-Century Carolina Health Conditions." *Journal of Southern History* 18 (August 1952): 289–302.

Dunn, Richard S. *Sugar and Slaves: The Rise of the Planter Class in the English West Indies, 1624–1713.* Chapel Hill: University of North Carolina Press, 1972.

Dusinberre, William. *Them Dark Days: Slavery in the American Rice Swamps.* New York: Oxford University Press, 1996.

Eaton, Clement. "A Dangerous Pamphlet in the Old South." *Journal of Southern History* 2 (August 1936): 323–34.

———. *Freedom of Thought in the Old South.* New York: P. Smith, 1951.

Egerton, Douglas R. *Gabriel's Rebellion: The Virginia Slave Conspiracies of 1800 and 1802.* Chapel Hill: University of North Carolina Press, 1993.

———. "Markets without a Market Revolution: Southern Planters and Capitalism." *Journal of Early American History* 16 (Summer 1996): 207–21.

Elkins, Stanley M. *Slavery: A Problem in American Institutional and Intellectual Life.* Chicago: University of Chicago Press, 1976.

Ellis, Richard E. *The Union at Risk: Jacksonian Democracy, States' Rights, and the Nullification Crisis.* New York: Oxford University Press, 1987.

Faust, Drew Gilpin. "Evangelicalism and the Meaning of the Proslavery Argument: The Reverend Thornton Stringfellow of Virginia." *Virginia Magazine of History and Biography* 85 (January 1977): 3–17.

———. *James Henry Hammond and the Old South: A Design for Mastery.* Baton Rouge: Louisiana State University Press, 1982.

———. "The Peculiar South Revisited: White Society, Culture, and Politics in the Antebellum Period, 1800–1860." In *Interpreting Southern History: Historiographical Essays in Honor of Sanford W. Higginbotham,* edited by John B. Boles and Evelyn Thomas Nolen, 78–119. Baton Rouge: Louisiana State University Press, 1987.

———. *A Sacred Circle: The Dilemma of the Intellectual in the Old South, 1840–1860.* Philadelphia: University of Pennsylvania Press, 1977.

————. "A Southern Stewardship: The Intellectual and the Proslavery Argument." *American Quarterly* 31 (Spring 1979): 63–80.

Fichtenau, Heinrich. *Living in the Tenth Century.* Translated by Patrick J. Geary. Chicago: University of Chicago Press, 1991.

Fladeland, Betty L. "Compensated Emancipation: A Rejected Alternative." *Journal of Southern History* 42 (May 1976): 169–86.

Fogel, Robert William. *Without Consent or Contract: The Rise and Fall of American Slavery.* New York: Norton, 1989.

Ford, Lacy K., Jr. *Origins of Southern Radicalism: The South Carolina Upcountry, 1800–1860.* New York: Oxford University Press, 1988.

Fox, Richard Wightman, and T. J. Jackson Lears, eds. *The Culture of Consumption: Critical Essays in American History, 1880–1980.* New York: Pantheon, 1983.

————. *The Power of Culture: Critical Essays in American History.* Chicago: University of Chicago Press, 1993.

Fox-Genovese, Elizabeth. *Within the Plantation Household: Black and White Women of the Old South.* Chapel Hill: University of North Carolina Press, 1988.

Fox-Genovese, Elizabeth, and Eugene D. Genovese. *Fruits of Merchant Capital: Slavery and Bourgeois Property in the Rise and Expansion of Capitalism.* New York: Oxford University Press, 1983.

Fraser, Walter J., Jr., and Winfred B. Moore Jr., eds. *The Southern Enigma: Essays on Race, Class, and Folk Culture.* Westport, Conn.: Greenwood, 1983.

Fredrickson, George M. *The Black Image in the White Mind: The Debate on Afro-American Character and Destiny, 1817–1914.* New York: Harper and Row, 1971.

Freehling, Alison G. *Drift toward Dissolution: The Virginia Slavery Debate of 1831–1832.* Baton Rouge: Louisiana State University Press, 1982.

Freehling, William W. *Prelude to Civil War: The Nullification Controversy in South Carolina, 1816–1836.* New York: Harper and Row, 1966.

————. *Road to Disunion: Secessionists at Bay, 1776–1854.* New York: Oxford University Press, 1990.

Freidel, Frank. "Francis Lieber, Charles Sumner, and Slavery." *Journal of Southern History* 9 (February 1943): 75–93.

Frey, Sylvia R. *Water from the Rock: Black Resistance in a Revolutionary Age.* Princeton: Princeton University Press, 1991.

Gallay, Alan. *The Formation of a Planter Elite: Jonathan Bryan and the Southern Colonial Frontier.* Athens: University of Georgia Press, 1989.

Gates, Paul W. *The Farmer's Age: Agriculture, 1815–1860.* New York: Holt, Rinehart and Wilson, 1960.

Geary, Susan. "The Domestic Novel as Commercial Commodity: Making a Best Seller in the 1850s." *Papers of the Bibliographical Society of America* 70 (Third Quarter 1976): 365–93.

Genovese, Eugene D. *From Revolution to Rebellion: Afro-American Slave Revolts in the Making of the Modern World.* Baton Rouge: Louisiana State University Press, 1979.

————. *The Political Economy of Slavery: Studies in the Economy and Society of the Slave South.* New York: Vintage, 1967.

――――. *Roll, Jordan, Roll: The World the Slaves Made.* New York: Pantheon, 1974.

――――. *The Slaveholders' Dilemma: Freedom and Progress in Southern Conservative Thought, 1820–1860.* Columbia: University of South Carolina Press, 1992.

――――. "The Southern Slaveholders' View of the Middle Ages." In *Medievalism in American Culture,* edited by Bernard Rosenthal and Paul E. Szarmach, 31–52. Binghamton, N.Y.: Center for Medieval and Early Renaissance Studies, State University of New York at Binghamton, 1989.

――――. *The World the Slaveholders Made: Two Essays in Interpretation.* New York: Pantheon, 1969.

Gibson, Gail. "Costume and Fashion in Charleston, 1769–1782." *South Carolina Historical Magazine* 82 (July 1981): 225–47.

Gilmore, William J. *Reading Becomes a Necessity of Life: Material and Cultural Life in Rural New England, 1780–1835.* Knoxville: University of Tennessee Press, 1989.

Gipson, Lawrence Henry. *The British Isles and the American Colonies: The Southern Plantations, 1748–1754.* Vol. 2 of *The British Empire before the American Revolution.* 1936. Reprint, New York: Knopf, 1960.

Godbold, E. Stanley, Jr., and Robert H. Woody. *Christopher Gadsden and the American Revolution.* Knoxville: University of Tennessee Press, 1982.

Gould, Christopher. "The South Carolina and Continental Associations: Prelude to Revolution." *South Carolina Historical Magazine* 87 (January 1986): 30–48.

Gray, Lewis Cecil. *History of Agriculture in the Southern United States to 1860.* 2 vols. Washington, D.C.: Carnegie Institute, 1933.

Green, Michael D. *The Politics of Indian Removal: Creek Government and Society in Crisis.* Lincoln: University of Nebraska Press, 1982.

Greenberg, Kenneth S. *Masters and Statesmen: The Political Culture of American Slavery.* Baltimore: Johns Hopkins University Press, 1985.

――――. "Revolutionary Ideology and the Proslavery Argument: The Abolition of Slavery in Antebellum South Carolina." *Journal of Southern History* 42 (August 1976): 365–84.

Greene, Jack P. "Colonial South Carolina and the Caribbean Connection." *South Carolina Historical Magazine* 88 (January 1987): 192–210.

Griffin, Clifford S. *Their Brothers' Keepers: Moral Stewardship in the United States, 1800–1865.* New Brunswick: Rutgers University Press, 1960.

Grimsted, David. *Melodrama Unveiled: American Theater and Culture, 1800–1850.* Chicago: University of Chicago Press, 1968.

Guilds, John Caldwell. *Simms: A Literary Life.* Fayetteville: University of Arkansas Press, 1992.

Gutmann, Myron P. *Toward the Modern Economy: Early Industry in Europe, 1500–1800.* Philadelphia: Temple University Press, 1988.

Hahn, Steven. *The Roots of Southern Populism: Yeoman Farmers and the Transformation of the Georgia Upcountry, 1850–1890.* New York: Oxford University Press, 1983.

Hall, David D., and John B. Hench, eds. *Needs and Opportunities in the History of the Book: America, 1639–1876.* Worcester, Mass.: American Antiquarian Society, 1987.

Hamer, Philip M. "Great Britain, the United States, and the Negro Seamen Acts, 1822–1848." *Journal of Southern History* 1 (February 1935): 3–28.

Hanawalt, Barbara A. *The Ties That Bound: Peasant Families in Medieval England.* New York: Oxford University Press, 1986.

Hart, James L. *The Popular Book: A History of America's Literary Taste.* New York: Oxford University Press, 1950.

Harwood, Thomas F. "British Evangelical Abolitionism and American Churches in the 1830's." *Journal of Southern History* 28 (August 1962): 287–306.

Haskell, Thomas L. "Capitalism and the Origins of the Humanitarian Sensibility." *American Historical Review* 90 (April–June 1985): 339–61, 547–66.

Hatch, Nathan O. *The Democratization of American Christianity.* New Haven: Yale University Press, 1989.

Heimert, Alan. *Religion and the American Mind, from the Great Awakening to the Revolution.* Cambridge: Harvard University Press, 1966.

Herlihy, David. *Medieval Households.* Cambridge: Harvard University Press, 1985.

Heyrman, Christine L. *Southern Cross: The Beginnings of the Bible Belt.* New York: Knopf, 1997.

Higginbotham, A. Leon, Jr. *In the Matter of Color: The Colonial Period.* New York: Oxford University Press, 1978.

Hill, Samuel S., Jr., ed. *Encyclopedia of Religion in the South.* Macon: Mercer University Press, 1984.

———. *The South and the North in American Religion.* Athens: University of Georgia Press, 1980.

Hindus, Michael Stephen. *Prison and Plantation: Crime, Justice, and Authority in Massachusetts and South Carolina, 1767–1878.* Chapel Hill: University of North Carolina Press, 1980.

Holton, R. J., ed. *The Transition from Feudalism to Capitalism.* London: Macmillan, 1985.

Hont, Istan, and Michael Ignatieff. "Needs and Justice in the *Wealth of Nations*: An Introductory Essay." In *Wealth and Virtue: The Shaping of Political Economy in the Scottish Enlightenment,* 1–44. Cambridge: Cambridge University Press, 1983.

Hood, Fred J. *Reformed America: The Middle and Southern States, 1783–1837.* University: University of Alabama Press, 1980.

Hoole, W. Stanley. *The Ante-Bellum Charleston Theatre.* University: University of Alabama Press, 1946.

Horsman, Reginald. *Race and Manifest Destiny: The Origins of American Racial Anglo-Saxonism.* Cambridge: Harvard University Press, 1981.

Hubbell, Jay B. *The South in American Literature, 1607–1900.* Durham: Duke University Press, 1954.

Hudson, Larry E., Jr. *To Have and to Hold: Slave Work and Family Life in Antebellum South Carolina.* Athens: University of Georgia Press, 1997.

———, ed. *Working toward Freedom: Slave Society and Domestic Economy in the American South.* Rochester: University of Rochester Press, 1994.

Huff, Archie Vernon. *Langdon Cheves of South Carolina.* Columbia: University of South Carolina Press, 1977.

Hunt, Alfred N. *Haiti's Influence on Antebellum America: Slumbering Volcano in the Caribbean.* Baton Rouge: Louisiana State University Press, 1988.

Inscoe, John C. "Carolina Slave Names: An Index to Acculturation." *Journal of Southern History* 49 (November 1983): 527–54.

Isaac, Rhys. *The Transformation of Virginia, 1740–1790.* New York: Norton, 1982.

Jackson, Harvey H. "Hugh Bryan and the Evangelical Movement in Colonial South Carolina." *William and Mary Quarterly*, 3d ser., 43 (October 1986): 594–614.

———. *Lachlan McIntosh and the Politics of Revolutionary Georgia.* Athens: University of Georgia Press, 1979.

Jenkins, William Sumner. *Pro-Slavery Thought in the Old South.* 1935. Reprint, Gloucester, Mass.: P. Smith, 1960.

Johnson, Michael P. "Planters and Patriarchy: Charleston, 1800–1860." *Journal of Southern History* 46 (February 1980): 45–72.

Johnson, Michael P., and James L. Roark. *Black Masters: A Free Family of Color in the Old South.* New York: Norton, 1984.

Jolley, Nicholas, ed. *The Cambridge Companion to Leibniz.* Cambridge: Cambridge University Press, 1995.

Jones, George Fenwick. "The Black Hessians: Negroes Recruited by the Hessians in South Carolina and Other Colonies." *South Carolina Historical Magazine* 83 (October 1982): 287–302.

Jones, Louis Pinckney. "William Elliott, South Carolina Nonconformist." *Journal of Southern History* 17 (August 1951): 361–81.

Jordan, Winthrop D. *Tumult and Silence at Second Creek: An Inquiry into a Civil War Slave Conspiracy.* Baton Rouge: Louisiana State University Press, 1993.

———. *White over Black: American Attitudes toward the Negro, 1550–1812.* Chapel Hill: University of North Carolina Press, 1968.

Joyner, Charles. *Down by the Riverside: A South Carolina Slave Community.* Urbana: University of Illinois Press, 1984.

Kelley, Mary. *Private Woman, Public Stage: Literary Domesticity in Nineteenth-Century America.* New York: Oxford University Press, 1984.

Kennedy, Michael L. "A French Jacobin Club in Charleston, South Carolina, 1792–1795." *South Carolina Historical Magazine* 91 (January 1990): 4–22.

Kenney, William Howland, III. "Alexander Garden and George Whitefield: The Significance of Revivalism in South Carolina, 1738–1741." *South Carolina Historical Magazine* 71 (January 1970): 1–16.

Kerber, Linda K. *Women of the Republic: Intellect and Ideology in Revolutionary America.* Chapel Hill: University of North Carolina Press, 1980.

Kirk, Russell. *Randolph of Roanoke: A Study in Conservative Thought.* Chicago: University of Chicago Press, 1951.

Klein, Rachel N. *Unification of a Slave State: The Rise of the Planter Class in the South Carolina Backcountry, 1760–1808.* Chapel Hill: University of North Carolina Press, 1990.

Klingberg, Frank J. *An Appraisal of the Negro in Colonial South Carolina: A Study in Americanization.* Washington, D.C.: Associated Publishers, 1941.

Kousser, J. Morgan, and James M. McPherson, eds. *Region, Race, and Reconstruction: Essays in Honor of C. Vann Woodward.* New York: Oxford University Press, 1982.

Kriedte, Peter. *Peasants, Landlords, and Merchant Capitalists: Europe and the World Economy, 1500–1800.* Translated by V. R. Berghahn. Cambridge: Cambridge University Press, 1983.

Kulikoff, Allan. "The Transition to Capitalism in Rural America." In *The Agrarian Origins of American Capitalism,* 13–33. Charlottesville: University Press of Virginia, 1992.

Kuykendall, John W. *"Southern Enterprize": The Work of National Evangelical Societies in the Antebellum South.* Westport, Conn.: Greenwood, 1982.

Lambert, Frank. "Subscribing for Profits and Piety: The Friendship of Benjamin Franklin and George Whitefield." *William and Mary Quarterly,* 3d ser., 50 (July 1993): 529–54.

———. "'Pedlar in Divinity': George Whitefield and the Great Awakening, 1737–1745." *Journal of American History* 77 (December 1990): 812–37.

Lane, Ann J., ed. *The Debate over "Slavery": Stanley Elkins and His Critics.* Urbana: University of Illinois Press, 1971.

Lane, Mills, ed. *Neither More nor Less Than Men: Slavery in Georgia.* Savannah: Beehive Press, 1993.

Latner, Richard B. "The Nullification Crisis and Republican Subversion." *Journal of Southern History* 43 (February 1977): 19–38.

Leach, William. *Land of Desire: Merchants, Power, and the Rise of a New American Culture.* New York: Pantheon, 1993.

Lehmann, Hartmutt, and Guenther Roth, eds. *Weber's Protestant Ethic: Origins, Evidence, Contexts.* New York: Cambridge University Press, 1993.

Lerner, Gerda. *The Grimké Sisters from South Carolina: Rebels against Slavery.* Boston: Houghton Mifflin, 1967.

Lewis, Jan. *The Pursuit of Happiness: Family and Values in Jefferson's Virginia.* Cambridge: Cambridge University Press, 1983.

Littlefield, Daniel C. "Plantations, Paternalism, and Profitability: Factors Affecting African Demography in the Old British Empire." *Journal of Southern History* 47 (May 1981): 167–82.

———. *Rice and Slaves: Ethnicity and the Slave Trade in Colonial South Carolina.* Baton Rouge: Louisiana State University Press, 1981.

Lofton, John. *Insurrection in South Carolina: The Turbulent World of Denmark Vesey.* Yellow Springs, Ohio: Antioch Press, 1964.

Loveland, Anne C. *Southern Evangelicals and the Social Order, 1800–1860.* Baton Rouge: Louisiana State University Press, 1980.

Lumpkin, Katharine Du Pre. *The Emancipation of Angelina Grimké.* Chapel Hill: University of North Carolina Press, 1974.

Lynch, Joseph H. *Godparents and Kinship in Early Medieval Europe.* Princeton: Princeton University Press, 1986.

Lynch, William O. "The Westward Flow of Southern Colonists before 1861." *Journal of Southern History* 9 (August 1943): 303–27.

McCardell, John. *The Idea of a Southern Nation: Southern Nationalists and Southern Nationalism, 1830–1860.* New York: Norton, 1979.

McCoy, Drew R. *The Elusive Republic: Political Economy in Jeffersonian America.* Chapel Hill: University of North Carolina Press, 1980.

McCracken, Grant. *Culture and Consumption: New Approaches to the Symbolic Character of Consumer Goods and Activities.* Bloomington: Indiana University Press, 1988.

McCrady, Edward. *The History of South Carolina under the Royal Government, 1719–1776.* New York: Macmillan, 1899.

McCurry, Stephanie. *Masters of Small Worlds: Yeoman Households, Gender Relations, and the Political Culture of the Antebellum South Carolina Low Country.* New York: Oxford University Press, 1995.

Machor, James L., ed. *Readers in History: Nineteenth-Century American Literature and the Contexts of Response.* Baltimore: Johns Hopkins University Press, 1993.

McKendrick, Neil, and J. H. Plumb. *The Birth of a Consumer Society: The Commercialization of Eighteenth-Century England.* Bloomington: Indiana University Press, 1982.

MacLeod, Duncan J. *Slavery, Race, and the American Revolution.* London: Cambridge University Press, 1974.

MacPherson, C. B. *The Political Theory of Possessive Individualism: Hobbes to Locke.* Oxford: Clarendon, 1962.

Maier, Pauline. *From Resistance to Revolution: Colonial Radicals and the Development of American Opposition to Britain, 1767–1775.* New York: Vintage, 1974.

Malone, Dumas. *The Public Life of Thomas Cooper, 1783–1839.* Columbia: University of South Carolina Press, 1961.

Marx, Karl. *Capital.* Translated by Ben Fowkes. 3 vols. New York: Vintage, 1977.

Massey, Gregory D. "The Limits of Antislavery Thought in the Revolutionary Lower South: John Laurens and Henry Laurens." *Journal of Southern History* 63 (August 1997): 495–530.

Mathews, Donald G. "Charles Colcock Jones and the Southern Evangelical Crusade to Form a Biracial Community." *Journal of Southern History* 41 (August 1975): 299–320.

———. *Religion in the Old South.* Chicago: University of Chicago Press, 1977.

———. *Slavery and Methodism: A Chapter in American Morality.* Princeton: Princeton University Press, 1965.

Matthewson, Tim. "Jefferson and Haiti." *Journal of Southern History* 61 (May 1995): 209–48.

Merrens, H. Roy, and George D. Terry. "Dying in Paradise: Malaria, Mortality, and the Perceptual Environment in Colonial South Carolina." *Journal of Southern History* 50 (November 1984): 533–50.

Miles, Edwin A. "After John Marshall's Decision: *Worcester v. Georgia* and the Nullification Crisis." *Journal of Southern History* 39 (November 1973): 519–44.

Miller, Joseph C. *Way of Death: Mercantilism and the Angolan Slave Trade, 1730–1830.* Madison: University of Wisconsin Press, 1988.

Miller, William C. *Arguing about Slavery: The Great Battle in the United States Congress.* New York: Knopf, 1996.

Miller, William T. "Nullification in Georgia and in South Carolina as Viewed by the New West." *Georgia Historical Quarterly* 14 (December 1930): 286–302.

Mooney, Chase C. *William H. Crawford, 1772–1834.* Lexington: University of Kentucky Press, 1974.

Moore, Glover. *The Missouri Controversy, 1819–1821.* Lexington: University of Kentucky Press, 1953.

Moore, R. Laurence. *Selling God: American Religion in the Marketplace of Culture.* New York: Oxford University Press, 1994.

Morgan, Philip. "Three Planters and Their Slaves: Perspectives on Slavery in Virginia, South Carolina, and Jamaica, 1750–1790." In *Race and Family in the Colonial South,* edited by Winthrop D. Jordan and Sheila L. Skemp, 37–89. Jackson: University Press of Mississippi, 1987.

Morris, Christopher. *Becoming Southern: The Evolution of a Way of Life, Warren County and Vicksburg, Mississippi, 1770–1860.* New York: Oxford University Press, 1995.

Morris, Colin. *The Discovery of the Individual, 1050–1200.* New York: Harper and Row, 1972.

Morrow, Ralph E. "The Proslavery Argument Revisited." *Mississippi Valley Historical Review* 48 (June 1961): 79–94.

Moss, Elizabeth. *Domestic Novelists in the Old South: Defenders of Southern Culture.* Baton Rouge: Louisiana State University Press, 1992.

Mott, Frank Luther. *A History of American Magazines.* 5 vols. Cambridge: Harvard University Press, 1930–68.

Mukerji, Chandra. *From Graven Images: Patterns of Modern Materialism.* New York: Columbia University Press, 1983.

Muller, Jerry Z. *Adam Smith in His Time and Ours: Designing the Decent Society.* New York: Free Press, 1993.

Murdoch, Richard K. "Citizen Mangourit and the Projected Attack on East Florida in 1794." *Journal of Southern History* 14 (November 1948): 524–40.

Nadelhaft, Jerome J. *The Disorders of War: The Revolution in South Carolina.* Orono: University of Maine at Orono Press, 1981.

Nagel, Paul C. "The Election of 1824: A Reconsideration Based on Newspaper Opinion." *Journal of Southern History* 26 (August 1960): 315–29.

Nash, Gary B. *Red, White, and Black: The Peoples of Early America.* Englewood Cliffs, N.J.: Prentice Hall, 1974.

Nash, Gary B., and Jean R. Soderlund. *Freedom by Degrees: Emancipation in Pennsylvania and Its Aftermath.* New York: Oxford University Press, 1991.

Nash, R. C. "Trade and Business in Eighteenth-Century South Carolina: The Career of John Guerard, Merchant and Planter." *South Carolina Historical Magazine* 96 (January 1995): 6–29.

Nevill, John Cranstoun. *Harriet Martineau.* London: Frederick Muller, 1943.

Nord, David Paul. "Systematic Benevolence: Religious Publishing and the Marketplace in Early Nineteenth-Century America." In *Communication and*

Change in American Religious History, edited by Leonard I. Sweet, 239–69. Grand Rapids, Mich.: Eerdmans, 1993.

Norton, Mary Beth. *Liberty's Daughters: The Revolutionary Experience of American Women, 1750–1800*. Boston: Little, Brown, 1980.

Oakes, James. *The Ruling Race: A History of American Slaveholders*. New York: Vintage, 1983.

————. *Slavery and Freedom: An Interpretation of the Old South*. New York: Knopf, 1990.

O'Brien, Conor Cruise. *The Long Affair: Thomas Jefferson and the French Revolution, 1785–1800*. Chicago: University of Chicago Press, 1996.

O'Brien, Michael. *A Character of Hugh Legaré*. Knoxville: University of Tennessee Press, 1985.

————, ed. *All Clever Men, Who Make Their Way: Critical Discourse in the Old South*. Athens: University of Georgia Press, 1992.

O'Brien, Michael, and David Moltke-Hansen, eds. *Intellectual Life in Antebellum Charleston*. Knoxville: University of Tennessee Press, 1986.

Ohline, Howard A. "Slavery, Economics, and Congressional Politics, 1790." *Journal of Southern History* 46 (August 1980): 335–60.

Ohmann, Richard M. *Selling Culture: Magazines, Markets, and Class at the Turn of the Century*. London: Verso, 1996.

Olwell, Robert A. "'Domestick Enemies': Slavery and Political Independence in South Carolina, May 1775–March 1776." *Journal of Southern History* 55 (February 1989): 21–48.

————. *Masters, Slaves, and Subjects: The Culture of Power in the South Carolina Low Country, 1740–1790*. Ithaca: Cornell University Press, 1998.

————. "'A Reckoning of Accounts': Patriarchy, Market Relations, and Control on Henry Laurens's Lowcountry Plantations, 1762–1785." In *Working toward Freedom: Slave Society and Domestic Economy in the American South*, edited by Larry E. Hudson Jr., 33–52. Rochester: University of Rochester Press, 1994.

Osterweis, Rollin G. *Romanticism and Nationalism in the Old South*. New Haven: Yale University Press, 1949.

Ott, Thomas O. *The Haitian Revolution, 1789–1804*. Knoxville: University of Tennessee Press, 1973.

Papenfuse, Eric Robert. *The Evils of Necessity: Robert Goodloe Harper and the Moral Dilemma of Slavery*. Transactions of the American Philosophical Society, vol. 87, pt. 1. Philadelphia: American Philosophical Society, 1997.

Parish, Peter J. *Slavery: History and Historians*. New York: Harper and Row, 1989.

Parks, Edd Winfield. *Ante-Bellum Southern Literary Critics*. Athens: University of Georgia Press, 1962.

Patrick, J. Max. *Savannah's Pioneer Theater from Its Origin to 1810*. Athens: University of Georgia Press, 1953.

Patrick, Rembert W. *Florida Fiasco: Rampant Rebels on the Georgia-Florida Border, 1810–1815*. Athens: University of Georgia Press, 1954.

Pease, Jane H. "A Note on Patterns of Conspicuous Consumption among Seaboard Planters, 1820–1860." *Journal of Southern History* 35 (August 1969): 381–93.

Pease, Jane H., and William H. Pease. "The Economics and Politics of Charleston's Nullification Crisis." *Journal of Southern History* 47 (August 1981): 335–62.

Pennington, Edgar Legare. "The Reverend Francis Le Jau's Work among Indians and Slaves." *Journal of Southern History* 1 (November 1935): 442–58.

———. *Thomas Bray's Associates and Their Work among the Negroes.* Worcester, Mass.: American Antiquarian Society, 1939.

Perdue, Theda. *Slavery and the Evolution of Cherokee Society, 1540–1866.* Knoxville: University of Tennessee Press, 1979.

Persons, Stow. *The Decline of American Gentility.* New York: Columbia University Press, 1973.

Peterson, Merrill D. *Olive Branch and Sword: The Compromise of 1833.* Baton Rouge: Louisiana State University Press, 1982.

Peterson, Thomas Virgil. *Ham and Japheth: The Mythic World of Whites in the Antebellum South.* Metuchen, N.J.: Scarecrow Press, 1978.

Phillips, Ulrich B. *American Negro Slavery: A Survey of the Supply, Employment, and Control of Negro Labor as Determined by the Plantation Regime.* New York: D. Appleton, 1918.

Pichanick, Valerie Kossew. *Harriet Martineau: The Woman and Her Work, 1802–76.* Ann Arbor: University of Michigan Press, 1980.

Poesch, Jessie. *The Art of the Old South: Painting, Sculpture, Architecture, and the Products of Craftsmen, 1560–1860.* New York: Knopf, 1983.

Poggi, Gianfranco. *Calvinism and the Capitalist Spirit: Max Weber's Protestant Ethic.* Amherst: University of Massachusetts Press, 1983.

Posey, Walter B. "The Advance of Methodism into the Lower Southwest." *Journal of Southern History* 2 (November 1936): 439–52.

———. "The Protestant Episcopal Church: An American Adaptation." *Journal of Southern History* 25 (February 1959): 3–30.

———. "The Slavery Question in the Presbyterian Church in the Old Southwest." *Journal of Southern History* 15 (August 1949): 311–24.

Preyer, Norris W. "Southern Support of the Tariff of 1816—a Reappraisal." *Journal of Southern History* 25 (August 1959): 306–22.

Prude, Jonathan. "'To Look upon the 'Lower Sort': Runaway Ads and the Appearance of Unfree Laborers in America, 1750–1800." *Journal of American History* 78 (June 1991): 124–59.

Quarles, Benjamin. *The Negro in the American Revolution.* 1961. Reprint, Chapel Hill: University of North Carolina Press, 1996.

Raboteau, Albert J. *Slave Religion: The "Invisible Institution" in the Antebellum South.* New York: Oxford University Press, 1978.

Radway, Janice A. *Reading the Romance: Women, Patriarchy, and Popular Literature.* Chapel Hill: University of North Carolina Press, 1984.

Rawley, James A. *The Transatlantic Slave Trade: A History.* New York: Norton, 1981.

Reid, Nina. "Loyalism and the 'Philosophic Spirit' in the Scientific Correspondence of Dr. Alexander Garden." *South Carolina Historical Magazine* 92 (January 1991): 5–14.

Reidy, Joseph P. *From Slavery to Agrarian Capitalism in the Cotton Plantation South: Central Georgia, 1800–1880*. Chapel Hill: University of North Carolina Press, 1992.

Remini, Robert B. *The Life of Andrew Jackson*. New York: Harper, 1988.

Reynolds, David S. *Faith in Fiction: The Emergence of Religious Literature in America*. Cambridge: Harvard University Press, 1981.

Reznek, Samuel H. "The Depression of 1819–1822: A Social History." *American Historical Review* 39 (October 1933): 28–47.

Ridgely, J. V. *Nineteenth-Century Southern Literature*. Lexington: University Press of Kentucky, 1980.

Roark, James L. *Masters without Slaves: Southern Planters in the Civil War and Reconstruction*. New York: Norton, 1977.

Robinson, Donald L. *Slavery in the Structure of American Politics, 1765–1820*. New York: Harcourt Brace Jovanovich, 1971.

Rodgers, Daniel T. "Republicanism: The Career of a Concept." *Journal of American History* 79 (June 1992): 12–38.

Rogers, George C., Jr. *Charleston in the Age of the Pinckneys*. Norman: University of Oklahoma Press, 1969.

————. *Evolution of a Federalist: William Loughton Smith of Charleston (1758–1812)*. Columbia: University of South Carolina Press, 1962.

Rogers, James A. *Richard Furman: Life and Legacy*. Macon, Ga.: Mercer University Press, 1985.

Rose, Willie Lee. "The Domestication of Domestic Slavery." In *Slavery and Freedom*, 18–36. Edited by William W. Freehling. New York: Oxford University Press, 1982.

Ross, Ian Simpson. *The Life of Adam Smith*. Oxford: Clarendon, 1995.

Rossiter, Clinton. *1787: The Grand Convention*. New York: Macmillan, 1966.

Rothbard, Murray N. *The Panic of 1819: Reactions and Policies*. New York: Columbia University Press, 1962.

Rothman, David J. *The Discovery of the Asylum: Social Order and Disorder in the New Republic*. Boston: Little, Brown, 1971.

Rozbicki, Michael J. "The Curse of Provincialism: Negative Perceptions of Colonial American Plantation Gentry." *Journal of Southern History* 63 (November 1997): 727–52.

Rubin, Louis D., Jr. *The Edge of the Swamp: A Study in the Literature and Society of the Old South*. Baton Rouge: Louisiana State University Press, 1989.

Scarborough, Ruth. *The Opposition to Slavery in Georgia prior to 1860*. Nashville: George Peabody College for Teachers, 1933.

Schantz, Mark S. "'A Very Serious Business': Managerial Relationships on the Ball Plantations, 1800–1835." *South Carolina Historical Magazine* 88 (January 1987): 1–22.

Schlatter, Richard. *Private Property: The History of an Idea*. New Brunswick, N.J.: Rutgers University Press, 1951.

Schmidt, Leigh Eric. *Consumer Rites: The Buying and Selling of American Holidays*. Princeton: Princeton University Press, 1995.

———. "'The Grand Prophet,' Hugh Bryan: Early Evangelicalism's Challenge to the Establishment and Slavery in the Colonial South." *South Carolina Historical Magazine* 87 (October 1986): 238–50.

Schneider, A. Gregory. *The Way of the Cross Leads Home: The Domestication of American Methodism.* Bloomington: Indiana University Press, 1993.

Scott, Anne Firor. *The Southern Lady: From Pedestal to Politics, 1830–1930.* Chicago: University of Chicago Press, 1970.

Sellers, Charles G. *The Market Revolution: Jacksonian America, 1815–1846.* New York: Oxford University Press, 1991.

———. *The Southerner as American.* Chapel Hill: University of North Carolina Press, 1960.

Shaffer, Arthur H. "Between Two Worlds: David Ramsay and the Politics of Slavery." *Journal of Southern History* 50 (May 1984): 175–96.

Shain, Barry Alan. *The Myth of American Individualism: The Protestant Origins of American Political Thought.* Princeton: Princeton University Press, 1994.

Shalhope, Robert E. *John Taylor of Carolina: Pastoral Republican.* Columbia: University of South Carolina Press, 1980.

———. "Race, Class, Slavery, and the Antebellum Southern Mind." *Journal of Southern History* 37 (November 1971): 557–74.

———. "Thomas Jefferson's Republicanism and Antebellum Southern Thought." *Journal of Southern History* 42 (November 1976): 529–56.

Shields, David S. *Civil Tongues and Polite Letters in British America.* Chapel Hill: University of North Carolina Press, 1997.

Shore, Laurence. *Southern Capitalists: The Ideological Leadership of an Elite, 1832–1885.* Chapel Hill: University of North Carolina Press, 1986.

Sidbury, James. *Ploughshares into Swords: Race, Rebellion, and Identity in Gabriel's Virginia, 1730–1810.* New York: Cambridge University Press, 1997.

Silver, Rollo G. *The American Printer, 1787–1825.* Charlottesville: University Press of Virginia, 1967.

Sirmans, M. Eugene. *Colonial South Carolina: A Political History, 1663–1763.* Chapel Hill: University of North Carolina Press, 1966.

———. "The Legal Status of the Slave in South Carolina, 1670–1740." *Journal of Southern History* 28 (November 1962): 462–73.

Smith, Alfred Glaze, Jr. *Economic Readjustment of an Old Cotton State: South Carolina, 1820–1860.* Columbia: University of South Carolina Press, 1958.

Smith, H. Shelton. *In His Image, but. . . : Racism in Southern Religion, 1780–1910.* Durham: Duke University Press, 1972.

Smith, Mark M. *Mastered by the Clock: Time, Slavery, and Freedom in the American South.* Chapel Hill: University of North Carolina Press, 1997.

———. "Old South Time in Comparative Perspective." *American Historical Review* 101 (December 1996): 1432–69.

Snay, Mitchell. *Gospel of Disunion: Religion and Separatism in the Antebellum South.* New York: Cambridge University Press, 1993.

Sobel, Mechal. *Trabelin' On: The Slave Journey to an Afro-Baptist Faith.* Westport, Conn.: Greenwood, 1979.

Soderlund, Jean R. *Quakers and Slavery: A Divided Spirit*. Princeton: Princeton University Press, 1985.

Solow, Barbara L., and Stanley L. Engerman, eds. *British Capitalism and Caribbean Slavery: The Legacy of Eric Williams*. Cambridge: Cambridge University Press, 1987.

Sparks, Randy J. *On Jordan's Stormy Banks: Evangelicalism in Mississippi, 1773–1871*. Athens: University of Georgia Press, 1994.

Staiger, C. Bruce. "Abolitionism and the Presbyterian Schism of 1837–1838." *Mississippi Valley Historical Review* 36 (December 1949): 391–414.

Stampp, Kenneth M. *The Peculiar Institution: Slavery in the Antebellum South*. New York: Knopf, 1956.

Steckel, Richard H. "Slave Mortality: An Analysis of Evidence from Plantation Records." *Social Science History* 3 (October 1979): 86–114.

Steffen, Charles G. "In Search of the Good Overseer: The Failure of the Agricultural Reform Movement in Lowcountry South Carolina, 1821–1834." *Journal of Southern History* 63 (November 1997): 753–802.

Stenberg, Richard R. "The Jefferson Birthday Dinner, 1830." *Journal of Southern History* 4 (August 1938): 334–45.

Stevenson, Brenda E. *Life in Black and White: Family and Community in the Slave South*. New York: Oxford University Press, 1996.

Stewart, Mart A. *"What Nature Suffers to Groe": Life, Labor, and Landscape on the Georgia Coast, 1680–1920*. Athens: University of Georgia Press, 1996.

Stone, Lawrence. *The Family, Sex, and Marriage in England, 1500–1800*. New York: Harper and Row, 1977.

Stout, Harry S. *The Divine Dramatist: George Whitefield and the Rise of Modern Evangelicalism*. Grand Rapids, Mich.: Eerdmans, 1991.

———. "Religion, Communications, and the Ideological Origins of the American Revolution." *William and Mary Quarterly*, 3d ser., 37 (October 1977): 519–41.

Stowe, Steven M. *Intimacy and Power in the Old South: Ritual in the Lives of the Planters*. Baltimore: Johns Hopkins University Press, 1987.

Stroupe, Henry Smith. *The Religious Press in the South Atlantic States, 1802–1865: An Annotated Bibliography with Historical Introduction and Notes*. Durham: Duke University Press, 1956.

Sydnor, Charles S. *The Development of Southern Sectionalism, 1819–1848*. Baton Rouge: Louisiana State University Press, 1948.

Tadman, Michael. *Speculators and Slaves: Masters, Traders, and Slaves in the Old South*. Madison: University of Wisconsin Press, 1989.

Taylor, William R. *Cavalier and Yankee: The Old South and American National Character*. Cambridge: Harvard University Press, 1979.

Temperley, Howard. "Capitalism, Slavery, and Ideology." *Past and Present*, no. 75 (May 1977): 94–118.

———. "The Ideology of Antislavery." In *The Abolition of the Atlantic Slave Trade: Origins and Effects in Europe, Africa, and the Americas*, edited by David Eltis and James Walvin, 21–36. Madison: University of Wisconsin Press, 1981.

Thomas, Gilian. *Harriet Martineau*. Boston: Twayne Publishers, 1985.

Thomas, J. P. "The Barbadians in Early South Carolina." *South Carolina Historical Magazine* 31 (April 1930): 75–92.

Thompson, Ernest Trice. *Presbyterians in the South*. 3 vols. Richmond: John Knox Press, 1963.

Thompson, H. P. *Thomas Bray*. London: Society for the Propagation of Christian Knowledge, 1954.

Thompson, John B. *Ideology and Modern Culture: Critical Social Theory in the Era of Mass Communication*. Stanford: Stanford University Press, 1990.

Thornton, J. Mills, III. *Politics and Power in a Slave Society: Alabama, 1800–1860*. Baton Rouge: Louisiana State University Press, 1978.

Tise, Larry E. *Proslavery: A History of the Defense of Slavery in America, 1701–1840*. Athens: University of Georgia Press, 1987.

Tompkins, Jane. *Reader-Response Criticism: From Formalism to Post-Structuralism*. Baltimore: Johns Hopkins University Press, 1980.

———. *Sensational Designs: The Cultural Work of American Fiction, 1790–1860*. New York: Oxford University Press, 1985.

Townsend, Leah. *South Carolina Baptists, 1670–1805*. Florence, S.C.: Florence Printing, 1935.

Tracy, Susan J. *In the Master's Eye: Representations of Women, Blacks, and Poor Whites in Antebellum Southern Literature*. Amherst: University of Massachusetts Press, 1995.

Trent, William P. *William Gilmore Simms*. Boston: Houghton, Mifflin, 1892.

Ullmann, Walter. *The Individual and Society in the Middle Ages*. Baltimore: Johns Hopkins University Press, 1966.

U.S. Department of Commerce, Bureau of the Census. *Historical Statistics of the United States: Colonial Times to 1970*. 2 vols. Washington, D.C.: Government Printing Office, 1975.

Van Horne, John C. "Joseph Solomon Ottolenghe (c. 1711–1775): Catechist to the Negroes, Superintendent of the Silk Culture, and Public Servant in Colonial Georgia." *Proceedings of the American Philosophical Society* 125 (October 1981): 398–409.

Vaughan, Alden T. "From White Man to Redskin: Changing Anglo-American Perception of the American Indian." *American Historical Review* 87 (October 1982): 917–53.

Verlinden, Charles. *The Beginnings of Modern Colonization*. Translated by Yvonne Freccero. Ithaca: Cornell University Press, 1970.

Vipperman, Carl J. *The Rise of Rawlins Lowndes, 1721–1800*. Columbia: University of South Carolina Press, 1978.

———. *William Lowndes and the Transition of Southern Politics, 1782–1822*. Chapel Hill: University of North Carolina Press, 1989.

Wade, Richard. "The Vesey Plot: A Reconsideration." *Journal of Southern History* 30 (May 1964): 148–61.

Wakelyn, Jon L. *The Politics of a Literary Man: William Gilmore Simms*. Westport, Conn.: Greenwood, 1973.

Wallace, David D. *South Carolina: A Short History, 1520–1948.* Columbia: University of South Carolina Press, 1966.

Wallerstein, Immanuel. *The Modern World-System.* 3 vols. New York: Academic Press, 1974–89.

Walsh, Richard. *Charleston's Sons of Liberty.* Columbia: University of South Carolina Press, 1959.

Warner, Michael. *The Letters of the Republic: Publication and the Public Sphere in Eighteenth-Century America.* Cambridge: Harvard University Press, 1990.

Waterhouse, Richard. *A New World Gentry: The Making of a Merchant and Planter Class in South Carolina, 1670–1770.* New York: Garland, 1989.

Watson, Charles S. *Antebellum Charleston Dramatists.* University: University of Alabama Press, 1976.

Watson, Ritchie D., Jr. *The Cavalier in Virginia Fiction.* Baton Rouge: Louisiana State University Press, 1985.

Wayne, Michael. *The Reshaping of Plantation Society: The Natchez District, 1860–1880.* Baton Rouge: Louisiana State University Press, 1983.

Webb, R. K. *Harriet Martineau: A Radical Victorian.* New York: Columbia University Press, 1960.

Weber, Max. *The Protestant Ethic and the Spirit of Capitalism.* Translated by Talcott Parsons. London: G. Allen and Unwin, 1930.

Weir, Robert M. *Colonial South Carolina: A History.* Millwood, N.Y.: KTO Press, 1983.

———. " 'The Harmony We Were Famous For': An Interpretation of Pre-Revolutionary South Carolina Politics." *William and Mary Quarterly,* 3d ser., 27 (October 1969): 473–501.

———. "South Carolinians and the Adoption of the U.S. Constitution." *South Carolina Historical Magazine* 89 (April 1988): 73–89.

West, E. G. *Adam Smith.* New Rochelle, N.Y.: Arlington House, 1969.

Wheatley, Vera. *The Life and Work of Harriet Martineau.* London: Secker and Warburg, 1957.

White, Shane. *Somewhat More Independent: The End of Slavery in New York City, 1770–1810.* Athens: University of Georgia Press, 1991.

Williams, Eric. *Capitalism and Slavery.* New York: G. P. Putnam, 1944.

Williams, Frances Leigh. *A Founding Family: The Pinckneys of South Carolina.* New York: Harcourt Brace Jovanovich, 1978.

Williams, Rosalind H. *Dream Worlds: Mass Consumption in Late-Nineteenth-Century France.* Berkeley: University of California Press, 1982.

Wiltse, Charles M. *John C. Calhoun: Nationalist, 1782–1828.* Indianapolis: Bobbs-Merrill, 1944.

Wimsatt, Mary Ann. *The Major Fiction of William Gilmore Simms: Cultural Traditions and Literary Form.* Baton Rouge: Louisiana State University Press, 1989.

Wood, Betty. *Slavery in Colonial Georgia, 1730–1775.* Athens: University of Georgia Press, 1984.

———. *Women's Work, Men's Work: The Informal Slave Economies of Lowcountry Georgia.* Athens: University of Georgia Press, 1995.

Wood, Gordon S. *The Radicalism of the American Revolution.* New York: Knopf, 1992.

Wood, Peter H. *Black Majority: Negroes in Colonial South Carolina from 1670 through the Stono Rebellion.* New York: Knopf, 1974.

Woolsey, Ronald C. "The West Becomes a Problem: The Missouri Controversy and Slavery Expansion as the Southern Dilemma." *Missouri History Review* 77 (July 1983): 409–32.

Woolverton, John F. *Colonial Anglicanism in North America.* Detroit: Wayne State University Press, 1984.

Wright, Gavin. *The Political Economy of the Cotton South: Households, Markets, and Wealth in the Nineteenth Century.* New York: Norton, 1978.

Wyatt-Brown, Bertram. "The Antimission Movement in the Jacksonian South: A Study in Regional Folk Culture." *Journal of Southern History* 36 (November 1970): 501–29.

———. "The Mask of Obedience: Male Slave Psychology in the Old South." *American Historical Review* 93 (December 1988): 1228–52.

———. "Modernizing Southern Slavery: The Proslavery Argument Reinterpreted." In *Region, Race, and Reconstruction: Essays in Honor of C. Vann Woodward,* edited by J. Morgan Kousser and James M. McPherson, 27–49. New York: Oxford University Press, 1982.

———. *Southern Honor: Ethics and Behavior in the Old South.* New York: Oxford University Press, 1982.

Yazawa, Melvin. *From Colonies to Commonwealth: Familial Ideology and the Beginnings of the American Republic.* Baltimore: Johns Hopkins University Press, 1985.

Young, Jeffrey R. "Ideology and Death on a Savannah River Rice Plantation, 1833–1867: Paternalism amidst 'A Good Supply of Disease and Pain.'" *Journal of Southern History* 59 (November 1993): 673–706.

Zahniser, Marvin R. *Charles Cotesworth Pinckney: Founding Father.* Chapel Hill: University of North Carolina Press, 1967.

Zboray, Ronald J. *A Fictive People: Antebellum Economic Development and the American Reading Public.* New York: Oxford University Press, 1993.

Zuckerman, Michael. "Penmanship Exercises for Saucy Sons: Some Thoughts on the Colonial Southern Family." *South Carolina Historical Magazine* 84 (July 1983): 152–66.

UNPUBLISHED DISSERTATIONS AND PAPERS

Cantrell, Clyde Hull. "The Reading Habits of Ante-Bellum Southerners." Ph.D. diss., University of Illinois, 1960.

Chesnutt, David R. "South Carolinian Expansion into Colonial Georgia." Ph.D. diss., University of Georgia, 1971.

Crouse, M. A. "The Manigault Family of South Carolina, 1685–1783." Ph.D. diss., Northwestern University, 1964.

DesChamps, Margaret Burr. "The Presbyterian Church in the South Atlantic States, 1801–1860." Ph.D. diss., Emory University, 1952.

Duncan, John Donald. "Servitude and Slavery in Colonial South Carolina." Ph.D. diss., Emory University, 1971.

Dye, Renée. "Sociology for the South: Representations of Caste, Class, and Social Order in the Fiction of William Gilmore Simms." Ph.D. diss., Emory University, 1994.

Forbes, Robert Pierce. "Slavery and the Meaning of America." Ph.D. diss., Yale University, 1994.

Laing, Annette. "'After Their Heathen Way': African Christianization and the Anglican Mission in Eighteenth-Century South Carolina and Georgia." Paper presented at the American Historical Association annual meeting, Seattle, Wash., January 1998.

McInnis, Maurie Dee. "The Politics of Taste: Classicism in Charleston, South Carolina, 1815–1840." Ph.D. diss., Yale University, 1996.

Miller, James. "South by Southwest: Planter Emigration and Elite Ideology in the Deep South, 1815–1861." Ph.D. diss., Emory University, 1996.

Ward, Susan Page. "The Development of the Theme of Chivalry in Nineteenth-Century Southern Literature." Ph.D. diss., Duke University, 1980.

INDEX

Franklin, Benjamin, 30
Fraser, Hugh, 145
Fredericksburg, Va., 140
Fredrickson, George, 129
Free blacks, 127
Freehling, William, 164, 202
Freeman, George, 213
French and Indian War, 18, 38–39
French Revolution, 92, 101–5, 117, 150, 177, 204, 225–26
Furman, Richard, 8–9, 10, 82, 102, 113–15, 118, 134, 141, 143, 145–47, 168–72, 175, 181, 191, 213

Gabriel's Rebellion, 123
Gadsden, Christopher, 53–54, 68–69, 86–87, 92, 120
Gaffney, Michael, 150
"Gag rule," 222
Galphin, George, 83
Garden, Alexander (colonial minister), 28–29, 31–32, 34–35, 37, 43, 50, 142, 170
Garden, Alexander (nineteenth-century S.C. resident), 215
Garden, Alexander, II, 37–38, 72
Garden, Alexander, III, 72
Garrison, William Lloyd, 216
Gender conventions. See Men; Women
George III (king of England), 42
Georgia, 5, 13, 18, 26, 29, 33–34, 36, 43, 46, 67, 82, 105, 107, 120, 134, 138, 162–63, 165, 186, 189; Assembly, 50, 62, 189; ban on slavery in, 21–22, 30; commitment to slavery in, 70, 76–77, 80, 94–97, 127, 155, 174, 175, 206, 225, 232; Native Americans in, 97–98, 185–86; politics in, 196–97, 207–11; religion in, 88, 144, 176, 190, 219; resistance against British government, 49–51, 57, 61–62; settlement of, 21–23; slave insurrection and fear of insurrection in, 21–22, 64, 71, 100, 104, 212; slavery in, 128, 182; and tensions with South Carolina, 52, 83

Georgia Gazette, 48, 64, 68
Georgia Trustees, 21–23, 28, 30, 33, 36
Genovese, Eugene D., 6, 9–10
Germain, George, 78
Gibson, Edmund, 28
Gignilliat, James, 28
Glen, James, 21, 38
Glover, Henry S., 211
Gordon, Thomas, 62
Gray, Alexander, 68
Greene, Catherine, 85
Greene, Cornelia L., 104
Greene, Nathanael, 73, 105; family of, 105
Grenville, George, Lord, 49
Grimball, John Berkley, 183
Grimké, Angelina, 221
Grimké, Thomas, 203
Guignard, John, 212
Guy Rivers, 213, 214, 227

Habersham, James, 41, 43, 45–47, 50, 60, 62–65, 71–72
Haiti. *See* St. Domingue
Hales, Stephen, 28
Ham (biblical figure), 122
Hamilton, Alexander, 99, 187
Hamilton, James, Jr., 168, 197–98, 204, 207, 217
Hammet, William, 100, 113–18, 168
Hammond, James Henry, 198, 222–23, 225–26, 232
Harden, Edward, 174, 207
Harden, Edward, Jr., 212, 219
Harden, Robert, 187
Harper, William, 232
Harrington, Henry William, 131
Hart, Anne, 69, 82
Hart, Caroline, 217
Hart, Oliver, 46, 73, 81–82
Hartford Convention, 187
Haskell, Thomas, 11
Havana, 36
Hayne, Robert Y., 161, 190, 192, 199, 205
Hemphill, James, 222

Prosser, J. R., 181
Publishing industry. *See* Print culture
Purrysburg, S.C., 73, 100

Quakers, 99, 111, 127
Quincy, Josiah, Jr., 66

Ramsay, David, 87, 96–97, 116, 119–20,
    134, 147
Randolph, John, 127–28, 133, 137, 188
Read, Jacob, 104, 143
Reading, 12. *See also* Novels; Print
    culture
Reformation, 23
*Remarkable Extracts and Observations
    on the Slave Trade*, 173
Republican Motherhood, 86, 118
Republican Party, 120, 159
Revivals. *See* Christianity; Evangelical-
    ism; Georgia: religion in; South Car-
    olina: religion in
Rhees, M. J., 114
Rhode Island, 66, 93
Riceboro, S.C., 138
Richard (slave belonging to William
    Alston), 108
Richardson, Elizabeth, 151
Richardson, James B., 182, 184
Richardson, John P., 151
Richardson, William, 182, 184
Rivers, Josiah, 145
Robert (slave belonging to Margaret
    Izard Manigault), 129
Robertson, James, 97
Roper, Benjamin, 172
Rose, Willie Lee, 13
Ross, John, 209
Royal Society of Arts, 37
Royer, Judith Giton, 17
Rush, Benjamin, 108–9
Rutledge, Edward, 73, 109
Rutledge, John, 74–75, 93–94
Rutledge, Rebecca Motte, 200, 206, 210,
    217, 225

Sabey (slave belonging to Samuel
    Dubose Jr.), 129
St. Augustine, Fla., 21, 79
St. Domingue, 92, 102–4, 119, 125, 156,
    167, 177, 225
Saint Paul, 33, 114
Saint Thomas Aquinas, 23–24
Salvation Army, 12
Sambo and Toney, 141–43, 176
Sarah (slave belonging to Louisa
    McAllister), 129
Savannah, Ga., 26, 29, 42–43, 62, 81,
    113–14, 122, 131, 145, 150, 162, 183–85,
    187, 212, 219
Savannah Female Asylum, 191
Scotland, 102, 134
Scott, Walter, 12, 134, 138, 179–80
Scottish Chiefs, 135–36, 151
Seabrook, Whitemarsh, 186, 189, 194
Sectionalism, 15, 158–61, 170, 187–94, 217
Self Control, 137
Seminole Indians, 185
Senate. *See* Congress, U.S.
Servants, white, 74, 79, 156, 224–25
Sexual relations, 66, 149
Shakespeare, William, 40, 133–34,
    137–38, 172, 215
Shays's Rebellion, 92
Shinner, Charles, 53
Shylock, 40–41
Simms, William Gilmore, 1–5, 8–9, 12,
    186, 190, 200–201, 213, 227, 234
Singleton, Marion, 215
Singleton, Richard, 215
Sinkler, Charles, 149
Slater, John, 132–33
Slaves: agricultural knowledge of,
    18–19; Christian mission to, 24–35,
    42, 113–16, 145; domestic trade in,
    180; fugitive, 94, 97–98, 115, 158; inter-
    national trade in, 17, 19–20, 40,
    44–45, 47, 63–64, 80, 94–97, 114, 116,
    126–27, 152–53; population of, 20,
    63–64, 80; resistance of, 14, 20–21, 23,
    31, 33–34, 36, 64, 80, 100, 110, 181;

slaveowners' recognition of humanity of, 2–3, 7–9, 31, 42–48, 50, 64, 70, 75–76, 79, 80–81, 88, 106–12, 119, 121, 123, 130, 142, 158, 172, 181, 212, 221, 232; white abuse of and suffering of, 1–2, 7, 14–15, 37, 46, 54, 74–75, 107, 132–33, 139, 149, 167, 174, 180, 182–84